ACCA

Paper

P5

Advanced performance management

D1390358

Welcome to IFP's study text for Paper P5 *Advanced Performance Management* which is:

- Written by tutors
- Comprehensive but concise
- In simple English
- Used around the world by Emile Woolf Colleges including China, Russia and the UK

ifp International Financial Publishing

in association with

EW **Emile Woolf** International
Training Professionals

First edition published by
International Financial Publishing Limited
Hitherbury House, 97 Portsmouth Road, Guildford, Surrey GU2 5DL
Email: info@ifpbooks.com
www.ifpbooks.com

Notice
International Financial Publishing Limited has made every effort to ensure that at the time of writing the contents of this study text are accurate, but neither International Financial Publishing Limited nor its directors or employees shall be under any liability whatsoever for any inaccurate or misleading information this work could contain.

British Library Cataloguing in Publications Data
A catalogue record for this book is available from the British Library

ISBN: 978-1-905623-45-7

Printed and bound in Great Britain

Acknowledgements
The syllabus and study guide are reproduced by kind permission of the Association of Chartered Certified Accountants.

Contents

International Financial Publishing Limited

S

Syllabus and study guide

AIM

To apply relevant knowledge, skills and exercise professional judgement in selecting and applying strategic management accounting techniques in different business contexts and to contribute to the evaluation of the performance of an organization and its strategic development.

MAIN CAPABILITIES

On successful completion of this paper, candidates should be able to:

A. Use strategic planning and control models to plan and monitor organisational performance

B. Assess and identify relevant macroeconomic, fiscal and market factors and key external influences on organisational performance

C. Identify and evaluate the design features of effective performance management information and monitoring systems

D. Apply appropriate strategic performance measurement techniques in evaluating and improving organisational performance

E. Advise clients and senior management on strategic business performance evaluation and on recognising vulnerability to corporate failure

F. Identify and assess the impact of current developments in management accounting and performance management on measuring, evaluating and improving organisational performance.

Rationale

The Advanced Performance Management syllabus further develops key aspects introduced in Paper F5, *Performance Management,* at the skills level and draws on aspects of the material covered from a more strategic and operational planning perspective in Paper P3, *Business Analysis*.

The syllabus introduces candidates to the strategic role of management accounting as a discipline for planning and controlling performance so that strategic objectives can be set, monitored and controlled. It also covers the impact of external factors on strategic management issues, such as macroeconomic, fiscal, market and environmental impacts on performance. From appreciating the strategic context of performance management and the impact of wider factors, the syllabus examines, at an operational level, the issues relating to performance measurement systems and their design.

The syllabus then moves from performance management systems and their design to the scope and application of high-level performance measurement techniques in a variety of contexts, including not-for-profit organisations and multinational businesses. Having covered the strategic aspects of performance management and operational systems for the measurement and control of performance in a variety of contexts, candidates are then expected to synthesise this knowledge in the role of an advisor to senior management or independent clients on how to assess and control the performance of an entity, including the recognition of whether a business is facing difficulties or possibly failure.

Finally, the syllabus deals with current developments in performance management and with emerging issues as they might affect or influence the management of performance within organisations.

Detailed syllabus

A   Strategic planning and control

1.   Introduction to strategic management accounting

2.   Appraisal of alternative approaches to budgeting for control

3.   Changes in business structure and management accounting

4.   Effect of Information Technology (IT) on modern management accounting

B   Economic, fiscal and environmental factors

1.   Impact of world economic and market trends

2.   Impact of national fiscal and monetary policy on performance

3.   Other environmental and ethical issues

C   Performance measurement systems and design

1.   Management accounting and information systems

2.   Internal sources of management information

3.   External sources of management information

4.   Recording and processing methods

5.   Management reports

D   Strategic performance measurement

1.   Performance hierarchy

2.   Scope of strategic performance measures in private sector

3.   Strategic performance issues in complex business structures

4.   Divisional performance and transfer pricing issues

5.   Scope of strategic performance measures in not-for-profit organisations

6.   Behavioural aspects of performance measurement

E   Performance evaluation and corporate failure

1.   Alternative views of performance measurement

2.   Non-financial performance indicators

3.   Predicting and preventing corporate failure

F   Current developments and emerging issues in management accounting and performance management

1.   Current developments in management accounting techniques

2.   Current issues and trends in performance management

Structure of the examination paper

The examination paper will comprise two sections:

- Section A will comprise two compulsory questions worth 60 marks. A maximum of 40 marks will be available for either question in Section A. Since Section A is compulsory it is expected that candidates will not only attempt it in the examination, but will also allocate the appropriate amount of time. The two questions in Section A may or may not be based upon the same scenario.

- Section B contains 3 optional questions worth 20 marks each. Candidates will be required to answer two of these questions. At least one of the questions in Part B will be entirely discursive in nature.

		Number of marks
Section A:	Answer both questions, total 60 marks	60
Section B:	Answer two from three questions, 20 marks each	40
		100

Study Guide

This study guide provides more detailed guidance on the syllabus. You should use this as the basis of your studies.

A   STRATEGIC PLANNING AND CONTROL

1.   Introduction to strategic management accounting

a)   Explain the role of strategic management accounting in strategic planning and control.

b)   Discuss the role of corporate planning in clarifying corporate objectives, making strategic decisions and checking progress towards the objectives.

c)   Compare planning and control at the strategic and operational levels within a business entity.

d)   Discuss how organisational survival in the long term necessitates consideration of life cycle issues.

e)   Assess the use of strategic management accounting in the context of multinational companies.

f)   Discuss the scope for potential conflict between strategic business plans and short term localised decisions.

g)   Evaluate how SWOT analysis may assist in the performance management process.

h)   Discuss the benefits and difficulties of benchmarking performance with best practice organisations.

i)   Evaluate how risk and uncertainty play an especially important role in long term strategic planning and decision-making that relies upon forecasts of exogenous variables.

j)   Assess the impact of government policy on an organisation and its strategy formulation and implementation.

2.   Appraisal of alternative approaches to budgeting for control

a)   Evaluate the strengths and weaknesses of alternative budgeting models and compare such techniques as fixed and flexible, rolling, activity based, zero based and incremental.

b)   Assess how budgeting may differ in not-for-profit organisations from profit-seeking organisations.

c)   Evaluate the issues raised by advocates of 'beyond budgeting'.

d)   Discuss the behaviour aspects of budgeting for control and the impact such behaviour may have on corporate performance.

3.   Changes in business structure and management accounting

a)   Assess the continuing effectiveness of traditional management accounting techniques within a rapidly changing business environment.

b)   Identify and discuss the particular information needs of organisations adopting a functional, divisional or network form and the implications for performance management.

c) Discuss the concept of business integration and the linkage between people, operations, strategy and technology.

d) Assess the influence of Business Process Reengineering on systems development and improvements in organisational performance.

e) Discuss and evaluate the application of activity-based management.

f) Identify and discuss the required changes in management accounting systems as a consequence of empowering staff to manage sectors of a business.

4. Effect of Information Technology (IT) on modern management accounting

a) Assess the changing accounting needs of modern service orientated businesses compared with the needs of traditional manufacturing industry.

b) Discuss how modern IT systems provide the opportunity for instant access to management accounting data throughout the organisation and their potential impact on business performance.

c) Discuss how modern IT systems facilitate the remote input of management accounting data in an acceptable format by non-finance specialists.

d) Explain how modern information systems provide instant access to previously unavailable data that can be used for benchmarking and control purposes and help improve business performance.

e) Assess the need for businesses to continually refine and develop their management accounting and information systems if they are to maintain or improve their performance in an increasingly competitive and global market.

B   ECONOMIC, FISCAL AND ENVIRONMENTAL FACTORS

1. Impact of world economic and market trends

a) Assess the impact and influence of external environmental factors on an organisation and its strategy.

b) Evaluate pricing and other business strategies in order to maintain or improve competitive position and performance.

2. Impact of national fiscal and monetary policy on performance

a) Discuss the need to consider the environment in which an organisation is operating when assessing its performance, including:

i) Political climate

ii) Market conditions

iii) Funding

b) Assess the impact of governmental regulation on performance measurement techniques used and the performance levels achieved (for example, in the case of utility services and former state monopolies).

3.   **Other environmental and ethical issues**

   a)   Discuss the ways in which stakeholder groups operate and how they effect an organisation and its strategy formulation and implementation.

   b)   Discuss the ethical issues that may impact on strategy formulation and business performance.

   c)   Discuss the ways in which stakeholder groups may influence business performance.

C   PERFORMANCE MEASUREMENT SYSTEMS AND DESIGN

1.   **Management accounting and information systems**

   a)   Identify the accounting information requirements for strategic planning, management control and operational control and decision-making.

   b)   Discuss, with reference to management accounting, ways in which the information requirements of a management structure are affected by the features of the structure.

   c)   Evaluate the objectives of management accounting and management accounting information.

   d)   Discuss the integration of management accounting information within an overall information system.

   e)   Define and discuss the merits of, and potential problems with, open and closed systems.

   f)   Highlight the ways in which contingent (internal and external) factors influence management accounting and its design and use.

   g)   Advise how anticipated human behaviour will influence the design of a management accounting system.

   h)   Discuss the impact of responsibility accounting on information requirements.

2.   **Internal sources of management information**

   a)   Identify and discuss the principal internal sources of management accounting information.

   b)   Demonstrate how these principal internal sources of management information might be used for control purposes.

   c)   Identify and discuss the direct data capture and process costs of internally generated management accounting information.

   d)   Identify and discuss the indirect costs of producing internally generated information.

   e)   Discuss those factors that need to be considered when determining the capacity and development potential of a system.

3.   **External sources of management information**

   a)   Identify and discuss common external sources of information.

   b)   Identify and discuss the costs associated with external sources.

c) Discuss the limitations of using externally generated information.

d) Identify and discuss the categories of external information that are likely to be a useful addition to an organisation's management accounting system.

e) Demonstrate how the information might be used in planning and controlling activities e.g. benchmarking against similar activities.

4. Recording and processing methods

a) Demonstrate how the type of business entity will influence the recording and processing methods.

b) Discuss how IT developments e.g. spreadsheets, accountancy software packages and electronic mail may influence recording and processing systems.

c) Discuss the difficulties associated with recording and processing data of a qualitative nature.

5. Management reports

a) Discuss the principal controls required in generating and distributing internal information.

b) Discuss the procedures that may be necessary to ensure security of highly confidential information that is not for external consumption.

D   STRATEGIC PERFORMANCE MEASUREMENT

1. Performance hierarchy

a) Discuss the purpose, structure and content of a mission statement and their potential impact on business performance.

b) Discuss the ways in which high level corporate objectives are developed.

c) Identify strategic objectives and discuss how they may be incorporated into the business plan.

d) Discuss how strategic objectives are cascaded down the organisation via the formulation of subsidiary performance objectives

e) Discuss social and ethical obligations that should be considered in the pursuit of corporate performance objectives.

f) Explain the performance 'planning gap' and evaluate alternative strategies to fill that gap. [3]

g) Identify and discuss the characteristics of operational performance.

h) Discuss the relative significance of planning as against controlling activities at different levels in the performance hierarchy.

2. Scope of strategic performance measures in private sector

a) Demonstrate why the primary objective of financial performance should be primarily concerned with the benefits to shareholders.

b) Justify the crucial objectives of survival and business growth.

c) Discuss the appropriateness of, and apply different measures of performance, including:

    i) Return on Capital Employed (ROCE)

    ii) Return on Investment (ROI)

    iii) Earnings Per Share (EPS)

    iv) Earning Before Interest, Tax and Depreciation Adjustment (EBITDA)

    v) Residual Income (RI)

    vi) Net Present value (NPV)

    vii) Internal Rate of Return (IRR)

d) Discuss why indicators of liquidity and gearing need to considered in conjunction with profitability.

e) Compare and contrast short and long run financial performance and the resulting management issues.

f) Explore the traditional relationship between profits and share value with the long term profit expectations of the stock market and recent financial performance of new technology/communications companies.

3. Strategic performance issues in complex business structures

a) Evaluate the use and the application of strategic models in planning and assessing the business performance of an entity, such as Ansoff, Boston Consulting Group and Porter.

b) Discuss the problems encountered in planning, controlling and measuring performance levels, e.g. productivity, profitability, quality and service levels, in complex business structures.

4. Divisional performance and transfer pricing issues

a) Describe, compute and evaluate performance measures relevant in a divisionalised organisation structure including ROI, RI and Economic value added (EVA).

b) Discuss the need for separate measures in respect of managerial and divisional performance. [2]

c) Discuss the circumstances in which a transfer pricing policy may be needed and discuss the necessary criteria for its design.

d) Demonstrate and evaluate the use of alternative bases for transfer pricing.

e) Explain and demonstrate issues that require consideration when setting transfer prices in multinational companies.

5. Scope of strategic performance measures in not-for-profit organisations

a) Highlight and discuss the potential for diversity in objectives depending on organisation type.

b) Discuss the need to achieve objectives with limited funds that may not be controllable.

c) Identify and discuss ways in which performance may be judged in not-for profit organisations.

d) Discuss the difficulties in measuring outputs when performance is not judged in terms of money or an easily quantifiable objective.

e) Discuss how the combination of politics and the desire to measure public sector performance may result in undesirable service outcomes.

f) Assess 'value for money' service provision as a measure of performance in not-for-profit organisations and the public sector.

6. Behavioural aspects of performance measurement

a) Discuss the relationship between performance measurement systems and behaviour and how the latter can influence performance.

b) Discuss the accountability issues that might arise from performance measurement systems.

c) Evaluate the ways in which performance measurement systems may send the 'wrong signals' and result in undesirable business consequences.

d) Assess the potential beneficial and adverse consequences of linking reward schemes to performance measurement.

e) Demonstrate how management style needs to be considered when designing an effective performance measurement system.

E PERFORMANCE EVALUATION AND CORPORATE FAILURE

1. Alternative views of performance measurement

a) Evaluate the 'balanced scorecard' approach as a way in which to improve the range and linkage between performance measures.

b) Evaluate the 'performance pyramid' as a way in which to link strategy, operations and performance.

c) Evaluate the work of Fitzgerald and Moon that considers performance measurement in business services using building blocks for dimensions, standards and rewards.

2. Non-financial performance indicators

a) Discuss the interaction of non-financial performance indicators with financial performance indicators.

b) Discuss the implications of the growing emphasis on non-financial performance indicators.

c) Discuss the significance of non-financial performance indicators in relation to employees.

d) Identify and discuss the significance of non-financial performance indicators in relation to product/service quality e.g. customer satisfaction reports, repeat business ratings, customer loyalty, access and availability.

e) Discuss the difficulties in interpreting data on qualitative issues.

    f)   Discuss the significance of brand awareness and company profile and their potential impact on business performance.

3. Predicting and preventing corporate failure

    a)   Assess the potential likelihood of corporate failure, utilising quantitative and qualitative performance measures.

    b)   Assess and critique quantitative and qualitative corporate failure prediction models.

    c)   Identify and discuss performance improvement strategies that may be adopted in order to prevent corporate failure.

F. CURRENT DEVELOPMENTS AND EMERGING ISSUES IN PERFORMANCE MANAGEMENT

1. Current developments in management accounting techniques

    a)   Discuss the ways through which management accounting practitioners are made aware of new techniques and how they evaluate them.

    b)   Assess the changing role of the management accountant in today's business environment as outlined by Burns and Scapens.

    c)   Discuss and evaluate the application of Japanese business practices and management accounting techniques, including Kaizen costing, Target costing, Just-in-time, and Total Quality Management.

    d)   Discuss and evaluate environmental management accounting.

2. Current issues and trends in performance management

    a)   Evaluate and apply the value-based management approaches to performance management.

    b)   Discuss and apply other recently developed performance measurement frameworks; e.g. Six Sigma; the Performance Prism.

    c)   Discuss contemporary issues in performance management.

    d)   Discuss how changing organisation's structure, culture and strategy will influence the adoption of new performance measurement methods and techniques.

DCF tables

Present value table

Present value of 1 i.e. $(1+r)^{-n}$ where r = discount rate, n = number of periods until payment

Periods					Discount rate (r)						
(n)	1%	2%	3%	4%	5%	6%	7%	8%	9%	10%	
1	0.990	0.980	0.971	0.962	0.952	0.943	0.935	0.926	0.917	0.909	1
2	0.980	0.961	0.943	0.925	0.907	0.890	0.873	0.857	0.842	0.826	2
3	0.971	0.942	0.915	0.889	0.864	0.840	0.816	0.794	0.772	0.751	3
4	0.961	0.924	0.888	0.855	0.823	0.792	0.763	0.735	0.708	0.683	4
5	0.951	0.906	0.863	0.822	0.784	0.747	0.713	0.681	0.650	0.621	5
6	0.942	0.888	0.837	0.790	0.746	0.705	0.666	0.630	0.596	0.564	6
7	0.933	0.871	0.813	0.760	0.711	0.665	0.623	0.583	0.547	0.513	7
8	0.923	0.853	0.789	0.731	0.677	0.627	0.582	0.540	0.502	0.467	8
9	0.914	0.837	0.766	0.703	0.645	0.592	0.544	0.500	0.460	0.424	9
10	0.905	0.820	0.744	0.676	0.614	0.558	0.508	0.463	0.422	0.386	10
11	0.896	0.804	0.722	0.650	0.585	0.527	0.475	0.429	0.388	0.350	11
12	0.887	0.788	0.701	0.625	0.557	0.497	0.444	0.397	0.356	0.319	12
13	0.879	0.773	0.681	0.601	0.530	0.469	0.415	0.368	0.326	0.290	13
14	0.870	0.758	0.661	0.577	0.505	0.442	0.388	0.340	0.299	0.263	14
15	0.861	0.743	0.642	0.555	0.481	0.417	0.362	0.315	0.275	0.239	15

(n)	11%	12%	13%	14%	15%	16%	17%	18%	19%	20%	
1	0.901	0.893	0.885	0.877	0.870	0.862	0.855	0.847	0.840	0.833	1
2	0.812	0.797	0.783	0.769	0.756	0.743	0.731	0.718	0.706	0.694	2
3	0.731	0.712	0.693	0.675	0.658	0.641	0.624	0.609	0.593	0.579	3
4	0.659	0.636	0.613	0.592	0.572	0.552	0.534	0.516	0.499	0.482	4
5	0.593	0.567	0.543	0.519	0.497	0.476	0.456	0.437	0.419	0.402	5
6	0.535	0.507	0.480	0.456	0.432	0.410	0.390	0.370	0.352	0.335	6
7	0.482	0.452	0.425	0.400	0.376	0.354	0.333	0.314	0.296	0.279	7
8	0.434	0.404	0.376	0.351	0.327	0.305	0.285	0.266	0.249	0.233	8
9	0.391	0.361	0.333	0.308	0.284	0.263	0.243	0.225	0.209	0.194	9
10	0.352	0.322	0.295	0.270	0.247	0.227	0.208	0.191	0.176	0.162	10
11	0.317	0.287	0.261	0.237	0.215	0.195	0.178	0.162	0.148	0.135	11
12	0.286	0.257	0.231	0.208	0.187	0.168	0.152	0.137	0.124	0.112	12
13	0.258	0.229	0.204	0.182	0.163	0.145	0.130	0.116	0.104	0.093	13
14	0.232	0.205	0.181	0.160	0.141	0.125	0.111	0.099	0.088	0.078	14
15	0.209	0.183	0.160	0.140	0.123	0.108	0.095	0.084	0.074	0.065	15

Annuity table

Present value of an annuity of 1 i.e. $\dfrac{1-(1+r)^{-n}}{r}$ where r = discount rate, n = number of periods

Periods **Discount rate (r)**

(n)	1%	2%	3%	4%	5%	6%	7%	8%	9%	10%	
1	0.990	0.980	0.971	0.962	0.952	0.943	0.935	0.926	0.917	0.909	1
2	1.970	1.942	1.913	1.886	1.859	1.833	1.808	1.783	1.759	1.736	2
3	2.941	2.884	20829	2.775	2.723	2.673	2.624	2.577	2.531	2.487	3
4	3.902	3.808	3.717	3.630	3.546	3.465	3.387	3.312	3.240	3.170	4
5	4.853	4.713	4.580	4.452	4.329	4.212	4.100	3.993	3.890	3.791	5
6	5.795	5.601	5.417	5.242	5.076	4.917	4.767	4.623	4.486	4.355	6
7	6.728	6.472	6.230	6.002	5.786	5.582	5.389	5.206	5.033	4.868	7
8	7.652	7.325	7.020	6.733	6.463	6.210	5.971	5.747	5.535	5.335	8
9	8.566	8.162	7.786	7.435	7.108	6.802	6.515	6.247	5.995	5.759	9
10	9.471	8.983	8.530	8.111	7.722	7.360	7.024	6.710	6.418	6.145	10
11	10.37	9.787	9.253	8.760	8.306	7.887	7.499	7.139	6.805	6.495	11
12	11.26	10.58	9.954	9.385	8.863	8.384	7.943	7.536	7.161	6.814	12
13	12.13	11.35	10.63	9.986	9.394	8.853	8.358	7.904	7.487	7.103	13
14	13.00	12.11	11.30	10.56	9.899	9.295	8.745	8.244	7.786	7.367	14
15	13.87	12.85	11.94	11.12	10.38	9.712	9.108	8.559	8.061	7.606	15

(n)	11%	12%	13%	14%	15%	16%	17%	18%	19%	20%	
1	0.901	0.893	0.885	0.877	0.870	0.862	0.855	0.847	0.840	0.833	1
2	1.713	1.690	1.668	1.647	1.626	1.605	1.585	1.566	1.547	1.528	2
3	2.444	2.402	2.361	2.322	2.283	2.246	2.210	2.174	2.140	2.106	3
4	3.102	3.037	2.974	2.914	2.855	2.798	2.743	2.690	2.639	2.589	4
5	3.696	3.605	3.517	3.433	3.352	3.274	3.199	3.127	3.058	2.991	5
6	4.231	4.111	3.998	3.889	3.784	3.685	3.589	3.498	3.410	3.326	6
7	4.712	4.564	4.423	4.288	4.160	4.039	3.922	3.812	3.706	3.605	7
8	5.146	4.968	4.799	4.639	4.487	4.344	4.207	4.078	3.954	3.837	8
9	5.537	5.328	5.132	4.946	4.772	4.607	4.451	4.303	4.163	4.031	9
10	5.889	5.650	5.426	5.216	5.019	4.833	4.659	4.494	4.339	4.192	10
11	6.207	5.938	5.687	5.453	5.234	5.029	4.836	4.656	4.486	4.327	11
12	6.492	6.194	5.918	5.660	5.421	5.197	4.988	4.793	4.611	4.439	12
13	6.750	6.424	6.122	5.842	5.583	5.342	5.118	4.910	4.715	4.533	13
14	6.982	6.628	6.302	6.002	5.724	5.468	5.229	5.008	4.802	4.611	14
15	7.191	6.811	6.462	6.142	5.847	5.575	5.324	5.092	4.876	4.675	15

CHAPTER

1

Revision: ABC and other accounting methods

Contents

Revision of selected management accounting topics

- Management accounting techniques and the P5 examination
- Revision topics

1 Revision of selected management accounting topics

1.1 Management accounting techniques and the P5 examination

The syllabus for Advanced Performance Management is concerned with the strategic role of management accounting systems in providing management with information for planning and controlling the performance of an entity.

It covers the strategic relevance of management accounting at a 'high' level of management and also performance measurement systems at an operational level.

In your examination, you may be required to comment on the relevance of some management accounting techniques, and the value of the information they provide in particular circumstances. For a variety of reasons, some 'traditional' management accounting techniques, such as absorption costing, budgeting and standard costing have all been criticised. These techniques may not be appropriate methods of providing information to management in a business environment where conditions are continually changing.

In your examination, you might also be asked to apply some management accounting techniques that are useful, or that might be useful in particular circumstances.

You should be familiar with these techniques from your previous studies. However, it is important that you should understand these techniques and why they are used. You should also be able to use the techniques and apply them, because they might be included in an examination question.

1.2 Revision topics

Some important techniques will be described later in this text. However, you should already be familiar with the following accounting methods and techniques:

- Activity based costing (ABC)
- Throughput accounting
- Backflush accounting
- Relevant costs for decision-making
- Capital investment appraisal techniques, in particular the NPV method of DCF analysis
- The analysis of risk and uncertainty.

These methods and techniques are described in this chapter and the chapters that follow.

Activity based costing (ABC)

- Activity based costing, overhead costs and cost drivers
- When using ABC might be appropriate
- ABC and the cost of processes
- The measurement of costs with ABC
- ABC and traditional absorption costing
- Using ABC information
- Advantages and limitations of ABC

2 Activity based costing (ABC)

2.1 Activity based costing, overhead costs and cost drivers

Activity based costing (ABC) is a form of absorption costing. However, it differs from traditional absorption costing, in which production overhead costs are traced to production departments and production activities, and absorbed at a direct labour hour rate.

Instead of tracing production overhead costs to departments (functions) and then to products, ABC traces overhead costs to activities and then to products or customers. ABC can be used to:

- measure product costs
- measure the costs (and so the profitability) of customers
- assess the value created by specific activities or processes (activity based management)

Activity based costing is based on the following assumptions:

- In a modern manufacturing environment, a large proportion of total costs consists of overhead costs, and direct labour costs are relatively small.
- Because overhead costs are large, it is appropriate to trace these costs as accurately as possible to the products that create the cost.
- Since direct labour is a fairly small element of cost, it is inappropriate to trace production overhead costs to products by absorbing overheads at a rate per direct labour hour.

Further assumptions are that:

- Many overhead costs are attributable to activities, such as customer order handling or product warehousing and despatch. These activities are not necessarily confined to single functional departments within the organisation.
- The costs of each of these activities are driven by one or more factors, called **cost drivers**. The cost driver for an activity is not necessarily production volume. For

example, the cost driver for order-handling costs might be the number of orders, not the quantity of items in each order.

■ Overhead costs are therefore caused by activities, and the costs of activities are driven by factors other than production volume.

ABC is a system of costing that attempts to:

■ Identify the activities that create (overhead) costs

■ Identify the cost driver or cost drivers for each of these activities

■ Charge overheads to products on the basis of the activities that are required to provide the product: each product should be charged with a fair share of overhead cost, that represents the activities that go into making and selling it.

There is also an argument that in the long run, all overhead costs are variable (even though they are fixed in the short term). Measuring costs with ABC might therefore provide management with useful information for controlling activities and long-term costs.

2.2 When using ABC might be appropriate

There are several reasons why traditional absorption costing and marginal costing systems might be considered inadequate, and an Activity based costing system much more appropriate.

■ Overhead costs are now a very large proportion of total costs, in manufacturing as well as service industries. Since overhead costs are such a large part of total costs, marginal costing provides only limited information for management, because it does not analyse fixed overhead costs.

■ Traditional absorption costing assumes that production overhead costs are 'driven' by production activity, and direct labour hours or machine hours worked. In many industries, this is not the case.

■ In highly competitive markets, management need much more than information merely about the profitability of products. They need to know about the profitability of particular markets, or distribution channels, and the profitability of different categories of customer. By relating costs to activities, ABC can be used to provide information about market profitability, channel profitability and customer profitability.

Activity based costing is a form of costing in which overheads are traced to each activity, and absorbed at a rate for each activity rather than a rate per direct labour hour. It is likely to be suitable as a method of costing in the following circumstances:

■ In a manufacturing environment, where absorption costing is required for inventory valuations.

■ Where a large proportion of production costs are overhead costs, and direct labour costs are relatively small.

■ Where products are complex.

■ Where products are provided to customer specifications.

■ Where order sizes differ substantially, and order handling and despatch activity costs are significant.

In addition, it might be possible to identify, for each activity, variable costs and fixed costs, and controllable and non-controllable costs. This will provide information to assist managers with the control of the costs of these activities.

As indicated earlier, activity based costing can also be used to analyse the costs of customers as well as products, and ABC can be used to assess:

■ the costs and profitability of different types of customer

■ the costs and profitability of different methods of selling (different channels of distribution).

An ABC system of costing is essential for an activity based management approach to improving systems and processes.

2.3   ABC and the cost of processes

Processes deliver satisfaction to the customer, not departments. The approach in ABC is to identify key processes (activities), and the factors that 'drive' the costs of those processes (activities). This is different from measuring costs of the work done by each department.

 Example

A company has a customer services department, which is responsible for dealing with customers.

The main activities performed by the department include:

■ preparing price quotations

■ receiving orders from customers

■ confirming orders after the finance department has checked the customer's credit

■ expediting orders ('progress chasing')

■ dealing with customer queries and complaints.

Although the customer relations department is responsible for dealing with the customer, most of these activities are performed in association with staff from other departments.

■ To prepare price quotations for customers, staff in the customer services department need to work closely with the sales staff and engineering staff.

■ To confirm orders after credit checks, staff in the customer services department must work closely with the finance department.

■ To expedite orders, customer services staff must work closely with staff in the production and distribution departments.

■ Dealing with customer complaints also involves other departments – sales, engineering, finance or production, depending on the nature of the complaint or query.

In an activity based costing system, if these five activities are identified as major activities within the company, costs should be identified for each activity separately. The costs will include not only the costs incurred in the customer services departments, but also significant costs incurred in the other departments. ABC crosses departmental boundaries.

2.4 The measurement of costs with ABC

To measure costs with ABC, the basic approach is a five-stage process:

(1) Identify the main activities or processes within an organisation that appear to be the reason for expenditures.

(2) Identify a cost driver for each activity.

(3) Create cost pools, for collecting costs that have the same cost driver.

(4) Measure the volume or incidence of the cost driver for each activity, and calculate an attribution rate (allocation rate or apportionment rate) for the activity costs. This is a rate per unit of cost driver.

(5) Attribute the costs from each pool to products, markets, channels of distribution or customers, based on their use of the cost drivers and using the attribution rate for each activity.

Pooled costs can be attributed directly to products. This contrasts with traditional absorption costing techniques, where production overhead costs are initially attributed to 'service departments' and then re-attributed from service centres to production departments and then individual products.

 Example

A manufacturing company has identified that a large part of its overhead costs are incurred in handling customer orders, and that the same effort goes into handling a small order as the effort required to deal with a large order. Order sizes differ substantially. The company makes four products, and the estimated costs of order handling are $250,000 per year.

The company uses ABC, and wants to establish an order-handling overhead cost for each product, based on the following budget:

Product	Number of orders	Total number of units ordered
W	15	60,000
X	22	33,000
Y	4	40,000
Z	9	27,000
	50	160,000

If the cost driver for order handling is the number of orders handled, the budgeted order handling cost will be $240,000/50 = $5,000 per order. Overhead costs will be charged to products as follows:

Product	Number of orders	Cost
		$
W	15	75,000
X	22	110,000
Y	4	20,000
Z	9	45,000
	50	250,000

2.5 ABC and traditional absorption costing

Although ABC is a form of absorption costing, the effect of ABC could be to allocate overheads in a completely different way between products. Product costs and product profitability will therefore be very different with ABC compared with traditional absorption costing.

Example

Entity Blue makes and sells two products; X and Y. Data for production and sales each month are as follows:

Sales demand	4,000 units	8,000 units
Direct material cost/unit	$20	$10
Direct labour hours/unit	0.1 hour	0.2 hours
Direct labour cost/unit	$2	$4

Production overheads are $500,000 each month. These are absorbed on a direct labour hour basis. The overhead absorption rate is $250 per direct labour hour.

An analysis of overhead costs suggests that there are four main activities that cause overhead expenditure.

Activity	Total cost	Cost driver	Total number	Product X	Product Y
	$				
Batch set-up	100,000	Number of set-ups	20	10	10
Order handling	200,000	Number of orders	40	24	16
Machining	120,000	Machine hours	15,000	6,000	9,000
Quality control	80,000	Number of checks	32	18	14
	500,000				

Required
Calculate the full production costs for Product X and Product Y, using:

(a)   traditional absorption costing

(b)   Activity based costing.

Answer

Traditional absorption costing	Product X	Product Y	Total
	$	$	
Direct materials	20	10	
Direct labour	2	4	
Overhead (at $250 per hour)	25	50	
Total production cost	47	64	
Number of units	4,000	8,000	
Total cost	$188,000	$512,000	$700,000

Activity based costing

Activity	Total cost	Cost driver		Product X	Product Y
	$		$	$	$
Batch set-up	100,000	Cost/set-up	5,000	50,000	50,000
Order handling	200,000	Cost/order	5,000	120,000	80,000
Machining	120,000	Cost/machine hour	8	48,000	72,000
Quality control	80,000	Cost/check	2,500	45,000	35,000
	500,000			263,000	237,000

	Product X	Product Y	Total
	$	$	$
Direct materials	80,000	80,000	
Direct labour	8,000	32,000	
Overheads	263,000	237,000	
Total cost	351,000	349,000	$700,000
Number of units	4,000	8,000	
Cost per unit	$87.75	$43.625	

In this example, the unit cost with a traditional absorption costing approach differs substantially from the unit costs with Activity based costing .

2.6 Using ABC information

ABC information can be used in a variety of ways. Applied to overhead costs, it provides information that could be of value for decision-making and better cost management.

Product costing and decision-making

ABC can provide a useful understanding of cost behaviour that is more meaningful than a simple division of costs into fixed and variable costs.

- It can often be assumed that many activity-based costs may be fixed in the short term, but are variable in the longer term.

- More activity-related costs are variable at the product-sustaining level than at the product or batch level. (The product-sustaining level is concerned with issues such as: 'should we continue to make this product or should we discontinue production?')

- Even more activity-related costs are variable at the facility-sustaining level than at the product-sustaining level. (The facility-sustaining level is concerned with issues such as: 'should we shut down this production plant or distribution centre?)

- As indicated earlier, activity-related costs can be attributed to markets, channels of distribution and customers, giving management more information with which to make their decisions.

Drivers of cost

ABC gives management more information about the activities that drive costs. Activities can be grouped into three categories:

- **Core activities**. These are activities that are the reason for the entity's existence and that are related to its critical success factors. These activities add value directly. Costs of these activities should be kept low, but not at the risk of failing to achieve objectives.

- **Support activities**. These are activities that enable core activities to be accomplished, and so are indirectly value-adding. The focus for management should be on performing these activities efficiently, and obtaining value for money. Is the activity worth the cost of delivering, and if so at what level or volume? How often does the activity need to be performed?

- **Diversionary activities**. These are activities caused by inadequate performance, such as the correction of errors. Diversionary activities do not add value. Management should try to minimise these activities, and reduce their costs.

Cost control and cost reduction

Activity based costing can also provide management with useful information about how costs might be cut, especially where a large proportion of the costs consist of fixed salaries paid to employees. The table below shows two methods of presenting the costs of an administration in a university.

Traditional costing	$000	ABC	$000
Salaries	225,000	Enrolling students	176,000
Depreciation	14,000	Input of examination marks	3,000
Materials	3,000	Preparing timetables	4,000
Other operating costs	21,000	Dealing with student queries	80,000
General expenses	6,000	General expenses	6,000
	269,000		269,000

The ABC format of cost reporting suggests that most resources are used in enrolling students and answering student queries. If management want to reduce costs, these are the activities where cost savings are most likely to be achieved.

In contrast, the traditional costing report does not provide information that is useful for the control of costs.

2.7 Advantages and limitations of ABC

Using ABC can have advantages and disadvantages.

Advantages

- ABC provides useful information about the activities that drive overhead costs. Traditional absorption costing and marginal costing do not do this.

- ABC therefore provides information that could be relevant to long-term cost control and long-term product selection or product pricing.

- ABC can provide the basis for a management information system to manage and control overhead costs.

- It might be argued that full product costs obtained with ABC are more 'realistic'; although it can also be argued that full product cost information is actually of little practical use or meaning for management.

- ABC might be useful for pricing products, where product pricing is on a cost-plus basis.

- Product cost and product profit information with ABC is possibly more useful than costs and profits based on traditional absorption costing.

Limitations

Activity based costing has several limitations.

- The analysis of costs in an ABC system may be based on unreliable data and weak assumptions. In particular, ABC systems may be based on inappropriate activities and cost pools, and incorrect assumptions about cost drivers.

- ABC provides an analysis of historical costs. Decision-making by management should be based on expectations of future cash flows. It is incorrect to assume that there is a causal relationship between a cost diver and an activity cost, so that increasing or reducing the activity will result in higher or lower activity costs.

- In some cases, ABC may be little more than a sophisticated absorption costing system.

- Within ABC systems, there is still a large amount of overhead cost apportionment. General overhead costs such as rental costs, insurance costs and heating and lighting costs may be apportioned between cost pools. This reduces the causal link between the cost driver and the activity cost.

- Many ABC systems are based on just a small number of cost pools and cost drivers. More complex systems are difficult to justify, on grounds of cost.

- Many activities and cost pools have more than one cost driver. Identifying the most suitable cost driver for a cost pool/activity is often difficult.

- Traditional cost accounting systems may be more appropriate for the purpose of inventory valuation and financial reporting.

- It might be a costly system to design and use. The costs might not justify the benefits. It must be remembered that full product costing is of little relevance for management decision-making.

The main advantages and disadvantages of ABC are summarised in the table below.

Advantages	Disadvantages
Gives management a better understanding of how resources are consumed by overhead activities.	There might be doubts about the quality of the information provided by ABC:
Focuses management attention on an important area of costs.	How are the major activities identified?
Can provide information for the control of activity/overhead costs.	How are overhead costs allocated to cost pools?
Can provide information to assist with budgeting activity costs/overhead costs (activity based budgeting).	How are cost drivers identified?
	What if there are two or more cost drivers for the same activity?
Can provide information to assist with activity based management.	Setting up an ABC system might be expensive. Will it provide sufficient value to justify the cost?

Throughput accounting

- Optimised production technology (OPT) and the Theory of Constraints.
- Assumptions in throughput accounting
- Throughput, inventory and operating expenses
- Profit and throughput accounting
- The value of inventory in throughput accounting
- Throughput accounting and the Theory of Constraints
- Throughput accounting ratio

---

3 Throughput accounting

3.1 Optimised Production Technology (OPT) and the Theory of Constraints

Throughput accounting is a method of accounting associated with Optimised production technology and the Theory of Constraints. Optimised Production Technology or OPT is a computer system for production planning and capacity management. OPT computer systems were developed in the 1980s by Eli Goldratt and are based on his Theory of Constraints.

The Theory of Constraints is based on the view that in a manufacturing system, the capacity of the system is limited (constrained) by one or more bottlenecks in the system. The production volume is restricted by these 'limiting factors' or bottlenecks. Production output will be optimised by focusing on the constraints that restrict production activity. By removing the constraint, or making the constraint less restricting, the ability of the system to produce more will be increased.

The key constraint may be sales, in which case the entity needs to produce just enough output to meet sales demand. However, the key constraint that creates the 'bottleneck' in production is something different.

- It may be a shortage of a particular resource, such as time on a particular type of machine or available skilled labour.
- It may be inefficiency in production, with stoppages and hold-ups caused by wastage, scrapped items and machine down-time.
- It may be unreliability in the supplies of key raw materials, and a shortage of key materials.
- The key resource might even be intangible, such as management competence.

To optimise output, management should focus on the key constraint and try to remove it.

When one key constraint is removed, there will be another key constraint to take its place, but total output capability will have increased. Until the key constraint is removed (for example, by obtaining more machines so more labour, or using

---

machines or labour more efficiently), management should try to optimise output within the limitations of the constraint.

To optimise production, management should therefore **continually** identify and remove constraints in order to raise output capacity.

The Theory of Constraints and inventory

Another aspect of OPT and the Theory of Constraints is that **holding inventory is considered wasteful**. Inventories do not add any value. Value is created only when finished goods inventory is sold.

■ If a production system could produce output just in time to meet the sales demand from customers, the finished output would be sold immediately, as soon as it is produced. There would be no need for inventories of finished goods.

■ Similarly, if a production system could acquire raw materials and components just in time to meet the need to use the materials in production, there would be no need for inventories of materials.

■ Inventory can sometimes hide bottlenecks in production, by providing 'buffer stock'. However, if there were no bottlenecks in production, and output could be produced immediately to meet customer demand, inventory would have no purpose. Inventory may therefore hide inefficiencies in production that management should be trying to eliminate.

The aim should therefore be to eliminate inventory.

An OPT computer system schedules production in a way that produces the maximum output possible within the limitations imposed by the existing key constraint. Eli Goldratt referred to 'throughput' rather than production output, and there is a close connection between Goldratt's Theory of Constraints and throughput accounting.

Concepts in OPT

It is useful to understand some of the main concepts in OPT.

■ A bottleneck or key constraint limits production capacity for the entire production system.

■ Losing time in a bottleneck activity means time lost – and output lost – for the entire production system.

■ However, saving time in a non-bottleneck activity is a wasted effort, because it has no effect on output.

■ There is no reason to produce items faster than a bottleneck activity can use them. Producing items at a faster rate than they can be used simply means that inventories will increase.

■ Inventories are wasteful and expensive. They add no value.

■ The process batch sizes should be variable, to optimise throughput, and should not be a fixed or standard size.

3.2   Assumptions in throughput accounting

Throughput accounting is associated with the Theory of Constraints. It is also based on the view that the only variable cost in operations is the cost of materials bought from external suppliers. All other operating expenses, including all labour costs, should be treated as fixed costs.

- In traditional marginal costing, it is assumed that direct labour costs are a variable cost, but in practice this is not usually correct. Employees are paid a fixed weekly or monthly wage or salary, and labour costs are a fixed cost.

- The only variable cost is the purchase cost of materials and components purchased from external suppliers.

- A business makes real profit by adding value. Value is added by selling goods or services to customers whose market value is more than the cost of the materials that go into making them. However, value is not added until the sale is actually made.

- Value added should be measured as the value of the sale minus variable cost, which is the cost of the materials.

3.3   Throughput, inventory and operating expenses

Throughput accounting is therefore based on three concepts:

- throughput
- inventory (investment) and
- operating expenses.

Throughput

Throughput is defined as 'the rate of production of a defined process over a stated period of time. Rates may be expressed in terms of units of products, batches produced, turnover or other meaningful measurements' (CIMA *Official Terminology*).

Value is added by creating throughput. The value of throughput can be measured as follows:

Throughput = Sales minus Variable costs

Throughput is not created until a sale occurs.

Throughput differs from contribution in traditional marginal costing because variable costs consist only of real variable costs, which are (mainly) materials costs.

It is therefore appropriate to define throughput as:

Throughput = Sales minus Cost of raw materials and components

Inventory (or investment)

Inventory or investment is all the money that is tied up in a business, in inventories of raw materials, WIP and finished goods. Inventory is eventually converted into throughput.

Operating expenses

All expenses other than raw materials and components costs should be treated as 'operating expenses'.

Operating expenses are all the expenditures incurred to produce the throughput. They consist of all costs that are not variable costs, and so include labour costs.

3.4   Profit and throughput accounting

Profit in throughput accounting is measured as throughput minus operating expenses.

 Example

	$
Sales	800,000
Raw materials and components costs	350,000
Throughput	450,000
Operating expenses	340,000
Net profit	110,000

A feature of throughput accounting that makes it different from other methods of costing, such as absorption costing and marginal costing, is that operating expenses are not charged to products. The throughput from individual products is measured, but nothing else except net profit.

3.5   The value of inventory in throughput accounting

Inventories do not have value, except the variable cost of the materials and components. Even for work in progress and inventories of finished goods, the only money invested is the purchase cost of the raw materials. No value is added until the inventory is sold.

In throughput accounting, all inventory is therefore valued at the cost of its raw materials and components, and nothing more.

It should not include any other costs, not even labour costs. No value is added by the production process, not even by labour, until the item is sold.

It is **impossible** to make extra profit simply by producing more output, unless the extra output is sold.

Throughput accounting and marginal costing

Throughput accounting has close similarities with marginal costing, because 'throughput' is similar in concept to 'contribution'. However:

■ In marginal costing, profit can be increased by increasing inventories of WIP and finished goods, because direct labour costs and variable production overhead costs are added to the cost of inventory, and kept out of cost of sales.

■ In throughput accounting, there is no increase at all in profit from an increase in WIP and finished goods.

3.6 Throughput accounting and the Theory of Constraints

According to the Theory of Constraints, a constraint is anything that limits the output from the system. If a system had no constraint:

■ its output would be zero, or

■ the system would continue to produce more and more output without limit.

Therefore for any system whose output is not zero, there must be a constraint that stops it from producing more output than it does. In a manufacturing system, constraints can be described as **bottlenecks** in the system.

If the aim of a business is to make money and profit, the most appropriate method of doing this is to:

■ increase throughput (per unit of constraining resource)

■ reduce operating expenses (per unit of constraining resource), or

■ reduce inventory, since there is a cost in holding inventory.

Goldratt argued that the most effective of these three ways of increasing profit is to increase throughput.

Throughput can be increased by identifying the bottlenecks in the system, and taking action to remove them or ease them.

Note: Throughput accounting is also relevant to **Just in Time production**. JIT production depends on avoiding breakdowns in the flow of production and production bottlenecks. JIT is described in more detail in a later chapter.

3.7 Throughput accounting ratio

Performance can be measured using three ratios:

■ Throughput per unit of the bottleneck resource

■ Operating expenses per unit of the bottleneck resource

■ Throughput accounting ratio.

The throughput accounting ratio is the ratio of [throughput in a period per unit of bottleneck resource] to [operating expenses per unit of bottleneck resource].

Units of a bottleneck resource are measured in hours (labour hours or machine hours). This means that the throughput accounting ratio can be stated as:

$$\text{Throughput accounting ratio} = \frac{\text{Throughput per hour of bottleneck resource}}{\text{Operating expenses per hour of bottleneck resource}}$$

Example

A business manufactures Product Z that has a selling price of $20. The materials costs are $8 per unit of Product Z. Total operating expenses each month are $120,000.

Machine capacity is the key constraint on production. There are only 600 machine hours available each month, and it takes three minutes of machine time to manufacture each unit of Product Z.

Required

(a)   Calculate the throughput accounting ratio.

(b)   How might this ratio be increased?

Answer

(a)   Throughput per unit of Product Z = $20 - $8 = $12.

Machine time per unit of Product Z = 3 minutes = 0.05 hours.

Throughput per machine hour = $12/0.05 = $240.

$$\text{Operating expenses per machine hour} = \frac{\$120,000}{600 \text{ hours}} = \$200$$

$$\text{Throughput accounting ratio} = \frac{\$240}{\$200} = 1.20$$

(b)   To increase the throughput accounting ratio, it might be possible to:

■   Raise the selling price for Product Z for each unit sold, to increase the throughput per unit.

■   Improve the efficiency of machine time used, and so manufacture Product Z in less than three minutes.

■   Find ways of reducing total operating expenses, in order to reduce the operating expenses per machine hour.

> ## Backflush accounting
>
> - The basic concept of backflush accounting
> - The difference between traditional costing and costing with backflush accounting
> - The features of backflush accounting
> - Backflush accounting with two 'trigger points'
> - Backflush accounting with one 'trigger point'
> - Backflush accounting: conclusion

4 Backflush accounting

4.1 The basic concept of backflush accounting

Backflush accounting is a method of accounting that begins by focusing on output and then works backwards, allocating costs between cost of goods sold and inventories. This is the complete opposite to traditional cost accounting, which begins by calculating the cost of production and inventories and works forwards to establish a cost of sales and value for closing inventory.

It simplifies costing accounting, because it ignores labour variances and work-in-progress value. Transfers between processes are often made at standard cost, and any variances are taken directly as a total variance to the income statement as a gain or a loss.

Backflush accounting is ideally suited to a **JIT system of purchasing and production**, and is suitable where inventory levels are low and so inventory values are immaterial.

JIT is described in more detail in a later chapter. Essentially, however, a JIT approach is to:

- purchase materials from suppliers just in time for when they are needed for production, and
- produce goods just in time for when customers want to buy them.

If JIT purchasing and production systems can be achieved, there is no requirement to hold inventories of materials or finished goods. In any JIT system, inventories should be small and financially immaterial - even if the ideal target of zero inventories cannot be achieved in practice.

4.2 The difference between traditional costing and costing with backflush accounting

Backflush accounting is a method of cost accounting that is consistent with JIT systems.

- Traditional cost accounting systems for manufacturing costs are 'sequential tracking' systems. They track the costs of items as they progress through the manufacturing process, from raw materials, through work in progress to finished goods. At each stage of the manufacturing process, more costs are added and recorded within the cost accounting system.

- The main benefit of sequential tracking costing systems is that they can be used to put a cost to items of inventory. When inventory is large, there is a need to measure inventory costs with reasonable 'accuracy'.

- With a JIT philosophy, this benefit does not exist. Inventory should be small, or even non-existent. The cost of inventory is therefore fairly insignificant. A costing system that measures the cost of inventory is therefore of little or no value, and is certainly not worth the time, effort and expenditure involved.

- Backflush accounting is an alternative costing system that can be applied in a JIT environment. It is ideally suited to a manufacturing environment where production cycle times are fairly short and inventory levels are low.

As the term 'backflush' might suggest, costs are calculated after production has been completed. They are allocated between the cost of goods sold and inventories in retrospect. They are not built up as work progresses through the production process.

4.3 The features of backflush accounting

With backflush accounting, the starting point for costing is the completion of production. Production costs are identified first. These are the costs of materials and other expenses that have been recorded and charged to production. If there is any inventory, this is given a value. The value should be immaterial so an estimate should be sufficient.

Gross profit is then calculated in the usual way:

	$	$
Sales		200,000
Opening inventory (immaterial)	50	
Costs of production	10,000	
	100,050	
Less closing inventory (immaterial)	(80)	
Cost of sales		99,970
Profit		100,030

It is important to recognise that the great advantage of backflush accounting is that costs can be worked 'backwards', after the goods have been produced and sold. There is no need for a complex cost accounting system that records costs of production sequentially.

4.4 Backflush accounting with two 'trigger points'

A backflush accounting system has one or two trigger points, when costs are recorded. When there are two trigger points, these are usually:

- the purchase of raw materials and

- the manufacture of completed products.

A numerical example will be used to illustrate the costing method.

Example

Suppose that a manufacturing company operates a JIT system. At the beginning of a period, it has no inventory of raw materials or finished goods. It manufactures a single product, Product P, which has the following standard cost:

	$
Raw materials	20
Direct labour	8
Overheads	22
	50

During the period, it incurred the following costs:

Raw materials purchased	$2,030,000
Direct labour costs incurred	$775,000
Overhead costs incurred	$2,260,000

The company made 100,000 units of Product P and sold 98,000 units.

The company uses a backflush costing system, with trigger points at raw materials purchase and at completion of production.

Trigger point 1

Record the purchase of raw materials

Raw materials inventory account

	$		$
Creditors	2,030,000		

Trigger point 2

Record the manufacture of the 100,000 units

Finished goods inventory account

		$		$
Raw materials	(100,000 × 20)	2,000,000		
Conversion costs	(100,000 × 30)	3,000,000		

Raw materials inventory account

	$		$
Creditors	2,030,000	Finished goods inventory	2,000,000
		Closing balance c/f	30,000
	2,030,000		2,030,000

Conversion costs account

	$		$
Bank (labour cost)	775,000	Finished goods inventory	3,000,000
Creditors (overheads)	2,260,000	Balance	35,000
	3,035,000		3,035,000

The closing balance on the raw materials account may represent the cost of closing inventory. If so, it is carried forward as an opening balance to the start of the next period. However, any cost variance (difference between standard and actual material cost) should be taken to the income statement for the period.

Similarly, the balance on the conversion costs account probably represents cost variances for labour and overhead, and this should be written off to the income statement for the period.

Management should identify the cause of any variances, and take control measures where appropriate. However, variances will probably be analysed using non-financial methods of investigation, and it is unlikely that detailed cost variances will be calculated in the backflush costing system.

The cost of sales and closing inventory of finished goods are simply recorded as follows:

Finished goods inventory account

		$			$
Raw materials	(100,000 × 20)	2,000,000	Cost of goods sold	(98,000 × 50)	4,900,000
Conversion costs	(100,000 × 30)	3,000,000	Closing inventory	(2,000 × 50)	100,000
		5,000,000			5,000,000

Example

An entity uses backflush accounting, with two trigger points, the purchase of raw materials and the manufacture of finished goods.

The following transactions occurred during a period when there was no opening inventory of raw materials or finished goods.

Purchase of raw materials	$25,600
Labour and overhead costs incurred	$15,700
Finished goods completed	1,000 units
Units sold	990 units

Standard cost per unit = $40, consisting of $25 materials and $15 conversion costs.

Using backflush accounting, material purchases are recorded when they occur but costs of production and sale can be established after the units have been produced and sold.

Recording initial costs:

Debit: Raw materials inventory	$25,600
Credit: Creditors/payables	$25,600
Debit: Conversion costs	$15,700
Credit: Creditors/payables	$15,700

When the units have been produced:

Debit: Finished goods (1,000 × $25)	$25,000
Credit: Raw materials inventory	$25,000
Debit: Finished goods (1,000 × $15)	$15,000
Credit: Conversion costs	$15,000

When the units are sold:

Debit: Cost of sales (990 × $40)	$39,600
Credit: Finished goods	$39,600.

This leaves a closing balance in finished goods of $400 (ten units). There is also a balance on the raw materials and conversion costs accounts. The raw materials balance may be a closing inventory value or may represent cost variances for materials. The conversion costs account balance will represent cost variances for conversion costs.

These accounting entries, made in retrospect, are sufficient to account for production costs and cost of sales in the period.

4.5 Backflush accounting with one 'trigger point'

An even simpler backflush accounting system has just one trigger point, the manufacture of finished units. Using the same example, the cost accounting entries would be as follows:

Finished goods inventory account

		$			$
Creditors	(100,000 × 20)	2,000,000	Cost of goods sold	(98,000 × 50)	4,900,000
Conversion costs	(100,000 × 30)	3,000,000	Closing inventory	(2,000 × 50)	100,000
		5,000,000			5,000,000

Conversion costs account

	$		$
Bank (labour cost)	775,000	Finished goods inventory	3,000,000
Creditors (overheads)	2,260,000	Balance	35,000
	3,035,000		3,035,000

The only difference is that there is no raw materials inventory account. The $30,000 of materials that has been purchased but not used is simply not recorded in the costing system, and is therefore not included in closing inventory at the end of the period.

4.6   Backflush accounting: conclusion

The examples above should illustrate that with backflush accounting, costs are not 'tracked' sequentially from raw materials through work in progress to finished goods and cost of sales. They are applied in retrospect, from finished goods and back to raw materials and conversion costs.

Backflush accounting therefore avoids the need to maintain a detailed cost accounting system, which can be regarded as a non-value added activity.

Management must monitor performance, but performance measurement is more likely to consist of non-financial performance indicators, rather than detailed cost variances.

CHAPTER

2

Accounting for decision-making

Contents
1   Decision-making and relevant costs
2   Short-term decisions
3   Cost-Volume-Profit (CVP) analysis

Decision-making and relevant costs

- Relevant costs
- Non-relevant costs
- Relevant cost of materials
- Relevant cost of labour
- Quantitative and qualitative factors in decision-making

---

1 Decision-making and relevant costs

Business decisions are often based on choosing a course of action that maximises profit or value. When a decision is made, there must be a choice between at least two different possible options. If the decision is based entirely on financial considerations, the choice should be the option with:

- the lowest expected cost, or
- the highest expected profit or return on capital.

When decisions are made to maximise profit or value, relevant costs and relevant revenues must be used in the financial evaluation of the decision.

1.1 Relevant costs

A **relevant cost** is a future cash flow arising as a direct consequence of the decision.

Relevant revenue is the extra revenue arising as a direct consequence of a decision.

Relevant costs include:
- incremental costs
- opportunity costs
- avoidable costs.

Incremental cost

An incremental cost is an extra cost (cash flow) that will be incurred as a direct consequence of a decision.

Opportunity cost

An opportunity cost is the benefit forgone by choosing one opportunity instead of the next best alternative course of action.

An opportunity cost is often measured as the extra contribution or profit that would have been earned by choosing the next best course of action.

Avoidable costs

Avoidable costs are future cash payments that will be avoided as a consequence of the decision. They are costs that can be identified with an activity or a business sector that would be avoided (saved) if that activity or sector did not exist. Avoidable costs are usually associated with shutdown or disinvestment decisions.

1.2   Non-relevant costs

A non-relevant cost is a cost that is not relevant to a decision. Non-relevant costs must be ignored for the financial analysis of a decision.
They are costs that are or will be incurred anyway, regardless of the decision that is made.

Non-relevant costs include:

■ sunk costs

■ committed costs

■ notional costs (or imputed costs)

Sunk costs

Sunk costs are costs that have already been incurred. Since they have been incurred, they are not relevant to any decision about the future.

An example of a sunk cost is the purchase cost of an asset that has already been acquired. (The relevant cost of an existing asset that would be used if a decision is taken is the benefit that would be obtained from using the asset in the next-most-profitable way. For example, the relevant cost of an asset might be the net revenue obtainable from disposing of it).

Historical costs are sunk costs. They are irrelevant for decision-making. However, historical costs might be used to estimate future costs that are relevant to a decision.

Committed costs

Committed costs are also irrelevant and should be ignored in the financial analysis of decisions. A committed cost is a future cost that will be incurred anyway, whatever decision is taken now.

A committed cost is a future cost that exists because of an existing obligation.

Notional costs (or imputed costs)

Notional costs are non-relevant costs. They are costs that do not represent cash flows. Examples of non-relevant costs, which must be ignored in decision-making, are:

■ apportioned or absorbed overhead costs

■ depreciation charges.

1.3 Relevant cost of materials

The relevant cost of raw materials is usually their current replacement cost. The relevant cost is the replacement cost when:

■ the materials will be purchased as a direct consequence of the decision

■ the materials have been purchased and are held in inventory, but if they are used as a consequence of the decision, they will be replaced (additional quantities will be purchased).

When materials are already held in inventory, and will not be replaced if they are used, the relevant cost is the higher of:

■ their current net disposal value, and

■ the savings or contribution that would be obtained by putting them to another use.

If the materials are already held in inventory and have no resale value and no other possible use, the relevant cost of using them is 0.

Relevant cost of materials

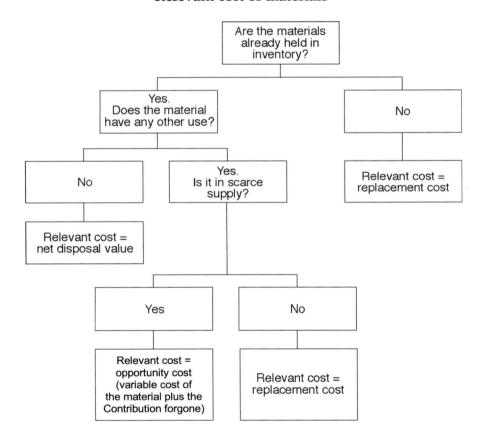

 Example

Entity Blue has been asked by a customer to quote for a job, and it is prepared to quote a price based on the relevant costs of the job plus a mark-up for profit. The job would require the following materials:

　　　　　　　　　　　　　　　　　　　© International Financial Publishing Limited

Material item	Total units required	Units held in inventory	Original purchase cost	Net disposal value	Replacement cost
			$ per unit	$ per unit	$ per unit
W	800	0	-	-	10.00
X	1,000	400	4.00	5.00	12.00
Y	1,000	700	6.00	4.00	8.00
Z	300	300	5.00	6.00	11.00

Material X is used regularly for other work.

Some units of materials Y and Z are held in inventory as the result of buying too many units in the past. There is no alternative use for Material Y which could be disposed of. The units of material Z could be used in another job as substitute for 400 units of Material V, which currently costs $7 per unit. Entity Blue currently has no units of Material V in inventory.

Required

Calculate the relevant costs of the materials for deciding whether or not to accept the contract.

Answer

Relevant costs of materials	$
Material W: (800 × $10)	8,000
Material X: (1,000 × $12)	12,000
Material Y: (700 × $4) + (300 × $8)	5,200
Material Z: (400 × $7)	2,800
	28,000

Notes on relevant costs

- All the units of **Material W** will have to be purchased in full at a cost of $10 per unit.

- **Material X** is in regular use. 400 units are held in inventory, but if these are used for the job, they will have to be replaced. Relevant costs are therefore 1,000 units at the replacement cost of $12 per unit.

- 1,000 units of **Material Y** are needed and 700 are already held in inventory. If they are used for the job, 300 extra units must be bought at $8 each. The existing inventory of 700 units will not be replaced when they are used. However, if they are not used for the job, they could be sold at $4 each. The disposal value of these 700 units is an opportunity cost.

- The units of **Material Z** needed for the job are already held in inventory. They will not be replaced if they are used for the job. However, there is an opportunity cost of using the materials because the units could either be disposed of for $6 per unit ($1,800 in total) or used instead of other materials (Material V) that would cost 400 × $7 = $2,800. Since substituting the Material Z in place of Material V is more beneficial, the opportunity cost is $2,800.

1.4 Relevant costs of labour

The relevant cost of labour should be established as follows:

Relevant cost of labour

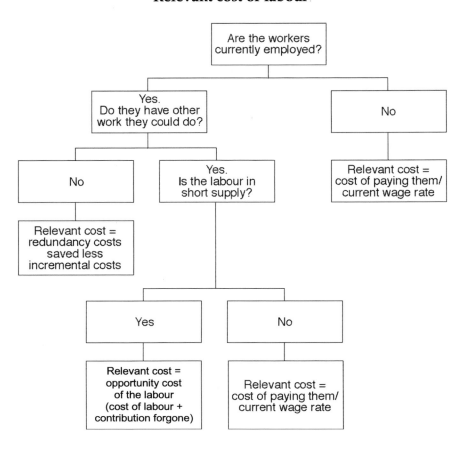

 Example

A printing company has been asked by a regular customer to do a special job at a competitive price. The management accountant has been asked to identify the minimum price to charge that would leave the printing company no worse off but no better off by doing the job.

The following estimates for the job have been prepared:

	$
Grade 1 labour (4 hours at $20 per hour)	80
Grade 2 labour (3 hours at $30 per hour)	90
Grade 3 labour: (2 hours at $15)	30
Paper	150
Variable overhead (9 hours at $5 per hour)	45
Fixed overhead (9 hours at $25 per hour)	225
	620

(a) Grade 1 employees are paid a fixed wage for a 40-hour working week. This job could be done mostly in normal working time, but two hours of Grade 1 overtime would be needed.

(b) Similarly, all Grade 2 employees are paid for a 40-hour working week. Two hours of Grade 2 overtime would be needed to do the work.

(c) All overtime is paid at 50% above normal hourly rates.

(d) The Grade 3 employees are already working at full capacity, and if they are used to do this job for the customer, a Grade 3 employee would be switched from doing other work where he is earning a contribution of $10 per hour.

(e) The paper will have to be purchased for the job.

Required

What is the price the company should charge for the job to make a 20% mark-up on the minimum price at which it would make no profit but no loss?

Answer

Relevant costs	$
Grade 1 labour: (2 hours × $20) plus 50%	60
Grade 2 labour: (2 hours × $30) plus 50%	90
Grade 3 labour: (2 hours × $25)	50
Paper	150
Variable overheads: (9 hours × $5)	45
Minimum price (relevant costs)	395
Mark-up (20%)	79
Price for the customer	474

Notes on relevant costs

■ **Grade 1 and Grade 2 labour.** Labour in normal time is a committed cost, and is not relevant to decision about the minimum price. However, overtime hours, paid at 50% over the normal rate, are relevant because they will be incremental costs.

■ **Grade 3 labour.** There is an opportunity cost of using the labour on this job instead of on another job, which would earn a contribution of $10 per hour. Opportunity cost = $15 + $10 = $25 per hour.

■ It is assumed that variable overhead is a relevant cost.

■ It is assumed that fixed overhead spending would be unaffected and the absorbed fixed overheads for the job are not relevant.

1.5 Quantitative and qualitative factors in decision-making

Relevant cost analysis is based on the assumption that the decision should be to choose the option where the financial benefit will be the greatest. For decisions with a short-term payback (short-term decisions), a decision should be taken if:

■ there is a net cash flow benefit and no other option offers a better net cash flow benefit

■ the net cost, measured in relevant cash flows, is less than with any other option.

For longer-term decisions (capital expenditure decisions), the timing of cash flows and the time value of money should be taken into consideration, using discounted cash flow analysis.

The assumption that decisions should be based on financial considerations alone might not be valid. Financial considerations are important, but a decision might be taken for non-financial reasons, or non-financial factors might affect the choice between two or more different courses of action.

Non-financial factors that could affect a decision include:

- **customer satisfaction**: it may be better to spend more to provide customers with a better service, or a higher **quality** of product
- **reputation**: a company might choose one course of action in preference to another in order to protect its reputation in the market
- **speed**: it is sometimes worth paying more to get a job finished more quickly, or to provide a faster delivery service
- **customer relationships**: a company might be willing to spend money in the short-term in order to protect a well-established relationship with a customer.

> ### Short-term decisions
>
> - Short-term decisions and long-term decisions
> - Types of short-term decision
> - Discontinuance decisions (shutdown decisions)
> - Short-term decisions based on limiting factors
> - Make or buy decisions
> - Decisions to accept or reject an order
> - Further processing decisions

2 Short-term decisions

2.1 Short-term decisions and long-term decisions

Relevant costs should be used for the evaluation of all decisions. However, a distinction might be made between short-term and long-term decisions because:

- with short-term decisions (typically, within a time period of one year or less) the cost of capital is not relevant
- with long-term decisions (typically, with a time period of more than one year) the cost of capital is relevant and future cash flows are discounted to a present value.

2.2 Types of short-term decision

There can be many types of short-term decision, but decisions that might be the subject of an examination question include:

- discontinuance decisions (or shutdown decisions)
- short-term decisions based on limiting factors
- make or buy decisions when there is a limiting factor
- decisions whether to accept or reject an order
- further processing decisions.

2.3 Discontinuance decisions (shutdown decisions)

A discontinuance decision, or shutdown decision, is a decision whether or not to shut down an operation or a part of the business.

The financial decision should usually be based on a comparison of:

- the loss in revenue from closing down the operation, and
- the saving in costs from closing down (avoidable costs).

Shutdown decisions are often long-term decisions and not short-term decisions, because a decision to shut down an operation will affect profits for several years in the future. However, you might also come across a shutdown decision where the consequences are only for the short-term.

Example

Luca Company has three operating divisions. The expected financial results of each division next year are as follows:

	Division X	Division Y	Division Z
	$	$	$
Sales	50,000	30,000	40,000
Variable costs	(30,000)	(18,000)	(20,000)
Specific fixed costs	(12,000)	(10,000)	(10,000)
Apportioned head office costs	(5,000)	(4,000)	(5,000)
Profit/(loss)	3,000	(2,000)	5,000

Required

Taking only the financial results next year into consideration, recommend whether or not Division Y should be closed down.

Answer

Division Y	$
Loss of sales from closure	(30,000)
Saving in variable costs	18,000
Fall in contribution from closure	(12,000)
Saving in specific fixed costs	10,000
Net loss from closure	(2,000)

On the basis of this information, Division Y should remain open as it will make a net addition to profit next year of $2,000.

This assumes that all the specific fixed costs will be saved if the division is closed but that there will be no savings in head office costs.

2.4 Short-term decisions based on limiting factors

A limiting factor is a resource that limits the volume of activity in a period, such as the volume of production and sales. A limiting factor could be a restricted supply of materials, or labour or machine time.

If there is a limiting factor, relevant cost analysis assumes that the decision should be to make and sell the items that will maximise profit in the period, making the best possible use of the scarce resource.

It is also assumed that profit will be maximised by **maximising total contribution.**

When there is just one scarce resource, contribution is maximised by making and selling the items that provide the maximum contribution per unit of the limiting factor (maximum contribution per unit of the scarce resource).

When the sales demand for any item is restricted, items should be ranked in order of contribution per unit of the scarce resource. Profit will be maximised by making and selling the top-ranked up to the sales demand limit.

 Example

Entity Yellow makes and sells three products, A, B and C. Budget estimates for each product for next year are as follows:

	Product A	Product B	Product C
	$	$	$
Sales price	21	22	15
Variable costs:			
Materials	7	12	9
Labour	9	6	3
Fixed cost	3	2	2
	units	units	units
Sales demand	6,000	5,000	4,000

All three products use the same direct materials and are made by the same employees. Labour is paid $12 per hour. In the next year, the available supply of materials will be restricted to $150,000 (at cost) and the available supply of labour to 7,100 hours.

Required

What products should the entity make and sell next year in order to maximise profit?

 Answer

There might be **two** scarce resources, materials and labour. The first step is to find out whether either of them (or both of them) is a limiting factor.

Materials	Product A	Product B	Product C	Total
	$	$	$	$
Required to meet budget	42,000	60,000	36,000	138,000
Available				150,000
Surplus				12,000

Materials are not a limiting factor.

Labour	Product A	Product B	Product C	Total
	hours	hours	hours	hours
Required to meet budget	4,500	2,500	1,000	8,000
Available				7,100
Shortage				900

Labour is a limiting factor. Total profit and total contribution will be maximised by earning the largest contribution possible for each labour hour worked.

	Product A	Product B	Product C
	$	$	$
Sales price	21	22	15
Variable costs	16	18	12
Contribution per unit	5	4	3
Labour hours per unit	0.75	0.50	0.25
Contribution per hour	$6.67	$8.00	$12.00
Ranking	3rd	2nd	1st

The profit-maximising schedule for production and sales is as follows:

Product	Number of units	Number of labour hours	Contribution
			$
C	4,000	1,000	12,000
B	5,000	2,500	20,000
		3,500	32,000
A (balance)	4,800	3,600	24,000
		7,100	56,000

Assumptions in limiting factor analysis

The following assumptions are made in limiting factor analysis. If any of these assumptions are not correct, the profit-maximising decision might be different.

■ **Fixed costs will be the same** regardless of the decision that is taken. This means that profit will be maximised if contribution is maximised. This assumption might be wrong. Some fixed costs might be **specific** to a product, and the decision to reduce the production volume might result in some saving in the fixed costs.

■ The **unit variable cost is constant** at all levels of production and sales.

■ The **estimates of sales demand** for each product are **known with certainty**. These estimates might be wrong.

2.5 Make or buy decisions

A make or buy decision is a decision about whether to make items internally, or whether to sub-contract their manufacture to an external supplier. Work that is sub-contracted to an external supplier is 'outsourced'.

A make or buy decision might arise when an entity has a limiting factor that prevents it from masking everything itself. In this situation, it could be profitable to sub-contract some of the work.

The decision to be made is:

■ Whether it is profitable to sub-contract work, and

■ If so, which items should be purchased and which should be made internally.

The decision is based on a comparison of:

- The relevant costs of in-house manufacture and
- The costs of external purchase.

If there is a limiting factor that prevents the entity from making everything itself, the decision about what to make and what to buy is reached by:

- calculating the additional cost of external purchase (extra cost) for each unit of limiting factor
- ranking the products in order of extra cost per unit of limiting factor
- buying the products where the extra cost is the lowest.

 Example

Entity Red makes four items W, X, Y and Z, for which costs and sales in the next year are expected to be as follows:

Item:	W	X	Y	Z
Sales	2,000 units	4,000 units	3,000 units	1,000 units
Variable cost/unit	$	$	$	$
Materials	10	5	7.5	12.5
Labour	7	2	4.5	6.5
	17	7	12.0	19.0
Sales price	29	11	18.0	39.0
Contribution	12	4	6.0	20.0

The entity is having difficulty in obtaining the materials. Each product uses the same material, and only one type of material is used in manufacture. The expected availability of materials next year is 11,000 kilos. The material costs $5 per kilo.

An overseas manufacturer is willing to supply the items to Entity Red at the following costs per unit (including delivery costs):

Item	$
W	20.00
X	11.00
Y	15.75
Z	21.50

Required

Which items should Entity Red make internally, and which should it buy from the external manufacturer?

Answer

Are materials a limiting factor?

Materials required to meet sales	kilos
W: (2,000 × 2 kilos)	4,000
X: (4,000 × 1 kilo)	4,000
Y: (3,000 × 1.5 kilos)	4,500
Z: (1,000 × 2.5 kilos)	2,500
	15,000
Available	11,000
Shortage	4,000

Materials are a limiting factor.

	W	X	Y	Z
	$	$	$	$
Variable cost/unit to make	17	7	12.00	19.0
Cost of buying	20	11	15.75	21.5
Extra cost of buying	3	4	3.75	2.5
Materials/unit	2 kilos	1 kilo	1.5 kilos	2.5 kilos
Extra cost of buying/kilo	$1.5	$4	$2.5	$1.0
Ranking for purchase	3rd	1st	2nd	4th

The make or buy decision should be as follows, to maximise contribution and profit.

Item	Number of units	Materials kilos	Contribution per unit	Contribution
Make			$	$
X	4,000	4,000	4	16,000
Y	3,000	4,500	6	18,000
		8,500		
W (balance)	1,250	2,500	12	15,000
		11,000		49,000
Buy				
W (balance)	750	(12 – 3)	9	6,750
Z	1,000	(20 – 2.5)	9	17,500
Total contribution				73,250

2.6 Decisions to accept or reject an order

Another type of decision is a decision whether or not to accept an order. The comparison here should be between:

■ the relevant costs of the order, including any opportunity cost of other opportunities forgone as a consequence, and

■ the incremental revenue from the order.

The normal rules of relevant costing should be applied.

Example

Entity Purple is considering whether or not to undertake an order from a customer. It is trying to establish the relevant costs of the order.

(1) The order would require 3,000 kilos of material P. There are over 3,000 kilos already held in inventory. Material P is no longer in regular use by Entity Purple and could be disposed of for scrap at $1.50 per kilo. It could also be used as a substitute for Material Q, which is in regular use for making another product. Material Q can be purchased for $4 per kilo. To use Material P as a substitute for Material Q, conversion costs of $1.60 per kilo would have to be spent on the Material P. One kilo of material P, after conversion, would be a substitute for one kilo of material Q.

(2) Skilled labour needed to fulfil the order would be specially recruited for $50,000.

(3) Unskilled labour needed to fulfil the order would be transferred from another department. The cost of the labour time (3,000 hours) would be $30,000 in wages. However, 1,500 of these hours would be idle time if the order is not undertaken. The other 1,500 hours would be spent on work that would provide a contribution of $5,000.

Required

Identify the relevant costs of materials and labour for this customer order.

Answer

The **relevant cost of Material P** is the benefit that would be obtained from its most profitable alternative use. The alternatives for using Material P are:

(a) to sell it for scrap and earn $1.50 per kilo.

(b) to use it as a substitute for material Q, and save ($4 – $1.60) $2.40 per kilo.

The relevant cost of material P is therefore $2.40 per kilo.

The **relevant cost of the unskilled labour**, which will be paid wages of $30,000 anyway, is the loss of cash flow from having to move the labour from other work. Contribution is calculated after deducting labour cost as a variable cost; therefore 50% of the labour cost – $15,000 – must be included in the relevant cost.

Relevant costs	$
Material P (3,000 kilos × $2.40)	7,200
Skilled labour	50,000
Unskilled workers	
Use of idle time	0
Use of other time (50% × $30,000) + $5,000	20,000
	77,200

2.7 Further processing decisions

A further processing decision may arise in a manufacturing company that produces an item in a process or a sequence of processes. The output from a process might have a market, and a selling price. However, there might also be an opportunity to further process the output to produce a finished item with a higher selling price.

The decision is whether to sell the item in its part-finished form, or whether to process it further and sell the finished item.

The relevant cash flows are:

■ the extra (net) revenue obtained by further processing the item, and

■ the incremental costs of further processing.

The financial decision should be to further process the item if the extra revenue exceeds the incremental costs.

Example

A company manufactures two cleaning fluids, X and Y. The two fluids are manufactured in a joint process. Every 8,000 litres of materials input to the joint process produces 4,000 litres of X and 3,200 litres of Y. The costs of processing are as follows:

	$
Direct materials: 8,000 litres	1,600
Direct labour	200
Variable production overhead	300
Fixed production overhead	2,000
	4,100

Product X sells for $1.10 per litre and product Y for $0.75 per litre.

The company could put product X through another production process, where there is spare production capacity. The further processing would produce another cleaning product, ZPlus. Every one litre of input to the further process will produce 0.90 litres of Zplus.

The costs of further processing would be:

	$
Product X: 4,000 litres	
Added materials in further processing	400
Direct labour	40
Variable production overhead	80
Fixed production overhead	400
	920

Zplus would sell for $1.40 per litre.

Required

Using financial reasons only to justify the decision, should the company sell product X or should it further process the product to make Zplus? Assume for the purpose of the analysis that direct labour is a variable cost.

Answer

The joint processing costs are irrelevant to the decision. They will be incurred in both cases, if product X is sold for $1.10 per litre or is processed further to make Zplus. The analysis of relevant cash flows is as follows:

Every 4,000 litres of product X can be further processed to make 3,600 litres of ZPlus.

		$
Revenue from sale of 3,600 litres of Zplus (× $1.40)		5,040
Revenue from sale of 4,000 litres of product X (× $1.10)		4,400
Incremental revenue from further processing		640
Incremental costs of further processing		
Added materials in further processing	400	
Direct labour	40	
Variable production overhead	80	
Fixed production overhead		520
Incremental gain from further processing		120

There would be an incremental gain of $120 from further processing, for every 4,000 litres of product X that are further processed. This analysis assumes that there would be no additional fixed costs from further processing, and that no capital expenditure would be required to make further processing possible.

> ### Cost-Volume-Profit (CVP) analysis
>
> - Calculating the break-even point
> - The margin of safety
> - CVP analysis and decision-making
> - CVP analysis and more than one product

3 Cost-volume-profit (CVP) analysis

Cost-volume-profit analysis, or CVP analysis should be familiar to you from your earlier studies. These notes are revision notes, and also explain the approach to CVP analysis when an organisation makes and sells several products, not just one product.

Cost analysis, sometimes called break-even analysis, is the study of the inter-relationships between costs, sales volume and profit at various levels of activity. CVP analysis is based on marginal costing, and assumes that costs can be categorised into variables costs and fixed costs.

To help with planning and decision-making, management should know not only what the budgeted profit will be, but also:

- the sales level at which there will be neither profit nor loss (the break-even point), and
- the amount by which actual sales can fall below the budgeted sales level, without incurring a loss (the margin of safety).

3.1 Calculating the break-even point

A break-even point can be calculated in either of two ways.

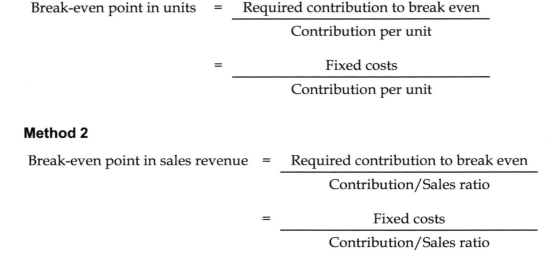

Method 1

$$\text{Break-even point in units} = \frac{\text{Required contribution to break even}}{\text{Contribution per unit}}$$

$$= \frac{\text{Fixed costs}}{\text{Contribution per unit}}$$

Method 2

$$\text{Break-even point in sales revenue} = \frac{\text{Required contribution to break even}}{\text{Contribution/Sales ratio}}$$

$$= \frac{\text{Fixed costs}}{\text{Contribution/Sales ratio}}$$

Example

An entity makes a single product that has a variable cost of $3 per unit. The selling price is $8 per unit. Fixed costs in each month are $200,000.

(a) **The break-even point in units**

Contribution per unit = $8 – $3 = $5.
Break-even point = $200,000/$5 per unit = 40,000 units each month.

(b) **The break-even point in sales revenue**

Contribution/sales (C/S) ratio = $5/$8 = 0.625
Break-even point = $200,000/0.625 = $320,000.

3.2 The margin of safety

The margin of safety is the difference in units between the budgeted sales volume and the break-even sales volume and it is usually expressed as a percentage of the budgeted sales volume.

The margin of safety may also be expressed as the difference between the budgeted sales revenue and break-even sales revenue, expressed as a percentage of either:

■ the budgeted sales revenue, or

■ the break-even sales volume.

It shows by how much actual sales could fall below the budget target without a loss being incurred. It is therefore a simple measure of risk in the budget estimates of sales.

Example

Entity ABC makes and sells a product that has a variable cost of $15 and a selling price of $20. Budgeted fixed costs for the year are $800,000 and budgeted sales are 200,000 units.

The contribution per unit is $5 ($20 – $15).

Break-even point is therefore $800,000/$5 per unit = 160,000 units.

The margin of safety is 40,000 units (200,000 – 160,000)

This is 25% of the break-even sales volume and 20% of the budgeted sales volume.

3.3 CVP analysis and decision-making

Simple CVP analysis can be used in decision-making. Some examples are shown below.

Example

Entity Blue makes and sells a single product, for which variable costs are as follows:

	$
Direct materials	12
Direct labour	8
Variable overheads	6
	26

The sales price is $35 per unit, and fixed costs per year are $468,000. The company wishes to make a profit of $180,000 next year.

Required
Calculate the sales volume required to achieve this target profit.

Answer

Target profit = $180,000

Therefore target contribution = $468,000 + $180,000 = $648,000.

Contribution per unit = $35 – $26 = $9

Therefore target sales = $648,000/$9 per unit = 72,000 units.

Alternatively:

C/S ratio = 9/35

Therefore target sales = $648,000/(9/35) = $2,520,000.

Example

Entity DEF makes a product whose variable cost is $0.60 per unit. The current selling price is $1.80 per unit. Fixed costs are $80,000 per month, and the monthly profit at current sales volume is $11,000.

The entity wishes to raise the sales price to $2.00 per unit, but is aware that an increase in the selling price will result in some loss of sales.

Required
If the selling price is increased to $2.00, what would be the minimum volume of sales each month needed to prevent a fall in profits?

Answer

Minimum target contribution = Fixed costs + Target profit
= $80,000 + $11,000 = $91,000.
If the selling price is increased to $2, the contribution per unit will be $1.40.

Required sales volume to earn a contribution of $91,000
= $91,000/$1.40 per unit = 65,000 units.

Example

Entity GHJ makes a product that has a variable cost of $18 and a sales price of $26 per unit. Fixed costs are $608,000 per year. The current annual volume of sales is 90,000 units.

The entity would like to increase the annual sales volume, but in order to increase annual production and sales above 90,000 units, it would have to hire additional equipment, at an annual cost of $64,000.

Required

What is the number of units that must be sold each year to achieve the same profit as is currently earned, if the additional equipment is hired?

Answer

The current unit contribution is $(26 – 18) = $8.

	$
Total contribution currently earned (90,000 × $8)	720,000
Extra fixed costs of hiring equipment	64,000
Minimum annual contribution required if equipment is hired	784,000

Minimum sales required = $784,000/$8 per unit = 98,000 units.

The minimum sales requirement is therefore 8,000 higher than the current annual sales volume, assuming that there will be no change in the selling price or the unit variable cost.

Example

Entity JKL issues mobile phones to all its sales representatives. The sales manager has been looking at two different tariffs for telephones.

(a)   Tariff 1: an annual rental of $600 plus calls charged at $0.05 per minute

(b)   Tariff 2: an annual rental of $360 plus calls charged at $0.08 per minute.

Below what volume of usage would Tariff 2 be cheaper?

Answer

Suppose that the annual usage of a telephone is x minutes.

Tariff 1 = 600 + 0.05x
Tariff 2 = 360 + 0.08x

Total costs are the same when:

600 + 0.05x = 360 + 0.08x
0.03x = 240,
x = 8,000 minutes.

Below annual usage of 8,000 minutes, Tariff 2 is cheaper.

3.4 CVP analysis and more than one product

CVP analysis can be used when an entity sells more than one product, but only if it is assumed that products are sold in a fixed proportion or ratio. Without this assumption of a fixed selling ratio, it is impossible to calculate a unique break-even point or target sales level to achieve a certain amount of profit.

To use CVP analysis, we must use either:

■ a weighted average contribution per unit, based on the budgeted units of sale, or

■ a weighted average contribution/sales ratio, based on the budgeted sales revenue (in $).

These weighted average amounts can be used to calculate a break-even point, and the units or sales revenues for each product are then calculated by applying the budgeted sales proportions.

Example

Entity MNP has the following budget for next year.

Product	Sales	Sales price	Variable cost	Contribution per unit	Total contribution
	units	$	$	$	$
A	5,000	7	5	2	10,000
B	5,000	14	6	8	40,000
C	20,000	4	1	3	60,000
D	5,000	10	4	6	30,000
	35,000				140,000

Fixed costs will be $100,000.

What is the break-even point?

Answer

Break-even point in units

Total contribution = $140,000
Weighted average contribution per unit = $140,000/35,000 units = $4 per unit.
Break-even point = $100,000/$4 per unit = 25,000 units.
Break-even point: sales of each unit:

Product		Sales	Contribution per unit	Total contribution
		units	$	$
A	(1/7)	3,571.4	2	7,142.8
B	(1/7)	3,571.4	8	28,571.2
C	(4/7)	14,285.8	3	42,857.4
D	(1/7)	3,571.4	6	21,428.4
		25,000.0		99,999.8

This is the break-even position, allowing for a rounding difference of $0.02.

Break-even point in sales revenue

Budgeted sales = (5,000 × $7) + (5,000 × $14) + (20,000 × $4) + (5,000 × $10) = $235,000.

Budgeted weighted average C/S ratio = $140,000/$235,000 = 140/235 = 0.59574468.
Break-even point = $100,000/0.59574468. = $167,857.

This break-even point is 71.42857% of budgeted sales (167,857/235,000).

Product	Break-even sales	Contribution/ Sales ratio	Total contribution
	$		$
A	25,000	2/7	7,142.9
B	50,000	8/14	28,571.4
C	57,143	3/4	42,857.3
D	35,714	6/10	21,428.4
	167,857		100,000.0

CHAPTER

3

Decision-making with risk and uncertainty

Contents	
1	Risk and expected values
2	Perfect and imperfect information
3	Decision trees
4	Assessing risk in decision-making

> ## Risk and expected values
>
> - Decision-making and risk and uncertainty
> - Risk preference
> - Worst, most likely and best possible outcomes
> - Maximax, maximin and minimax regret decision rules
> - Expected values

1 Risk and expected values

1.1 Decision-making and risk and uncertainty

Decision-making, particularly long-term decision-making, has to be taken under conditions of risk and uncertainty.

- **Uncertainty** occurs when there is insufficient information about what will happen, or what will probably happen, in the future. It is therefore likely that estimates of future values (future sales, future costs, and so on) will be inaccurate.

- **Risk** occurs when future events of the future outcome could be any of several different possibilities. However, the probabilities of each possible outcome can be assessed with reasonable accuracy.

Uncertainty in decision-making can be reduced by obtaining more reliable information. Risk cannot be removed from a decision, because risk exists in the situation itself. A decision-maker can try to analyse the risk, and must make a decision on the basis of whether the risk is justified or acceptable.

1.2 Risk preference

Risk preference describes the attitude of a decision-maker towards risk. Decision-makers might be described as risk averse, risk-seeking or possibly risk neutral.

- A **risk-averse decision maker** considers risk in making a decision, and will not select a course of action that is more risky unless the expected return is higher and so justifies the extra risk. It is not correct to state that a risk-averse decision-makerseeks to avoid risk as much as possible. However, a risk-averse decision-makermight expect a substantially higher return to make the extra risk worth taking.

- A **risk-neutral decision maker** ignores risk in making a decision. The decision of a risk neutral decision-makeris to select the course of action with the highest expected return, regardless of risk. The highest expected return could mean the highest EV of NPV or the highest EV of profit.

- A **risk-seeking decision maker** also considers risk in making a decision. A risk seeker, unlike a risk-averse decision-maker, will take extra risks in the hope of earning a higher return. Given two options with the same EV of NPV, a risk seeker will prefer the option with the higher risk.

Example

A company must make a choice between three different projects A, B and C. These three projects are mutually exclusive. The net present values of each project have been estimated as follows:

	Project A	Project B	Project C
	NPV	NPV	NPV
Probability 0.5	+ 800,000	+ 2,000,000	+ 100,000
Probability 0.5	- 500,000	- 1,700,000	+ 50,000
Expected value of NPV	+ 150,000	+ 150,000	+ 75,000

Projects A and B have a higher expected NPV than project C, but are more risky. Project C would have a positive NPV, whereas projects A and B have a 50% chance of a negative NPV. Project B is more risky than project A, although it has the same expected return (NPV) of + 150,000. With project B, the NPV could be as high as + 2,000,000, but could also be as low as – 1,700,000.

So which project should be undertaken?

- A risk-averse decision-maker would choose either project A or project C. Project C offers a lower return but lower risk, and project A has a higher expected return but higher risk. A risk-averse decision-maker would not choose project B, because project A offers the same expected return for less risk.

- A risk-seeking decision-maker would choose project B rather than project A, in the hope of making a return of + 2,000,000.

- A risk-neutral decision-maker might choose either project A or project B because they both offer the same expected return, which is higher than the expected return from project C.

1.3 Worst, most likely and best possible outcomes

The choice between two or more alternative courses of action might be based on the worst, most likely or best expected outcomes from each course of action. A simple example will be used to explain this point.

Example

A company must make a decision between three possible courses of action, 1, 2 and 3. The expected profit or loss from each course of action has been estimated as follows:

Course of action	Worst possible outcome	Most likely outcome	Best possible outcome
Course 1	- 1,000	+ 4,000	+ 5,000
Course 2	- 500	+ 2,500	+ 7,000
Course 3	- 3,000	+ 1,000	+ 9,000

The course of action chosen by the company will depend on the attitude to risk of its decision-maker.

- A decision might be taken to select the project where the possible loss is the lowest. This would be course of action 2, where the worst outcome is – 500. This is not as bad as the worst outcome for courses of action 1 and 3. A risk-averse decision-maker might choose this course of action.

- A decision might be taken on the basis of the most likely outcome. The preferred course of action would then be the one where the expected return is highest. In this example, the preferred course of action would be course 1, where the most likely return is + 4,000. This is better than course 2 (+ 2,500) or course 3 (+ 1,000).

- A decision might be taken on the basis of the best possible return. The preferred course of action would then be the one that offers the highest return. Here, the preferred course of action would be course 3 (+ 9,000). This course of action would be the choice of a risk-seeking decision-maker.

The main disadvantage of choosing between mutually-exclusive courses of action on the basis of the worst, most likely or best possible outcome is that the choice **ignores the likelihood or probability** of the worst, most likely or best outcomes actually happening.

1.4 Maximax, maximin and minimax regret decision rules

Choosing between mutually-exclusive courses of action on the basis of worst, most likely or best possible outcome can be stated as 'decision rules'. The choice may be based on a maximax, maximin or a minimax regret decision rule.

- **Maximax decision rule**. The decision-maker will select the course of action with the highest possible pay-off. The decision-maker seeks the highest return, assuming that events turn out in the best way possible. The maximax decision rule is a decision rule for the risk-seeker.

- **Maximin decision rule**. The decision-maker will select the course of action with the highest expected return under the worst possible conditions. This decision rule might be associated with a risk adverse decision maker.

- **Minimax regret decision rule**. The decision-maker selects the course of action with the lowest possible 'regret'. 'Regret' is the opportunity cost of having made the wrong decision, given the actual conditions that apply in the future.

 Example

The previous example will be used again as an example, but with one number changed.

A business entity has to decide which of three projects to select for investment. The three projects are mutually exclusive, and only one of them can be selected.

The expected profits from investing in each of the projects will depend on the state of the market. The following estimates of net present value have been prepared:

State of market	Diminishing	Static	Expanding
Probability	0.4	0.3	0.3
	$000	$000	$000
Project 1	100	200	950
Project 2	0	500	600
Project 3	180	190	200

Which options would be selected?

(a)   under the maximax decision rule

(b)   under the minimax decision rule

(c)   under the minimax regret decision rule?

Answer

(a)   **Maximax decision rule**. The most favourable outcome is an expanding market. Project 1 offers the highest return in an expanding market; therefore project 1 will be selected.

(b)   **Minimax decision rule**. The least favourable outcome is a diminishing market. The most favourable outcome in a diminishing market is project 3; therefore project 3 will be selected.

(c)   **Minimax regret decision rule**. To establish the decision under the minimax regret decision rule, we must first prepare a pay-off table showing the regret the decision-maker would have choosing option 1, option 2 or option 3, and the actual market conditions turn out diminishing, static or expanding.

The regret with each course of action is shown in the pay-off table below. The right-hand column of the table shows the maximum regret.

State of market	Diminishing	Static	Expanding	Maximum regret
	$000	$000	$000	
Project 1	80	300	0	300
Project 2	180	0	350	350
Project 3	0	310	750	750

If you are not sure how regret is calculated, the following notes might be helpful:

■   If project 1 is selected and the market condition turns out to be diminishing, the regret will be not having chosen option 3, because the NPV with option 1 would be 100 and with option 3 it would be 180. The regret is therefore 180 – 100 = 80.

■   If project 1 is selected and the market condition turns out to be static, the regret will be not having chosen option 2, because the NPV with option 1 would be 200 and with option 2 it would be 500. The regret is therefore 500 – 200 = 300.

■   If project 1 is selected and the market condition turns out to be expanding, there is no regret because the best possible option has been chosen.

■   The maximum regret with option 1 is the highest of 180, 300 and 0. This is 300.

The minimum 'maximum regret' is 300 with option 1. Option 1 would therefore be selected if the minimax regret rule is applied.

1.5 Expected values

Expected values can be used to analyse information where risk can be assessed. Where probabilities are assigned to different outcomes, we can evaluate the worth of a decision as the expected value or weighted average of these outcomes.

Expected value (EV) = weighted average of possible outcomes.

The weighted average value is calculated by applying the probability of each possible outcome to the value of the outcome.

$$EV = \sum px$$

Where
p = the probability of each outcome and
x = the value of each outcome

An EV is a measurement of **weighted average value**.

A decision might be based on selecting the course of action that offers the highest EV of profit, or the lowest EV of cost. In other words, the 'decision rule' is to select the course of action with the highest EV of profit or the lowest EV of cost.

The main advantage of using EVs to make a decision, compared to the decision rules explained earlier, is that it takes into consideration the probability or likelihood of each different possible outcome.

Example

A business entity has to decide which of three projects to select for investment. The three projects are mutually exclusive, and only one of them can be selected.

The expected profits from investing in each of the projects will depend on the state of the market. The following estimates of net present value have been prepared:

State of market	Diminishing	Static	Expanding
Probability	0.4	0.3	0.3
	$000	$000	$000
Project 1	100	200	900
Project 2	0	500	600
Project 3	180	190	200

(**Note**: This type of table is called a 'pay-off table' or a 'pay-off matrix'. It shows all the possible 'pay-offs' or results – NPV, profit and so on – from different possible decisions or strategies).

Required

Identify which project would be selected if the decision is to choose the project with the highest expected value of NPV.

Answer

State of market	Probability	Project 1		Project 2		Project 3	
		NPV	EV of NPV	NPV	EV of NPV	NPV	EV of NPV
		$000	$000	$000	$000	$000	$000
Diminishing	0.4	100	40	0	0	180	72
Static	0.3	200	60	500	150	190	57
Expanding	0.3	900	270	600	180	200	60
			370		330		189

Based on expected values, project 1 should be selected.

Advantages of using expected values

Using EVs to make a decision has some advantages.

■ An EV is a weighted average value, that is based on all the different possible outcomes and the probability that each will occur.

■ It recognises the risk in decisions, based on the probabilities of different possible results or outcomes.

■ It expresses risk in a single figure.

Disadvantages of using expected values

Using EVs to make a decision also has some disadvantages.

■ The probabilities of the different possible outcomes may be difficult to estimate.

■ The EV is unlikely to be an actual outcome that could occur. In the example above, the EVs for projects 1, 2 and 3 (370, 330 and 189) are not expected to occur. They are simply weighted average values.

■ Unless the same decision has to be made many times, the average will not be achieved. It is therefore not a valid way of making a decision about the future when the outcome will happen only once.

■ An EV is an average value. It gives no indication of the range or spread of possible outcomes. It is therefore an inadequate measurement of risk.

Example

A business entity has a choice of three different projects. They all involve the same amount of capital expenditure, and the entity can only afford one of the three projects. The expected NPV of the three projects will depend on future market conditions, which may be poor (probability 30%) moderate (probability 50%) or good (probability 20%).

The following table sets out the NPV for each product for each possible market condition. It also shows the EV of the NPV. (Workings are not shown, but make sure that you can calculate the EVs).

Project	Poor (0.3) NPV $m	Moderate (0.5) NPV $m	Good (0.2) NPV $m	EV of NPV $m
1	(20)	15	60	+ 13.5
2	1	10	20	+ 9.1
3	(10)	22	38	+ 15.6

Using EV as a basis for decision-making, the decision should be to select Project 3.

However, an EV is just a weighted average of different possible outcomes. The NPV is more likely to be positive than negative, but there is some risk of a negative NPV. And if the market conditions are good, it would be much better to choose Project 1.

There are other ways of making a logical choice between mutually-exclusive projects.

- Using the **maximin decision criterion**, the decision would be to choose the project with the maximum minimum profit or NPV.

  (This is also called the minimax decision criterion, which is to choose the project with the minimum worst possible outcome. This is the same concept.)

  Using the maximin approach, Project 2 should be selected because its worst possible outcome is + $1 million, better than the other two projects. Whatever happens, the NPV will be at least $1 million.

Using the **minimax regret decision criterion**, the choice should be the project where the maximum possible regret is minimised. The following table sets out the regrets:

Project	Poor (0.3) Regret $m	Moderate (0.5) Regret $m	Good (0.2) Regret $m	Maximum regret $m
1	21	7	0	21
2	0	12	40	40
3	11	0	22	22

For example, if the market conditions are moderate, we would not regret choosing Project 3, but if we had chosen Project 1 we would have regretted the decision by $7 million (NPV 22 - NPV 15).

Using the minimax regret basis for decision-making, Project 1 should be selected because the maximum amount by which we would regret making this choice is $21 million. This will happen if the market conditions turn out to be poor.

There is no 'correct' basis for making decisions in conditions of risk or uncertainty. There are, however, different logical approaches to making the choice.

> ## Perfect and imperfect information
>
> - Perfect information
> - The value of perfect information
> - Imperfect information and the value of imperfect information
> - Summary: the value of information

2 Perfect and imperfect information

Information reduces uncertainty in decision-making, and clarifies the position on risk. Information might be perfect, although in practice it is more likely to be imperfect.

2.1 Perfect information

With perfect information, the future outcome can be predicted with certainty. For example, if you had perfect information about the rolling of a dice, you would know in advance which number would turn up when the dice is rolled – 1 2, 3, 4, 5 or 6 – even though the probability of each is still 1/6.

Perfect information can be used to make decisions. With perfect information, the decision-maker can make the decision knowing exactly what is going to happen in the future.

It is possible to calculate the value of having perfect information about what is going to happen in the future.

2.2 The value of perfect information

The value of perfect information is the maximum amount a decision-maker would be willing to pay for advance information about which outcome will occur, in the certain knowledge that the information will be correct.

The value of perfect information is calculated with expected values.

$$\text{Value of perfect information} = \text{Expected value with perfect information} - \text{Expected value without perfect information}$$

The value of perfect information is the difference between:

- the expected value of profit or cost if the perfect information is available and
- the expected value of profit or cost if the decision is taken on the basis of known probabilities, but the perfect information is not available about which possibility is actually going to occur.

Example

A business entity has to decide which of three projects to select for investment. The three projects are mutually exclusive, and only one of them can be selected.

The expected profits from investing in each of the projects will depend on the state of the market. The following estimates of net present value have been prepared:

State of market	Diminishing	Static	Expanding
Probability	0.4	0.3	0.3
	$000	$000	$000
Project 1	100	200	900
Project 2	0	500	600
Project 3	180	190	200

(This is the same example as was used earlier to illustrate expected values).

What would be the value of perfect information about what the state of the market will be?

Answer

Without perfect information, the decision will be to invest in project 1, because it has the highest EV of net present value, $370,000.

With perfect information, the decision will be to select the project that offers the largest NPV, given the actual state of the market.

State of market	Best project (highest NPV)	NPV	Probability	Expected value
		$000		$000
Diminishing	Project 3	180	0.4	72
Static	Project 2	500	0.3	150
Expanding	Project 1	900	0.3	270
EV of NPV with perfect information				492
EV of NPV without perfect information				370
Value of perfect information				122

2.3 Imperfect information and the value of imperfect information

Imperfect information is information that might be incorrect in predicting what will happen.

The value of imperfect information can be calculated in a similar way to calculating the value of perfect information.

$$\text{Value of imperfect information} = \text{Expected value with imperfect information} - \text{Expected value without imperfect information}$$

A numerical question on this topic will not arise in the examination. However, you might be required to understand the nature of imperfect information and how to calculate its value for a written examination question.

2.4   Summary: the value of information

Information is rarely perfect. Predictions about future results are not correct all the time. However, even though it might sometimes be inaccurate, information reduces uncertainty. Having information, even if it is not 100% reliable, will reduce the likelihood of making bad decisions, compared with having no information at all.

Similarly, it is worth more to have better information. It is worth paying to have better information because, even though it is not perfect, it will improve the quality of decision-making.

EV analysis is a method of trying to put a value to information, perfect or imperfect. Knowing how much information is worth will help managers to decide whether it is worth paying to obtain the information. If the expected benefit from having information exceeds the cost of obtaining it, there is financial justification for obtaining it.

The theory of the value of information is important for information providers, such as management accountants, who need to understand the value of the information they are providing.

Decision trees

- The purpose of decision trees
- Drawing a decision tree
- Decision trees and two-stage decisions
- Decision trees and joint probabilities

---

3 Decision trees

3.1 The purpose of decision trees

A decision tree is a diagram that can be drawn to show:

- the decision options that are available
- the different possible outcomes from each decision option.

A decision tree also shows the probabilities of each possible outcome and can be used to demonstrate the expected value (EV) of each decision option.

Decision trees are not an essential technique for analysing risk or uncertainty in decision-making. However, they can present decision options in a way that is easy to understand, especially when the decision options are fairly complex.

A decision tree gets its name because it starts at a fixed point – the decision that has to be made now– and it branches out to show the different decision options and the possible outcomes from each of those options.

3.2 Drawing a decision tree

A simple decision tree consists of:

- a decision point or decision node, representing the decision to be made now
- lines drawn from the decision node, with each line representing a decision option
- a probability node for each decision option: the line for each decision option drawn from the decision node leads to a probability node
- lines drawn from each probability node, showing the different possible outcomes resulting from the decision, and the associated probabilities of each.

A decision node is shown as a box shape.

A probability node is shown as a circle.

Example

A company is about to launch a new product on the market, and a decision has to be made about pricing. The product will be priced at either $10 or $15 per unit. The variable cost of manufacturing and sale will be $6 per unit.

Market research suggests that:

■ if the product is priced at $10, there is a 0.4 probability that monthly sales demand will be 10,000 units and a 0.6 probability that monthly sales demand will be 15,000 units

■ if the product is priced at $15, there is a 0.6 probability that monthly sales demand will be 3,000 units and a 0.4 probability that monthly sales demand will be 9,000 units

Fixed costs each month will not be affected by the sales volume.

Required

Draw a decision tree.

Answer

The decision is whether to price the product at $10 or $15. These are the two decision options to be drawn from the decision node in the decision tree.

Each decision option leads to a probability node. Out of each probability node, the different possible outcomes should be shown. In this example, the different possible outcomes for each option are the different possible volumes of sales demand.

The EV of each decision option can be shown in the decision tree. One way of doing this is to show the value of each possible outcome at the end of the decision tree, and to calculate the EV of each option from these. This is shown in the decision tree below.

A decision tree can be drawn vertically, from top to bottom. Alternatively, it can be drawn horizontally, from left to right. A horizontal presentation is shown here.

3.3 Decision trees and two-stage decisions

Decision trees can be used to show more complex decisions, involving two-stage decision-making. Two-stage decision making means that one decision must be made now, and another decision will have to be made at a later time. The decision that is taken for the future second-stage decision will depend on the outcome from the first-stage decision. The basic principles of drawing a decision tree remain the same.

An important difference is that the second stage decision should be evaluated first. The EV of the current decision cannot be calculated until it has been established what the second-stage decision will be.

Again, an example will be used to show how these decision trees are drawn.

Example

A trader wants to rent space in a new shopping mall for one year, and has to decide how much space to rent. The terms of the rental are that there will be a one-year rental arrangement for the space that is rented initially, but the trader will have the option after six months to rent some additional space for a further six months, until the end of the year.

Net cash flows for the first six months of trading will depend on the success of the new mall in attracting shoppers. Estimates of net cash flows in the first six months are as follows:

Amount of space rented initially	Outcome	Probability	Net cash flow, 1st six months
Small	Mall is very successful	0.4	160
	Mall is fairly successful	0.6	80
Large	Mall is very successful	0.4	200
	Mall is fairly successful	0.6	40

Cash flows in the second six months will depend partly on trading in the first six months, partly on whether or not a decision is made to take additional space, and partly on the success of the shopping mall in the second six months.

If the shopping mall is very successful in the first six months, there is a 0.7 probability that it will be very successful in the second six months, and a 0.3 probability that it will be only fairly successful.

If the shopping mall is only fairly successful in the first six months, there is a 0.2 probability that it will be very successful in the second six months, and a 0.8 probability that it will be fairly successful.

Estimates of cash flows in the second six months are as follows:

- If a decision is taken to expand after six months, net cash flows will be 25% higher in the second six months than in the first six months if the mall is very successful in the second six months.

- If a decision is taken to expand after six months, net cash flows will be 30% lower in the second six months than in the first six months if the mall is only fairly successful in the second six months.

- If the decision is not to expand after six months, net cash flows will be the same in the second six months as in the first six months if the mall is very successful in the second six months.

- If the decision is not to expand after six months, net cash flows will be 10% lower in the second six months than in the first six months if the mall is only fairly successful in the second six months.

Required

Draw a decision tree and evaluate the decision.

 ### Answer

Study the decision tree carefully. First, you should try to understand how it has been drawn. When you understand the logic of its structure, you should look at how the current decision has been evaluated. The current decision cannot be evaluated until after the second stage decision has been evaluated, and you know what the second stage decision will be.

Decision now	Second stage decision		Probability	Cash flow 2nd six months	EV of 2nd stage decision
	Very successful 2 (0.4)	Expand → Very	0.7	200	140.0
		Fairly	0.3	112	33.6
					173.6
		Don't → Very	0.7	160	112.0
		Fairly	0.3	144	43.2
					155.2
Small space	Fairly successful 3 (0.6)	Expand → Very	0.2	100	20.0
		Fairly	0.8	56	44.8
					64.8
		Don't → Very	0.2	80	16.0
		Fairly	0.8	72	57.6
					73.6
1	Very successful 4 (0.4)	Expand → Very	0.7	250	175.0
		Fairly	0.3	140	42.0
					217.0
		Don't → Very	0.7	200	140.0
		Fairly	0.3	180	54.0
					194.0
Large space	Fairly successful 5 (0.6)	Expand → Very	0.2	50	10.0
		Fairly	0.8	28	22.4
					32.4
		Don't → Very	0.2	40	8.0
		Fairly	0.8	36	28.8
					36.8

The second stage decision must be evaluated first.

- **Decision nodule 2**. If the trader takes the small space and the mall is very successful in the first six months, the decision after six months will be to expand, and the EV of cash flows in the second six months will be 173.6.

- **Decision nodule 3**. If the trader takes the small space and the mall is only fairly successful in the first six months, the decision after six months will be **not** to expand, and the EV of cash flows in the second six months will be 73.6.

- **Decision nodule 4**. If the trader takes the large space and the mall is very successful in the first six months, the decision after six months will be to expand, and the EV of cash flows in the second six months will be 217.0.

- **Decision nodule 5**. If the trader takes the large space and the mall is only fairly successful in the first six months, the decision after six months will be **not** to expand, and the EV of cash flows in the second six months will be 36.8.

The current decision can now be evaluated, using the EVs for the second stage decisions.

Decision now	Mall success in 1st six months	1st 6 months	Net cash flows EV of 2nd six months	Total	Probability	EV
Small	Very	160	173.6	333.6	0.4	133.44
	Fairly	80	73.6	153.6	0.6	92.16
						225.60
Large	Very	200	217.0	417.0	0.4	166.80
	Fairly	40	36.8	76.8	0.6	46.08
						212.88

On the basis of expected value, the decision now should be to rent the small space for the first six months.

3.4 Decision trees and joint probabilities

Decision trees can also be used to illustrate joint probabilities, where the outcome from a decision depends on two or more different factors.

A joint probability is a probability that two things will happen together. The joint probability of both event A and event B happening is calculated as follows:

$$P(a, b) = P(a) \times P(b)$$

Where
$P(a, b)$ = the joint probability that both A and B will happen
$P(a)$ = the probability that A will happen
$P(b)$ = the probability that B will happen.

In a decision tree, joint probabilities are shown by two stages of probability nodes for each decision option.

Example

A company has to decide which version of a new product to launch on the market, Version 1 or Version 2. Because the products are very similar, only one of them can be launched, and it will have an expected market life of 12 months.

Due to the differences in the product designs, however, the sales demand for each will be different. The net cash flows from launching either product will depend on two factors, which are unrelated to each other:

- the size of the market
- the speed of response of a major competitor.

The expected cash flows are as follows:

Size of market	Speed of competitor's response	Net cash flow (000s)
Version 1		
Large	Fast	300
	Slow	500
Medium	Fast	150
	Slow	200
Small	Fast	50
	Slow	100
Version 2		
Large	Fast	400
	Slow	700
Medium	Fast	200
	Slow	300
Small	Fast	100
	Slow	120

The size of the market for each product has been estimated from market research as follows:

Size of market	Version 1	Version 2
	probability	probability
Large	0.3	0.1
Medium	0.3	0.4
Small	0.4	0.5

The probability that the major competitor will respond quickly is 0.6 in the case of Version 1 and 0.5 in the case of Version 2. If the competitor does not respond quickly, it will be judged to have responded slowly.

Required

Draw a decision tree to show whether Version 1 or Version 2 should be launched on the market.

Answer

Notice how there are two stages of probability node in the decision tree. The joint probabilities and EV calculations are shown on the right hand side of the decision tree.

Decision	Market size	Competitor response	Joint probability		Net cash flow	EV
		Fast	(0.3 x 0.6)	0.18	300	54
	Large	Slow	(0.3 x 0.4)	0.12	500	60
		Fast	(0.3 x 0.6)	0.18	150	27
Version 1	Medium	Slow	(0.3 x 0.4)	0.12	250	30
		Fast	(0.4 x 0.6)	0.24	50	12
	Small	Slow	(0.4 x 0.4)	0.16	100	16
						199
		Fast	(0.1 x 0.5)	0.05	400	20
	Large	Slow	(0.1 x 0.5)	0.05	700	35
Version 2		Fast	(0.4 x 0.5)	0.20	200	40
	Medium	Slow	(0.4 x 0.5)	0.20	300	60
		Fast	(0.5 x 0.5)	0.25	100	25
	Small	Slow	(0.15x 0.5)	0.25	120	30
						210

On the basis of expected value, the decision should be to launch Version 2 on the market.

> ## Assessing risk in decision-making
>
> - Standard deviation of the expected return
> - Sensitivity analysis
> - Simulation

4   Assessing risk in decision-making

The decision rules considered so far do not measure risk mathematically. However, when a probability distribution of possible outcomes is available, the decision-maker can analyse the risk using a statistical or mathematical method.

The decision is then made by considering both the expected return (for example, the EV of NPV) and the risk.

Three approaches to measuring and analysing risk are:

- calculating the standard deviation of the expected return
- sensitivity analysis
- simulation modelling.

4.1   Standard deviation of the expected return

When the possible outcomes from a decision are estimated as a probability distribution, we can calculate both the EV of the expected return and the standard deviation of the expected return.

Standard deviation is a statistical measurement of risk or variation. A higher standard deviation indicates higher risk (higher potential variation above or below the EV of return).

The formula for calculating the standard deviation of a probability distribution is:

$$s = \sqrt{S(x - x)^2 \, prob \, (x)}$$

 Example

The original example will again be used.

A business entity has to decide which of three projects to select for investment. The three projects are mutually exclusive, and only one of them can be selected.

The expected profits from investing in each of the projects will depend on the state of the market. The following estimates of net present value have been prepared:

State of market	Diminishing	Static	Expanding	EV of NPV
Probability	0.4	0.3	0.3	
	$000	$000	$000	$000
Project 1	100	200	900	370
Project 2	0	500	600	330
Project 3	180	190	200	189

Required

(a) Calculate the standard deviation of the expected NPV for each project.

(b) Consider how the measurements of standard deviation might affect the choice of project.

Answer

Project 1	NPV	Probability		
$\bar{x} = 370$	x	p	$x - \bar{x}$	$p(x - \bar{x})^2$
Diminishing	100	0.4	- 270	29,160
Static	200	0.3	- 170	8,670
Expanding	900	0.3	570	84,270
				122,100

$$s = \sqrt{122,100} = \text{(in \$000s) } 349.4$$

Project 2	NPV	Probability		
$\bar{x} = 330$	x	p	$x - \bar{x}$	$p(x - \bar{x})^2$
Diminishing	0	0.4	- 330	43,560
Static	500	0.3	+ 170	8,670
Expanding	600	0.3	+ 270	21,870
				74,100

$$s = \sqrt{74,100} = \text{(in \$000s) } 272.2$$

Project 3	NPV	Probability		
$\bar{x} = 189$	x	p	$x - \bar{x}$	$p(x - \bar{x})^2$
Diminishing	180	0.4	- 9	32.4
Static	190	0.3	+ 1	0.3
Expanding	200	0.3	+ 11	36.3
				69.0

$$s = \sqrt{69} = \text{(in \$000s) } 8.3$$

Summary

Project	EV of NPV	Standard deviation
	$000	$000
Project 1	370	349.4
Project 2	330	272.2
Project 3	189	8.3

The choice between the three projects can take risk into consideration, as well as the EV of the NPV. In this example the project with the highest EV also has the highest risk, and the project with the lowest EV has the lowest risk.

With simple probability distributions, such as the probabilities shown in this example, the standard deviation has no further meaning or practical value.

However, if a probability distribution showed the characteristics of a normal distribution (or another recognised probability distribution), it would be possible to carry out further detailed analysis of the risk using normal distribution tables.

Advantages of measuring standard deviation

There are several advantages to measuring the standard deviation of possible outcomes.

- A standard deviation gives a numerical value to the spread of possible results around the average or expected value.

- It gives recognition to risk in a decision, and quantifies the risk.

- It can be used for statistical analysis when it can be assumed that the probability distribution is a normal distribution.

Disadvantages of measuring standard deviation

The meaning or significance of a standard deviation is limited when the probability distribution is not a normal distribution or (other recognisable probability distribution).

4.2 Sensitivity analysis

Sensitivity analysis is a method of risk or uncertainty analysis in which the effect on the expected outcome of changes in the values of key 'variables' or key factors are tested. For example, in budget planning, the effect on budgeted profit might be tested for changes in the budgeted sales volume, or the budgeted rate of inflation, or budgeted materials costs, and so on.

There are several ways of using sensitivity analysis.

- We can estimate by how much an item of cost or revenue would need to differ from their estimated values before the decision would change.

- We can estimate whether a decision would change if estimated sales were x% lower than estimated, or estimated costs were y% higher than estimated. (This is called 'what if…?' analysis: for example: 'What if sales volume is 5% below the expected amount)?

The starting point for sensitivity analysis is the original plan or estimates, giving an expected profit or value. Key variables are identified (such as sales price, sales volume material cost, labour cost, completion time, and so on). The value of the selected key variable is then altered by a percentage amount (typically a reasonable estimate of possible variations in the value of this variable) and the expected profit or value is re-calculated.

In this way, the sensitivity of a decision or plan to changes in the value of the key items or key factors can be measured.

An advantage of sensitivity analysis is that if a **spreadsheet model** is used for analysing the original plan or decision, sensitivity analysis can be carried out quickly and easily, by changing one value at a time in the spreadsheet model.

4.3 Simulation

Simulation modelling is used when a plan or budget is represented by a mathematical model. The model will contain a large number of inter-related variables (sales volumes of each product, sales prices of each product, availability of constraining resources, resources per unit of product, costs of materials and labour, and so on).

The model is then used to calculate the value of the outcome or result, for a given set of values for each variable. It is then used to produce the expected outcome or result again, with a different set of values for each variable. The model is used to prepare a large number of different possible outcomes, each time with different combinations of values for all the variables.

As a result, the model will produce a range of many different possible results or outcomes that can be analysed statistically, by putting the possible outcomes into a probability distribution.

Simulation modelling therefore leads on to further statistical analysis of risk.

One example of simulation is a mathematical model which could be approached using the 'Monte Carlo' method. With Monte Carlo simulation, a probability distribution for the possible different values for each variable is used to allocate random numbers to each possible value. Random number allocations are given to all the different possible values for every input variable in the model. (The random number allocation should reflect the probability distribution).

A special computer program can be used to generate random numbers, and the random numbers generated by the program are used to give a value to each variable in the model. These values are then used to calculate the result or outcome that would occur.

Repeating the simulation many times produces a probability distribution of the possible outcomes.

Advantage of the Monte Carlo method

The advantages of Monte Carlo simulation modelling are as follows:

- It gives more information about the possible outcomes and their relative probabilities.
- It is useful for problems which cannot be solved analytically.

Limitation of the Monte Carlo method

It is not a technique for making a decision, only for getting more information about the risk and the probability of different possible outcomes.

CHAPTER

4

Quantitative techniques in budgeting

Contents

Analysing costs into fixed and variable

- The need to estimate fixed and variable costs
- High low method
- Linear regression analysis

---

1 Analysing costs into fixed and variable

1.1 The need to estimate fixed and variable costs

To prepare accurate cost budgets, it is important to understand how costs 'behave'. Cost behaviour refers to the way in which total costs increase as the volume of an activity increases.

It is commonly assumed that total costs can be analysed into fixed costs and a variable cost per unit of activity, such as a variable cost per unit of product or per hour of service. Some overhead costs are a mixture of fixed costs and variable costs, but these can be separated into a fixed cost portion and a variable cost portion.

To prepare reliable cost budgets or cost estimates, it may be necessary to estimate fixed costs and variable costs.

- Direct material costs are normally 100% variable costs.
- Direct labour costs may be treated as variable costs. However, when there is a fixed labour force, direct labour costs may be budgeted as a fixed cost.
- Overhead costs maybe treated as fixed costs. However, for an accurate analysis of overhead costs, it may be necessary to make an estimate of fixed costs and variable costs. These estimates are often based on an analysis of historical costs.

You should be familiar already with two techniques for estimating fixed and variable costs:

- the high low method
- linear regression analysis.

It is unlikely that you will be expected to use either technique in your examination. However, you might be required to comment on each technique, and its reliability as a forecasting/budgeting technique to estimate costs.

1.2 High low method

The high low method provides an estimate of fixed and variable costs for an activity by taking two historical costs:

- the total costs for the highest recorded volume of the activity, and
- the total costs for the lowest recorded volume of the activity.

Where appropriate, one or both cost figures is adjusted to allow for price inflation, to bring them to the same price level.

It is assumed that these two historical records of cost are an accurate guide to expected costs for the activity.

Example

A company is trying to estimate its fixed and variable production overhead costs in each month. It has the following historical data of costs in the previous five months:

Production volume	Total cost
000 units	$000
8	25
6	22
6	19
9	24
5	16

Required

(a) Use this data to estimate fixed costs each month and the variable cost per unit, using the high low method.

(b) What should be the estimated costs for production overheads next month if the expected volume of production is 8,000 units?

Answer

Using this data and the high low method, the fixed production overhead costs per month and the variable production overhead cost per unit would be estimated as follows:

- The highest production volume in the available data is 9,000 units.

- The lowest production volume in the available data is 5,000 units.

- These are assumed to be reliable measures of cost.

The difference between the two total cost figures consists of variable costs only, because fixed costs are the same at each output volume.

		units		$
High	Total overhead cost of	9,000	=	24,000
Low	Total overhead cost of	5,000	=	16,000
Difference	Variable cost of	4,000	=	8,000

Variable production overhead cost per unit = $8,000/4,000 = $2.

This variable cost per unit should be used with either the high or low output volume and total cost to calculate the fixed costs per month.

	$
Total cost of 9,000 units	24,000
Variable cost of 9,000 units (× $2)	18,000
Fixed costs per month	6,000

For the purpose of budgeting or cost estimation, production overhead costs will be fixed costs of $6,000 per month and a variable cost of $2 per unit produced.

Comment on the high low method

The high low method is a simple method of separating mixed costs into fixed and variable cost elements. However, it is based on the assumption that two historical records of cost are reliable indicators of cost behaviour. This assumption may be invalid, and estimates of fixed and variable costs may therefore be unreliable.

1.3 Linear regression analysis

Linear regression analysis is a technique for estimating a 'line of best fit' from historical data. It can be used for analysing historical data for costs in order to estimate fixed costs and variable costs. It can also be used to analyse a historical trend, for example a historical trend in sales volume, in order to prepare a forecast for future periods, on the assumptions that the trend:

- is upward or downward in a 'straight line', and

- the historical trend will continue in a straight line in the future.

Linear regression analysis is a more accurate forecasting method than the high low method. Like the high low method, it assumes that there is a straight-line formula y = a + bx. It also uses historical data to produce an estimate for the values of a and b.

However, unlike the high low method, it uses any number of historical data items, not just two (the high and the low data items).

The formulae are, for y = a + bx:

$$a = \frac{\sum y}{n} - \frac{b \sum x}{n}$$

$$b = \frac{n \sum xy - \sum x \sum y}{n \sum x^2 - \left(\sum x \right)^2}$$

Where
a = fixed costs in each period
b = variable cost per unit
x, y = historical data, for example for activity level (x) and total cost (y)
n = the number of data items used

It is most unlikely that you will be asked to estimate fixed and variable costs using linear regression analysis. However, you should be familiar with the techniques from your earlier studies. For your examination, you might be required to comment on the reliability of linear regression analysis as a technique for estimating fixed and variable costs.

The technique will be illustrated using the same data that was used earlier to demonstrate the high low method.

Example

A company is trying to estimate its fixed and variable production overhead costs in each month. It has the following historical data of costs in the previous five months:

Production volume	Total cost
000 units	$000
8	25
6	22
6	19
9	24
5	16

Required

(a) Use this data to estimate fixed costs each month and the variable cost per unit, using the high low method.

(b) What should be the estimated costs for production overheads next month if the expected volume of production is 8,000 units?

Answer

The number of items of data: n = 5

The other values for the formulae are calculated as follows:

Production volume	Total cost		
x	y	xy	x^2
8	25	200	64
6	22	132	36
6	19	114	36
9	24	216	81
5	16	80	25
34	106	742	242

The values for y are the total costs and the values for x are the activity/output volumes.

Σ x = 34
Σ y = 106
Σ xy = 742
Σ x^2 = 242
n = 5

The formulae can now be used to establish a value for b and then a.

$$b = \frac{5(742)-(34)(106)}{5(242)-(34)^2}$$

$$= \frac{3,710-3,604}{1,210-1,156} = \frac{106}{54}$$

$$b = 1.96$$

$$a = \frac{106}{5} - \frac{1.96(34)}{5}$$

$$a = 21.2 - 13.3 = 7.9$$

The estimate of costs is therefore = 7,900 + 1.96x.

When output x = 8,000 units, the estimated total costs will be:

Total costs = $7,900 + (8,000 × $1.96) = $23,580, say $23,600.

The estimate of total costs using the high low method was $22,000.

Comment on linear regression analysis

Linear regression analysis should be more reliable than the high low method as a method of estimating fixed and variable costs, because it is based on more items of historical data.

However, it is not necessarily reliable. It assumes that total costs vary with changes in the selected activity. This assumption might be incorrect. Total costs may change in response to other factors, not the selected activity. For example, it might be assumed that the total costs of distribution will vary with the volume of sales, when it might be more appropriate to assume that total costs vary with the number of customer orders handled.

An advantage of linear regression analysis is that the reliability of estimates can be tested by calculating a correlation coefficient.

Correlation

Correlation refers to the extent to which values for y can be predicted from any given value for x, using the values for a and b obtained from linear regression analysis.

- A high degree of correlation indicates that values for y can be estimated with a reasonable degree of confidence from values of x.
- A low degree of correlation indicates that values for y estimated from any given value of x will not be particularly reliable.

The extent of correlation between values of x and values of y can be measured by a correlation coefficient, r. The correlation coefficient is calculated using the following formula:

$$r = \frac{n\sum xy - \sum x \sum y}{\sqrt{\left[n\sum x^2-(\sum x)^2\right]\left[n\sum y^2-(\sum y)^2\right]}}$$

If you look at the formula carefully, you should notice that most of the values in the formula are the same as the values used to calculate b in the linear regression analysis formula. The only additional values you need are for $n\sum y^2$ and $(\sum y)^2$.

The value of r produced by this formula must always be within the range – 1 to + 1.

■ When r is close to + 1, there is a high degree of positive correlation. When r = + 1, there is perfect positive correlation, and all the pairs of data for x and y that have been used to estimate the values for a and b lie on a straight line, y = a + bx, when drawn graphically.

■ When r is close to - 1, there is a high degree of negative correlation. When r = - 1, there is perfect negative correlation, and all the pairs of data for x and y that have been used to estimate the values for a and b lie on a straight line, y = a - bx, when drawn graphically.

■ When r is 0, there is no correlation at all between the values of x and the values of y, and the linear regression formula would be completely unreliable. Correlation probably needs to be at the very least between 0.80 and 1.00 or between – 0.80 and – 1.00 to be considered of much significance.

Example

The correlation coefficient can be calculated for the previous example, as follows:

Production volume	Total cost			
x	y	xy	x^2	y^2
8	25	200	64	625
6	22	132	36	484
6	19	114	36	361
9	24	216	81	576
5	16	80	25	256
34	106	742	242	2,302

$$r = \frac{106}{\sqrt{[54]\left[5(2,302)-(106)^2\right]}} = \frac{106}{\sqrt{(54)(274)}}$$

r = 106/121.6 = + 0.87.

Here, there is a reasonably strong positive correlation between the values of x and the values of y that are estimated using the linear regression formula.

Linear regression analysis and forecasting

Linear regression analysis can also be used in forecasting, where it can be assumed that there has been a linear trend in the past, and this same linear trend will continue into the future.

Exactly the same method is used in forecasting as for estimating fixed and variable costs. The trend line is a formula y = a + bx, where x is the year or month.

To simplify the arithmetic, you should number the years 1, 2, 3, 4 and so on (or even start at year 0, and number the years 0, 1, 2, 3 and so on).

> **Forecasting techniques**
>
> ■ The nature of a time series
> ■ Trends and seasonal variations
> ■ Estimating seasonal variations

2 Forecasting techniques

In order to prepare budgets, it is necessary to make forecasts. The learning curve and linear regression analysis are both techniques for forecasting costs, and linear regression analysis can also be used to prepare other forecasts, such as forecasts of sales.

You need to be aware of other forecasting techniques that might be used in budgeting, why they are used, and the extent to which management can rely on them.

A common type of forecast is a forecast of a trend or time series, where there are likely to be seasonal variations in the trend.

2.1 The nature of a time series

A time series is a record of amounts or values in each period of time over a longer time period. Examples of a time series are sales each month over a period of five years, or the volume of production each year over a period of ten years.

It is sometimes assumed that a time series has a predictable pattern, so that what has happened in the past can be used to predict the future.

If it is assumed that there has been a straight-line trend in the past that will continue into the future, linear regression analysis can be used to forecast future values in future periods. This has been explained earlier.

2.2 Trends and seasonal variations

Sometimes, it might be assumed that there is an underlying trend, possibly a straight-line trend, but there are seasonal variations. For example, sales every month might be rising in a straight-line trend, but with variations up or down each month according to the month of the year. Regularly, sales in some months are higher than sales in other months.

A straight-line trend can be assumed to exist in the long run, provided that the average seasonal variations above the line equal the average seasonal variations below the line.

Average seasonal variations can be estimated, and to prepare budgets or forecasts for the future, the seasonal variation is added to or subtracted from the straight-line trend forecast, to obtain a seasonal forecast.

2.3 Estimating seasonal variations

A method of estimating seasonal variations and using these to prepare forecasts will be illustrated with an example.

Example

A company has used sales records for each quarter of the year for the past few years to prepare an estimate of the trend in sales each quarter.

The straight-line trend in quarterly sales is
y = 150,000 + 10,000x

where
x = the quarter in the time series, where 0 = the sales in the first quarter of 20X1.

The actual sales in each quarter are shown in the table below. These are compared with the sales that would be forecast, using a straight-line trend of y = 150,000 + 10,000x. The differences are shown in the right-hand column as seasonal variations.

Time period	Actual sales	Estimated sales, using trend line y = 150,000 + 10,000x	Difference = seasonal variation
	$	$	$
Quarter 1, 20X1	119,200	150,000	- 30,800
Quarter 2, 20X1	167,500	160,000	+ 7,500
Quarter 3, 20X1	219,200	170,000	+49,200
Quarter 4, 20X1	151,500	180,000	- 28,500
Quarter 1, 20X2	162,000	190,000	- 28,000
Quarter 2, 20X2	203,700	200,000	+ 3,700
Quarter 3, 20X2	258,400	210,000	+ 48,400
Quarter 4, 20X2	199,700	220,000	- 20,300
Quarter 1, 20X3	200,400	230,000	- 29,600
Quarter 2, 20X3	248,000	240,000	+ 8,000
Quarter 3, 20X3	296,200	250,000	+ 46,200
Quarter 4, 20X3	237,200	260,000	- 22,800
Quarter 1, 20X4	242,000	270,000	- 27,000
Quarter 2, 20X4	284,800	280,000	+ 4,800
Quarter 3, 20X4	341,200	290,000	+ 41,200
Quarter 4, 20X4	276,400	300,000	- 23,600

These figures can be used to calculate an average seasonal variation for each quarter of the year.

However, the total seasonal variations must add up to 0, otherwise a straight-line trend does not exist. A simple adjustment is therefore made so that the seasonal variations do add up to 0.

Seasonal variations	Quarter 1	Quarter 2	Quarter 3	Quarter 4	Total
	$	$	$	$	$
20X1	- 30,800	+ 7,500	+ 49,200	- 28,500	
20X2	- 28,000	+ 3,700	+ 48,400	- 20,300	
20X3	- 29,600	+ 8,000	+ 46,200	- 22,800	
20X4	- 27,000	+ 4,800	+ 41,200	- 23,600	
Total	- 115,400	+ 24,000	+ 185,000	- 95,200	
Average	- 28,850	+ 6,000	+ 46,250	- 23,800	- 400
Adjustment to 0	+ 100	+ 100	+ 100	+ 100	+ 400
Adjusted average	- 28,750	+ 6,100	+ 46,350	- 23,700	

Sales forecast for 20X5

Time period	Estimated sales, using trend line y = 150,000 + 10,000x	Seasonal variation	Sales forecast
	$	$	$
Quarter 1, 20X5 (x = 16)	310,000	- 27,750	282,250
Quarter 2, 20X5 (x = 17)	320,000	+ 6,100	326,100
Quarter 3, 20X5 (x = 18)	330,000	+46,350	376,350
Quarter 4, 20X5 (x = 19)	340,000	- 23,700	316,300

The reliability of forecasts of trends and seasonal variations

Forecasts using estimated trends and seasonal variations are based on the assumptions that the past is a reliable guide to the future. This assumption may be incorrect. However, forecasts must be made; otherwise it is impossible to make plans beyond the very short term.

The techniques described in this chapter, although they might prove inaccurate, are used because there is no better alternative.

Uncertainty in budgeting

- The nature of uncertainty in budgeting
- Flexible budgets
- Probabilities and expected values
- Spreadsheets and 'what if' analysis

3 Uncertainty in budgeting

3.1 The nature of uncertainty in budgeting

Uncertainty arises when there is a lack of reliable information. In budgeting, there is uncertainty because estimates and forecasts may be unreliable. Information is almost never 100% reliable (or 'perfect'), and some uncertainty in budgeting is therefore inevitable.

Risk arises in business because actual events may turn out better or worse than expected. For example, actual sales volume may be higher or lower than forecast. The amount of risk in business operations varies with the nature of the operations. Some operations are more predictable than others. The existence of risk means that forecasts and estimates in the budget, which are based on expected results, may not be accurate.

Both risk and uncertainty mean that estimates and forecasts in a budget are likely to be wrong.

Management should be aware of risk and uncertainty when preparing budgets and when monitoring performance.

- When preparing budgets, it may be appropriate to look at several different forecasts and estimates, to assess the possible variations that might occur. In other words, managers should think about how much better or how much worse actual results may be, compared with the budget.
- When monitoring actual performance, managers should recognise that adverse or favourable variances might be caused by weaknesses in the original forecasts, rather than by good or bad performance.

Several approaches may be used for analysing risk and uncertainty in budgets. These include:

- flexible budgets
- using probabilities and expected values
- using spreadsheet models and 'what if' analysis (sensitivity analysis)
- stress testing.

3.2 Flexible budgets

Flexible budgets may be prepared during the budget-setting process. A flexible budget is a budget based on an assumption of a different volume of output and sales than the volume in the master budget or 'fixed budget'.

For example, a company might prepare its master budget on the basis of estimated sales of $100 million. Flexible budgets might be prepared on the basis that sales will be higher or lower – say $80 million, $90 million, $110 million and $120 million. Each flexible budget will be prepared on the basis of assumptions about fixed and variable costs, such as increases or decreases in fixed costs if sales rise above or fall below a certain amount, or changes in variable unit costs above a certain volume of sales.

During the financial year covered by the budget, it may become apparent that actual sales and production volume will be higher or lower than the fixed budget forecast. In such an event, actual performance can be compared with a suitable flexible budget.

Flexible budgets can be useful, because they allow for the possibility that actual activity levels may be higher or lower than forecast in the master budget. The main disadvantage of flexible budgets could be the time and effort needed to prepare them. The cost of preparing them could exceed the benefits of having the information that they provide.

3.3 Probabilities and expected values

Estimates and forecasts in budgeting may be prepared using probabilities and expected values. An expected value is a weighted average value calculated with probabilities.

Example

A company is preparing a sales budget. The budget planners believe that the volume of sales next year will depend on the state of the economy.

State of the economy	Sales for the year
	$ million
No growth	40
Low growth	50
Higher growth	70

It has been estimated that there is a 60% probability of no growth, a 30% probability of low growth and a 10% probability of higher growth.

The expected value (EV) of sales next year could be calculated as follows:

State of the economy	Sales for the year	Probability	EV of sales
	$ million		$ million
No growth	40	0.6	24
Low growth	50	0.3	15
Higher growth	70	0.1	7
EV of sales			46

The company might decide to prepare a sales budget on the assumption that annual sales will be $46 million.

The problems with using probabilities and expected values

There are two problems that might exist with the use of probabilities and expected values.

■ The estimates of probability might be subjective, and based on the judgement or opinion of a forecaster. Subjective probabilities might be no better than educated guesses. Probabilities should have a rational basis.

■ An expected value is most useful when it is a weighted average value for an outcome that will happen many times in the planning period. If the forecast event happens many times in the planning period, weighted average values are suitable for forecasting. However, if an outcome will only happen once, it is doubtful whether an expected value has much practical value for planning purposes.

This point can be illustrated with the previous example of the EV of annual sales. The forecast is that sales will be $40 million (0.60 probability), $50 million (0.30 probability) or $70 million (0.10 probability). The EV of sales is $46 million.

■ The total annual sales for the year is an outcome that occurs only once. It is doubtful whether it would be appropriate to use $46 million as the budgeted sales for the year. A sales total of $46 million is not expected to happen.

■ It might be more appropriate to prepare a fixed budget on the basis that sales will be $40 million (the most likely outcome) and prepare flexible budgets for sales of $50 million and $70 million.

When the forecast outcome happens many times in the planning period, an EV might be appropriate. For example, suppose that the forecast of weekly sales of a product is as follows:

Weekly sales	Probability	EV of weekly sales
$		$
7,000	0.5	3,500
9,000	0.3	2,700
12,000	0.2	2,400
		8,600

Since there are 52 weeks in a year, it would be appropriate to assume that weekly sales will be a weighted average amount, or EV. The budget for annual sales would be (52 × $8,600) = $447,200. If the probability estimates are fairly reliable, this estimate of annual sales should be acceptable as the annual sales budget.

3.4 Spreadsheets and 'what if' analysis

Preparing budgets is largely a 'number crunching' exercise, involving large amounts of calculations. This aspect of budgeting was made much easier, simpler and quicker with IT and the development of computer-based models for budgeting. Spreadsheet models, or similar planning models, are now widely used to prepare budgets.

A feature of computer-based budget models is that once the model has been constructed, it becomes a relatively simple process to prepare a budget. Values are input for the key variables, and the model produces a complete budget.

Amendments to a budget can be made quickly. A new budget can be produced simply by changing the value of one or more input variables in the budget model.

This ability to prepare new budgets quickly by changing a small number of values in the model also creates opportunities for **sensitivity analysis** and **stress testing**. The budget planner can test how the budget will be affected if forecasts and estimates are changed, by asking 'what if' questions. For example:

■ What if sales volume is 5% below the budget forecast?

■ What if the sales mix of products is different?

■ What if the introduction of the new production system or the new IT system is delayed by six months?

■ What if interest rates go up by 2% more than expected?

■ What if the fixed costs are 5% higher and variable costs per unit are 3% higher?

Sensitivity analysis and stress testing are similar.

■ Sensitivity analysis considers variations to estimates and input values in the budget model that have a reasonable likelihood of happening. For example, variable unit costs might be increased by 5% or sales forecasts reduced by 5%.

■ Stress testing considers the effect of much greater changes to the forecasts and estimates. For example, what might happen of sales are 20% less than expected? Or what might happen if the price of a key raw material increases by 50%?

The answers to 'what if' questions can help budget planners to understand more about the risk and uncertainty in the budget, and the extent to which actual results might differ from the expected outcome in the master budget. This can provide valuable information for risk management, and management can assess the 'sensitivity' of their budget to particular estimates and assumptions.

> ## The learning curve
>
> - Learning curve theory
> - The learning curve model
> - Graph of the learning curve
> - Formula for the learning curve
> - Conditions for the learning curve to apply
> - Implications of the learning curve
> - Weaknesses in the application of learning curve theory

4 The learning curve

4.1 Learning curve theory

When a work force begins a task for the first time, and the task then becomes repetitive, it will probably do the job more quickly as it learns. It will find quicker ways of performing tasks, and will become more efficient as knowledge and understanding increase.

When a task is well-established, the learning effect wears out, and the time to complete the task becomes the same every time the task is carried out.
However, during the learning period, the time to complete each subsequent task can fall by a very large amount.

The learning curve effect was first discovered in the US during the 1940s, in aircraft manufacture. Aircraft manufacture is a highly-skilled task, where:

- the skill of the work force is important, and
- the labour time is a significant element in production resources and production costs.

The time taken to produce the first unit of a new model of an aeroplane might take a long time, but the time to produce the next unit is much less, and the time to produce the third is even less, and so on. Labour times per extra unit therefore fall.

4.2 The learning curve model

The effect of the learning curve can be predicted mathematically, using a learning curve model. This model was developed from actual observations and analysis in the US aircraft industry.

The learning curve is measured as a percentage learning curve effect. For example, for a particular task, there might be an 80% learning curve effect, or a 90% learning curve effect, and so on.
When there is an 80% learning curve, the cumulative average time to produce units of an item is 80% of what it was before, every time that output doubles.

- The **cumulative average time per unit** is the average time for all the units made so far, from the first unit onwards.

- This means, for example, that if an 80% learning curve applies, the average time for the first two units is 80% of the average time for the first one unit. Similarly, the average time for the first four units is 80% of the average time for the first two units.

Example

The time to make a new model of a sailing boat is 100 days. It has been established that in the boat-building industry, there is an 80% learning curve.

Required

Calculate:

(a) the cumulative average time per unit for the first 2 units, first 4 units, first 8 units and first 16 units of the boat

(b) the total time required to make the first 2 units, the first 4 units, the first 8 units and the first 16 units

(c) the additional time required to make the second unit, the 3rd and 4th units, units 5 – 8 and units 9 – 16.

Answer

Total units (cumulative)	Cumulative average time per unit	Total time for all units	Incremental time for additional units	Average time for additional units
	days	days	days	days
1	100	100	100	
2	80	160	60	60
4	64	256	96	48
8	51.2	409.6	153.6	38.4
16	40.96	655.36	245.76	30.72

Example

The first unit of a new model of machine took 1,600 hours to make. A 90% learning curve applies. How much time would it take to make the first 32 units of this machine?

Answer

Average time for the first 32 units = 1,600 hours × 90% × 90% × 90% × 90% × 90% = 944.784 hours

Total time for the first 32 units = 32 × 944.784 hours = 30,233 hours.

4.3   Graph of the learning curve

The learning curve can be shown as a graph. There are two graphs following.

The left-hand graph shows the cumulative average time per unit. This falls rapidly at first, but the learning effect eventually ends and the average time for each additional unit becomes constant (a standard time).

The right hand graph shows how total costs increase. The total cost line is a curved line initially, because of the learning effect.

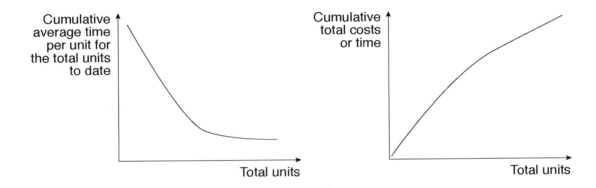

4.4   Formula for the learning curve

The learning curve is represented by the following formula (mathematical model).

Learning curve: $y = ax^b$

Where
y = the cumulative average time per unit for all units made
x = the number of units made so far (cumulative number of units)
a = the time for the first unit
b = the learning factor.

$$\text{The learning factor b} = \frac{\text{Logarithm of learning rate}}{\text{Logarithm of 2}}$$

The learning rate is expressed as a decimal, so if the learning curve is 80%, the learning factor is: (logarithm 0.80/logarithm 2)

To use this formula you must be able to calculate logarithms. Make sure that you know how to use the logarithms function on your calculator.

 Example

If there is an 80% learning curve, the learning factor is calculated as follows:

$$\frac{\text{Logarithm} \;\; 0.80}{\text{Logarithm} \;\; 2} = \frac{-0.09691}{0.30103} = -0.32193$$

The learning curve formula is therefore: $y = ax^{-0.32193}$

It might help to remember that $x^{-0.32913}$ is another way of writing $\dfrac{1}{X^{0.32193}}$

Going back to the previous example, the cumulative average time to produce eight units can therefore be calculated as:

$$y = 100 \times \dfrac{1}{8^{0.32193}}$$

= 100 (0.512)

= 51.20

$$y = 100 \times \left(\dfrac{1}{8^{0.32913}} \right)$$

Example

It will take 500 hours to complete the first unit of a new product. There is a 95% learning curve effect.

Calculate how long it will take to produce the seventh unit.

Answer

The time to produce the seventh unit is the difference between:

■ the total time to produce the first six units, and

■ the total time to produce the first seven units.

(1) **Learning factor**

$$\dfrac{\text{Logarithm } 0.95}{\text{Logarithm } 2} = \dfrac{-0.02227639}{0.30103} = -0.074$$

(2) **Average time to produce the first 6 units**

$$y = 500 \times \dfrac{1}{6^{0.074}}$$

= 500 (0.8758239)

= 437.9 hours per unit

(3) **Average time to produce the first seven units**

$$y = 500 \times \dfrac{1}{7^{0.074}}$$

$$= 500 \ (0.86589)$$

$$= 432.9 \text{ hours per unit}$$

(4)   Time to produce the 7th unit

	Hours
Total time for the first 7 units (7 × 432.9)	3,030.3
Total time for the first 6 units (6 × 437.9)	2,627.4
Time for the 7th unit	402.9

4.5   Conditions for the learning curve to apply

The learning curve effect will only apply in the following conditions:

■ There must be stable conditions for the work, so that learning can take place. For example, labour turnover must not be high; otherwise the learning effect is lost. The time between making each subsequent unit must not be long; otherwise the learning effect is lost because employees will forget what they did before.

■ The activity must be labour-intensive, so that learning will affect the time to complete the work.

■ There must be no change in production techniques, which would require the learning process to start again from the beginning.

■ Employees must be motivated to learn.

In practice, the learning curve effect is not used extensively for budgeting or estimating costs (or calculating sales prices on a cost plus basis).

4.6   Implications of the learning curve

When a process benefits from a learning curve effect, there are implications for budgeting and pricing.

■ Budgets should allow for the reduction in the average labour time per unit. Total labour requirements (the size of the work force required) will be affected.

■ Pricing. If prices are calculated on a 'cost plus' basis, prices quoted to customers should allow for future cost savings. The sales budget will be affected by expected reductions in the sales price.

■ Any system of budgetary control should make allowance for the expected reduction in the production time per unit. Actual hours taken should be compared with expected hours, allowing for the learning curve effect.

4.7   Weaknesses in the application of learning curve theory

Learning curve theory assumes that stable production conditions will exist, and all subsequent units will be produced to the same specifications as the original product. In practice, the product may go through several major design changes after the first unit has been produced.

It may be difficult to measure the learning rate with sufficient accuracy. It also may be difficult to measure the time taken for the first unit accurately.

CHAPTER

5

Discounted cash flow (DCF) and long-term decisions

Contents

1	DCF: basic revision points
2	DCF and taxation
3	DCF and inflation
4	Other aspects of DCF analysis

DCF: basic revision points

- Introduction
- Net present value (NPV) method of investment appraisal
- Calculating the NPV of an investment project
- Discount tables
- Annuities
- Layout of NPV calculations
- Calculating cash flows: other points to remember

---

1 DCF: basic revision points

1.1 Introduction

You should be familiar already with discounted cash flow analysis as a technique for evaluating proposed investments, to decide whether they are financially worthwhile.

The expected future cash flows from the investment (cash payments and cash receipts) are all converted to a present value by discounting at the cost of capital. The present value of investment costs and the present value of the investment returns (cash benefits of returns) can be compared.

This chapter provides a brief description of the NPV method of DCF analysis, so that you can revise the topic if you need to. An examination question might expect you to calculate an NPV as part of the solution.

1.2 Net present value (NPV) method of investment appraisal

With the NPV method of investment appraisal, all the future cash flows from an investment are converted into a present value, by discounting the cash flow at the investment cost of capital. This cost of capital is the return required from the investment.

The PV of a cash flow is calculated by multiplying the cash flow by a discount factor. The discount factor is $1/(1+r)^n$
where:
r is the discount rate as a proportion: for example 12% = 0.12
n is the year in which the cash flow will occur.

Cash flows at the beginning of the investment, in Year 0, are already stated at their present value. The present value of $1 in Year 0 is $1.

Assumptions about the timing of cash flows

In DCF analysis, the following assumptions are made about the timing of cash flows during each year:

- All cash flows for the investment are assumed to occur at the end of the year
- If a cash flow will occur early during a particular year, it is assumed that it will occur at the end of the previous year. Therefore an item of cash expenditure early in Year 1, for example, is assumed to occur in Year 0.

1.3 Calculating the NPV of an investment project

The net present value (NPV) of a project is the net difference between the present value of all the costs incurred and the present value of all the cash flow benefits (savings or revenues).

- If the present value of benefits exceeds the present value of costs, the NPV is positive.
- If the present value of benefits is less than the present value of costs, the NPV is negative.
- The NPV is 0 when the PV of benefits and the PV of costs are equal.

The **decision rule** is that, ignoring other factors such as risk and uncertainty, and non-financial considerations, a project is worthwhile financially if the NPV is positive or zero. It is not worthwhile if the NPV is negative.

The **net present value** of an investment project is also **a measure of the value of the investment**. For example, if a company invests in a project that has a NPV of $2 million, the value of the company should increase by $2 million.

1.4 Discount tables

Discount tables are available. They take away the need to calculate the value of discount factors $[1/(1 + r)^n]$.

Discount tables will be provided in your examination, if required, and the discount factors in the tables are rounded to three decimal places.

An extract from discount tables is shown below.

Periods (n)	Discount rates (r)									
	1%	2%	3%	4%	5%	6%	7%	8%	9%	10%
1	0.990	0.980	0.971	0.962	0.952	0.943	0.935	0.926	0.917	0.909
2	0.980	0.961	0.943	0.925	0.907	0.890	0.873	0.857	0.842	0.826
3	0.971	0.942	0.915	0.889	0.864	0.840	0.816	0.794	0.772	0.751
4	0.961	0.924	0.888	0.855	0.823	0.792	0.763	0.735	0.708	0.683
5	0.951	0.906	0.863	0.822	0.784	0.747	0.713	0.681	0.650	0.621

For example, suppose that you need to calculate the present value of $60,000 in Year 4 if the cost of capital (discount rate) is 7%.

PV = $60,000 × 0.763 = $45,780.

1.5 Annuities

An annuity is a constant cash flow for a given number of time periods.

Examples:
$30,000 each year for years 1 – 5
$20,000 each year for years 3 – 10
$500 each month for months 1 – 24.

Calculating the PV of an annuity

If you need to calculate the present value of $50,000 per year for years 1 – 3 at a discount rate of 9%, you could calculate this as follows:

Year	Cash flow $	Discount factor at 9%	Present value $
1	50,000	1/(1.09) = 0.917	45,850
2	50,000	1/(1.09)· = 0 842	42,100
3	50,000	1/(1.09)· = 0.772	38,600
		NPV	126,550

The PV of the constant annual cash flows =
[Annual cash flow] × [Sum of the discount factors for each year].

In this example, the PV = $50,000 × (0.917 + 0.842 + 0.772)
= $50,000 × 2.531 = $126,550.

The factor 2.531 is the annuity factor for years 1 – 3 at a discount rate of 9%.

A table of annuity factors, giving the discount factor for an annuity from Year 1 to Year n inclusive, will be available in your examination, if you need it.

An extract is shown below.

Extract from annuity tables

Periods (n)	1%	2%	3%	4%	5%	6%	7%	8%	9%	10%
1	0.990	0.980	0.971	0.962	0.952	0.943	0.935	0.926	0.917	0.909
2	1.970	1.942	1.913	1.886	1.859	1.833	1.808	1.783	1.759	1.736
3	2.941	2.884	2.829	2.775	2.723	2.673	2.624	2.577	2.531	2.487
4	3.902	3.808	3.717	3.630	3.546	3.465	3.387	3.312	3.240	3.170
5	4.853	4.713	4.580	4.452	4.329	4.212	4.100	3.993	3.890	3.791

Discount rates (r)

The annuity factors are for periods starting in period 1 (year 1). For example, the annuity factor for years 1 – 3 at 9%, from the table, is 2.531.

Using annuities and annuity factors for investment appraisal

Annuity discount factors can be used in DCF investment analysis, mainly to make the calculations easier and quicker.

Example

What is the present value of the cash flows for a project, if the cash flows are $60,000 each year for years 1 – 7, and the cost of capital is 15%?

Answer

$60,000 × 4.160 (annuity factor at 15%, n = 7) = $249,600.

Example

What is the present value of the following cash flows, when the cost of capital is 12%?

Year	Annual cash flow $	Discount factor at 12%	Present value $
0	(100,000)		
1	10,000		
2	15,000		
3 – 15	20,000		
NPV			

Answer

Annuity factor at 12%, years 1 – 15 = 6.811

Annuity factor at 12%, years 1 – 2 = 1.690

Therefore annuity factor at 12%, years 3 – 15 = 6.811 – 1.690 = 5.121

Year	Annual cash flow $	Discount factor at 12%	Present value $
0	(100,000)	1.000	(100,000)
1	10,000	0.893	8,930
2	15,000	0.797	11,955
3 – 15	20,000	5.121	102,420
		NPV	+23,305

Example

A company is considering an investment of $70,000 in a project. The project life would be five years.

What must be the minimum annual cash returns from the project to earn a return of at least 9% per annum?

Answer

Investment = $70,000

Annuity factor at 9%, years 1 – 5 = 3.890

Minimum annuity required = $17,995 ($70,000 / 3.890)

1.6   Layout of NPV calculations

If you are required to present NPV calculations in the answer to an examination question, it is important that you should be able to present your calculations and workings clearly. There are two normal methods of presenting calculations, and you should try to use one of them.

The two methods of presentation are shown below, with illustrative figures.

Format 1

Year	Description of item	Cash flow $	Discount factor at 10%	Present Value $
0	Machine	(40,000)	1.000	(40,000)
0	Working capital	(5,000)	1.000	(5,000)
1-3	Cash profits	20,000	2.487	49,740
3	Sale of machine	6,000	0.751	4,506
3	Recovery of working capital	5,000	0.751	3,755
			NPV	13,001

Format 2

Year	0	1	2	3
Description of item	$	$	$	$
Machine/sale of machine	(40,000)			6,000
Working capital	(5,000)			5,000
Cash receipts		50,000	50,000	50,000
Cash expenditures		(30,000)	(30,000)	(30,000)
Net cash flow	(45,000)	20,000	20,000	31,000
Discount factor at 10%	1.000	0.909	0.826	0.751
Present value	(45,000)	18,180	16,520	23,281
NPV	+ 12,981			

For computations with a large number of cash flow items, the second format is probably easier. This is because the discounting for each year will only need to be done once.

1.7   Calculating cash flows: other points to remember

To calculate cash flows for a project, the following points should also be remembered:

Cash flows should be calculated using **relevant costs**. The same rules apply to the calculation of relevant costs for long-term decisions as for short-term decisions. If the project involves the purchase of capital assets, these might have a residual value at the end of the project. This residual value should be included as a cash inflow in the appropriate year.

A project may require an investment in **working capital**.

- When there is an increase in working capital, cash flows are lower than cash profits by the amount of the increase.

- Similarly, when there is a reduction in working capital, cash flows are higher than cash profits by the amount of the reduction.

Working capital is usually included in DCF analysis as follows:

- The working capital for the project is included as a cash outflow at the beginning of the project, in Year 0.

- At the end of the project, when working capital is reduced to $0, the reduction in working capital is included as a cash inflow. The cash inflow is normally included as a cash flow in the final year of the project.

DCF analysis should normally take **taxation** into consideration, and possibly also **inflation**. The effects of taxation and inflation are explained in the following sections.

> ### DCF and taxation
>
> - Taxation cash flows in investment appraisal
> - Interest costs and taxation
> - Timing of cash flows for taxation
> - Tax-allowable depreciation (capital allowances)
> - Straight-line method and reducing balance method
> - Balancing charge or balancing allowance on disposal

2 DCF and taxation

2.1 Taxation cash flows in investment appraisal

In project appraisal, cash flows arise due to the effects of taxation.

When an investment results in higher profits, there will be higher taxation. For example, if taxation on profits is 25% and a company earns $10,000 each year from an investment, the pre-tax cash inflow is $10,000, but there is a tax payment of $2,500.

Similarly, if an investment results in lower profits, tax is reduced. For example, if an investment causes higher spending of $5,000 each year and the tax on profits is 30%, there will be a cash outflow of $5,000 but a cash benefit from a reduction in tax payments of $1,500.

Tax cash flows should be included in DCF analysis.

2.2 Interest costs and taxation

Interest costs are allowable for tax purposes. However, interest cash flows are not included in DCF analysis, because the interest cost is in the cost of capital (discount rate). In DCF analysis, an **after-tax cost of capital** is used to calculate present values. An after-tax cost of capital is a discount rate that allows for the tax relief on interest payments.

2.3 Timing of cash flows for taxation

The tax on extra profits or the tax savings due to lower profits could occur either:

- in the same year as the profits or losses to which they relate, or
- one year later ('one year in arrears').

Either of these assumptions could be correct. An examination question should specify which assumption you should use.

Example

The after-tax cost of capital is 8%. A project costing $60,000 will be expected to earn cash profits of $40,000 in year 1 and $50,000 in year 2. Taxation at 30% occurs one year in arrears of the profits or losses to which they relate.

For the purpose of this exercise, assume that the cost of the project is not an allowable cost for tax purposes.

Required: Calculate the NPV of the project.

Answer

Year	Investment/pre-tax cash profit	Tax at 30%	Net cash flow	Discount factor at 8%	Present value
	$	$	$		$
0	(60,000)		(60,000)	1.000	(60,000)
1	40,000		40,000	0.926	37,040
2	50,000	(12,000)	38,000	0.857	32,566
3		(15,000)	(15,000)	0.794	(11,910)
	NPV				(2,304)

2.4 Tax-allowable depreciation (capital allowances)

When a business buys a non-current asset, depreciation is charged in the financial accounts. However, depreciation in the financial accounts is not an allowable expense for tax purposes. Instead, the tax rules provide for 'tax-allowable depreciation' or capital allowances.

Tax-allowable depreciation affects the cash flows from an investment, and the tax effects must be included in the project cash flows.

2.5 Straight-line method and reducing balance method

There are two ways of allowing depreciation for tax purposes:

- the straight-line method
- the reducing balance method.

Straight-line method

With the straight-line method of tax-allowable depreciation, the depreciation expense allowed for tax purposes =
(The cost of the asset minus any expected residual value)/Expected years of life

Example

An asset costs $80,000 and has an expected economic life of four years with no residual value. If depreciation is allowed for tax purposes over four years using the straight-line method, the allowable depreciation would be $20,000 each year.

If the rate of tax on profits is 25%, the annual reduction in tax from the capital allowance is $20,000 × 25% = $5,000 for four years.

Reducing balance method

With the reducing balance method, the tax-allowable depreciation expense in each year is a constant percentage each year of the written down value (WDV) of the asset as at the beginning of the year. The WDV of the asset is its cost less all accumulated capital allowances to date.

Example

An asset costs $80,000. Tax-allowable depreciation is 25% on a reducing balance basis. Tax on profits is payable at the rate of 30%. Tax is payable/saved one year in arrears. The cash flow benefits from the tax depreciation are calculated as follows:

Year		WDV at start of year	Tax allowable depreciation (25%)	Tax saved (30%)	Year of cash flow benefit
		$	$	$	
0		80,000	20,000	6,000	1
1	(80,000 – 20,000)	60,000	15,000	4,500	2
2	(60,000 – 15,000)	45,000	11,250	3,375	3
3	(45,000 – 11,250)	33,750	8,438	2,531	4
4	(33,750 – 8,438)	25,312	6,328	1,898	5
5	(25,312 – 6,328)	18,984			

(Note: WDV = the tax written-down value of the asset.)

2.6 Balancing charge or balancing allowance on disposal

When an asset reaches the end of its useful life, it will be scrapped or disposed of. On disposal, there might be a balancing charge or a balancing allowance. This is the difference between:

- the written-down value of the asset for tax purposes, and
- its disposal value (if any).

If the written-down value of the asset for tax purposes is higher than the disposal value, the difference is a balancing allowance. The balancing allowance is set against taxable profits, and so it will result in a reduction in tax payments of:

Balancing allowance × Tax rate = Cash saving

If the written-down value of the asset for tax purposes is lower than the disposal value, the difference is a balancing charge. The balancing charge is a taxable amount, and will result in an increase in tax payments of:

Balancing charge × Tax rate = Cash payment.

Example

A company is considering an investment in a non-current asset costing $80,000. The project would generate the following cash profits:

Year	$
1	50,000
2	40,000
3	20,000
4	10,000

The asset is eligible for tax-allowable depreciation at 25%, by the reducing balance method. It is expected to have a residual value of $20,000 at the end of year 4. The after-tax cost of capital is 9%. The rate of tax on profits is 30%. Taxation cash flows occur one year in arrears.

Required
Calculate the NPV of the project.

Answer

The solution to the previous example shows the calculations of the tax allowance each year for depreciation. It also shows that at the beginning of year 4, the year of disposal, the written down value of the asset will be $33,750. The disposal value of the asset at the end of year 4 is $20,000. At the end of the project life (Year 4), there will therefore be a balancing allowance of:
$33,750 - $20,000 = $13,750.

The tax saved in Year 5 will therefore be $13,750 × 30% = $4,125.

(If the residual value had been higher than $33,750, there would have been an amount chargeable to tax for the year).

Year	Investment	Cash profits	Tax on profits at 30%	Tax-allowable dep'n – tax saved	Net cash flow	DCF factor at 9%	PV
	$	$	$	$	$		$
0	(80,000)				(80,000)	1.000	(80,000)
1		50,000		6,000	56,000	0.917	51,352
2		40,000	(15,000)	4,500	29,500	0.842	24,839
3		20,000	(12,000)	3,375	11,375	0.772	8,782
4	20,000	10,000	(6,000)	2,531	26,531	0.708	18,784
5			(3,000)	4,125	1,125	0.650	731
						NPV	+ 24,488

> ## DCF and inflation
>
> - Inflation and long-term projects
> - The rules for inflation in DCF analysis

3 DCF and inflation

3.1 Inflation and long-term projects

When a company makes a long-term investment, there will be costs and benefits for a number of years. In all probability, the future cash flows will be affected by inflation in sales prices and inflation in costs.

In practice, it is common to carry out DCF analysis for investment appraisal on the assumption that:

- there will be no inflation in prices and costs, or
- it is impossible to predict what inflation will be, but it should be assumed that inflation will be insignificant and immaterial.

It is certainly difficult to predict what the rate of inflation will be over the next few years, and this is probably why inflation is normally ignored for DCF analysis.

However, inflation might be a significant factor in some investments. Inflation should be taken into consideration:

- when it is likely to be significant, and
- when reasonable estimates of the future rate of inflation can be made.

3.2 The rules for inflation in DCF analysis

The cost of capital used in DCF analysis is normally a 'money' cost of capital. In other words, it is a cost of capital based on current market returns and yields.

When estimates are made for inflation in future cash flows, the rules are as follows:

- Estimate all cash flows at their inflated amount. Since cash flows are assumed to occur at the year-end, they should be increased by the rate of inflation for the full year.
- To estimate a future cash flow at its inflated amount, you can apply the formula:

  Cash flow in year n at inflated amount =
  [Cash flow at current price level] $\times (1 + i)^n$

  - where i is the annual rate of inflation.
- Discount the inflated cash flows at the cost of capital, to obtain the NPV.

Example

A company is considering an investment in an item of equipment costing $150,000. The equipment would be used to make a product. The selling price of the product at today's prices would be $10 per unit, and the variable cost per unit (all cash costs) would be $6.

The project would have a four-year life, and sales are expected to be:

Year	Units of sale
1	20,000
2	40,000
3	60,000
4	20,000

At today's prices, it is expected that the equipment will be sold at the end of Year 4 for $10,000. There will be additional fixed cash overheads of $50,000 each year as a result of the project, at today's price levels.

The company expects prices and costs to increase due to inflation at the following annual rates:

Item	Annual inflation rate
Sales	5%
Variable costs	8%
Fixed costs	8%
Equipment disposal value	6%

The company's cost of capital is 12%. Ignore taxation.

Required
Calculate the NPV of the project.

Answer

All the cash flows must be re-stated at their inflated amounts.

An assumption needs to be made about what the cash flows will be in Year 1. Are 'today's' price levels the price levels to use in Year 1, or should the cash flows in Year 1 be increased to allow for inflation?

Since Year 1 cash flows relate to the end of Year 1, the appropriate assumption is usually to start inflating the cash flows in Year 1. This assumption is used here.

Item		Year 1 $	Year 2 $	Year 3 $	Year 4 $
Revenue					
At today's prices		200,000	400,000	600,000	200,000
At inflated prices (5% per year)	A	210,000	441,000	694,575	243,101

Costs

Variable, today's prices		120,000	240,000	360,000	120,000
Fixed, today's prices		50,000	50,000	50,000	50,000
Total, today's prices		170,000	290,000	410,000	170,000
At inflated prices	B	183,600	338,256	516,482	231,283
(8% per year)					
Net cash profit (A − B)		26,400	102,744	178,093	11,818
Equipment disposal					12,625
($10,000 × (1.06)·)					

The NPV can now be calculated in the normal way.

Year		Cash flow	Discount factor at 12%	Present value
		$		$
0	Equipment	(150,000)	1.000	(150,000)
1	Cash profit	26,400	0.893	23,575
2	Cash profit	102,744	0.797	81,887
3	Cash profit	178,093	0.712	126,802
4	Cash profit	11,818	0.636	7,516
4	Disposal value	12,625	0.636	8,030
	NPV			+ 97,810

Other aspects of DCF analysis
■ Sensitivity analysis
■ Asset replacement decisions
■ Using DCF with other project evaluation methods
■ Evaluation of a DCF analysis

4 Other aspects of DCF analysis

4.1 Sensitivity analysis

Sensitivity analysis should be used as a method of providing information about the risk or uncertainty in a decision. Techniques such as sensitivity analysis and expected values have been described in an earlier chapter, for the purpose of short-term decisions and budgeting. The same techniques may be applied to DCF and long-term capital investment decisions.

Sensitivity analysis can be used in the following ways:

■ To calculate the effect on the NPV of a given percentage reduction in benefits or a given percentage increase in costs. For example, what would the NPV of the project be if sales volumes were 10% below estimate, or if annual running costs were 5% higher than estimate?

■ To calculate the percentage amount by which benefits must fall below estimate or costs rise above estimate before the project NPV becomes negative. For example, by how much would sales volumes need to fall below the expected volumes, before the project NPV became negative?

 Example

A company is considering the following project:

Year	Equipment	Income	Running costs	Net cash flow	DCF factor at 10%	PV
	$	$	$	$		$
0	(8,000)				1.000	(8,000)
1		6,000	3,500	2,500	0.909	2,273
2		8,000	4,500	3,500	0.826	2,891
3		10,000	5,500	4,500	0.751	3,379
4		4,000	2,500	1,500	0.683	1,025
NPV						+ 1,568

Required
Estimate the sensitivity of the project to:

■ income being lower than estimate, and

■ running costs being higher than estimate.

Solution

Year	Equipment		Income	Running costs	NPV
	PV		PV	PV	NPV
	$		$	$	$
0	(8,000)				
1			5,454	(3,181)	
2			6,608	(3,717)	
3			7,510	(4,131)	
4			2,732	(1,707)	
PV	(8,000)		22,304	(12,736)	+ 1,568

The sensitivity of the project to errors in the estimates can now be assessed as follows:

- Income. The project would cease to have a positive NPV if income is below the estimate by more than: $\dfrac{1,568}{22,304} = 0.070$ or 7.0%.

- Running costs. The project would cease to have a positive NPV if running costs are above the estimate by more than: $\dfrac{1,568}{12,736} = 0.123$ or 12.3%.

An assessment of risk and uncertainty could then be made on the basis of the likelihood that income will fall below estimate or running costs will increase above the estimate by more than these amounts.

4.2 Asset replacement decisions

An asset replacement decision involves deciding how frequently a non-current asset should be replaced, when it is in regular use, so that when the asset reaches the end of its useful life, it will be replaced by an identical asset.

In other words, this type of decision is about what is the most appropriate useful economic life of a non-current asset, and how soon should it be replaced?

Here we are not dealing with a one-off decision about whether or not to acquire an asset. Instead we are deciding when to replace an asset we are currently using with another new asset; and then when the new asset has been used up, replacing it again with an identical asset; and so on in perpetuity. We are evaluating the cycle of replacing the machine – considering the various options for how long we should keep it before replacing it.

The **decision rule** is that the preferred replacement cycle for an asset should be the least-cost replacement cycle. This is the frequency of replacement that minimises the PV of cost.

The cash flows to consider

The cash flows that must be considered when making the asset replacement decision are:

- the capital cost (purchase cost) of the asset

- the maintenance and operating costs of the asset: these will usually increase each year as the asset gets older
- tax relief on the asset (tax-allowable depreciation)
- the scrap value or resale value of the asset at the end of its life.

The main problem with evaluating an asset replacement decision is comparing these costs over a similar time frame. For example, how can we compare the PV of costs for asset replacement cycles of one, two, three, four and five years?

For example, you cannot simply compare the PV of cost over a two-year replacement cycle with the PV of cost over a three-year replacement cycle, because you would be comparing costs over two years with costs over three years, which is not a fair comparison.

Methods of evaluation

A method is needed for comparing the different replacement cycles over a common period of time. There are three methods of doing this:

- the lowest common multiple method
- the finite time method
- the equivalent annual cost method: this is the method normally used.

The equivalent annual cost method is the method normally used, and the only one of these three methods that you need to know for your examination. It is the only method described here.

The equivalent annual cost method

The equivalent annual cost method of calculating the most cost-effective replacement cycle for assets is as follows:

- For each choice of replacement cycle, the PV of cost is calculated over one full replacement cycle, with the asset purchased in year 0 and disposed of at the end of the life cycle.
- This PV of cost is then converted into an equivalent annual cost or annuity. The equivalent annual cost is calculated by dividing the PV of cost of the life cycle by the annuity factor for the cost of capital, for the number of years in the life cycle.
- The replacement cycle with the lowest equivalent annual cost is selected as the least-cost replacement cycle.

 Example

ABC Company is considering its replacement policy for a particular machine which it intends to replace every year, every two years or every three years. The machine has a purchase cost of $17,000 and a maximum useful life of three years. The following information is also relevant:

Year	Maintenance/running costs of machine	Scrap value if sold at end of year
	$	$
1	1,900	8,000
2	2,400	5,500
3	3,750	4,000

The cost of capital for ABC Company is 10%.

What is the optimum replacement cycle? Ignore taxation. Use the equivalent annual cost method.

 Answer

Replace every year

Year		Cash flow	Discount factor at 10%	PV
		$		$
0	Purchase	(17,000)	1.000	(17,000)
1	Maintenance costs	(1,900)	0.909	(1,727)
1	Resale value	8,000	0.909	7,272
	PV of cost			(11,455)

Equivalent annual cost = PV of cost/Annuity factor at 10% for 1 year
= $11,455/0.909 = $12,602.

Replace every two years

Year		Cash flow	Discount factor at 10%	PV
		$		$
0	Purchase	(17,000)	1.000	(17,000)
1	Maintenance costs	(1,900)	0.909	(1,727)
2	Maintenance costs	(2,400)	0.826	(1,982)
2	Resale value	5,500	0.826	4,543
	PV of cost			(16,166)

Equivalent annual cost = PV of cost/Annuity factor at 10% for 2 years
= $16,166/1.736 = $9,312.

Replace every three years

Year		Cash flow	Discount factor at 10%	PV
		$		$
0	Purchase	(17,000)	1.000	(17,000)
1	Maintenance costs	(1,900)	0.909	(1,727)
2	Maintenance costs	(2,400)	0.826	(1,982)
3	Maintenance costs	(3,750)	0.751	(2,816)
1	Resale value	4,000	0.751	3,004
	PV of cost			(20,521)

Equivalent annual cost = PV of cost/Annuity factor at 10% for three years
= $20,521/2.487 = $8,251.

Summary

Replace	Equivalent annual cost
	$
Every year	12,602
Every two years	9,312
Every three years	8,251

Conclusion: The least-cost decision is to replace the asset every three years, because a three-year replacement cycle has the lowest equivalent annual cost.

4.3 Using DCF with other project evaluation methods

DCF (NPV or IRR) might be used together with other methods of project appraisal.

- A DCF project appraisal might be used together with an ROI or residual income assessment. The weaknesses of the ROI and residual income methods for project appraisal have already been explained in an earlier chapter.

- A DCF project appraisal might also be used with the **payback method**. The payback of a project is the number of years it will take before the net cash inflows from the project 'pay back' the initial expenditures in Year 0.

A company might have a rule, for example, that capital projects will not be undertaken unless they are expected to have a positive NPV and are also expected to pay back within, say, four years.

4.4 Evaluation of a DCF analysis

In your examination, you might be asked to comment on a DCF evaluation. When managers are given a DCF analysis and intend to use the analysis to make their investment decision, it is important to ask some basic questions.

To assess the figures provided by a DCF analysis, there are several factors that might need consideration.

- Are the figures in the DCF evaluation reliable? Has anything been omitted? Are any of the figures incorrect?

- Could the NPV be improved by delaying some costs of the project, or by reducing the investment in working capital?

- Has the most appropriate discount rate been used?

- Use sensitivity analysis to asses the risk in the project. What would happen if costs were to increase by 5%, say, or revenues were to be 5% lower than expected?

Example
A company is considering whether to invest in a new product, for which a market is developing. The product is expected to have a four-year life, and during the life of the product, the company wants to maintain a 10% share of the total market. Its marketing team has estimated the expected market size in each year, and the price that would probably have to be charged for the product to maintain a 10% market share, as follows:

Year	Total market size units	Sales price to win 10% share per unit
1	400,000	$60
2	600,000	$65
3	500,000	$60
4	300,000	$40

A DCF analysis for the project is shown below. The company normally uses 12% as the discount rate for project evaluation.

	Year 0	Year 1	Year 2	Year 3	Year 4	Year 5
Sales units		40,000	60,000	50,000	30,000	
Sales price ($/unit)		$60	$65	$60	$40	
	$000	$000	$000	$000	$000	$000
Capital expenditure/ residual value	(2,500)					500
Working capital	(700)				700	
Revenue		2,400	3,900	3,000	1,200	
Advertising	(900)	(500)	(300)	(200)		
Variable costs ($20/unit)		(800)	(1,200)	(1,000)	(600)	
Extra fixed costs		(400)	(400)	(400)	(400)	
Net cash flow	(4,100)	700	2,000	1,400	900	500
Discount factor at 12%	1.000	0.893	0.797	0.712	0.636	0.567
PV at 12%	(4,100.0)	625.1	1,594.0	996.8	572.4	283.5
NPV at 12% (in $000)	**(28.2)**					
Discount factor at 10%	1.000	0.909	0.826	0.751	0.683	0.621
PV at 10%	(4,100.0)	636.3	1,652.0	1,051.4	614.7	310.5
NPV at 10% (in $000)	**+ 164.9**					

At a discount rate of 12%, the project has a small negative NPV, indicating that it should not go ahead. However, a further analysis of the figures might suggest the following points.

Are the figures reliable?

The figures are not reliable, because there are some obvious omissions.

The cash flows do not include any cash flows for taxation; therefore the DCF analysis is probably incomplete.

The cash flows do not allow for inflation in prices. If there is inflation in sales prices and running costs, and the cost of capital remains 12%, the project might have a small positive NPV after allowing for inflation.

Could the NPV be improved by managing cash flows?

The NPV could be improved if it is possible to delay some of the costs, particularly advertising costs.

The NPV would also be improved if the investment in working capital could be reduced.

Cash flows might be improved by charging higher prices and taking a share of the market that is less than 10%.

Is the discount rate suitable?

It is interesting to note that the project would have a positive NPV at a lower discount rate of 10%, and it might be appropriate to check that 12% is a suitable discount rate for this project.

Sensitivity analysis

It might be useful to carry out some sensitivity analysis, by varying the sales volume each year, or the sale price per unit, or the variable cost per unit, or the residual value of the capital equipment. Sensitivity analysis would provide information about the amount of risk in the project, and possible variations in the NPV.

CHAPTER

6

Introduction to strategic management accounting

Contents
1   Introduction to strategic planning and control
2   Levels of management and management information
3   Strategic management accounting
4   Strategic objectives, customer satisfaction and adding value
5   The effect of IT on management accounting

Introduction to strategic planning and control

- Definition of strategic planning and control
- Advantages of formal strategic planning
- The strategic planning process
- Performance management systems
- Linking performance measurement to strategy

1 Introduction to strategic planning and control

1.1 Definition of strategic planning and control

'Strategic planning and control' within an entity is the continuous process of:
- identifying the goals and objectives of the entity
- planning strategies that will enable these goals and objectives to be achieved
- setting targets for each strategic objective (performance targets)
- implementing the strategy
- converting strategies into shorter-term operational plans
- monitoring actual performance (performance measurement and review)
- taking control measures where appropriate when actual performance is below the target.

Other aspects of strategic planning and control are:
- re-assessing plans and strategies when circumstances in the business environment change
- where necessary, changing strategies and plans.

1.2 Advantages of formal strategic planning

Companies usually have a formal strategic planning process, because a formal system of planning:
- clarifies objectives
- helps management to make strategic decisions. Strategic planning forces managers to think about the future: companies are unlikely to survive unless they plan ahead
- establishes targets for achievement
- co-ordinates objectives and targets throughout the organisation, from the mission statement and strategic objectives at the top of a hierarchy of objectives, down to operational targets
- provides a system for checking progress towards the objectives.

However, planning must also be flexible. Plans and targets must often be changed in response to events in the business environment, or in response to changes in the business environment. For example, to succeed in a fast-changing and competitive business, it may be necessary to react to a new initiative by a rival company.

Changes in strategic plans

Strategic plans often cover a period of several years, typically five years or longer. They are prepared on the basis of the best information available at the time, using assumptions about the nature of the business environment – competitive conditions, market conditions, available technology, the economic, social and political climate, and so on.

However, the business environment can change very quickly, in unexpected ways. Changes can create new threats to a company, or they can create new business opportunities. Whenever changes occur, a company should be able to respond – taking measures to deal with new threats, or to exploit new opportunities.

The response of a company to changes in its environment could mean having to develop new strategies and abandon old ones. When changes are made, the original strategic plan will no longer be entirely valid, although large parts of it might be unaffected.

Strategic planning in practice is therefore often a mixture of:

■ formal planning, and

■ developing new strategies and making new plans whenever significant changes occur in its business environment.

Responding to unexpected changes by doing something that is not in the formal plan is sometimes called 'freewheeling opportunism'. It means making unplanned decisions, to take advantages of opportunities as they arise, or to deal with unexpected threats.

1.3   The strategic planning process

Different methods and approaches may be used to develop strategic plans. Some of these methods will be described in more detail in later chapters.

A basic approach to strategic planning is shown in the following diagram.

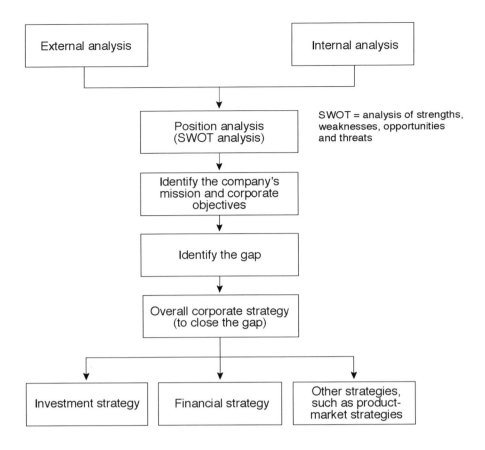

External analysis

External analysis involves an analysis of developments outside the organisation that are already affecting the organisation or could affect the organisation in the future. These are external factors that might affect the achievement of objectives and strategy selection.

An external analysis might consider:

- the political situation in each country where it has operating subsidiaries
- changes in the law, and how these affect the organisation
- changes in economic conditions
- social factors and cultural factors, such as an increasing average age in the population
- technology changes: the development of the internet and e-commerce, for example, have had enormous consequences for business within the past few years
- the competitive environment, such as the entry of a new competitor into the market, or the 'globalisation' of the market.

An external analysis should identify opportunities and threats that face the organisation. Strategies might be developed to exploit opportunities or take counter-measures to deal with threats.

Internal analysis

Internal analysis looks at the strengths and weaknesses within the organisation – its products, existing customers, management, employees, technical skills and 'know-how', its operational systems and procedures, its reputation for quality, the quality of its suppliers, its liquidity and cash flows, and so on.

SWOT analysis

SWOT analysis is the analysis of the strengths and weaknesses of an organisation, and the opportunities and threats in its environment. This method of strategic analysis is often used by organisations as a starting point for strategic planning.

Strategic management accounting can assist with SWOT analysis by trying to put costs or benefits to particular strengths, weaknesses, opportunities and threats, so that strategic managers are able to assess their importance.

SWOT analysis is explained in more detail later.

Gap analysis

Gap analysis involves:

■ identifying the corporate objectives for the organisation, and what strategic management wants the organisation to achieve each year over the planning period

■ comparing these strategic targets with the expected actual results, if there are no changes in strategy and no new planning initiatives.

■ The gap is the difference between these two. Strategies should be developed to close the gap, so that expected performance is in line with the strategic aims and objectives.

(Note: Gap analysis is sometimes described as an analysis of the difference between 'Where we are' and 'Where we want to be'.)

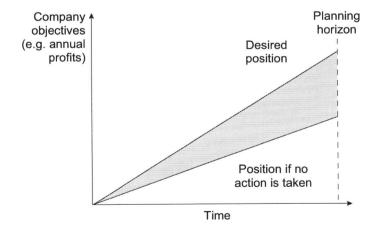

Strategies have to be developed to 'close the gap'. Operational plans are then formulated in order to implement each chosen strategy.

1.4   Performance management systems

A system of performance management is concerned with the following:

- setting targets for the achievement of the entity's main strategic objective
- setting targets for each strategy that is implemented for achieving the main strategic objective
- setting targets at all levels of management within the entity: all planning targets (at all levels within the entity) should be consistent with the strategic targets and objectives
- measuring actual performance
- comparing actual performance with the targets
- where appropriate, taking control measures
- where appropriate, changing the targets.

In many organisations, performance measurement systems are also used in a system of incentives and rewards, and managers are given a reward (often a cash bonus) for achieving or exceeding one or more agreed performance targets.

Performance measurement is therefore concerned with planning and controlling, at all levels within an organisation.

1.5   Linking performance measurement to strategy

The measures of performance used throughout an organisation should be linked to the corporate strategy of the organisation, and should be consistent with corporate strategy. This means that there has to be consistency between performance measures at all levels in the organisation, from operating levels up.

The performance measures that are used should focus on targets where success is a critical factor.

The performance measures that are chosen should do the following:

- Measure effectiveness – the effectiveness of processes, and the effectiveness of products and services in meeting customer needs
- Measure efficiency – the use of resources within the organisation
- Include 'external' measures from outside the organisation as well as internal measures
- Be a mixture of financial and non-financial measurement, and qualitative and quantitative measurements
- Focus on the long-term as well as the short-term
- Be flexible so that the measures used are continually changed in response to a changing business environment

- Recognise the trade-off between different measures of performance: for example, it is often necessary to make compromises to reach a suitable balance between short-term and long-term targets

- Recognise the motivational effect that performance measurements can have on employee and management behaviour.

> ## Levels of management and management information
>
> - Levels of management
> - Information for different management levels
> - Performance management and management accounting
> - Strategic and operational information for performance measurement
> - Potential conflict between strategic plans and short-term decisions

2 Levels of management and management information

In 'traditionally-structured' large organisations, there is a hierarchy of managers, from senior management down to junior managers and supervisors. The responsibilities of managers vary according to their position in the management hierarchy.

Even in small organisations, the nature of management activities can be analysed into different levels.

The purpose of this chapter is to consider the differing information requirements of managers at different levels in the decision-making hierarchy, and in particular at the information requirements for strategic decision-making. Management accounting systems should be capable of providing the information required by managers at all levels.

2.1 Levels of management

A common approach to analysing levels of management and management decision-making is to identify three levels:

- strategic management
- tactical management
- operational management.

Strategic management

Strategic management is concerned with:

- deciding on the objectives and strategies for the organisation
- making or approving long-term plans for the achievement of strategic targets
- monitoring actual results, to check whether these are in line with strategic targets
- where appropriate, taking control action to bring actual performance back into line with strategic targets
- reviewing and amending strategies.

A strategy is a plan for the achievement of a long-term objective. The main objective of a profit-making entity may be to maximise the wealth of its owners. Several strategies are selected for the achievement of this main objective, and each individual strategy might have its own specific objective.

Strategic planning is often concerned with developing products and markets and for long-term investment. For example, a company seeking to increase its profits by 10% a year for the next five years might select the following strategies:

■ Marketing strategy: to expand into markets in other countries (with specific countries selected as planning targets for each year of the plan)

■ Innovation strategy: to invest in research and development (with a target to launch, say, two new products on the market each year for the next five years)

■ Investment strategy: to invest in new technology (with a target, say, of replacing all existing equipment with new technology within the next five years).

Tactical management

Tactical management is associated with the efficient and effective use of an organisation's resources, and the control over expenditure. In a large organisation, tactical managers are the 'middle managers'.

Tactical management is concerned with implementation and control of medium-term plans, within the guidelines of the organisation's strategic plans. For example, budgeting and budgetary control are largely tactical management responsibilities.

Operational management

Operational management is the management of day-to-day operating activities. It is usually associated with operational managers and supervisors.

At an operational level, managers need to make sure on a day-to-day basis that they have the resources they need and that those resources are being used efficiently. It includes scheduling of operations and monitoring output, such as daily efficiency levels.

There isn't a clear dividing line between tactical management and operational management, but essentially the differences are a matter of detail. Tactical management may be concerned with the performance of an entire department during a one-week period, whereas operational management may be concerned with the activities of individuals or small work groups on a daily basis.

2.2   Information for different management levels

Information should be provided to managers to help them to make decisions. The nature of the information required varies according to the level of management and the type of decision. Within organisations, there are management information systems that provide this information. A major element of the overall management information system should be the management accounting system.

A management accounting system should provide information for strategic management, tactical management and operational management.

The requirements of management for information vary with the level of management. This concept is set out simply in the diagram below.

Levels of management and information requirements

Strategic management information

Strategic management information is information that helps strategic managers to:

■ make long-term plans

■ assess whether long-term planning targets will be met, and

■ review existing strategies and make changes or improvements.

Strategic management needs strategic information. The characteristics of strategic information may be summarised as follows:

■ It is often information about the organisation as a whole, or a large part of it.

■ It is often in summary form, without too much detail.

■ It is generally relevant to the longer-term.

■ It is often forward-looking.

■ The data that is analysed to provide the information comes from both internal and external sources (from sources inside and outside the organisation).

■ It is often prepared on an 'ad hoc' basis, rather than in the form of regular and routine reports.

■ It may contain information of a qualitative nature as well as quantified information.

■ There is often a high degree of uncertainty in the information. This is particularly true when the information is forward-looking (for example, a forecast) over a number of years in the future.

Tactical information

Tactical information is information reported to middle managers in a large organisation, or for the purpose of annual planning and budgetary control.

Tactical information is used to decide how the resources of the organisation should be used, and to monitor how well they are being used. It is useful to relate tactical information to the sort of information that is contained in an annual budget. A budget is planning at a tactical management level, where the plan is expressed in financial terms.

The general features of tactical information are as follows:

- It is often information about individual departments and operations.
- It is often in summary form, but at a greater level of detail than strategic information.
- It is generally relevant to the short-term and medium-term.
- It may be forward-looking (for example, medium-term plans) but it is often concerned with performance measurement. Control information at a tactical level is often based on historical performance.
- The data that is analysed to provide the information comes from both internal and external sources (from sources inside and outside the organisation), but most of the information comes from internal sources.
- It is often prepared on a routine and regular basis (for example, monthly or weekly performance reports).
- It consists mainly of quantified information.
- There may be some degree of uncertainty in the information. However, as tactical plans are short-term or medium-term, the level of uncertainty is much less than for strategic information.

Control reports might typically be prepared every month, comparing actual results with the budget or target, and much of the information comes from internal sources. Examples of tactical information might be:

- variance reports in a budgetary control system
- reports on resource efficiency, such as the productivity of employees
- sales reports: reports on sales by product or by customer
- reports on capacity usage.

Operational information

Operational information is needed to enable supervisors and front line (operational) managers to organise and monitor operations, and to make on-the-spot decisions whenever operational problems arise. Operational information may also be needed by employees, to process transactions in the course of their regular work.

The general features of operational information are as follows:

- It is normally information about specific transactions, or specific jobs, tasks, daily work loads, individuals or work groups. (It is 'task-specific'.)

- It may be summarised at a work group or section level, but is in a more detailed form than tactical information.

- It is generally relevant to the very short-term.

- It may be forward-looking (for example, daily plans) but it is often concerned with transactions, procedures and performance measurement at a daily level.

- The data that is analysed to provide the information comes almost exclusively from both internal sources (from sources inside the organisation).

- It consists mainly of quantified information. Most of this information is 'factual' and is not concerned with uncertainty.

Operational information is provided regularly, or is available online when required. It is concerned with operational details, such as:

- the number of employees in the department absent from work

- wastage rates in production

- whether the scheduled work load for the day has been completed

- delays and hold-ups in work flow, and the reasons for the delay

- whether a customer's order will be completed on time.

In many respects, strategic information, tactical information and operational information are all concerned with the same things – business plans and actual performance. They are provided in different amounts of detail and with differing frequency. However, with the development of IT systems and internal and external databases, it is possible for all levels of information to be available to managers online and on demand.

Example

An accountancy tuition company has a strategic target of increasing its annual sales. What strategic, tactical and operational decisions might be taken towards achieving this target?

Answer

Here is a suggested answer.

(a) At a strategic level management may decide it is necessary to increase sales by 20%. It will then need to study the company and its business environment and decide how this might be done – for example by developing the existing business, buying a competitor company, or diversifying into other forms of training, such as training lawyers or bankers.

(b) At a tactical level, a budget should be prepared for the next year, based on strategic decisions already taken. Middle management should consider a variety of plans for achieving targets, such as spending more money on advertising, recruiting more trainers and running more training programmes. Targets might be set for each type of course or each geographical training centre location.

(c)   Operational management will make decisions about the courses and their administration, such as making special offers (free study materials) to attract more students, running additional courses when demand is strong, and making sure that all student fees are collected.

Example

What do you think might be the information requirements of the manager in each of the following scenarios?

Scenario 1

Wang Chung is the production director of a large Chinese factory producing music compact discs (CDs). He is considering a joint venture with a TBC Limited, a small CD producer in the UK, with the aim of supplying lower-cost CDs to the UK and European markets and thereby increasing profitability.

Scenario 2

James Pearce is a supervisor of a department responsible for making alterations to motor vans so that people can sleep in them and use them for overnight accommodation. He is in charge of the six people in his department and receives daily performance data on times taken by staff to complete their work compared to predetermined standard times. The department operates two eight-hour shifts each day. Two members of staff have requested time off on the same shift. This would disrupt the work production schedule. James can only permit one member of staff to take the time off, and so he has decided to accept one request and turn down the other.

Answer

Here is a suggested answer.

Scenario 1

Wang Chung needs strategic information to help him with the strategic planning for the joint venture. The information he is likely to need includes:

- How the joint venture will operate. What will be the responsibilities of the joint venture partners?
- Information about the business history and financial status of the joint venture partner.
- The target markets for the CDs.
- Conditions within these target markets.
- The products that the joint venture will plan to sell.
- The target selling price
- Details of how the lower-cost production and selling will be achieved.
- The nature (and prices) of competitors in these markets
- The term of the joint venture agreement.
- Financial data: the size of investment required, including working capital. Estimated sales and costs over the planning period.
- The risk in the project.

Scenario 2

James Pearce has to make an operational decision, and decide which of the two employees should be given the time off.

The information he needs might be:

■ The reasons why each employee wants the particular day off work, and whether either is willing to change to another day

■ How much holiday each employee has taken so far during the year, and the total number of days to which each is entitled

■ Whether there are policy guidelines or rules within the company about how this type of decision should be made

■ Whether there might be an available substitute worker who could be used for a day, so that both employees can take the same day off work.

2.3 Performance management and management accounting

Performance management is an important aspect of management accounting systems, because:

■ Management must set targets for achievement, and most targets must be measurable. Management information is needed so that realistic targets can be set, and managers responsible for achieving targets are informed clearly about what they are expected to achieve.

■ Progress towards the achievement of targets should be monitored, either by comparing:

- actual results with the original target, or

- the current/latest forecast with the original target.

However, as suggested above, performance targets and measurements should relate to long-term targets as well as short-term targets, strategic targets as well as operational targets and non-financial as well as financial targets.

2.4 Strategic and operational information for performance measurement

The differences between the information needs of strategic and operational managers for **measuring performance** are summarised in the following table:

Strategic management	Operational management
Mainly a longer-term focus	Short-term focus: day-to-day operational issues.
Feedback may be occasional	Regular feedback about performance
Broad 'higher level' issues, such as acquisitions and disposals, as well as the development of internal resources. Approach to measuring performance: Where are we? Where do we want to be?	Often routine information and concerned with the current use of resources and improving the efficiency and effectiveness of resources, and with cost control.

How do we get there?
What are the risks?

Largely external in focus	Mainly internal focus
Non-routine issues	Concerned with detailed plans and controls

Both types of performance measurement are needed.

2.5 Potential conflict between strategic plans and short-term decisions

Problems may occur in any organisation, but especially large organisations with a large number of managers, when 'local' operational managers take decisions that are inconsistent with long-term strategic objectives.

There a several reasons why this might happen.

■ 'Local' managers might be rewarded for achieving short-term planning targets, such as keeping actual expenditure within the budget limit. However, although there is a short-term benefit, there might be longer-term damage. For example, a local manager might decide to cut the training budget for his staff in order to reduce costs, but in the long-term the future success of the company might depend on having well-trained and skilled employees.

■ 'Local' managers might be unaware of the strategic plans and objectives, due to poor communication within the entity.

In any system of performance management, especially in systems where managers are rewarded for achieving planning targets, it is important to make sure that the short-term planning targets are consistent with longer-term strategic objectives.

Strategic management accounting
■ Criticisms of traditional management accounting
■ The nature of strategic management accounting
■ Issues in strategic management accounting

3 Strategic management accounting

The purpose of management accounting is to provide relevant and reliable information so that managers can make well-informed decisions. The value of management accounting depends on the quality of the information provided, and whether it helps managers to make better decisions.

3.1 Criticisms of traditional management accounting

Management accounting is often associated with long-established methods of costing and financial reporting, such as absorption costing, standard costing, variance analysis and budgetary control reports. Some of these traditional methods are now criticised because they do not provide useful information for managers in a business environment that is continually changing.

■ Traditional management accounting systems do not provide enough information that is relevant to strategic issues and the long-term objectives of the entity.

■ They focus on financial information. Although financial information is important, non-financial information is also needed by managers for decision-making. Traditional management accounting systems therefore provide incomplete information.

■ They focus on information that is gathered from within the organisation, such as information about the efficiency and effectiveness of operations and processes, and the control of costs. They do not provide information:

  - from sources outside the entity, or

  - about the effect that the business environment (and change in the business environment) is having on the entity.

■ They are more appropriate for stable business conditions, where changes are slow and gradual. They do not provide information that managers need to make decisions when circumstances are continually changing.

■ Traditional management accounting systems do not make full use of the capabilities of IT systems, for storing, analysing, accessing and communicating information.

The criticisms of traditional management accounting methods will be considered in more detail in later chapters.

3.2   The nature of strategic management accounting

Strategic management accounting is a system of management accounting that provides managers with information that is relevant to making and monitoring strategic decisions. This includes information from both inside and outside the organisation (internal and external information), information with a longer-term perspective and non-financial as well as financial information.

It provides information:

■ about longer-term strategic issues, as well as the shorter term

■ of a non-financial nature as well as financial information

■ obtained from external as well as internal sources

■ about the business environment as well as internal operations

■ that recognises the significance of change and the need to anticipate major changes in the business environment

■ where the focus is on being competitive and succeeding in a competitive market environment.

Strategic management accounting systems also provide information that links strategy to decision-making and actions at the operational level.

 Example

The corporate strategy for a business organisation might be to increase profits by 15% each year for the next ten years. A strategic management accounting system will need to inform management whether the operational strategies of the organisation are likely to result in the achievement of the overall corporate strategy – sales and marketing strategy, research and development strategy, product-market strategy, competitive strategies, IT strategies, employee recruitment strategy, and so on.

Management information also needs to forecast the probable effects on profitability of current strategies, or what the effects of new strategies might be. Providing reliable long-term forecasts is difficult.

3.3   Issues in strategic management accounting

As stated earlier, strategic management accounting involves planning and decision-making for the longer-term, and is concerned with non-financial strategic objectives as well as financial objectives. Strategic management accounting information should be provided for the purpose of strategic planning.

Issues in strategic management accounting include:

■ providing information about strategic objectives

■ the concepts of customer satisfaction and adding value

■ the product life cycle

■ internal and external analysis: SWOT analysis

■ benchmarking.

These issues are relevant to strategic management accounting. In order to provide relevant information to management, it is important that management accounting systems should recognise these strategic issues and provide information relating to them.

Risk and uncertainty

The analysis of **risk** is also significant: as a general rule, the risk in decision-making increases with the time period over which the consequences of the decision will have effect.

Business decisions inevitably involve risk. Actual results and actual events in the future might turn out differently from what is expected. There is also uncertainty about the future due to a lack of reliable information. Risk and uncertainty increase with the length of the planning period, and are important aspects of strategic planning.

Strategic planners should also consider the risks in the strategies they choose, as well as the potential profits and returns.

Strategic management accounting will therefore involve the measurement and assessment of risk in strategic decisions.

Strategic objectives, customer satisfaction and adding value

- trategic objectives
- Strategic objectives and customer satisfaction
- Customer satisfaction
- Value and adding value

4 Strategic objectives, customer satisfaction and adding value

4.1 Strategic objectives

The purpose of strategic planning and control is to help an entity to achieve its strategic objectives. It is normally assumed that the objective of a company is to provide a high return to its owners, the shareholders, consistent with the level of risk in the business.

Not-for-profit entities also have strategic objectives, which relate to the purpose for which they exist. These objectives are non-financial in nature.

Government influence on corporate strategies

Although the main objective of a company might be to maximise returns to its shareholders (for a given level of risk), strategy formulation and implementation is often strongly influenced by government policy. The influence of government policy on strategy varies from one company to another. Some examples are listed below.

- In some countries such as the UK, state-owned industries have been privatised (converted into public companies). The privatised companies are allowed to operate as normal commercial companies, except that they are also required to meet minimum specified levels of performance. For example, water supply companies are required to ensure supplies of water and also to maintain and replace water pipes and systems. Companies operating train services are expected to maintain minimum standards of service, or risk the loss of their operating franchise.

- In many countries, the government is a major customer of commercial companies. Government economic policy might therefore affect strategy formulation. For example, if a government announces a large and sustained increase in spending on hospitals and the health service, this could affect the investment plans of companies that supply the health service.

- A national government might have a policy of protecting important domestic industries against takeovers by foreign companies. This could affect strategic planning by companies that could become a takeover target, and also planning by multinational companies wishing to expand through foreign acquisitions.

- Government policy on competition in markets affects some industries. Mergers or takeovers that would create a monopoly in a market could be prevented, because they are against the 'public interest'.

- Taxation policies of national governments could affect the decisions of multinational companies about where to locate their operations. A government might try to attract inward investment by offering subsidies to companies that invest in the country. High taxation could persuade companies to re-locate in another country.

4.2 Strategic objectives and customer satisfaction

In order to achieve their overall strategic objectives, it is argued that all entities – both profit-making businesses and not-for-profit entities – need to meet the needs of their customers, and provide customer satisfaction.

If an entity fails to satisfy its customers, it will also fail to achieve its overall strategic objectives. This is because the long-term success of an entity depends on providing customer satisfaction.

The concepts of customer satisfaction and adding value are therefore important for strategic planning and control. Strategic management accounting systems should also be capable of providing information about customer satisfaction and added value.

4.3 Customer satisfaction

There are three ways in which a company might try to do business with its customers: a product-driven approach, a sales-driven approach and a marketing-led approach.

- In a product-driven approach, the company manufactures a product or range of products, and makes them available for customers to buy. It is assumed that customers will want to buy the products, possibly because there are no alternative products to buy.

- In a sales-driven approach, the company manufactures a product or range of products, and makes them available for customers to buy. However, the company recognises that the customer might be unsure about whether or not to buy the products. It therefore needs to make an effort to sell the products, using a sales force, advertising or sales promotions. This approach is sometimes called 'hard selling'.

- In a **marketing-led approach**, the company recognises that the best way to succeed is the make products that the customer wants to buy. Instead of making products that might attract customers, and then trying to sell them, a company learns as much as it can about what customers want and how much they would be willing to pay for it. 'What customers want' is called 'customer needs'. Providing a product that meets these customer needs is called 'customer satisfaction'.

Most companies in a competitive market environment adopt a marketing-led approach. It is widely accepted that a company will sell a product much more successfully if the product is designed and delivered in a form – and at a price – that attracts customers and makes them want to buy it.

It is important to understand that what customers want from a product is not simply a product that performs a particular function. There are several ways in which customer needs can be met.

- The product can be designed with features that are attractive to all customers or to a particular group of customers. For example, all sunglasses should provide users with some protection against the light from the sun. First-class travel is offered to customers who want comfortable and luxurious travel arrangements.

- Customers might want a product to be reliable or to last for a long time. On the other hand, they might not be concerned if the product has only a short useful life. For example, this is why some handkerchiefs are made from cloth and some from tissue, and why some books have a hard back and some a paper back.

- Customers sometimes want a product to be available in a convenient place, where it can be purchased when they want it. For example, airports and railway stations provide shops and stalls where travellers can buy food, drinks and other items.

- Customers might want a product to be available immediately or within a very short time; otherwise they will not buy it.

- The price that customers are willing to pay for a product or service depends on:
  - whether the product meets their needs ('satisfies' the customer's needs), and
  - the value that the customer gives to the satisfaction of those needs.

4.4 Value and adding value

Customer satisfaction is also linked to the concept of value.

'Value' can be defined as something that adds to customer satisfaction. Value might be provided by an improvement in product quality, or new features (such as greater reliability and a longer useful life). Value can also be created by making the product available more easily and conveniently, or by providing a service more quickly and with fewer mistakes.

When extra value is added to a product or service:
- customers are more likely to want to buy it, or
- customers will be prepared to pay a higher price to obtain it.

Adding value should therefore benefit the company – by selling more of the product, or by selling it at a higher price. Companies need to ensure, however, that the costs of providing added value do not exceed the benefits from the extra value created.

The term 'adding value' is also used to describe measures that make a process more efficient. The customer gets the same product or service, but it is provided at a lower cost. This means that the customer gets the same value, but it costs less. Lower costs mean that the company can make higher profit margins, or they can pass on some of the benefits to the customer in the form of a lower sales price.

The concept of customer satisfaction and adding value has extended from the products and services sold by companies to services provided by not-for-profit entities, such as hospitals, state-owned schools and the fire service. In not-for-profit entities, the purpose of adding value and meeting customer needs is to deliver a better service, and in doing so achieve the strategic objectives of the entity more successfully.

The 'value chain' and 'value analysis', which will be described in more detail later, relate to these concepts of value and providing customer satisfaction.

> ## The effect of IT on management accounting
>
> - IT systems and management accounting
> - IT systems for providers of services
> - IT systems and competitive advantage
> - Modelling and management information

5 The effect of IT on management accounting

5.1 IT systems and management accounting

Management accounting systems are information systems, and the development of information technology (IT) continues to have a significant impact on management accounting and on:

- collecting data
- storing data and information: (Note: data is unprocessed, whereas information is data that has been processed into something that has meaning or purpose)
- the ability to process data into valuable information
- access to information
- communication of information.

In many traditional management accounting systems, data was input to the computer system by specialist staff. There was often a high rate of input errors, and data validation checks were included in the software to reduce the error rate. In many systems, the process of collecting data and input to a computer system was fairly slow.

Many modern IT systems provide for **automatic input of data by non-finance operating staff**, often with minimal risk of errors. One example is the automatic input of sales data and inventory data at check-out points in stores and supermarkets, using bar codes and automatic bar code readers. Information is available about sales and reductions in inventory at the exact moment that the items are being sold.

IT systems also provide for **access to external sources of data** and information. External data can be obtained from the Internet, either:

- free of charge, for example, from the web sites of government departments and public news agencies, or
- through subscription (payments to an external information provider).

Another significant feature of many IT systems is **instant access to information**. Information might be held on a central database, and accessible to all authorised personnel through a network connection. Instant access means that managers do not have to wait for information to come to them, for example in routine reports. They can search for and obtain the information they want at any time.

A **wide range of complex data analysis** can be performed with computer software. Many managers can use models for planning and forecasting, including the application of sensitivity analysis to plans and forecasts.

5.2 IT systems for providers of services

For companies that provide services (rather than manufacturing goods), IT systems can make substantial improvements in the quality of service provision. A key feature of many services is the contact between a representative of the company (the service provider) and the customer. This may be face-to-face contact, or contact by telephone or even e-mail or text message.

IT systems can improve the quality of service in a number of different ways.

■ The service provider has instant access to the customer's files or to other key information. Instant access means that a customer's requests can be dealt with immediately. This makes it possible, for example, to sell and renew insurance policies by telephone.

■ In some cases, the customer is given the opportunity to take control over his own service provision. For example, customers can book seats on air flights and at theatres using the Internet and the service provider's web site.

■ Some services can be provided through IT systems. For example, customers can download media items (music and film) through the Internet.

Immediate service provision, made possible by IT systems, is likely to increase customer satisfaction with the service.

The Internet often makes it possible for customers to compare the products or services of different suppliers, and to make an informed choice about which supplier to buy from. It may therefore be important for companies to provide extensive information to customers on their web site, to help them make their purchase decisions.

5.3 IT systems and competitive advantage

Companies operating in a competitive market need to acquire a **competitive advantage** over their rivals, and offer better value to customers.

IT systems can be used to create a competitive advantage, by providing a better service (or cheaper service) to customers.

Significantly, **IT systems can also create a competitive advantage by providing management with better information**. In this respect, a well-designed management accounting system will provide a competitive advantage.

However, to remain competitive it is necessary to improve performance continually; otherwise rival firms will catch up and take the lead. In order to improve continually, IT systems must be renewed and updated.

5.4 Modelling and management information

The nature of models

A large amount of management information is prepared using IT software and models. Models are used for decision-making (such as planning decisions) and for monitoring performance for control purposes.

Information about actual performance might be recorded on a database, so that managers can access it online to obtain the information they need, whenever they need it.

■ Information about planned and actual performance might be set out in a **spreadsheet**, which produces performance measurements (such as variance information) automatically.

■ The term **'simulation model'** refers to any model that represents something else. In business, models are used to represent the real world. The simulation models used by management accountants are mathematical models.

A mathematical model establishes relationships between different items or 'variables'. For example, you might be familiar with the Economic Order Quantity (EOQ) model for inventory management. The variables in the basic EOQ model are the annual demand for an inventory item, the cost of placing an order for the item and the annual cost of holding an item in inventory. By giving values to each of these 'input' variables, the model can be used to identify a fourth variable (an 'output variable') – the size of purchase order to place with the supplier in order to minimise annual inventory costs.

Mathematical models can be classified as:

■ deterministic models or

■ probabilistic models (or stochastic models).

Deterministic models

A deterministic model is one that gives a specific value to each of the input variables.

For example, in a deterministic EOQ model, a specific value is given to the volume of annual demand, the cost of placing an order and the annual cost of holding one unit in inventory. The economic order quantity is then calculated from these variables. (A specific value for a variable is sometimes called a 'point estimate').

The advantage of a deterministic model is that it can be used to obtain a result or optimal value, often with a fairly simple mathematical formula.

The main disadvantage of a deterministic model is that it does not recognise the risk or uncertainty in a situation – for example, it does not recognise that the actual value of variables in the model might be in a range, or might be any of several different possibilities.

Probabilistic models (stochastic models)

A probabilistic model recognises that the value of input variables could be anywhere within a range of values, or any of several different possible values. For example:

- sales demand next year might be anywhere in the range, say, $2 million to $2.5 million
- the number of orders from a major customer next year might be 0, 1, 2 or 3.

A probabilistic model recognises the risk or uncertainty in the real world, by using probabilities. A probability distribution is identified for the different possible values for a variable, and these probabilities are used in the model to produce the management information required.

For example, a deterministic model might include a variable for annual sales demand next year and sales demand might be given the value '500,000 units'. A probabilistic model might give sales demand the following probability distribution:

Probability	Annual sales demand
	units
0.2	400,000
0.2	450,000
0.4	500,000
0.2	650,000

The advantage of probabilistic models is that risk and uncertainty can be analysed, providing managers with better-quality information for making decisions.

CHAPTER

7

Strategic planning techniques

Contents
1   Product life cycle and life cycle costing
2   SWOT analysis
3   Value chain analysis
4   Benchmarking

This chapter describes a variety of strategic planning concepts and techniques. A strategic management accounting system must be able to provide the information that is needed in order to use the techniques in practice.

The relevant information is obtained from a combination of internal and external sources.

Product life cycle and life cycle costing

- The product life cycle
- Financial aspects of the product life cycle
- Strategic significance of the product life cycle
- Product life cycle costing
- Why is life cycle costing significant?
- The product life cycle and the need for management information
- The product life cycle and key financial performance measures

1 Product life cycle and life cycle costing

1.1 The product life cycle

Many products have a life cycle. A 'normal' life cycle has four phases:

- Introduction
- Growth
- Maturity
- Decline.

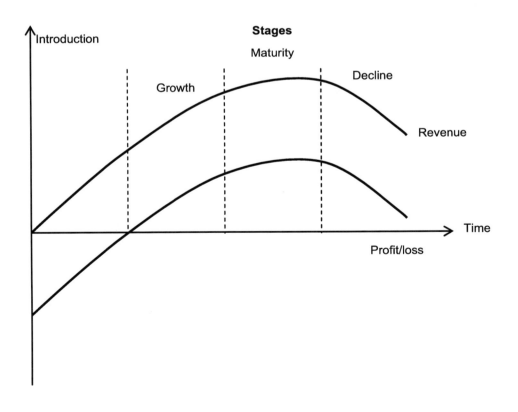

A new product is introduced to the market, and it goes through a period of growth in market demand and profitability. The market then 'matures' and sales stop growing. Eventually, the market declines and sales fall: the product becomes unprofitable and production is ended. The life of a product can be made longer, by re-designing the product regularly, and through advertising and other marketing methods.

The **length of a product life cycle** varies. As a general rule:

■ a broad type of product may have a long life of several decades

■ the product may be produced in several different forms, and the life cycle of each form of the product may be shorter than the total life of the broad product

■ companies may produce a form of the product, and the life cycle of a company's product may be shorter than the total life of broad product form.

For example, the life of the television has already been many decades long, and shows no obvious sign of coming to an end. However, the life cycle of the black-and-white picture television set has been shorter, and the end of the life of the analogue television can now be foreseen. Many companies have produced black and white picture televisions in the past, but the life cycle of their particular product will often have been quite short. For example, some companies may have stopped producing black and white televisions and switched entirely to colour televisions, long before other manufacturers stopped making black and white televisions. There is now a possibility that internet-based video systems will eventually replace the 'traditional' television.

As some products of a company reach the end of their life cycle, they need to be replaced with new products. **Product innovation** is essential to survival. Companies need to have a portfolio of products that:

■ provides a profit, and also

■ ensures the survival of the company's business in the longer term.

1.2   Financial aspects of the product life cycle

As explained earlier, the 'traditional' product life cycle has four phases: introduction, growth, maturity and finally, decline. At each phase in its life cycle:

■ selling prices will be altered

■ costs may differ

■ the amount invested (capital investment) may vary

■ spending on advertising and other marketing activities may change.

Sales volume, sales revenue, profitability, investment and cash flow will all vary as the product goes through the different stages of its life.

Introduction phase

When a product is new to the market, and a competitor has not already established a rival product in the market, a company may be able to choose its pricing strategy for the new product.

- If a **'market penetration' strategy** is chosen, the aim should be to sell the product at a low price in order to obtain a large share of the market as quickly as possible. This pricing strategy is therefore based on low prices and high volumes.

- If a **'market skimming' strategy** is chosen, the aim is to sell the product at a high price in order to maximise the gross profit per unit sold. Sales volumes will be low, and the product will be purchased only by customers who are willing to pay a high price to obtain a 'unique' item. Gradually, the selling price will be reduced, although it will be kept as high as possible for as long as possible.

Growth phase

In the growth phase of a product's life, sales demand grows rapidly, but more competitors enter the market. Companies need to focus on cost control, mainly by achieving economies of scale by producing in larger quantities. However, it is also important to ensure that customers believe that they are receiving good value and quality for the price.

Maturity phasem

In the maturity phase of a life cycle, the objective should be to maintain market share. It may be necessary to use changes in price to sustain market share. Alternatively, a company may look for new distribution channels that offer an opportunity to sell at higher prices or at lower costs.

Decline phase

In the decline phase, total sales in the market fall. Sales price might be increased in order to maximise profitability. Almost inevitably, this will result in a continuing fall in sales volumes.

1.3 Strategic significance of the product life cycle

The **strategic significance of the product life cycle** for the purpose of management accounting is as follows:

- Every product should be expected to go through a life cycle, although the length of the life cycle will vary for different products. In competitive markets, there is a tendency for the product life cycle to become shorter.

- Companies therefore need to innovate to remain competitive, and replace products reaching the end of their life cycle with new (successful) products.

- The financial performance of products changes over the different stages of its life cycle. Products start by needing large capital investment and make losses initially because sales demand has not yet grown. As they progress through their life cycle, they start to make profits and provide cash to the business.

- Profit targets and the assessment of performance for different products should recognise the stage of their life cycle that they have reached.

Strategic accounting information about the product life cycle can help managers to:

- assess the likely return on investment from a new product over its full life cycle, and

- predict when current products might reach the end of their life cycle, so that strategic managers can plan for new product development, and design of new products to take the place of those reaching the end of their life.

1.4 Product life cycle costing

Product life cycle costing is concerned with planning the costs of a product over the full course of its life, with the intention of:

- Identifying what those costs are likely to be: in particular, a product may require significant investment early in its life and substantial spending on marketing during its growth phase. In some cases, there may be decommissioning costs or clean-up costs at the end of its life.

- Trying to ensure that the product will prove an adequate return on investment over the full course of its life cycle.

Life cycle costing is the estimation of the costs for a product over its entire life cycle. These are not just the costs of producing the product, but all costs directly associated with making and selling the product. These include:

- costs of production

- costs of acquiring capital equipment to make and sell the product

- advertising and other marketing costs

- costs of repairs under guarantee or warranty

- product design costs and testing costs

- possibly, costs associated with the removal of equipment at the end of the product's life.

The purpose of life cycle costing is to ensure that the product will provide the required return on investment over the full course of its expected life.

1.5 Why is life cycle costing significant?

The significance of life cycle costing is that the costs of a product over its full life cycle should be considered at an early stage in the product's life, when it is in the early stage of product design.

It is recognised that a large proportion of the total life cycle costs of a product (possibly as much as 70% or 80%) are determined when the product is designed. For example, at the design stage, decisions are taken about:

- the number of components that will be in the product

- the quality of the materials that will be used

- whether components will be a standard design or not
- the packaging that will be used
- the quality of the end product, and
- its expected useful life for customers.

A new product should be expected to provide sufficient revenues to cover all its expected costs over the life cycle, and make a suitable return. If it seems possible that the product will not be profitable, changes can be made at the design stage to reduce costs and improve profitability.

Life cycle costing, like target costing, is therefore a method of managing and controlling the costs of a new product at the design and development stage.

1.6 The product life cycle and the need for management information

The need for management information about a product varies at different stages in the life cycle. Some factors are more important than others at each stage.

The following table suggests how the key performance measures change through the product life cycle:

	Introduction	Growth	Maturity	Decline
Business risk	High. The product might not be successful. A competitor might enter the market earlier.	High. The market might not grow as much as expected. The company might fail to win the expected share of the market.	Normal business risks, for example from competitors' activities or from the threat of a new competitor entering the market.	Low risk.
Main financial characteristics of this stage of the life cycle	Negative cash flows and losses. The decision to invest in the product is taken on the basis of NPV analysis over the product's life cycle.	Cash flows improving but may still be negative due to capital investment. The product becomes profitable.	The product is profitable and provides positive cash flows.	The product is still profitable and providing positive cash flows, but they are now smaller

Table continues

	Introduction	Growth	Maturity	Decline
Critical success factors	Speed in developing the product for the market.	Market growth and market share. Achieving a competitive advantage.	Sustaining competitive advantage. Retaining customers and market share. Making profitable use of limited resources.	Leaving the market at the most appropriate time. Avoiding losses and negative cash flows.
Key information requirements	Market research into customer needs and attitudes. Rate of adoption of new product by customers.	Information about market size, market growth and market share. Information about competitors and their strategies.	Costs of rival products or services. The nature and amount of limiting factor resources.	Rate of decline in the market.
Financial information requirements	NPV of the project (product development project).	Profits and cash flows. Sales: are marketing objectives being met?	Profitability, return on investment	Disposal value of main non-current assets. Free cash flows earned by the product.

1.7 The product life cycle and key financial performance measures

The financial performance of a product should be monitored, but the key performance measures will vary over the product's life cycle.

■ During the **introductory phase**, the new product is expected to make a loss and the cash flows will be negative. This is because early sales will be low and initial set-up costs could be high. Cash flows will also be affected by new capital expenditure and probably also by initial marketing costs. The key performance indicator should relate to the success of the product in winning its first customers, and the focus should be on the rate of growth in sales.

In order to achieve the required early growth in sales demand, the company might use a 'market penetration' pricing strategy. Market penetration pricing is explained in a later chapter.

Also during the introductory phase, it is important to make sure that actual spending is controlled, and that money is not wasted.

■ During the **growth phase**, the product will change from making losses to making a profit. By the end of the growth phase, it will also be a contributor of cash to the business instead of a user of cash. Profits and cash flows will therefore be monitored. However, return on capital (ROCE/ROI) will be low.

The rate of growth in sales remains important, and this will be monitored closely (in addition to the total market size and market share).

The company should also try to reduce average costs per unit as sales volumes increase. Costs should fall due to 'economies of scale' – for example because fixed costs can now be spread over a larger volume of output. Various improvements in efficiency should be achievable as sales volume grows.

■ During the **maturity phase**, the product will maximise its potential for making profits and contributing cash. The return on investment should be high. Profitability, ROI and cash flow are all significant performance indicators.

Another important factor is the length of this phase of the life cycle. An entity should want to maximise the length of time that the product remains profitable and a strong contributor of cash. The maturity phase might be extended, for example, by re-designing the product or by trying to sell the product to a new group of potential customers (for example, in a different geographical region). The company might also look for new distribution channels to continue the maturity phase of the product.

■ During the **decline phase**, the entity will probably continue to make and sell the product as long as it is contributing cash to the business. Profitability and cash flow are both important, even though sales are falling. The entity might use several financial measures to monitor performance, such as profit, EBITDA (earnings before interest, depreciation and amortisation), ROI and cash flow.

The key financial indicators are summarised in the following table.

	Introduction phase	Growth phase	Maturity phase	Decline phase
Profit	Not significant	Important: how soon does the product become profitable?	Important	Important
Cash flow	Negative. Not significant	Important. How soon do cash flows stop being negative?	Important	Important. When will they become negative? When should the product be abandoned?
ROI/residual income	Not significant	Low. Not significant	Important	Important

Table continues

	Introduction phase	Growth phase	Maturity phase	Decline phase
Sales growth	Important	Important	Less important. Sales growth should be low or possibly slightly negative	Not important
Other financial performance indicators	Control costs	Average costs (economies of scale)	Customer retention/ sales to new customers	EBITDA

> ## SWOT analysis
>
> - The nature of SWOT analysis
> - Strengths and weaknesses
> - Threats and opportunities
> - Preparing a SWOT analysis
> - Management accounting and SWOT analysis

2 SWOT analysis

2.1 The nature of SWOT analysis

SWOT analysis is a technique used in strategic planning for identifying key factors that might affect business strategy. These factors are both internal to the company and external, in its environment. SWOT analysis can be used in the strategic planning process to analyse the company's capabilities and core competencies (or lack of them) and also to carry out an environmental analysis.

SWOT analysis is an analysis of strengths, weaknesses, opportunities and threats.

- **S** – Strengths. Strengths are internal strengths that come from the resources of the entity.

- **W** – Weaknesses. Weaknesses are internal weaknesses in the resources of the entity.

- **O** – Opportunities. Opportunities are factors in the external environment that might be exploited, to the entity's strategic advantage.

- **T** – Threats. Threats are factors in the external environment that create an adverse risk for the entity's future prospects.

Strengths and weaknesses are concerned with the internal capabilities and core competencies of an entity. Threats and opportunities are concerned with factors and developments in the environment.

In order to prepare a SWOT analysis, it is necessary to:

- analyse the internal resources of the entity, and try to identify strong points and weak points

- analyse the external environment, and try to identify opportunities and threats.

2.2 Strengths and weaknesses

Strengths and weaknesses relate to factors within the entity, such as the strength and weaknesses of its processes and systems, its resources, its management and its track record of success or failure in the past.

Senior management in a company might have their own opinion of the strengths and weaknesses of the company, but a management information system should be able to provide **measured** and reliable information about strengths or weaknesses.

The table below contains examples of activities, processes and resources where there might be strengths or weaknesses that could have strategic significance.

Products and brands	Strength of the brand name
	Quality of products (or services)
	The portfolio of products, assessed in terms of (1) stages in their life cycle, or (2) a Boston Consulting Group portfolio analysis
	Profitability and return on capital
	Contribution to cash flow
Research and development	Number of innovations
	Success rate for new innovations
	Speed of innovation: speed in responding to new products of competitors
	Costs
Marketing	Abilities of the sales force
	Success in the past in selling products
	Efficiency of 'channels of distribution' – making the product available to customers
	Network of intermediaries – retail stores, agents or distributors
	Market size
	Market share
	Numbers of regular customers
	Customer service operations
Distribution/delivery	Location of distribution centres
	Cost of distribution
	Fleet of delivery vehicles
Finance	Availability of long-term capital
	Availability of short-term funding (cash)
	Profitability
	Operational cash flows
	Return on investment
	Credit control, collection of receivables, bad debts
Assets (buildings, equipment)	Type and value of assets
	Quality of assets
	Production capacity
	Location of assets
Employees and managers	Skills and experience
	Training
	Loyalty
	Motivation
	Industrial relations
Organisation and management	Centralised/decentralised management
	Management style
	Information systems

Suppliers and inventory	Relationship with key suppliers Storage capacity for inventory Speed of inventory turnover

2.3 Threats and opportunities

An information system should provide information to management about threats and opportunities in the environment. The sources of this information are outside the entity itself. There might be a wide range of information sources, such as official publications, newspaper reports, government statistics, physical observation of competitors and customers, and discussions with suppliers.

The nature of threat and opportunities in the environment can be classified into several broad groups. One method of classification is known as PESTEL:

Political threats and opportunities	Government regulations, for example, towards giving permission for new business developments and construction projects. Government policy, for example towards government spending programmes. Consequences of a change of government.
Economic threats and opportunities	Economic change: rate of economic growth or recession Exchange rates Interest rates Anti-monopoly regulations Rate of inflation Taxation
Social threats and opportunities	Social change: for example changes in the age distribution of the population Cultural change: for example, changes in leisure activities Movements in the population
Technological threats and opportunities	Any technological or scientific development
Environmental threats and opportunities	Cost and availability of forms of energy Pollution Preservation of the environment: sustainable business
Legal threats and opportunities	New laws Decisions by a court of law

2.4 Preparing a SWOT analysis

A SWOT analysis might be presented as four lists, in a cruciform chart, as follows: (Illustrative items have been inserted, for a small company producing pharmaceuticals).

Strengths	Weaknesses
Extensive research knowledge	Slow progress with research projects
Highly-skilled scientists in the work force	Poor record of converting research projects into new product development
High investment in advanced equipment	Recent increase in labour turnover
Patents on six products	
High profit margins	
Opportunities	**Threats**
Strong growth in total market demand	Recent merger of two major competitors
New scientific discoveries have not yet been fully exploited	Risk of stricter regulation of new products

In order to prepare a SWOT analysis, it is necessary to:

■ analyse the internal resources of the entity, and try to identify strong points and weak points

■ analyse the external environment, and try to identify opportunities and threats.

2.5   Management accounting and SWOT analysis

Management accounting systems should be able to support SWOT analysis by management, by providing relevant information. Much of this information can be quantified.

In the example above of the pharmaceuticals company, it should be possible to provide quantified data about items such as:

■ time to complete research projects

■ percentage of research projects that move on to a development phase

■ amount invested in capital equipment

■ labour turnover rates (compared to average labour turnover in the industry)

■ profit margins

■ growth in total market demand and annual sales.

Value chain analysis

- Creating value and competitive advantage
- The value chain
- A value chain for a company handling physical resources
- A value chain for service operations
- The value system

---

3 Value chain analysis

3.1 Creating value and competitive advantage

Value relates to the benefit that a customer obtains from a product or service. Value is provided by the attributes of the product or service. Customers are willing to pay money to obtain goods or services because of the benefits they receive. The price they are willing to pay puts a value on those benefits.

- A customer will often be willing to pay more for something that provides more value.
- Given a choice between two competing products or services, a customer will select the one that provides more value (in terms of value for money, quality, reliability, functions, convenience, and so on).

Business entities create added value when they make goods and provide services. For example, if a business entity buys a quantity of components for $100 and converts them into a wrist watch that it sells for $1,000, it has created value of $900.

In a competitive market, the most successful companies are those that are best at creating value. Michael Porter has argued that companies in a competitive market must seek competitive advantage over their rivals. They do this by creating more value and by creating value more effectively, more efficiently or at less cost.

Porter suggested that an entity can adopt either of two competitive strategies:

- a cost leadership strategy, where its aim is to create the same value as its competitors in the products it makes or the services it provides, but at a lower cost
- a differentiation strategy, where its aim is to create more value than its competitors, for a competing product or service, so that customers are willing to pay more to buy it.

3.2 The value chain

Porter (**Competitive Strategy**) developed the concept of the value chain. A **value chain** refers to inter-connected activities that create value. He argued that activities within an organisation can be analysed into different categories.

- Value can be created by any of these activities.

- Management should analyse these value-creating activities to identify where the organisation was most effective at creating value, and where it was least effective.

- Similarly, management can identify which activities give them a competitive advantage over rivals.

By analysing value-creating activities, decisions can be made about:

- how the creation of value can be improved

- how to improve a competitive advantage over rivals, and

- whether some activities should be stopped because they cost more than the value they create.

3.3 A value chain for a company handling physical resources

Porter's value chain is most commonly associated with the analysis of value creation in a company that handles physical resources, such as a manufacturing company or a retailing company.

Value-creating activities are grouped into two broad categories:

- primary activities and

- support activities.

These are divided into five primary activities and four support activities.

Porter's value chain

Most value is usually created in the primary value chain.

- **Inbound logistics**. These are the activities concerned with receiving and handling purchased materials and components, and storing them until needed.

- **Operations**. These are the activities concerned with converting the purchased materials into an item that customers will buy. In a manufacturing company, operations might include machining, assembly, packing, testing and equipment maintenance.

- **Outbound logistics**. These are activities concerned with the storage of finished goods before sale, and the distribution and delivery of goods (or services) to the customers.

- **Marketing and sales**.

- **Service**. These are all the activities that occur after the point of sale, such as installation, repairs and maintenance, and after-sales service.

The nature of the activities in the value chain varies from one industry to another, and there are also differences between the value chain of manufacturers, retailers and other service industries. However, the concept of the primary value chain is valid for all types of business entity.

It is important to recognise that value is added by all the activities on the primary value chain, including logistics. Customers might be willing to pay more for a product or a service if it is delivered to them in a more convenient way. For example, customers might be willing to pay more for household shopping items if the items are delivered to their home, so that they do not have to go out to a supermarket or a store to get them.

Secondary value chain activities: support activities

In addition to the primary value chain activities, there are also secondary activities or support activities. Porter identified these as:

- **Procurement**. These are activities concerned with buying the resources for the entity – materials, plant, equipment and other assets.

- **Technology development**. These are activities related to any development in the technological systems of the entity, such as product design (research and development) and IT systems.

- **Human resources management**. These are the activities concerned with recruiting, training, developing and rewarding people in the organisation.

- **Corporate infrastructure**. This relates to the organisation structure and its management systems, including planning and finance management.

- Support activities are often seen as necessary 'overheads' to support the primary value chain, but value can also be created by support activities. For example:
  - procurement can add value by identifying a cheaper source of materials or equipment
  - technology development can add value to operations with the introduction of a new IT system
  - human resources management can add value by improving the skills of employees through training.

Primary activities	Examples
Inbound logistics	Delivery systems for materials and components, warehouses for accepting deliveries
Operations	For a manufacturing company, manufacturing operations and methods: total quality management methods, just-in-time production methods and so on.
Outbound logistics	Warehousing for finished goods, methods of delivering goods to customers
Marketing and sales	Advertising and sales promotion methods, taking and processing sales orders, pricing
Service	After-sales service, handling customer queries and complaints

Support activities	Examples
Firm infrastructure	Centralised/decentralised management structure, size of head office, head office services, size of management hierarchy, decision-making processes
Human relations management	Recruitment policies, training policies, incentive (bonus) pay arrangements, employee skill levels
Technology development	Use of IT and IT systems, age of IT systems, use of e-commerce
Procurement	Choice of suppliers, arrangements with suppliers, just-in-time purchasing, negotiation of prices, credit terms and discounts with suppliers.

For each individual activity listed within each of these categories of activity, it should be possible to analyse what the company does well (creating value) and what it does less effectively.

It is also possible to use value chain analysis to identify the **information requirements** for each activity, to ensure that it can create value.

3.4 A value chain for service operations

Although Porter's value chain is normally associated with companies that handle physical goods, the same approach to analysis can be applied to companies in service industries.

An article by Malcolm Eva in Student Accountant ('The adaptability of strategic models', June 2005) suggested how value chain analysis could be applied to a service organisation. The article gave as an example an organisation providing distance learning courses. This example was based on a study by Woudstra and Powell (1989) in the American Journal of Distance Education.

The article suggests that the only difference between value chain analysis for organisations handling physical materials and for service organisations is the approach to analysing the primary activities. For a service organisation, it might be helpful to think of the five primary activities in terms of a process model, as follows:

Process model

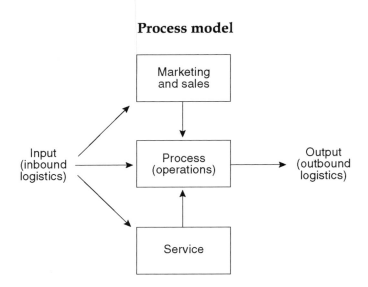

Using a distance learning organisation as an example, the article went on to suggest that the primary activities in the value chain could be identified. A simplified analysis is given below.

Review curriculum Obtain funding Obtain accreditation Establish hardware and software for learning	Register students Develop course content Prepare multimedia Mark assignments Give feedback to students	Distribute materials Place courses on-line Notify students of results Publish results	Promote the scheme Receive enquiries	Receive student feedback Provide telephone tuition support Provide tutorials
Inbound logistics	Operations (Process)	Outbound logistics	Marketing and sales	Service

The value chain can be analysed, to identify those activities that add value most effectively, and give the organisation a competitive advantage. Activities that do not add value can be analysed to see whether they should be done differently, or scrapped.

3.5   The value system

There is a value chain within every business entity. There is also a supply chain from the producers of raw materials and equipment through to the entities that sell the end consumer product to customers.

For example, food products might go from the original food producer to a food processor (who makes the processed food item) to a retailer. Here, there are three firms in the supply chain from the original food source to the end consumer. Each firm in the supply chain has its own value chain.

The value system is the sum of the value chains in all the firms in a supply chain.

The value that customers pay for when they buy goods or services comes from the value created by the entire value system.

This has an important implication for each firm in the supply chain. The firm should try to improve the efficiency and effectiveness of its own activities in creating value. However, it should also consider the entire value system, and think about how value might be added across the system, not just within its own internal value chain.

Collaboration between business entities and their key suppliers, for example in developing new materials or improving delivery systems, can help to add value across the supply chain, to the benefit of both entities.

Management accounting systems should be able to provide information to managers to help them identify ways of adding value across the entire length of the value chain, in its relationships with suppliers as well as in its own internal systems.

Benchmarking

- The purpose of benchmarking
- The potential benefits of benchmarking
- Methods of benchmarking
- Internal benchmarking
- Competitive benchmarking
- Process benchmarking
- Customer benchmarking
- Strategic benchmarking
- Functional benchmarking
- Product benchmarking (reverse engineering)
- Requirements for successful benchmarking
- Problems with benchmarking

4 Benchmarking

4.1 The purpose of benchmarking

Benchmarking is a process of setting standards or targets for products, services or work processes with reference to organisations that are recognised as models of 'best practice'. A benchmark is an organisation that provides the 'best practice' for comparison. An entity uses benchmarking to evaluate its own products, services or work processes by comparing them with the 'best practice' of the benchmark organisation.

The purpose of benchmarking is to identify measures that need to be taken to improve or change, so that the organisation becomes as good as, or better than, the benchmark.

Definition of benchmarking

'Benchmarking is the continuous process of measuring products, services and practices against the toughest competitors or the companies recognised as industry leaders ("best in class")' (The Xerox Company).

The benchmarking process

Benchmarking should be a continuous process, and it usually consists of the following stages:

- Identify aspects of performance that should be compared with a 'benchmark partner'.
- Select a suitable benchmark (a 'benchmark partner').
- Compare the product, service or process with the benchmark.

- Identify gaps in performance between the benchmark and the entity's own product, service or process.
- Identify changes that can be made to improve performance.
- Implement the improvements.
- Monitor the success of the changes in improving performance, and measure the benefits.

4.2 The potential benefits of benchmarking

Benchmarking can offer several benefits.

- It can be used to identify aspects of performance that are weak, where improvements are necessary.
- It can be used to set targets for improvement that are realistic and practicable.
- It can be used to look at practices in companies in different industries, and to learn from them.
- It encourages continuous improvement: benchmarking encourages managers and employees to make improvements, and to believe that changes are necessary.

4.3 Methods of benchmarking

There are several methods of benchmarking:

- internal benchmarking
- competitive benchmarking
- process benchmarking
- customer benchmarking.

Benchmarking can also be grouped into the following categories:

- strategic benchmarking
- functional benchmarking
- 'best practices' benchmarking (process benchmarking)
- product benchmarking.

4.4 Internal benchmarking

Internal benchmarking uses a benchmark inside the organisation itself. Other parts of the same organisation are compared with the benchmark.

For example, a company might have several regional or area offices. The best-performing regional office might be taken as a benchmark, and the other regional offices are compared with it. The benchmarking exercise should identify the reasons why each region has not performed as well as the benchmark. When the reasons for the worse performance are recognised, plans can be made to deal with the problems and achieve improvements.

4.5 Competitive benchmarking

Competitive benchmarking uses a successful competitor as the benchmark. A company compares its own products and systems with those of the competitor, and the purpose is to discover the reasons why the competitor is more successful.

When the reasons are identified, plans can be made to improve competitiveness, either by copying what the competitor does, or devising new products or systems that are even better then those of the competitor.

Comparing yourself with the main competitors makes good sense in a competitive business environment. A practical difficulty with competitive benchmarking, however, may be a lack of detailed information about the competitor.

- It should be possible to fully analyse a competitor's products – by buying them and looking at them in close detail.

- However, it may be more difficult to study a competitor's systems and methods of operation in detail. For example, a competitor may have a superior system for handling customers' calls, or a more efficient warehousing system, or a better order processing and despatch system. A rival company will not be allowed to examine these systems in detail.

Example

In 1991, the Massachussetts Institute of Technology and J D Power and Associates published a survey of car manufacturing plants in Japan, the USA and Europe. Japanese car production was used as a benchmark, and the survey found that productivity was much higher in Japan (where the average time to produce a car was 16.2 man hours) than in Europe (where the average time to produce one car was 36.2 man hours). The survey analysed possible reasons for the superior performance of Japanese producers, and made comparisons of performance in the areas of training time for new employees, absenteeism and the number of defects per vehicle produced.

The survey provided useful information for US and European car producers, but they had a huge gap to close before they could begin to compete effectively with their Japanese competitors.

Example

Benchmarking began with the Xerox Corporation in the US in 1982. Xerox, a manufacturer of photocopier machines, was in financial difficulties and losing market share to Japanese competitors, who were selling high-quality photocopiers at a much lower price. Xerox set up a management team that:

- identified key performance indicators for operations such as order fulfilment, distribution, production costs, retail selling prices and product features, and

- compared the performance of Xerox in each of these areas against those of its most successful competitors.

Xerox used the findings of its benchmarking exercise to identify areas for improvement. Improvements were made, and as a result customer satisfaction improved, costs were cut and Xerox improved its competitive position in the market.

Other companies followed the example of Xerox, and benchmarking became an established practice for performance measurement.

Competitive benchmarking and competitor analysis

Competitive benchmarking is not the same as competitor analysis. Competitor analysis involves a comparison by a company of its own performance with the performance of its main rivals. A company might draw up a 'league table' consisting of itself and its competitors, with the best performer at the top of the table and the worst performer at the bottom. For example, in the UK, some of the major supermarket chains draw up a league table of prices, with the chain offering the cheapest prices at the top of the table and the chain with the highest-price food stores at the bottom.

However, this is not benchmarking. Benchmarking is used to identify differences, and then to develop new ways of doing things, in order to make improvements in performance. The aim should be to make improvements that make the company better than its competitors, rather than improvements than help the company to close the gap with its competitors.

4.6 Process benchmarking

Process benchmarking is the most common method of benchmarking. It involves a comparison of the performance of the entity in one particular activity or process with the performance of another entity in a different industry. This type of benchmarking seeks to identify best practice anywhere, by looking at organisations with a reputation for excellence.

The purpose of process benchmarking is to use a benchmarking approach to analyse operational systems, such as purchasing, call handling (by call centres), order processing, delivery systems, information systems, and so on.

An organisation compares its own practices in an aspect of its operations with those of a benchmark organisation that is in an **unrelated industry** (and so is not a competitor). For example, a company may compare its warehousing and distribution systems with a benchmark organisation, its customer call centre operations or its IT system maintenance arrangements.

A process benchmarking programme is agreed between two organisations, which then share information about their systems and compare their performance. Each organisation is able to use the benchmarking process to review its system and procedures, and look for ways of improving their performance.

Benchmarking can be used as an approach to **improving quality** – in products, services and systems. Comparisons with the 'best' can provide ideas:

- for copying the benchmark organisation, or
- for doing something in a different way, not necessarily in exactly the same way as the benchmark organisation

Example

The Xerox Company wanted to improve its performance in dealing with customer orders. It identified Bean, a catalogue retailer specialising in outdoor clothing, as a benchmark for excellence in this area. The two organisations, Xerox and Bean, collaborated with each other in comparing their systems, exchanging information. Xerox management studied the order fulfilment process at Bean and used its findings to improve its own systems.

Process benchmarking can be very effective in helping a company to gain a competitive advantage over its rivals. 'Benchmarking ... is not a method for copying the best practices of competitors, but a way of seeking superior process performance outside the industry. Benchmarking makes it possible to gain competitive superiority rather than competitive parity.'

4.7 Customer benchmarking

Customer benchmarking is a completely different approach. This uses the customer as a benchmark, by trying to establish what the customer wants and expects. A company can compare what a customer wants with what the company actually provides.

Gaps can be identified between customer expectations and 'reality', and the company can then look for ways to close the gap.

4.8 Strategic benchmarking

Strategic benchmarking involves a comparison of the strategies of different companies. A company can compare its own strategies with those of its most successful competitor, or with the strategies of successful companies in other industries.

Strategic benchmarking usually involves a comparison with the most successful competitor. A company will use benchmarking to find out why the competitor is more successful. A starting point for the comparison is usually a survey of customers and shared suppliers, to find out what the competitor does better.

Aspects of strategy that might be considered include:

- strategic objectives
- core competencies
- process capability
- products
- strategic alliances
- the use of technology.

4.9 Functional benchmarking

Functional benchmarking is a form of competitor benchmarking. It involves a comparison of performance of a core business function in the company with the performance of the same function in a successful competitor. For example, functional benchmarking might involve a comparison of:

■ the sales and marketing function

■ the research and development function.

The aim should be to find out why the competitor appears to perform this function more successfully, in order to identify changes and improvements that should be made.

Process benchmarking compares processes in more detail.

4.10 Product benchmarking (reverse engineering)

Product benchmarking, also called reverse engineering, is a form of competitor benchmarking. It involves a comparison of an entity's products with the products manufactured by its main competitors.

The comparison will usually look at:

■ the competitor's costs

■ product concepts

■ strengths and weaknesses in product design and quality.

This product analysis will usually involve obtaining some products of the competitor and analysing them in the workshop or laboratory.

4.11 Requirements for successful benchmarking

There are several requirements for benchmarking to be effective as a way of improving competitiveness.

■ It is important to select key aspects of performance for benchmarking. These are the aspects of performance that have to be successful (and improved) in order to gain a competitive advantage over rivals.

■ It must be a continuous process, not a 'once only' exercise. Competitors do not 'stand still', and successful competitors will continually innovate and improve. It is essential to keep repeating benchmarking exercises in order to avoid falling behind again as the business environment changes.

■ Benchmarking should be a method for becoming better than competitors, not just for closing the gap on competitors and 'catching up'. The aim should be to achieve superior performance.

■ When benchmark partners are used for process benchmarking, the collaboration should be open and honest. A company should be prepared to give more information to its benchmark partner than it is hoping to obtain from the benchmark partner.

4.12 Problems with benchmarking

There are several problems that can make it difficult to use benchmarking successfully.

- It might be difficult to identify a critical process where benchmarking could provide valuable information to help an entity improve its performance. Benchmarking might select processes that are not critical to performance. The value of any benefits achieved will therefore be small and insignificant.

- It might be difficult to obtain reliable information for comparison with a benchmark. Even when a 'benchmark partner' is identified for process benchmarking, it could be difficult to get the 'partner' to agree to a benchmarking exercise and then to obtain the required information.

CHAPTER

8

Budgets and alternative budgeting models

Contents

1	Preparing budgets
2	Functional budgets
3	Flexible budgets and rolling budgets
4	Zero based budgeting (ZBB) and activity based budgeting (ABB)

> ## Preparing budgets
>
> - The purpose of budgeting
> - Budgeting: planning and co-ordination
> - Budgetary control

1 Preparing budgets

1.1 The purpose of budgeting

A budget is a plan covering an entire organisation, and stated mainly in money values. Typically, a budget is prepared annually for the next financial year. However, capital expenditure budgets will cover a longer planning period, but may be reviewed and updated every year.

There are several reasons for preparing budgets.

- A budget is an (annual) **plan** for the entire organisation. Like other types of plan, it is used to set targets for achievement.
- Since it is a plan for the entire organisation, a budget should **co-ordinate** the activities of everyone within the organisation, so that everyone works towards consistent goals.
- It is used for **control purposes**. Actual results can be compared with the budget, and differences reported as variances.
- It can be used to **communicate** information about plans and actual results, so that managers and other employees are aware of their expected and actual performance.
- Budgets might be used to **motivate** individuals, particularly managers, by setting them targets for performance for the year and rewarding them if they achieve their targets. Rewards may take the form of a cash bonus at the end of the year. Alternatively, rewards may be given in the form of eventual promotion, or (for senior managers) the award of shares or share options in the company.

1.2 Budgeting: planning and co-ordination

Budgeting can be described as planning at the 'tactical' management level. As annual plans, they must be consistent with the longer-term strategic plans of the organisation. They can also provide a useful benchmark for setting shorter-term operational targets, such as monthly sales volumes and output volumes, efficiency targets, capacity utilisation targets, and so on.

Budgets can also be an effective method of co-ordinating activities throughout an organisation, because:

- targets for all activities are set within the budget, and the targets for all managers should therefore be consistent with each other

■ as indicated above, budgets provide a co-ordinating link between longer-term strategic plans and shorter-term operational targets and plans.

These are the recognised strengths of 'traditional' budgeting systems.

1.3 Budgetary control

Budgets are used for control.

■ The budget may be divided into control periods, typically periods of one month. Actual results for a control period are then compared with the budget, and differences reported as variances. You should already be familiar with variance reporting from your earlier studies. Budgeting and variance reporting (and standard costing and variance reporting) are examples of a **feedback control system**.

- When actual results are worse than budget, there is an adverse variance. If the variance is significant, and the cause of the variance is controllable, the manager responsible may be expected to take control action to bring actual results back towards the budgeted performance level. Adverse variances are an example of **negative feedback**, where control action is needed to correct weaknesses or inefficiencies.

- When actual results are better than budget, there is a favourable variance. If the variance is significant, and the cause of the variance is controllable, the manager responsible may be expected to take control action to continue the favourable results in the future. Favourable variances are an example of **positive feedback**, where control action is expected to take actual results even further away from the budget or target.

■ Another method of control reporting is to prepare an up-to-date forecast of the results for the budget period. An up-to-date forecast is compared with the budget. The comparison may show that actual results for the year may be better or worse than originally budgeted. The control information provided by comparisons of current forecasts with the budget is an example of **feedforward control**.

A combination of feedback and feedforward control information can be used to keep management informed about performance.

■ An advantage of feedforward control is that it is forward-looking. Managers can act to alter future results, but cannot change what has already happened. Looking forward is therefore practical. However, up-to-date forecasts might not be entirely reliable, and when forecasts are uncertain or unreliable, the value of feedforward control information is limited.

■ An advantage of feedback information is that it uses historical information for comparison with the budget or standard costs. The differences between actual results and budget should therefore be a useful measurement of actual performance.

Variance analysis is not described in this chapter. It is assumed that you are sufficiently familiar with variances. It is most unlikely that you will be required to calculate any variances in your examination.

> **Functional budgets**
>
> - The master budget
> - The sales budget
> - The production budget
> - The direct materials usage budget
> - The direct labour budget
> - The purchases budget
> - Budgeted income statement

2 Functional budgets

2.1 The master budget

A 'master budget' is the budget for an entire organisation, and consists of functional budgets, together with:

- a budgeted income statement for the financial year
- a cash budget
- a budgeted balance sheet as at the year end
- possibly, a capital expenditure budget (covering more than one financial year, but updated on a 'rolling' basis each year).

An examination question might ask you to prepare functional budgets or a cash budget. This chapter describes the logical approach that can normally be used to prepare budgets for a manufacturing organisation. (The mathematics of budgeting for service industry organisations are usually easier).

It is assumed here that the key budget factor is sales demand, and the initial function budget to prepare is the sales budget.

The following example will be used to illustrate the preparation of the functional budgets.

In practice, budgets are usually prepared with computer models, such as a **spreadsheet model**. This chapter demonstrates the logic of budget preparation.

Example

Entity Yellow makes and sells two products, Product P and Product Q. The direct production costs of these products are as follows:

	Product P	$	Product Q	$
Direct materials				
Material A	(2 kg × $0.80)	1.60	(0.5 kg × $0.80)	0.40
Material B	(0.5 kg × $2)	1.00	(3 kg × $2)	6.00
Material C	(1 kg × $4)	4.00		-
		6.60		6.40
Direct labour				
Grade X	(0.25 hrs × $10)	2.50	(0.5 hrs × $10)	5.00
Grade Y	(0.25 hrs × $8)	2.00	(0.75 hrs × $8)	6.00
		4.50		11.00
Total direct cost		11.10		17.40

The sales price and expected sales volume for each product next year are as follows:

	Product P	Product Q
Sales price per unit	$20	$30
Budgeted sales volume	20,000 units	30,000 units

Budgeted overhead costs are as follows:

Production overheads	$80,000	including depreciation charges of $20,000
Administration overheads	$120,000	including depreciation charges of $10,000
Selling and distribution overheads	$190,000	including depreciation charges of $10,000

Bad debts are expected to be 2% of sales, and should be provided for. Bad debts are actually written off at the end of the second month following the sale. The costs of bad debts and allowances for doubtful debts are not included in the overhead costs above.

Inventories of raw materials at the beginning of January, and planned closing inventories at the end of January, are as follows:

Direct material	Inventory	
	At beginning of January	At end of January
	kilos	kilos
Material A	5,000	6,000
Material B	5,500	4,000
Material C	1,000	2,500

No further changes in inventory levels are planned during the year.

2.2 The sales budget

The sales budget is prepared for each product individually, and for sales revenue in total.

Product	Sales quantity	Sales price	Sales revenue
	units	$	$
P	20,000	20	400,000
Q	30,000	30	900,000
Total			1,300,000

2.3 The production budget

The production budget is calculated initially in units, although a production cost budget can be prepared later. The production budget in units is prepared for each product, as follows:

	Units
Sales budget in units	S
Plus budgeted closing inventory	C
Minus opening inventory	(O)
Production budget	(S+C-O)

In other words, the production budget for each product in units is the sales budget in units plus any planned increase in finished goods inventories (and work-in-progress inventories) minus the opening inventories of finished goods (and work in progress).

In the example, there are no planned changes in finished goods inventories; therefore the production budget in units is the same as the sales budget.

2.4 The direct materials usage budget

The direct materials usage budget is a statement of the quantities of direct materials required for production, and their cost. The budget is prepared for each item of material separately, but a total usage cost can also be shown.

	Material A	Material B	Material C	Total
	kilos	kilos	kilos	
To make 20,000 P	40,000	10,000	20,000	
To make 30,000 Q	15,000	90,000	0	
Total quantities	55,000	100,000	20,000	
Price per kilo	$0.80	$2	$4	
Total cost	$44,000	$200,000	$80,000	$324,000

2.5 The direct labour budget

The direct labour budget is similar to the direct materials usage budget. It is a statement of the quantities of direct labour required for production, and its cost. The budget is prepared for grade of labour separately, but a total direct labour cost can also be shown.

	Grade X	Grade Y	Total
	hours	hours	
To make 20,000 P	5,000	5,000	
To make 30,000 Q	15,000	22,500	
Total hours	20,000	27,500	
Cost per hour	$10	$8	
Total cost	$200,000	$220,000	$420,000

2.6   The purchases budget

The purchases budget is the budget for materials purchases. The purchases budget might be prepared for all materials, direct and indirect, or for direct materials only. The purchases budget differs from the materials usage budget by the amount of the planned increase or decrease in inventory levels of materials in the budget period.

The purchase quantities are calculated first, and these are converted into a purchases cost at the budgeted price for each material item. Purchase quantities are calculated as follows:

	Units
Material usage budget in units	S
Plus budgeted closing inventory	C
Minus opening inventory	(O)
Purchases budget, in units	(S+C-O)

The purchases budget in our example is as follows:

	Material A	Material B	Material C	Total
	kilos	kilos	kilos	
Usage budget	55,000	100,000	20,000	
Closing inventory	6,000	4,000	2,500	
	61,000	104,000	22,500	
Opening inventory	(5,000)	(5,500)	(1,000)	
Budgeted purchases	56,000	98,500	21,500	
Price per kilo	$0.80	$2	$4	
Purchases budget in $	$44,800	$197,000	$86,000	$327,800

2.7   Budgeted income statement

The functional budgets, together with budgets for the overhead costs and any other items of cost, should be sufficient to prepare a budgeted income statement for the period.

In our example, we need to remember that the bad and doubtful debt provisions for the year are expected to be 2% × $1,300,000 = $26,000

The budgeted income statement below is presented using marginal costing.

	Product P	Product Q	Total
	$	$	$
Sales	400,000	900,000	1,300,000
Variable cost of sales			
Direct materials	132,000	192,000	324,000
Direct labour	90,000	330,000	420,000
Total variable costs	222,000	522,000	744,000
Contribution	178,000	378,000	556,000
		$	
Production overheads		80,000	
Administration overheads		120,000	
Sales and distribution overheads		190,000	
Bad and doubtful debts		26,000	
			416,000
Budgeted profit			140,000

Flexible budgets and rolling budgets
■ Limitations of a 'fixed' budget
■ The nature of uncertainty in budgeting
■ Flexible budgets
■ Probabilities and expected values
■ Spreadsheets and 'what if' analysis
■ Rolling budgets (continuous budgets)

3 Flexible budgets and rolling budgets

3.1 Limitations of a 'fixed' budget

Weaknesses in the traditional budgeting process have been recognised, and alternative budgeting models have been developed to improve the quality of budgets and budgetary control.

A major weakness with an annual budget is that it is a fixed annual plan. Once it has been prepared, it usually remains the 'official' plan until it is replaced by the next annual budget 12 months later.

'Fixed' annual budgets are unsatisfactory for two important reasons.

- When a budget is prepared, there is a great deal of uncertainty about what will happen, and the budget will be based on estimates. Even when estimates are reasonable, there is no certainty that they will turn out to be 'correct'.

- Unexpected events will happen during the year, and conditions in the business environment will change. The changes might be significant, and the 'fixed' budget will cease to be realistic and achievable. It might therefore be appropriate to re-consider and revise the budget.

3.2 The nature of uncertainty in budgeting

Uncertainty arises when there is a lack of reliable information. In budgeting, there is uncertainty because estimates and forecasts may be unreliable. Information is almost never 100% reliable (or 'perfect'), and some uncertainty in budgeting is therefore inevitable.

Risk arises in business because actual events may turn out better or worse than expected. For example, actual sales volume may be higher or lower than forecast. The amount of risk in business operations varies with the nature of the operations. Some operations are more predictable than others. The existence of risk means that forecasts and estimates in the budget, which are based on expected results, may not be accurate.

Both risk and uncertainty mean that estimates and forecasts in a budget are likely to be wrong.

Management should be aware of risk and uncertainty when preparing budgets and when monitoring performance.

■ When preparing budgets, it may be appropriate to look at several different forecasts and estimates, to assess the possible variations that might occur. In other words, managers should think about how much better or how much worse actual results may be, compared with the budget.

■ When monitoring actual performance, managers should recognise that adverse or favourable variances might be caused by weaknesses in the original forecasts, rather than by good or bad performance.

Several approaches may be used for analysing risk and uncertainty in budgets. These include:

■ flexible budgets

■ using probabilities and expected values

■ using spreadsheet models and 'what if' analysis (sensitivity analysis)

■ stress testing.

3.3 Flexible budgets

Flexible budgets may be prepared during the budget-setting process. A flexible budget is a budget based on an assumption of a different volume of output and sales than the volume in the master budget or 'fixed budget'.

An organisation might prepare several flexible budgets in addition to the main budget (the master budget or fixed budget). If the actual level of activity differs significantly from the expected level, the fixed budget can be substituted by a suitable flexible budget.

For example, a company might prepare its master budget on the basis of estimated sales of $100 million. Flexible budgets might be prepared on the basis that sales will be higher or lower – say $80 million, $90 million, $110 million and $120 million. Each flexible budget will be prepared on the basis of assumptions about fixed and variable costs, such as increases or decreases in fixed costs if sales rise above or fall below a certain amount, or changes in variable unit costs above a certain volume of sales.

During the financial year covered by the budget, it may become apparent that actual sales and production volume will be higher or lower than the fixed budget forecast. In such an event, actual performance can be compared with a suitable flexible budget.

Flexible budgets can be useful, because they allow for the possibility that actual activity levels may be higher or lower than forecast in the master budget. The main disadvantage of flexible budgets could be the time and effort needed to prepare them. The cost of preparing them could exceed the benefits of having the information that they provide.

3.4 Probabilities and expected values

Estimates and forecasts in budgeting may be prepared using probabilities and expected values. An expected value is a weighted average value calculated with probabilities.

Example

A company is preparing a sales budget. The budget planners believe that the volume of sales next year will depend on the state of the economy.

State of the economy	Sales for the year
	$ million
No growth	40
Low growth	50
Higher growth	70

It has been estimated that there is a 60% probability of no growth, a 30% probability of low growth and a 10% probability of higher growth.

The expected value (EV) of sales next year could be calculated as follows:

State of the economy	Sales for the year	Probability	EV of sales
	$ million		$ million
No growth	40	0.6	24
Low growth	50	0.3	15
Higher growth	70	0.1	7
EV of sales			46

The company might decide to prepare a sales budget on the assumption that annual sales will be $46 million.

The problems with using probabilities and expected values

There are two problems that might exist with the use of probabilities and expected values.

■ The estimates of probability might be subjective, and based on the judgement or opinion of a forecaster. Subjective probabilities might be no better than educated guesses. Probabilities should have a rational basis.

■ An expected value is most useful when it is a weighted average value for an outcome that will happen many times in the planning period. If the forecast event happens many times in the planning period, weighted average values are suitable for forecasting. However, if an outcome will only happen once, it is doubtful whether an expected value has much practical value for planning purposes.

This point can be illustrated with the previous example of the EV of annual sales. The forecast is that sales will be $40 million (0.60 probability), $50 million (0.30 probability) or $70 million (0.10 probability). The EV of sales is $46 million.

- The total annual sales for the year is an outcome that occurs only once. It is doubtful whether it would be appropriate to use $46 million as the budgeted sales for the year. A sales total of $46 million is not expected to happen.

- It might be more appropriate to prepare a fixed budget on the basis that sales will be $40 million (the most likely outcome) and prepare flexible budgets for sales of $50 million and $70 million.

When the forecast outcome happens many times in the planning period, an EV might be appropriate. For example, suppose that the forecast of weekly sales of a product is as follows:

Weekly sales	Probability	EV of weekly sales
$		$
7,000	0.5	3,500
9,000	0.3	2,700
12,000	0.2	2,400
		8,600

Since there are 52 weeks in a year, it would be appropriate to assume that weekly sales will be a weighted average amount, or EV. The budget for annual sales would be (52 × $8,600) = $447,200. If the probability estimates are fairly reliable, this estimate of annual sales should be acceptable as the annual sales budget.

3.5 Spreadsheets and 'what if' analysis

Preparing budgets is largely a 'number crunching' exercise, involving large amounts of calculations. This aspect of budgeting was made much easier, simpler and quicker with IT and the development of computer-based models for budgeting. Spreadsheet models, or similar planning models, are now widely used to prepare budgets.

A feature of computer-based budget models is that once the model has been constructed, it becomes a relatively simple process to prepare a budget. Values are input for the key variables, and the model produces a complete budget.

Amendments to a budget can be made quickly. A new budget can be produced simply by changing the value of one or more input variables in the budget model.

This ability to prepare new budgets quickly by changing a small number of values in the model also creates opportunities for **sensitivity analysis** and **stress testing**. The budget planner can test how the budget will be affected if forecasts and estimates are changed, by asking 'what if' questions. For example:

- What if sales volume is 5% below the budget forecast?

- What if the sales mix of products is different?

- What if the introduction of the new production system or the new IT system is delayed by six months?

- What if interest rates go up by 2% more than expected?
- What if the fixed costs are 5% higher and variable costs per unit are 3% higher?

Sensitivity analysis and stress testing are similar.

- Sensitivity analysis considers variations to estimates and input values in the budget model that have a reasonable likelihood of happening. For example, variable unit costs might be increased by 5% or sales forecasts reduced by 5%.
- Stress testing considers the effect of much greater changes to the forecasts and estimates. For example, what might happen if sales are 20% less than expected? Or what might happen if the price of a key raw material increases by 50%?

The answers to 'what if' questions can help budget planners to understand more about the risk and uncertainty in the budget, and the extent to which actual results might differ from the expected outcome in the master budget. This can provide valuable information for risk management, and management can assess the 'sensitivity' of their budget to particular estimates and assumptions.

3.6   Rolling budgets (continuous budgets)

Some entities operate in a rapidly-changing environment. After preparing an annual budget, there may be changes in the business environment that soon make the budget irrelevant and out-of-date. For example, the rate of inflation may be much higher than expected, or a competitor might take action that changes conditions in the market. Social tastes and attitudes may change suddenly, affecting the sales demand for a company's products.

Unexpected and sudden changes affect budgets by making them irrelevant. Rolling budgets are a way of dealing with the problem. Rolling budgets, also called **continuous budgets**, are budgets covering a set period of time, such as one year, but prepared more frequently.

 Example

A company might prepare rolling annual budgets every three months. It will prepare four annual budgets each year. If its year-end is 31st December, its preparation of rolling budgets would be as follows:

Date of budget preparation	Period covered by the budget
December Year 1	1st January – 31st December Year 2
March Year 2	1st April Year 2 – 31st March Year 3
June Year 2	1st July Year 2 – 30th June Year 3
September Year 2	1st October Year 2 – 30th September Year 3
December Year 2	1st January – 31st December Year 3
and so on	

The main **advantages** of rolling budgets are as follows:

■ Budgets are continually reviewed and revised in response to changes in business conditions. The entity is not committed to a fixed annual budget that is no longer relevant.

■ Control can be exercised through comparisons between current forecasts and strategic targets. This is a form of **feedforward control**. When the business environment is continually changing, this may be a more effective method of budgetary control than comparing actual results with the fixed budget or standard costs.

The main **disadvantages** of rolling budgets are as follows:

■ They can be **time-consuming**, and divert management attention from the task of managing actual operations.

■ Whenever a new rolling budget is prepared, the new plans must be communicated to all managers affected by the changes. There is a risk that some managers will not be informed about changes to plans and targets.

> ## Zero based budgeting (ZBB) and activity based budgeting (ABB)
>
> - Incremental budgeting and zero based budgeting: a comparison
> - The framework for a ZBB system
> - Advantages of ZBB
> - Disadvantages of ZBB
> - ZBB and performance monitoring
> - Activity based budgeting (ABB)

4 Zero based budgeting and activity based budgeting (ABB)

4.1 Incremental budgeting and zero based budgeting: a comparison

Zero based budgeting (ZBB) is a method of preparing expenditure budgets that is an alternative to incremental budgeting.

Incremental budgeting

With **incremental budgeting**, the starting point for preparing the budget for next year's expenditure is actual expenditure in the current year. Adjustments are then made to the current year's expenditure, to allow for estimated inflation next year and also for known changes in expenditure (such as an increase or reduction in employee numbers next year, or higher or lower depreciation charges).

Essentially, however, incremental budgeting means budgeting by adding extra amounts of expenditure onto the costs actually incurred in the financial year just ended.

In many cases, there is inefficiency and excessive spending in the budget for the previous year. There is no incentive to identify inefficiency and reduce costs.

Zero based budgeting (ZBB)

Zero based budgeting was developed as a method of eliminating inefficiency and wasteful spending from the budget.

The **zero based budgeting approach** requires an expenditure budget to be built up from zero, so that all expenditure within the budget is properly considered and estimated.

- Its aim is to eliminate wasteful allowances for spending from expenditure budgets. Spending is not provided for in the budget unless it has been justified.
- ZBB is particularly appropriate for preparing overhead expenditure budgets. A problem arises with budgeting for overhead costs, whenever overhead spending levels cannot be related to particular activities (as in activity based costing) or to

volumes of production output. The temptation is to budget for next year's spending by assuming that spending next year will be much the same as in the current year, with perhaps an increase for inflation or a reduction for 'cost control measures'. This is incremental budgeting.

4.2 The framework for a ZBB system

If an entity wishes to introduce ZBB, it must divide its operations into **'decision units'**. These may also be called budget cost centres. Each decision unit should have a manager who is responsible for the budget for the unit. A decision unit, for the purpose of ZBB, is an operating division for which **'decision packages'** can be associated.

Each decision unit starts with a budget allowance of zero. The manager of the decision unit must then justify every programme and every item of spending for inclusion in the budget for next year. Each of these programmes or items of spending is called a 'decision package'.

- A decision package is a program of activity that will achieve a specific purpose.
- Each decision package must have a clearly-stated purpose that contributes to the goals and objectives of the entity.
- An expenditure estimate must be prepared for each decision package.

For each decision package, the decision unit manager should:

- identify the goal or objective of the programme
- identify the activities that must be carried out to perform the programme
- identify the resources required for the programme and their cost
- explain how the programme will contribute to the goals of the entity as a whole.

For each decision package, the decision unit manager must:

- justify the need for the decision package
- consider what would be the consequences of eliminating the decision package
- consider whether the decision package can be performed in a different way, more effectively or more efficiently.

Decision unit managers must therefore justify all their spending. As a result, the budget should eliminate wasteful spending ('budget slack') and spending that is no longer required due to changes in business conditions.

In preparing a zero based budget, each decision package is costed, and the budget planners must decide whether to accept the decision package for the budget, or whether to reject it. If a decision package is accepted, the cost estimate for the package goes into the budget.

Two types of decision package: ranking packages in order of priority

There are two types of decision package.

- **Decision packages for a minimum level of operation**. For example, there may be a minimum acceptable level of training for a group of employees. There may be several alternative decision packages for providing the training – internal courses, external courses, or computer-based training programmes. An expenditure estimate should be prepared for each alternative basic decision package.

- **Incremental decision packages**. These are programmes for conducting a more extensive operation than the minimum acceptable level. For example, there may be incremental decision packages for providing some employees with more training, or for having more extensive supervision, or more extensive quality control checks. For incremental decision packages, an estimate should be made of the cost of the incremental operation, and the expected benefits.

A zero based budget is then prepared as follows:

- A decision must be taken to provide for a minimum level of operation. This means deciding for each basic operation:

    - whether or not to perform the operation at all – do the benefits justify the costs?

    - If the operation is performed at a basic level, which of the alternative basic decision packages should be selected?

- Having decided on a basic level of operations, a basic expenditure budget can be prepared.

- The next step is to consider each incremental decision package, and decide whether this additional operation, or additional level of operations, is justified. An incremental decision package is justified if the expected benefits exceed the estimated costs.

- A budget can then be prepared consisting of all the selected basic decision packages and incremental decision packages.

- If the total expenditure budget is too high when all these decision packages are included, some incremental decision packages should be eliminated from the budget. One method of doing this is to rank the incremental decision packages in an order of priority (typically in order of net expected benefits, which are the expected benefits minus the estimated incremental costs). The decision packages at the bottom of the priority list can then be eliminated from the budget, until total budgeted expenditure comes within the maximum permitted spending limit.

Extensive use of value judgements by managers will be needed to rank decision packages in a priority order. This is because the expected benefits from incremental activities or incremental programmes are often based on guesswork and opinion, or on forecasts that might be difficult to justify.

4.3 Advantages of ZBB

The potential advantages of zero based budgeting, particularly when budgeting for overhead costs, are that:

- all spending levels in the budget must be justified: wasteful spending ('budget slack') should be eliminated

- all activities are reviewed and their value is assessed.

ZBB can be particularly useful in budgeting for 'discretionary costs'. These are costs that an entity does not have to incur, but chooses to incur because the expected benefits exceed the expected costs.

Managers of decision units are required to answer several key questions about their operational activities:

- Does each decision package support the goals and objectives of the entity?

- What would be the consequences for the entity if a decision package were to be eliminated?

- Can the same operation be performed in a different way, and at less cost?

- At what level of activity should each operation be conducted? Would it be appropriate to put in fewer resources, and conduct the operation at a lower level?

4.4 Disadvantages of ZBB

There are many difficulties and disadvantages with zero based budgeting.

- A large effort is required to establish a framework for zero based budgeting. Decision units must be identified, and for each decision unit, there must be a system for identifying decision packages. This takes time and effort. Once established, the framework must be kept up to date.

- Managers of decision units must spend much more time preparing budgets than they would with a traditional system of incremental budgeting.

- An effective system of ZBB requires an excellent management accounting system that can help managers to identify the incremental costs and benefits of different decision packages.

- Estimates, particularly estimates of the benefits of decision packages, are often based on the value judgements of managers.

- ZBB might be seen as a threat, to cut back expenditure allowances in the next budget year.

- When incremental decision packages are ranked in priority order, there may be disputes between managers of different decision units (budget cost centres), as each tries to protect his own spending levels and argue that budget cuts should fall on other cost centres.

ZBB can therefore be a very effective budgeting process for an occasional review of costs, as a cost-cutting exercise. However, it is not suitable as a regular budgeting system, because it would be too expensive and time-consuming.

In view of the large amount of management time that is required to prepare a zero based budget, an entity may decide to produce a zero based budget periodically, say every three years, and to prepare incremental budgets in the intervening years.

In order to maintain the support of budget cost centre managers for a system of ZBB, it is also necessary to make sure that any system of performance-based rewards (such as annual bonuses for keeping spending within budget limits) is not affected by the use of ZBB. If managers feel that their rewards will be threatened – for example because it will be difficult to keep spending within the ZBB limits – they are unlikely to give their support to the ZBB system.

Zero based budgeting techniques can be difficult to apply in practice. Decision unit managers will be expected to identify and evaluate each decision package, and then rank decision packages in order of priority. This calls for some skill and knowledge.

When a company is introducing ZBB for the first time, or when a new manager is appointed, it is therefore advisable to provide suitable training in ZBB methods.

4.5 ZBB and performance monitoring

Within a system of zero based budgeting, actual performance should be monitored.

■ For each decision package, there should be a measurable performance target.

■ Actual results should be compared with this target.

Each decision package must therefore have one or more measurable performance objective. The package must specify the objective or objectives, and the activities or operations that will be required to achieve those objectives.

Actual performance should be measured and compared with the objectives. Management must be informed whether or not the performance objectives are achieved.

4.6 Activity based budgeting (ABB)

Activity based budgeting (ABB) is similar in concept to activity based costing (ABC). When an entity uses activity based costing, it should be able to prepare activity based budgets. These are budgets prepared using activity based costing methods, and budgets for overheads are therefore prepared as activity costs.

Total budgeted overhead costs for the budget period are the sum of:

■ overhead costs associated with specific activities, and

■ general overhead costs that are not associated with any specific activities.

Failure to analyse overhead costs accurately: activity-based budgeting

Another criticism of traditional budgeting is that overhead costs are not estimated with enough accuracy. It has often been assumed that overhead costs are mainly fixed costs. In reality, this might not be true.

Overhead costs now make up a large proportion of total costs of many organisations. Since overhead costs are a substantial part of total costs, it would be inappropriate to assume that these costs are largely fixed from one year to the next, if the assumption is incorrect.

Activity based costing is based on the view that many overhead costs arise from certain key activities that make use of resources. For each activity, there is one (or more) 'cost drivers'. A cost driver is something that results in the use of resources. Cost drivers may therefore be seen as something that causes overhead costs to happen. Many overhead costs may vary according to the activity level associated with a cost driver.

Organisations that use activity based costing are able to budget for overhead costs using activity based budgeting. This analyses overhead costs into fixed costs and 'variable' costs that vary with a particular activity. Overhead cost budgets can be prepared, for each key activity, by:

- estimating the volume of activity in the budget period (this is the number of units of the cost driver)

- from this, estimating the amount of resources required to carry out the activities, and

- preparing a cost budget for these resources.

In principle, a system of ABB might help to remove 'slack; and wasteful overhead spending from the budget, because budgets are based on expected activity levels.

CHAPTER

9

Behavioural aspects of budgeting. Beyond budgeting

Contents
1   The behavioural aspects of budgeting
2   Beyond budgeting

The behavioural aspects of budgeting

- The relevance of attitudes and behaviour to effective budgeting
- Misunderstanding and worries about cost-cutting
- Opposition to unfair targets set by senior management
- Sub-optimisation
- Budget slack (budget bias)
- Corporate and individual aspirations
- Argyris: four behavioural issues in budgeting
- Budgeting as a bargaining process
- Budgets as a method of motivating individuals
- Behavioural aspects of budgetary control
- Management styles and budgetary control

1 The behavioural aspects of budgeting

1.1 The relevance of attitudes and behaviour to effective budgeting

The effectiveness of budgeting and budgetary control depends largely on the behaviour and attitudes of managers and (possibly) other employees.

- Budgets provide performance targets for individual managers. If managers are rewarded for achieving or exceeding their target, budgets could provide them with an incentive and a motivation to perform well.

- It has also been suggested that budgets can motivate individuals if they are able to participate in the planning process. Individuals who feel a part of the planning and decision-making process are more likely to identify with the plans that are eventually decided. By identifying with the targets, they might have a powerful motivation to succeed in achieving them.

When budgeting helps to create motivation in individuals, the human aspect of budgeting is positive and good for the organisation.

Unfortunately, in practice, human behaviour in the budgeting process has a negative effect. There are several possible reasons why behavioural factors can be harmful:

- Misunderstanding and worries about cost-cutting.
- Opposition to unfair targets set by senior management
- Sub-optimisation
- Budget slack or budget bias

1.2 Misunderstanding and worries about cost-cutting

Budgeting is often considered by the managers affected to be an excuse for cutting back on expenditure and finding ways to reduce costs. Individuals often resent having to reduce their spending, and so have a hostile attitude to the entire budgeting process. This fear and hostility can exist even when senior management do not have a cost-cutting strategy.

1.3 Opposition to unfair targets set by senior management.

When senior managers use the budgeting process to set unrealistic and unfair targets for the year, their subordinates may unite in opposition to what the senior managers are trying to achieve. Senior managers should communicate and consult with the individuals affected by target-setting, and try to win their agreement to the targets they are trying to set. Targets need to be reasonable.

A distinction can be made between:

- **aspirational budgets**, which are budgets based on performance levels and targets that senior managers would like to achieve, and

- **expectational budgets**, which are budgets based on performance levels and targets that senior managers would realistically expect to achieve.

Aspirational budgets might be considered unfair, especially if the individuals affected have not been consulted. Expectational budgets, based on current performance levels, do not provide for any improvements in performance.

Ideally perhaps, budgets might be set with realistic targets that provide for some improvements in performance.

In addition to opposing budgets that are unfair, operational managers may resent budgets because:

- they have been imposed by senior managers, without consulting the managers who will be responsible for achieving the budget targets

- they are unachievable

- they are irrelevant.

1.4 Sub-optimisation

There may be a risk that the planning targets for individual managers are not in the best interests of the organisation as a whole. For example, a production manager might try to budget for production targets that fully utilise production capacity. However, working at full capacity is not in the best interests of the company as a whole if sales demand is lower. It would result in a build-up of unwanted finished goods inventories. The planning process must be co-ordinated in order to avoid sub-optimal planning. In practice, however, effective co-ordination is not always achieved.

1.5 Budget slack (budget bias)

Budget slack has been defined as 'the intentional overestimation of expenses and/or underestimation of revenue in the budgeting process' (CIMA *Official Terminology*). Managers who prepare budgets may try to overestimate costs so that it will be much easier to keep actual spending within the budget limit. Similarly, managers may try to underestimate revenue in their budget so that it will be easier for them to achieve their budget revenue targets. As a result of slack, budget targets are lower than they should be.

When managers are rewarded for achieving their budget targets, the motivation to include some slack in the budget is even stronger.

An additional problem with budget slack is that when a manager has slack in his spending budget, he may try to make sure that actual spending is up to the budget limit. There are two reasons for this:

- If there is significant under-spending, the manager responsible might be required to explain why.

- Actual spending needs to be close to the budget limit in order to keep the budget slack in the budget for the next year.

The problem of budget slack is particularly associated with spending on 'overhead' activities and **incremental budgeting**. One of the advantages of **zero based budgeting** is that it should eliminate a large amount of slack from budgets.

In some cases, budget bias operates the other way. Some managers might prepare budgets that are too optimistic. For example, a sales manager might budget for sales in the next financial year that are unrealistic and unachievable, simply to win the approval of senior management.

1.6 Corporate and individual aspirations

The behavioural problems with budgeting arise because the corporate aims of an organisation are usually not the same as the aspirations of the individuals who work for it. For example, the aim of a company might be to maximise shareholder wealth, but there is no reason at all why this should be the aim of the company's employees and managers. Individuals have their own aims and ambitions, that working might (or might not) satisfy.

The potential conflict between corporate objectives and the aspirations of the company's employees can become apparent in the budgeting process, when an organisation sets its targets for the next year.

The accepted wisdom is that there is a potential conflict between corporate and individual aspirations. Individuals will be inclined to do what they want for themselves, regardless of whether this is good for the organisation.

The solution to the problem should be to bring the aspirations of individual managers and other employees as closely as possible into line with the objectives of the organisation. This is the rationale for measures to motivate individuals, such as reward schemes and motivation through **participation.**

1.7 Argyris: four behavioural issues in budgeting

Chris Argyris (1953) was one of the early writers on the behavioural aspects of budgeting. He suggested that four behavioural issues were involved in the budgeting process.

Behavioural issue	Comment
Budgets are a 'pressure device'	Many employees regarded the budgeting process as a way in which managers put pressure on 'lazy' workers and try to get them to work harder. Managers try to budget for improvements in performance, but employees resist the pressure and do not co-operate. Argyris commented that employee resistance against management pressure 'seems to be at the core of the budget problem'.
'Budget men' want to see operational managers fail	The accounting department is usually responsible for preparing the master budget and preparing budgetary control reports. Management accountants regard themselves as 'successful' in their work if they can identify significant adverse variances and poor operational performance. Their 'success' therefore arises out of the failures and poor performance of operational managers. The budgeting and budgetary control process is therefore damaged by hostility and poor communication between the management accounts (the 'budget men') and operational managers.
Departmental targets and goal congruence	A budget usually sets targets for each department, and departmental managers are considered successful if they achieve their budget target. However, one department might achieve its target in a way that is damaging to other departments and to the entity as a whole. There is often a lack of 'goal congruence' in departmental targets, which prevents co-operation between different departments.
Management style	Managers use budgets to impose their character and management style on their subordinates. Subordinates do not like the way that their manager behaves, but they blame the budget and not the manager for the problem.

1.8 Budgeting as a bargaining process

Budgeting should be a process where an organisation prepares short-term plans that are consistent with its objectives and strategies. In practice, however, planning often involves compromises, and balancing the requirements of different long-term and short-term objectives.

As a result, budgeting can become a bargaining process between managers. The managers with the greatest power and influence are the most likely to get what they want. In many cases, managers will make 'deals' and reach compromises on what should be included in the budget.

The bargaining process is evident perhaps in the annual round of budgeting in central government, when spending departments (health, education, social services, defence and so on) argue and negotiate with each other and with the treasury department. They try to reach agreement through bargaining on spending allowances for the next financial year.

In companies, managers might also use the budgeting process to bargain, giving way on some demands in order to get what they want in other matters.

Anthony Hopwood has commented on the bargaining process as follows: 'Behind the essential technical façade of the budgetary procedures lies a prior and less formal bargaining process in which the managers compete for … resources. In practice, budget requests can vary from being a statement of a manager's anticipations to being one of his most optimistic aspirations. Since the amounts requested often have an important effect on the amounts received and hence on … control over … resources, the requests are themselves strategies in a bargaining process in which the issues … include personal motives for status, recognition and advancement.'

1.9   Budgets as a method of motivating individuals

Instead of creating resistance and opposition, the budgeting process might possibly be used to motivate individual managers and employees, so that they have a personal interest in wanting to set a challenging budget and to achieve the budget targets that are set.

One approach to motivating individuals is to reward them for achieving their budget targets. Systems of rewards, such as annual cash bonuses, are widely used. Rewards systems are considered in more detail in a later chapter, in the context of performance targets.

It has also been suggested that individuals will be more committed to achieving budget targets if they are able to participate in the budgeting process, and contribute to the decision about what the budget targets should be.

■ Participation in budgets is achieved by inviting subordinates to discuss budget targets and suggest what these might be. However, the final decision about budget targets is the responsibility of senior managers.

■ The value of participation could therefore depend on the attitude of senior managers to the participation process. Is the participation by subordinates 'genuine'? Is the manager really listening to what the subordinates have to say?

The effect of participation on the motivation of subordinates will also depend on circumstances. Hopwood suggested that the effectiveness of participation on employee motivation depends on three key factors.

Factor	Comment
The nature of the task	The effectiveness of participation will depend on the nature of the work, and the extent to which employees have control over the way in which the work is done. 'In highly-programmed ... and technically constrained areas, where speed and detailed control are essential for efficiency, participative approaches have less to offer.... In contrast, in areas where flexibility, innovation and the capacity to deal with un-anticipated problems are important, participation in decision-making may offer a more immediate ... payoff....' (Hopwood).
Organisation structure	Participation is likely to be more effective in an organisation where management responsibilities are decentralised, and local managers have more influence over their own budgets.
Personality of the employees	Some types of individual are more likely than others to be motivated by participation in the budgeting process. This is a matter of different personalities.

1.10 Behavioural aspects of budgetary control

The performance of operational managers may be measured by comparing actual performance with the budget. The manager might be rewarded for achieving budget targets but criticised for failing to meet the budget.

This tendency to 'blame' managers for failing to meet the budget targets will have an adverse effect on the motivation and attitude of the operational managers in the following circumstances:

- The budget might not make any distinction between costs that are controllable and costs outside the manager's control. The manager might therefore be criticised for excess spending on items over which he has no control.

- Circumstances might change and events might occur that make the original budget unrealistic. Even so, the manager might be criticised for failing to meet the budget targets, even when changed circumstances have made the budget targets unrealistic.

1.11 Management styles and budgetary control

In the 1970s, research was carried out by Anthony Hopwood into performance evaluation by managers, and how the performance of managers with cost centre responsibility is judged. He identified three types of management style:

- A **budget-constrained style**. With this style of management, the performance of managers is based on their ability to meet budget targets in the short term. With this style of performance evaluation, the focus is mainly on budgeted costs actual costs and variances. Managers are under considerable pressure to meet their short-term budget targets. Stress in the job is high. Managers might be tempted to manipulate accounting data to make actual performance seem better in comparison with the budget.

■ A **profit-conscious style**. The performance of managers is evaluated on the basis of their ability to increase the general effectiveness of the operations under their management. Increasing general effectiveness means being more successful in achieving the longer-term aims of the organisation. For example, success in reducing costs in the long term would be considered an increase in general effectiveness.

With a profit-conscious style, budgets and variances are not ignored, but they are budgetary control information which is treated with caution, and variances are not given the same importance as with a budget-constrained style.

Hopwood found that with this style of management evaluation, costs remain important, but there is much less pressure and stress in the job. As a consequence, there was a good working relationship between managers and their subordinates. In addition, there was less manipulation of accounting data than with a budget-constrained style.

■ A **non-accounting style**. With this style, budgetary control information plays a much less important part in the evaluation of managers' performance. Other (non-accounting) measures of performance were given greater prominence.

Hopwood appeared to suggest that a profit-conscious style of evaluation was the most effective of the three.

This conclusion has been challenged by David Otley. His research into profit centre managers in the UK coal mining industry (1978) found that there was a fairly close link between good performance and a budget-constrained style of management evaluation. Managers whose performance was judged on success in meeting budget targets were generally more successful in actually meeting their targets.

The differing conclusions between the research of Hopwood and Otley suggest that the most appropriate approach to the evaluation of performance depends on the circumstances and conditions in which the organisations and their managers operate. This conclusion is consistent with the **contingency theory of management accounting** (described in an earlier chapter).

Beyond budgeting
■ Origins of 'beyond budgeting'
■ Weaknesses in traditonal budgeting
■ The 'beyond budgeting model'
■ Performance management in the 'beyond budgeting' model
■ Beyond budgeting: concluding comments

2 Beyond budgeting

2.1 Origins of 'beyond budgeting'

The Beyond Budgeting Round Table (BBRT) was set up in 1998. It is a European-wide research project investigating whether entities would benefit from the abolition of budgets and budgeting. The BBRT claims that several successful European companies have stopped preparing budgets. Instead, they use a 'responsibility model' for decision-making and performance measurement. As a result, their performance has improved.

In the UK, the ideas of 'beyond budgeting' are associated with the writing of Jeremy Hope and Robin Fraser.

2.2 Weaknesses in traditional budgeting

Hope and Fraser have argued that the traditional budgeting system is inefficient and inadequate for the needs of modern businesses. In a continually-changing business world, traditional budgeting systems can have the effect of making business organisations fixed and rigid in their thinking, and unable to adapt. As a result, business organisations may be much too slow and inflexible in reacting to business developments.

The budgeting system establishes 'last year's reality' as the framework for the current year's activities. When the business environment is changing rapidly, this approach is inadequate. Managers should respond quickly to changes in the environment, but traditional budgeting and budgetary control systems act as a restraint on innovation and initiative.

Consequences of the inadequacy of the traditional budgeting system are that:

- operational managers regard the budgeting process as a waste of their time and resent having to prepare and then continually revise budget plans

- management accountants are involved in the budgetary planning and control system, but their work adds little or no value to the business. As a result, it may be difficult to justify the existence of the management accounting function.

According to the Beyond Budgeting Round Table, there are ten major problems with the traditional budgeting and budgetary control system.

(1) Budgets are **time-consuming and expensive**. In spite of computer technology and the use of budget models, it can take four to five months in a large company to prepare the annual budget for next year. The work on budget preparation has been found to use over 20% of the time of senior managers and financial controllers.

(2) **Traditional budgeting adds little value** and uses up valuable management time that could be used better in other ways. Preparing a budget does nothing, or very little, to add value to the entity. Budgets 'are bureaucratic, time-consuming exercises, and the time taken would be better deployed in more value-creating activities' (Hope and Fraser).

(3) **Fails to consider shareholder value**. The traditional budgeting process focuses too much on **internal matters** and not enough on external factors and the business environment, and it fails to focus on shareholder value.

(4) **Rigid and inflexible: budgeting systems prevent fast response**. Managers concentrate on achieving 'agreed' budget targets, which may not be in the best interests of the organisation as a whole, particularly when circumstances change after the budget has been agreed. Budgets are therefore 'rigid' and prevent fast and flexible responses to changing circumstances and unexpected events.

(5) **Budgets 'protect' spending and fail to reduce costs**. In many entities, managers are expected to spend their entire budget allowance. If they don't, money will be taken away from their budget allowance next year. This is certainly no incentive to cut costs.

(6) Traditional budgeting and budgetary control **discourages innovation**. Managers are required to achieve fixed budget targets, and the fixed budget does not encourage continuous improvement. Managers will be reluctant to exceed their budgeted spending limits, even though extra spending would be necessary to react to events, possibly because spending above budget will put their bonus at risk. In a dynamic business environment, business organisations should be seeking continuous improvement and innovation.

(7) Budgets **focus on sales targets, not customer satisfaction**. This will possibly increase sales in the short-term, even if the products are not as good as they should be, but long-term success depends on satisfying customers.

(8) In practice, it has been found that although most companies have a budgeting system, they are poor at executing strategy. This suggests that budgeting systems are not effective systems for implementing strategy.

(9) Budgeting systems encourage a **culture of 'dependency'**, in which junior managers do what they are told by their boss, and do not argue. 'They reinforce the "command and control" management model and ... undermine attempts at organisational change, such as team working, delegation and empowerment' (Hope and Fraser).

(10) Budgets can lead to 'unethical' behaviour, such as including 'slack' within the budgeted spending allowance.

There are other major criticisms of budgeting systems.

- Traditional budgeting is seen as a method of imposing financial control, by comparing actual results with budget. Budgeting should be a system for communicating corporate goals – setting objectives and improving performance.

- Budgets are also plans that focus on financial numbers. 'They fail to deal with the most important drivers of shareholder value ... - knowledge or intellectual capital. Strong brands, skilled people, excellent management processes, strong leadership and loyal customers are assets that are outside the ... accounting system' (Hope and Fraser).

- In many cases, budget plans are not the result of a rational decision-making process. Often, budgets are a political compromise between different departments and managers, and budgeted spending limits for each manager are the outcome of a bargaining process.

- Traditional budgetary control encourages managers to achieve fixed budget targets, but does not encourage continuous improvement. Managers will be reluctant to exceed their budgeted spending limits, even though extra spending would be necessary to react to events, possibly because spending above budget will put their bonus at risk. In a dynamic business environment, business organisations should be seeking continuous improvement and innovation.

- Traditional budgeting shows the costs of departments and functions, but not the costs of activities that are performed by employees. The traditional budget figures do not give managers information about the cost drivers in their business. In addition, traditional budgets do not help managers to identify costs that do not add value.

2.3 The 'beyond budgeting model'

The Beyond Budgeting view is that budgeting, as practised by most companies, should be abolished. The traditional hierarchical form of management structure should also be abolished. In its place, there should be a system in which authority and responsibility is given to operational managers, who should work together to achieve the strategic objectives of the entity.

Traditional budgeting is based on a 'dependency model' of management and organisation culture. It is a system for centralised control by senior management. Control is exercised by requiring operational managers to meet (or exceed) budget targets.

The 'Beyond Budgeting' alternative is a 'responsibility model' in which decision-making and performance management are delegated to 'line managers' (operating managers). Instead of having fixed annual plans, these managers agree performance targets: these targets are reviewed regularly and amended as necessary in response to changing circumstances and unexpected events.

A solution to the lack of flexibility in traditional budgeting may be **continuous rolling forecasting** (or even continuous budgets), so that the business organisation can adapt much more quickly to changes in its environment and to new events.

Responsibility should be delegated to operational managers, who should be empowered to take decisions in response to changing circumstances, that the managers believe would be in the best interests of the organisation.

- Goals should be agreed by reference to external benchmarks (such as increasing market share, or beating the competition in other ways) and targets should not be fixed and internally-negotiated.

- Operational managers should be motivated by the challenges they are given and by the delegation of responsibility.

- Operational managers can use their direct knowledge of operations to adapt much more quickly to changing circumstances and new events.

- Operational managers may be expected to work within agreed parameters, but they are not restricted in their spending by detailed line-by-line budgets.

- Delegated decision-making should encourage more transparent and open communication systems within the organisation. Managers need continuous rolling forecasts to make decisions and apply control. Efficient IT systems are therefore an important element in the 'beyond budgeting' model.

2.4 Performance management in the 'beyond budgeting' model

In the Beyond Budgeting model of performance management, there are 12 basic principles.

(1) **Governance**. The basis for taking action should be a set of clear values. Mission statements and plans should not be used to guide action.

(2) **Responsibility for performance**. Managers should be responsible for achieving competitive results, not for meeting the budget target.

(3) **Delegation**. People should be given the ability and the freedom to act. They should not be controlled and constrained by senior managers.

(4) **Structure**. Operations should be organised around processes and networks, and should not be organised on the basis of departments and functions.

(5) **Co-ordination**. There should be effective co-ordination between people within the company, and this should be achieved by process design and fast information systems.

(6) **Leadership**. Senior managers should challenge and 'coach'. They should not command and control.

(7) **Setting goals**. The goal should be to beat competitors, not meet budget.

(8) **Formulating strategy**. Formulating and implementing strategy should be a continuous process, not an annual event imposed by senior management.

(9) **Anticipatory management**. Management should use anticipatory systems for managing strategy. (Anticipatory systems are systems that provide information about events that are anticipated in the future.)

(10) **Resource management**. Resources should be made available to operational managers at a fair cost, when they are required. Resources should not be allocated to departments in a fixed budget.

(11) **Measurement and control**. Performance measurement and control should be based on a small number of key performance indicators, not a large number of detailed reports.

(12) **Motivation and rewards**. Rewards, at a company level and a business unit level, should be based on competitive performance, not meeting predetermined budget targets.

Principles (1) to (6) are concerned with establishing an effective organisation and culture of behaviour. Principles (7) to (12) are concerned with establishing an effective system of performance measurement.

'Beyond Budgeting entails a shift from a performance emphasis based on numbers to one based on people. It assumes that performance improvement is more likely to come from giving capable people control over decisions (and making them accountable for results), than simply from adopting different measures and incentives' (Hope and Fraser).

Hope and Fraser set out the 12 principles, and their effect, as follows:

Effective organisation and behaviour		Effective performance		Management of competitive success
■ Clear values		■ Relative targets		■ Fast response
■ Responsibility for results		■ Adaptive strategies		■ Best people
■ Freedom and capability to act	×	■ Anticipatory management	=	■ Innovative strategies
■ Fast networks and processes		■ Internal market for resources		■ Low costs
■ Co-ordination		■ Fast, distributed controls		■ Loyal customers
■ Challenge and stretch		■ Relative team rewards		■ Satisfied customers

To compete successfully, management have to be very good at the six issues in the box on the right-hand side of this diagram.

■ They must create a climate and culture for fast response. An ability to respond quickly to unexpected changes and events will mean that the company can deal with uncertainty successfully. Change should be seen as an opportunity, not a threat.

  - Managers must be given responsibility for strategy, and they should monitor strategy continuously, not just once a year (as in the traditional budget model).

- If new initiatives are needed, managers should be able to obtain the resources they need quickly. 'They need, for example, the authority to acquire key people when they are available (not when there is room in the budget); to react to competitive threats and opportunities as they arise (not as predicted in an outdated plan); and to acquire and deploy resources when necessary (not as allocated by head office)' (Hope and Fraser).

■ They must employ the best people. A challenging environment to work in is likely to attract and retain top-quality employees.

■ They must innovate and generate new business ideas. Bureaucracy does not encourage innovation and creativity. The 'Beyond Budgeting' model does.

■ They must operate with low costs. Competitive pressures in markets are forcing down prices. In the 'Beyond Budgeting' model managers will adapt strategies to the requirements of the competitive environment, and will find ways to reduce costs if this is appropriate. The traditional budgeting model does not encourage effective cost reduction.

■ They must create and retain loyal customers. The 'Beyond Budgeting' model encourages managers to focus on satisfying customer needs. Satisfied customers are likely to be loyal customers.

■ They must create value for shareholders. The 'Beyond Budgeting' model should help a company to improve its profitability and create additional value for its shareholders.

2.5   Beyond budgeting: concluding comments

Hope and Fraser have argued that traditional budgeting systems are weak and should not be used. However, in practice most companies and other organisations continue to use them.

It has been argued that the 'beyond budgeting' model is much more easily applied in the private sector than in the public sector. Government activity is managed through expenditure budgets and spending controls, and there is accountability for spending to politicians (government ministers and elected representatives) and to the general public. There may also be uncertainty about the objectives of particular government activities or departments. In such circumstances, it is difficult to apply a flexible system of decision-making or to devolve decision-making to lower levels of management.

There have been attempts to improve traditional budgeting systems: for example, zero based budgeting, continuous budgets and activity based budgeting are all attempts to improve the budgeting system. Hope and Fraser argue, however, that these are 'valiant efforts to update the process, but they only deal with part of the [problem] and are both time-consuming and complicated to manage.'

CHAPTER

10

Changes in business structure and management accounting

Contents	
1	Contingency theory of management accounting
2	New institutional theory and management accounting
3	The relevance of traditional management accounting systems: 'relevance lost'
4	The relevance of standard costing and variance analysis
5	Activity based management (ABM)
6	Business Process Re-engineering (BPR)

Contingency theory of management accounting

- Theories of management accounting
- The nature of contingency theory in management accounting
- Contingent variables
- Contingency theory and the changing requirements for management accounting information

1 Contingency theory of management accounting

1.1 Theories of management accounting

Several theories have been developed to suggest:

- whether management accounting techniques are relevant to the modern business environment
- what factors affect the choice of which management accounting techniques to use
- reasons why the use of management accounting techniques might change over time, particularly with technological changes and other changes in the business environment.

You might be expected to show an awareness of these theories in your examination.

1.2 The nature of contingency theory in management accounting

Contingency theory is a theory that the most appropriate solution or system in a particular situation is dependent upon ('contingent' upon) the circumstances of the case. A contingency theory has been developed for management accounting, by writers such as Otley, to suggest what management accounting methods are most appropriate in any particular set of circumstances.

Otley has described the contingency theory of management accounting as follows:
'The contingency theory of management accounting is based on the premise that there is no universally appropriate accounting system applicable to all organisations in all circumstances. Rather a contingency theory attempts to identify specific aspects of an accounting system that are associated with certain defined circumstances and to demonstrate an appropriate matching.'

Contingency theory may therefore be summarised as follows:

- There is no unique management accounting system that is best for all organisations.
- So the important question is: 'What is the most effective management accounting system for my organisation'?
- The most effective management accounting system for an organisation depends on the circumstances of the organisation.

- It is therefore necessary to study the circumstances of the organisation, and identify the key features affecting the type of management accounting system that it needs.

Otley called these key features 'contingent variables'.

1.3 Contingent variables

The contingent variables that influence the type of management accounting system that should be applied include:

- the environment
- technology
- size and complexity of the organisation
- strategy
- culture
- other information systems within the organisation.

The environment

The type of management information system, for example whether it should be centralised or decentralised, depends largely on:

- whether the environment of the organisation is predictable or unpredictable
- the amount of competition in the market
- the number of product-markets in which the organisation competes.

 ### Example

When there is intense competition in a particular market, a key factor for business success might be to develop innovative products at a competitive price. When product innovation and pricing are significant factors, a company may use **target costing** and **target pricing**. Target pricing means deciding in advance a price at which a new product should be offered to the market. Target costing is an accounting technique concerned with developing a new product at a cost that will allow the company to sell it at the target price, and make a profit at that price.

Technology

In product costing, the nature of the manufacturing process determines how costs can be traced to products – for example, process costing and job costing are designed for different types of manufacturing system.

Similarly, with the development of new manufacturing methods, new management accounting techniques might be appropriate. For example, **backflush accounting** might be appropriate in a Just in Time manufacturing environment.

Size and complexity

Management accounting systems should be designed differently for organisations of differing sizes and complexity.

As an organisation grows, its organisation structure is likely to change and become more complex. From consisting of simple functional departments, it might grow into a large organisation with several investment centres. The management accounting requirements of the organisation will change as it grows and becomes more complex. In large organisations, where authority is delegated to divisional managers, new systems might be needed by head office to monitor the performance of the divisions and to make the divisional managers accountable for the division's performance. Responsibility accounting might be applied to investment centres, with performance of each centre measured by **Return on Investment (ROI)** or **Residual Income (RI)**.

Strategy

It has been argued that the cost appropriate management accounting system for an organisation will also depend on its choice of competitive strategy, and in particular whether it adopts:

- a 'cost leadership' strategy based on cost minimisation, or
- a 'product differentiation' strategy of offering customers an appropriate quality of product for a given price.

When a company has a 'cost leadership' strategy, it tries to be the lowest-cost producer in the market, and competes on the basis of sales price. Management accounting systems should focus on costs and cost control or cost reduction.

Many companies pursue a 'product differentiation' strategy, in which they do not try to be the least cost producer. Instead, they seek to offer products or services that create more 'value' for the customer, by satisfying their needs better. In these circumstances, a focus on cost control alone is inappropriate: management information systems need to provide managers with information about other factors that create value, such as product or service quality. Techniques such as **quality costing** might be appropriate.

Culture

The management accounting system should be consistent with the culture and value systems of the managers who will use it; otherwise, managers will resist the system and find fault with it.

Corporate culture describes the ethics and attitudes of management and employees within an organisation. A management accounting system is more effective if senior management can maintain a corporate culture that supports the aims of the organisation and objectives and its methods of working.

Other information systems within the organisation

Otley also argued that the requirements for an effective management accounting system also depend on the other information systems and control systems within the organisation.

A contingency approach to selecting a management accounting systems might be considered within the context of the factors set out in the following diagram:

Contingent variables	
Variables that the organisation cannot control	Objectives of the organisation

Control systems in the organisation			
Accounting information systems design	Other management information systems design	Organisation design	Other control systems and procedures

Intervening variables
Controllable items

Effectiveness of the organisation
(measured in terms of achieving its objectives)

1.4 Contingency theory and the changing requirements for management accounting information

A 'traditional' management accounting system may have provided management information for a manufacturing company where:

■ The management structure is highly centralised, and information about costs and profits was provided for the company as a single 'profit centre'.

■ All the support services and activities were performed by the company's own employees.

■ The company used only full-time employees.

■ Customers were willing to hold large inventories of goods purchased from the company, and would allow long supply lead times for the delivery of new supplies.

■ The manufacturing operations involved long production runs of standardised products.

In this type of environment, a traditional management accounting system – with budgeting, standard costing and budgetary control systems – was probably adequate for many of management's information requirements.
In modern-day manufacturing organisations:

■ Management authority may be much more decentralised, and a company may be organised on the basis of several profit centres or investment centres. If these profit centres provide goods or services to each other, a system is needed for deciding and recording transfer prices for work done by each profit centre for the others. In addition, there must be systems for reporting the performance of each separate centre – perhaps using return on investment or residual income as key measures of performance for investment centres.

■ Many activities are outsourced to external organisations. For example, manufacturing companies might outsource some parts of manufacturing operations, IT support services, some accounting services, security, cleaning services, management of the company's fleet of motor vehicles, and so on. When operations are outsourced, management need information to help them to:

- decide whether it is better to outsource work or do the work 'in-house'

- monitor the **quality** as well as the cost of the outsourced work.

■ Many part-time and temporary employees are used. Managers need information to help them plan the work and then monitor the performance of these employees.

■ Some customers have adopted a just-in-time (JIT) approach to purchasing, and do not hold large inventories. These customers need reliable suppliers who can deliver fresh supplies immediately. When customers expect to use JIT methods for purchasing, this has implications for the inventories of suppliers. Managers in supplier companies need information about optimum inventory levels, or about JIT production, so that they can meet the expectations of their customers.

■ In many industries, customers expect products to be adapted to their specific requirements. Product design is more significant, and many companies now commit significant resources to design work. Standard products, long production runs and standard costing systems are not appropriate.

A management information system must be capable of providing information that managers need. This can be information from external sources as well as from sources within the organisation itself. Managers may also need information for strategic decision-making as well as information for day-to-day operational control or shorter-term planning. In many cases, managers need non-financial information as well as financial information.

The challenge for management accounting systems is to satisfy all these information needs. In addition, as the needs of management change, accounting systems should change too. Contingency theory can therefore be used to explain why traditional management accounting systems can become irrelevant, and why new techniques should be used.

New institutional theory and management accounting

- Comparison of institutional theory and contingency theory
- The nature of new institutional theory
- New institutional theory and changes in management accounting practice
- Criticisms of new institutional theory

---

2 New institutional theory and management accounting

2.1 Comparison of institutional theory and contingency theory

An institution, for the purpose of institutional theory, is something that gives stability and meaning to social behaviour. It is an established way of behaving and thinking. 'Institution' therefore has a meaning that relates to 'something becoming an established institution' or 'something becoming institutionalised'.

- Contingency theory, as applied to management accounting, is based on the view that the most effective or appropriate management accounting system depends on the circumstances of the organisation.

- Institutional theory, as applied to management accounting, takes a different view. It starts by asking why so many organisations are similar in the way that they structure their accounting systems, and the methods that they use.

- Institutional theory also considers how systems might change as well as new ways of doing things might become institutionalised. This might be relevant to changes in management accounting systems.

2.2 The nature of new institutional theory

New institutional theory is an approach to the study of behaviour in organisations. The theory is based on the view that the attitudes, habits and established views within an organisation are influenced by its 'institutional environment'.

Established rules, beliefs and practices within an organisation are formulated by adopting the rules, beliefs and practices within other organisations. The way that an organisation operates is therefore decided not so much by what is best for the organisation, but by how things are done generally in all other similar organisations. Institutional theorists promote the concepts of 'isomorphism' whereby organisations become similar to others in the industry and institutionalised; they emerge as a common framework within the same field. These accepted norms have found their way into modern management thinking.

New institutional theory has been described as follows: 'People live in a socially constructed world that is filled with taken-for-granted meanings and rules. Much of their action is neither intentional nor conscious, for it is undertaken unconsciously and as a matter of routine (Carruthers, 1995).

DiMaggio and Powell are two leading exponents of new institutional theory. They suggested that organisations operating in similar environments are subject to the influence of established views about what is generally regarded as 'acceptable' behaviour'. As a result, all these organisations tend to have similar structures and processes. Quite simply, the theory is that all organisations become institutionalised. They adopt the common practices of other organisations in the industry, and the same attitudes.

This institutionalisation extends to management accounting systems, as well as to other aspects of organisational behaviour. This is why it is usual to find that certain management accounting methods are used in particular industries and not in others. There is a tendency for all organisations to use the same management accounting techniques because they are generally established and widely accepted, not because they are techniques that are necessarily useful and relevant to the organisation itself.

Powell and diMaggio identified three factors that make organisations copy the practices and processes of other organisations:

- pressures imposed on organisations to behave in a particular way by government, regulations and possibly by supplier relationships

- attitudes that are adopted when an organisation faces uncertainty and, in response to this uncertainty, it copies the practices of another organisation that it considers to be more successful or 'legitimate'

- attitudes of professionalism and the view that it is necessary to conform to a set of norms or rules developed by a professional body or group. Management accountants, for example, tend to conform to practices established by their professional bodies.

2.3 New institutional theory and changes in management accounting practice

A theory about changes in management accounting systems and practice is as follows.

Accounting is a social and institutional practice that inter-reacts with social relations within an organisation. When social relations within an organisation change, accounting systems will also change. For example, consider a situation in which a large company acquires control over a new subsidiary.

- The board of directors of the company will require information about the new subsidiary in order to monitor its performance.

- To meet the requirements of the new owner, practices and procedures in the subsidiary will change. The management accounting reporting system will also have to change, in response to the changes in practices and procedures.

- New accounting practices will be introduced.

- The new accounting procedures and practices will then be reproduced by other individuals who are responsible for introducing the new reporting system.

■ The new accounting practices might gain widespread acceptance, so that they come to be regarded as essential. In other words, they become institutionalised within the organisation.

This view perceives organisations needing legitimacy to survive. The organisation then adopts structures, job roles and policies e.g. Health and Safety, Equal Opportunities to appease outsiders. Unfortunately for the firm these do not increase efficiency or profitability.

2.4   Criticisms of new institutional theory

There are some criticisms of new institutional theory, as a method of explaining behaviour and processes within organisations.

■ It ignores the fact that behaviour within an organisation may be decided by the interests and views of powerful individuals or groups, rather than by generally-accepted practice. Practices may become established because they are actually appropriate for the requirements of the organisation rather than because they are generally-accepted and widely-used.

■ The theory does not satisfactorily explain how change occurs in established practices and views. It is more concerned with how practices become established than with how they change.

However, institutional theory might help to explain why some organisations use management accounting techniques and reporting systems that are not actually the most appropriate for the information requirements of the organisation's managers.

> **The relevance of traditional management accounting systems: 'relevance lost'**
>
> - The purpose of management accounting systems
> - Are traditional management accounting methods still relevant?
> - Kaplan: 'relevance lost'
> - Making management accounting relevant
> - Trends in management accounting

3 The relevance of traditional management accounting systems: 'relevance lost'

3.1 The purpose of management accounting systems

A management accounting system is a part of the management information system within an organisation. The purpose of management accounting is to provide information to managers that can be used to help them with making decisions. Traditionally, management accounting systems have provided financial or accounting information, obtained from accounting records and other data within the organisation. Commonly-used management accounting techniques have included absorption costing, marginal costing and cost-volume-profit analysis, budgeting, standard costing and budgetary control and variance analysis.

For various reasons, questions have been raised about the relevance of traditional management accounting to the needs of management in the modern business environment.

- Traditional management accounting techniques such as standard costing and variance analysis do not provide all the information that managers need in manufacturing companies where Total Quality Management or Just in Time management approaches are used.

- Traditional absorption costing is probably of limited value in a manufacturing environment where production processes are highly automated, and production overhead costs is a much more significant element of cost than direct labour.

- Traditional management accounting focuses on manufacturing costs, whereas many companies (and other organisations) operate in service industries and provide services rather than manufactured products.

- The traditional focus of management accounting has been on cost control or cost reduction. Lower costs mean that lower prices can be charged to customers, or higher profits can be made. However, many companies now seek to increase customer satisfaction and meet customer needs. To meet customer needs, other factors in addition to cost can be important – particularly product (or service) quality. Traditional management accounting ignores factors such as quality, reliability or speed of service.

- Many traditional management accounting techniques have a short-term focus. There are exceptions. Discounted cash flow, for example, is used to evaluate long-term capital projects. However, traditional management accounting systems do not provide senior managers with the information they need for making strategy decisions. Strategic decision-making needs information about competitors, customers, developments in technology and other environmental (external) factors.

Management information systems should be capable of providing the information that managers need. For the management accounting system to be the main management information system within an organisation, it must be able to provide the necessary variety of information – financial and non-financial, long-term as well as short-term – using suitable techniques of analysis.

3.2 Are traditional management accounting methods still relevant?

Many businesses compete with each other on the basis of:

- product or service quality and price
- delivery
- reliability
- after-sales service
- customer satisfaction – meeting customer needs.

These are critical variables in competitive markets and industries. Business organisations, faced with an increasingly competitive global market environment, must be able to deliver what the customer wants more successfully than their rivals. This means making sure that they provide quality for the price, and customer satisfaction, including the delivery, reliability and after-sales service that customers want or expect.

3.3 Kaplan: 'relevance lost'

Some years ago, Robert Kaplan put forward an argument that management accounting systems had lost their relevance and did not provide the information that managers need to make their decisions.

When these ideas were first published, they were ground-breaking because they challenged the value and 'relevance' of management accounting methods that were in widespread use at the time.

He suggested that the information needs of management had changed, but the information provided by management accountants had not. There was a danger that management accounting would lose its relevance – and value – entirely.

Kaplan made the following criticisms of traditional management accounting systems:

■ Traditional overhead costing systems, where overheads were absorbed into costs at a rate per direct labour hour, were irrelevant. (Activity based costing has been developed as just one alternative for overhead cost analysis.)

■ Standard costing systems are largely irrelevant, because in many markets customers do not want to buy standard products. They want product differentiation.

■ Traditional management accounting systems fail to provide information about aspects of performance that matter – product and service quality (and price), delivery, reliability, after-sales service and customer satisfaction.

He argued that in today's competitive market environment 'traditional cost accounting systems based on an assumption of long production runs of a standard product, with unchanging characteristics and specifications, [are not] relevant in this new environment.'

The need for a change of focus in providing information to management

Traditional management accounting systems focus on reducing costs and budgetary control of costs. Kaplan argued that the focus was wrong:

■ In modern production systems, products are often designed and manufactured to specific customer demands and often have a short life cycle. Their design is often sophisticated, and they are overhead-intensive. Traditional management accounting systems, in contrast, assume standard products whose manufacture is directly labour-intensive.

■ Machinery used in production is often flexible, and can be switched between different uses and purposes. Traditional manufacturing systems assume that standard tasks require particular types of machine. Although they may focus on minimising the machine time per product manufactured, these systems do not provide information to help with optimising the use of available multi-purpose machinery.

3.4 Making management accounting relevant

If it is accepted that traditional management accounting systems are no longer relevant to the information needs of managers in a competitive business world, the obvious next question is what has to be done to make them relevant?

The suggested answer is that management accounting systems need to recognise the factors that are critical for business success, and that management need to know about. These factors may be:

■ non-financial, as well as financial

■ longer-term (strategic) in nature, as well as short-term

■ strategic (concerned with objectives and strategies), as well as tactical (concerned with day-to-day management control)

- related to factors in the business environment as well as to factors within the business entity itself (in other words, making use of external as well as internal information).

3.5 Trends in management accounting

New techniques have been developed in management accounting, in response to changes in the business environment. Examples of techniques that have been developed include activity based costing and activity based management, backflush accounting, throughput accounting, target costing, life cycle costing, environmental management accounting and the balanced scorecard approach to performance measurement.

Some of these techniques have been developed in response to changes in manufacturing methods and systems.

Evaluating a management accounting technique

If the contingency theory of management accounting is valid, it should be expected that the management accounting techniques used in practice will vary with the particular information needs of the organisation.

For your examination, you may be required to give your views about whether a particular management accounting technique is appropriate for the specific requirements of a particular organisation.

The management accounting techniques used within an organisation must provide information that management need and will use. The key questions to ask, when assessing the usefulness of a management accounting system, are as follows:

The information needs of management

- What decisions do managers need to make?
- What are they key factors that will affect their decisions?
- What are the critical items of information they need for their decisions?

The information provided by the management accounting system

- Is the information provided:
    - **relevant** to the decision-making needs of the managers?
    - sufficiently **comprehensive** for these needs?
    - reliable?
    - available when needed?
- Is the information provided in a clear and understandable form?
- Are key items of information drawn to the attention of the manager, such as issues relating to **controllability**, **trend** or **materiality**?
- Does the benefit of having the information justify the cost of providing it?

The relevance of standard costing and variance analysis
■ Problems with standard costing and variances
■ The continuing relevance of standard costing systems

4 The relevance of standard costing and variance analysis

4.1 Problems with standard costing and variances

Writers such as Kaplan and Johnson have argued that standard costing and standard cost variances should not be used in a modern manufacturing environment for either:

■ cost control, or

■ performance measurement.

They argue that standard costs are no longer relevant in a modern manufacturing environment. Standard costing is used for standard products and the focus is on keeping production costs under control.

Kaplan and Johnson argued that using variance analysis to control costs and measure performance is **inconsistent with a focus on the objectives of quality, time and innovation,** which are now key factors in successful manufacturing operations.

■ Standard cost variances ignore quality issues and ignore quality costs. However, in a competitive market quality is a key success factor.

■ Manufacturing companies might have a system of Total Quality Management (TQM) in place, or something similar. An aim of TQM is to continue to find ways of achieving quality improvements, including cost reductions. With continuous improvement, there should be continual (small) reductions in costs. Standard costs – which are a fixed cost per unit – are inconsistent with the TQM objective of continuous improvement and cost reductions.

■ Another aim of the TQM approach is to eliminate waste from operations. Kaplan and Johnson argued that achieving standard costs is inconsistent with this TQM objective of eliminating waste. If waste is gradually eliminated, there should be continual reductions in costs.

■ When a company relies for success on innovation and new product design, many of its resources are committed to product design and development, and so many of its costs are incurred at this early stage of the product's life. Cost control should therefore focus on design and development costs, whereas standard costing provides information about production costs for products that have already been developed and are now in production.

■ When product design and innovation are important, product life cycles will be short. It may therefore be appropriate to look at all the costs of a product over its full life cycle (including its design and development stages, and including marketing costs as well as production costs).

- Standard costing variance analysis is restricted to monitoring the manufacturing costs of products during just a part of their life cycle.

- Standard costs are only likely to apply in a stable and non-changing business environment. In many industries, the environment is continually changing, and products are adapted to meet the changing circumstances and conditions.

4.2 The continuing relevance of standard costing systems

However, there are still some **advantages** to be obtained from using a standard costing system.

- Standard costs can be a useful aid for budgeting even in a Total Quality Management environment. Standard costs can be established for making products within the budget period to a target level of quality. If the TQM goals of continuous improvement and elimination of waste are achieved, the standard costs can be adjusted down for the next budget period.

- Managers need short-term ('real time') feedback on costs. They need to know whether costs are under control, and they also need to understand the financial consequences of their decisions and actions. Variance analysis is a useful method of providing 'real time' feedback on costs.

- Cost control is still an important aspect of management control. Quality, time and innovation may be critical factors, but so too is cost control. Standard costing and variance analysis provides a system for controlling costs in the short term.

- Standard costs for existing products can provide a useful starting point for planning the cost for new products.

- Standard costs can also be useful for target costing. The difference between the target cost for a product and its current standard cost is a 'cost gap'. Standard costs can be used to measure the size of the cost gap. In order to achieve the target cost, managers can focus on this cost gap and consider ways in which it can be closed.

- Overhead variances can provide useful information for cost control when many overhead costs are volume-driven.

> **Activity based management (ABM)**
>
> - Changes in business structure
> - The features of activity based management (ABM)
> - ABM: value-added activities and non-value added activities
> - Uses of ABM

5 · Activity based management (ABM)

5.1 Changes in business structure

Many entities operate in a rapidly-changing business environment. In response to the changes in their environment, they undergo changes themselves. Changes in business structures and processes are necessary in order to remain competitive. When business circumstances change significantly, it might be necessary to make big changes to organisation structures and processes.

Two techniques for introducing changes in business organisations are:

- Activity based management (ABM), and
- Business process re-engineering (BPR).

For each of these methods of managing change, information is needed to assist management. Much of this information should be provided by the management accounting system.

5.2 The features of activity based management (ABM)

In the past thirty years or so, there have been developments in management approaches to the re-design of activities, in order to improve the efficiency and effectiveness of activities and to reduce costs. The growing interest in activity management was due largely to the increase in overhead costs relative to other costs in an organisation. The 'traditional' focus of manufacturing companies on the control of direct costs was inadequate for controlling the much more significant costs of overhead activities.

Definitions

Activity based management (ABM) is the process of '... focusing on the management of activities to improve the value received by the customer and the profit achieved by providing this value' (CAM-I *Glossary of Activity Based Management*).

Activity based management (ABM) is 'the management processes that use the information provided by an activity-based cost analysis to improve organisational profitability. [ABM] includes performing activities more efficiently, eliminating the need to perform ... activities that do not add value for customers, improving the design of products, and developing better relationships with customers and suppliers. The goal of ABM is to enable customer needs to be satisfied while making fewer demands on [the resources of the entity]' (Horngren).

ABM has also been described as is the process of taking action based on Activity Based Costing (ABC) analysis. Activity based management developed out of activity based costing, which has been in use since the 1980s. The underlying concepts have been in existence for much longer, but the practice of ABM and ABC was given a boost by the use of spreadsheet models.

By identifying the costs of the activity or process, it is possible to decide whether it is profitable, or whether it adds value. This helps management to make more informed decisions about matters such as pricing, product mix, capital investment, and organisational change/process change.

Traditional cost accounting and ABC

Traditional cost accounting measured the costs of functions and departments, rather than the costs of the activities that are carried out within the organisation (such as the cost of receiving, and the processing and despatch of orders). In many organisations (especially those with high overhead costs) activities are the real 'cost drivers' of the business.

In addition:

■ a traditional budget often contains a significant amount of non-value-added costs that an ABM approach would possibly identify and eliminate

■ the annual budget often includes overhead costs as a fixed cost, based on a fixed output capacity for the budget period; in contrast, an ABM/ABC approach would begin with the activities required to meet customer demand, and plan capacity – and costs – accordingly.

5.3   ABM: value-added activities and non-value added activities

One aspect of ABM is that activities should be eliminated if they do not add value. An activity adds value when it contributes towards customer satisfaction, or increases the value of a product or service in the mind of the customer.

■ It might be possible to make value-added activities more efficient, or to add even more value.

■ Non-value added activities are a waste of time and expense. When these are identified, they should be eliminated.

■ Where activities add some value, but at great expense, the aim should be to reduce the cost of performing the activity.

For example, it is often suggested that a major activity in many public services, such as the hospitals service or the police service, is the completion of forms and preparing other official documents such as reports. Forms and reports add some value to a public service, but they should not take up excessive amounts of time for employees, such as doctors and policemen.

In a system of activity based costing, a key activity might be identified as 'keeping records'. If so, the costs of preparing reports and completing forms would be identified, and the factor or factors that drive the cost of this activity would be identified.

5.4 Uses of ABM

ABM can be used as a **cost reduction technique**. However, it can also be used to achieve **significant re-design of processes**, and is an alternative to Business Process Re-engineering as an approach to process re-design. By analysing the cost and the value-added element of various elements in a process or in a product or service mix, it is possible to re-design it radically to obtain competitive advantage.

Activity based management (ABM) analyses the management of activities in order to improve the value obtained ('value added'). ABM/ABC can help managers to improve their understanding of the value of what the organisation is doing, and whether it is using its available resources in the best way. It can provide useful information for answering questions such as:

- Does the organisation understand the purpose and true cost of all of the activities it performs?

- Which activities are a part of the 'core service'? Which activities are discretionary, but add value? Which activities are non-value-added activities and which activities are a waste of resources?

- When resources are in limited supply, do we prioritise activities properly, in order to maximise value?

ABM should be a recurring process, and not a 'once-only' exercise. This is because a common problem for organisations is to start with an effective value-adding process, but then over time to introduce 'nice-to-have' but costly additional features, which reduce their cost-effectiveness.

Example

An example of the application of ABM is the 'ticket-less airline' model used by airlines such as RyanAir or Easyjet in Europe and Southwest Airlines in the US.

- The concept of the 'ticket-less airline' challenged the existing assumption that passengers should be allocated a specific seat on an aircraft. Not issuing tickets might seem a relatively small cost saving, but it has enormous implications for the way the activity – booking passengers on flights –is carried out.

- A 'ticket-less airline' operates a 'one class' seating system. There is no distinction between first class, business class and economy class. This reduces the time at check-in and requires less check-in staff

- The ticket-less airlines use laminated cards instead of tickets. This reduces printing costs.

- Most passengers buy their tickets on the Internet. In doing so, they print their own ticket receipts and process their own payments. The costs of intermediaries – travel agents' commissions – are eliminated.

- Not having to allocate seats on the aircraft reduces time and administration costs at the airport.

- By limiting the service to the core offering – a flight – the cost of providing airline food is eliminated. In addition, it increases its revenue from on-board paid-for snacks.

- The large transaction cost savings (compared with traditional airline ticket costs) are passed on to customers in the form of highly flexible pricing, with many low-price ticket offers. The customer gains value from the improvements in the ticketing process.

Without activity based costing and activity based management, the model of the ticket-less airline would not have been possible.

Business Process Re-engineering (BPR)
■ BPR and changing processes
■ Principles of BPR
■ BPR and empowerment of employees
■ Conducting a BPR exercise
■ BPR projects: radical solutions

6 Business Process Re-engineering (BPR)

6.1 BPR and changing processes

To achieve a big competitive advantage, it is often necessary to take risks and to re-engineer processes in a radical way.

Business process re-engineering (BPR) is an approach to improving business operations and processes by re-designing them extensively. Changes introduced by BPR are major changes, completely altering the way that the process was carried out before.

Business Process Re-engineering (BPR) is defined by Hammer and Champy (*Re-engineering the Corporation: a Manifesto for Business Revolution, 1993*) as 'the fundamental re-thinking and rational re-design of the business processes to achieve dramatic improvements in critical contemporary measures of performance such as cost, quality, speed and service.'

(Note: Philosophically, BPR is the complete opposite of Total Quality Management (TQM), which believes in continuous but small improvements as the best way of achieving better performance. TQM is described in a later chapter.)

The aim of BPR is to take an operation or 'process' and radically re-design the way that it is carried out. Examples of processes may be:

■ handling customer orders, from taking an order to delivery to the customer

■ requisitioning of materials and purchasing system

■ the quality control process

■ in a hospital, the process for dealing with a particular type of patient, such as accident and emergency patients

BPR is a radical approach to the improvement of processes, and a BPR programme results in extensive and fundamental changes. It is therefore different from activity-based management, because the solutions provided by a BPR approach are often more radical and extreme. BPR is sometimes associated with radical shake-up, extensive job losses and heavy cost-cutting.

Like ABM, a BPR approach requires an analysis of costs that traditional management accounting systems do not provide.

6.2 Principles of BPR

Key principles of BPR are as follows:

- There must be a total re-think of business processes. Work must not be looked at from a departmental or functional perspective. It must be looked at in a cross-functional manner.

- Work should be organised around the natural flow of information, or materials or customers.

- Work should be organised around what the process produces, not around the tasks that go into it.

- The objective of a BPR programme is to achieve substantial improvements in performance by re-designing the process.

Hammer (1990) described the main principles of BPR as follows:

- There must be a **completely different way of thinking about a process**. A process should be seen as something that is done to achieve a desired objective. The focus should be on the end result, not the functions and activities involved in the existing process. The work should therefore be organised around the outcome from the process, not the tasks that go into performing it.

  For example, at one time the process of producing a daily newspaper was seen as a series of tasks, each carried out by different functions – reporting, writing copy, editing copy, producing the 'artwork' for print, producing printing plates and printing. These tasks were carried out by news reporters, editors, typesetters and printing staff.

  However, the purpose of this process is to produce daily newspapers for sale. This process has now been completely re-engineered. Reporting, writing and editing copy and producing artwork for print are now carried out by the same journalist, with minimal external interference, using IT technology.

- The aim is to achieve **dramatic improvements** in the process through major re-design.

- Whenever possible, the 'customer' for an operation or process should be required to carry out the process himself. A 'customer' should therefore be his own supplier.

  For example, suppose that when an individual re-orders supplies for a task, he sends a purchase order requisition to the buying department, and the buying department places the order. In this situation, the individual is an 'internal customer' of the buying department. A BPR consultant would possibly recommend that the individual should re-order supplies direct from the external supplier, and the intermediary function of the buying department should be scrapped. In this way, the individual would become his own supplier. In theory, this should simplify and speed up the buying process.

  Similarly, if the users of a computer system currently use the services of a help desk to sort out problems with using the system, a BPR recommendation might be that the team should take on the responsibility itself for system maintenance.

- The **decision points for controlling the process should be located where the work is done**. The people who do the work should also be the people who manage it. The distinction between managers and other employees, for the purposes of operating a process, should not exist.

6.3 BPR and empowerment of employees

Changes introduced by BPR will often involve the 'empowerment' of individual employees. This means giving an employee the 'power' to make decisions, without having to ask a supervisor or manager first. Similarly, junior operational managers may be empowered to take decisions without having to ask for the approval of a senior manager.

Empowerment of employees and junior managers has implications for management accounting systems and IT systems. If employees and junior operational managers are given authority to make certain operational decisions themselves, they need immediate access to relevant information in order to make a sensible decision.

This will probably require a management accounting system that provides:

- immediate access to information and
- information that is easy to find and easy to understand, for individuals with a non-financial background.

6.4 Conducting a BPR exercise

A BPR exercise seeks to transform the way in which a process is performed, with the aim of performing it better – more effectively, efficiently or economically.

In a BPR exercise, investigators (usually management consultants) will look at all the activities that are involved in performing the process under review. They might consider why each activity is performed, and what value it provides. Having investigated the existing process, the investigators will consider:

- whether it can be radically re-designed, so as to achieve the same results but more cheaply and efficiently, or – more usually –
- whether it can be radically re-designed to achieve even better results, perhaps more cheaply and efficiently.

The focus should be on the **outcome** from the process, and **how this affects customer satisfaction** and **how it adds value**.

A process is a series of activities. A BPR exercise into a food catering service would be looking for ways in which the customer can be provided with the product or service they expect, but in a cheaper and more effective way.

- Can the service or product provided in a way that increases customer satisfaction? Can the quality of the service or product be improved by changing the process?

- Can the product or service be provided in a way that is more convenient to the customer, or quicker?
- Can the process be carried out at a lower cost, without reducing customer satisfaction?
- Activities that do not add value should be eliminated.

Some of the features of changes that might be introduced by a BPR project include the following:

- The new process will often involve delegating more responsibility to employees who deal directly with suppliers and customers. In some cases, it might involve outsourcing – paying an external supplier to carry out some activities instead of performing the activities with the entity's own staff.
- Information should be captured once, at source, and made available to everyone who needs it through an efficient IT system.
- The need for checks and controls is often reduced by improving the quality of the process. Checking and controlling are activities that add no value.
- Employees might be required to perform several different tasks, not just one specialised task.

 Example

A food catering company provides meals at lunchtime to a large number of schools and workplaces. Before a BPR exercise, meals were provided as follows:

Each school or workplace had a kitchen, where the food was prepared and cooked. Staff included a trained chef at each location. Meals were served to individuals at their table by waitresses, who cleared up the used plates and cutlery for cleaning.

The BPR exercise discovered that what mattered most to 'customers' was getting a meal that they could enjoy but eat quickly. Speed was a key requirement of the meals service.

As a result of the BPR exercise, the following changes were introduced. All food for schools and workplaces in a local area were prepared and cooked centrally by a highly-qualified chef. This improved the quality of the meals. The meals were then delivered to each school or workplace ready-cooked, and the food was then heated up on site at the appropriate time. 'Customers' were asked to queue for their meals rather than have waitress service. This made the process of providing the meals much quicker. Finally, disposable plates and cutlery were introduced, removing the need for cleaning the dishes at the end of the mealtime.

As a result of the changes, 'customers' received better-quality meals that they were able to obtain and eat more quickly. Non-value adding activities – a waitress service and cleaning the dishes – were removed from the process.

6.5   BPR projects: radical solutions

BPR projects are often led by external business consultants. They look at a particular process, and consider ways in which its purpose or objective could be achieved better in a completely different way. The aim of a BPR project is to design a completely new system of operating that will provide **very large benefits** to the organisation.

For example, BPR consultants may look at the processes that a company uses for inventory control. Its solution may be to get rid of inventory entirely, and switch to a just-in-time purchasing and production system.

Similarly, BPR consultants investigating the branch network of a commercial bank may recommend that the bank should close its branch network entirely, and switch all its customers to on-line banking services.

Some BPR projects recommend solutions that are not quite as radical, but even so, the recommended changes are always substantial. Because the recommended changes are radical, the risks are often high.

CHAPTER

11

Economic, fiscal and environmental factors. Pricing strategy

Contents
1   PEST analysis
2   Pricing strategies
3   Pricing decisions: cost-based pricing methods
4   Pricing decisions: market-based approaches to pricing

> ## PEST analysis
>
> - The elements of PEST analysis
> - PEST analysis at the 'macro' level
> - PEST analysis at the departmental or divisional level
> - Economic and market trends
> - The influence of fiscal policy and monetary policy
> - Environmental and ethical issues

1 PEST analysis

1.1 The elements of PEST analysis

An earlier chapter explained the use of SWOT analysis in strategic planning. A part of SWOT analysis is the analysis of opportunities and threats in the business environment. PEST analysis is a technique that can be used to assess the influence and impact of environmental factors on an entity, its business strategies, its competitive position and its performance.

In your examination, you might be required to analyse the business environment of a company, and comment on factors that could influence its future strategies. PEST analysis can provide a useful framework for this type of analysis.

PEST analysis is used as a structured approach to analysing the influence of external factors on an organisation or system. The name 'PEST' relates to four categories that are used to analyse these external factors:

- **P** – Political influences
- **E** – Economic influences
- **S** – Sociological/cultural influences
- **T** – Technological influences

This approach to analysis is also called:

- SLEPT analysis, when 'legal influences' are added as a separate category of influences, or
- PESTLE analysis when 'legal influences' and 'environmental/ecological influences' are added as separate categories of influence.

1.2 PEST analysis at the 'macro' level

PEST analysis is normally used at the 'macro' level. This means that it is used to analyse environmental influences on the company or organisation as a whole.

- **Political influences**. Political influences include government policy, legislation and regulations (and the possibility of new legislation).

- **Economic influences**. These include the current and expected future estate of the economy, future movements in exchange rates and interest rates, volatility in the market place, and the expected economic growth or decline in an industry.

- **Sociological influences**. These include fashions, trends, social attitudes and habits and demographic changes. For companies involved in IT for example, the growth in the use of computers and communications technology has been a crucially important change in sociological habits in the past few decades.

- **Technological influences**. These are changes in technology that are having or will have an effect on the organisation. Changes in technology can have an impact on the design products and services, processes, IT systems and so on.

1.3   PEST analysis at the departmental or divisional level

PEST analysis can also be used to analyse the influences within an organisation on a department or division within an organisation. The 'environmental' influences in this case are factors outside the department, but relating to the organisation as a whole.

This use of PEST analysis can be helpful for considering the effect of a planned 'business solution' in a department.

The method of analysis is the same as for PEST analysis at the macro level. The tables below give examples of what organisational influences on a department might be.

Political influences	Company policies
	Organisational strategy
	The attitude of the board of directors
	A change in the CEO or any other member of the board of directors
	The management structure in the organisation, and lines of reporting and control
	Management style
Economic influences	Budget spending allocations
	Cross-charging policies (transfer pricing)
	Accounting models and methods used
Sociological influences	Work practices in the organisation
	Expected working hours
	Flexibility allowed in working time
	Autonomy given to individual members of staff
	The likelihood of organisational change and employee attitudes
	The likelihood of redundancies and employee attitudes
Technological influences	The capabilities of existing IT systems

1.4 Economic and market trends

Companies need to be aware of trends in the economy generally and in the markets for their products and services. Many companies operate in a global market place, and they need to monitor global economic developments and market trends.

In other words:

■ Some economic and market factors should influence strategic planning.

■ Unexpected changes in the economy and in particular markets will affect performance, so that performance exceeds expectation or is worse than expected, for reasons outside management's control.

Here are just a few examples.

■ There appears to be a major shift in worldwide production from countries in North America and Europe towards countries such as China and India, where production costs are lower. A multinational company planning its future manufacturing or outsourcing strategy should consider this trend. Decisions about where to produce goods, or whether to purchase (outsource) rather than manufacture internally, will affect the competitive position of the company in the future.

■ There might be a forecast of an economic downturn in the USA. North America is an important market for companies in many other countries of the world. A fall in demand in US markets could have significant consequences for these companies.

■ There is a growing recognition that energy might become more restricted in supply and more expensive in future years. Supply shortages might occur with other natural resources, such as hard wood and fish stocks. Companies might decide to develop strategies to deal with expected shortages in order to remain competitive, such as becoming more energy-efficient and trying to secure future supplies of key materials.

Unexpected changes in economic and market conditions will also affect the performance of companies. For example:

■ If total demand for a product falls unexpectedly, all companies operating in the market should expect profits to be lower than expected. Provided that the market is still profitable, companies should expect to maintain their percentage share of total market sales (in other words, maintain their competitive strength).

■ A company might have a growth strategy, expecting to achieve large increases in sales and profitability. The success of this strategy might depend on having access to new capital funding, in order to finance the growth in business. The success of this strategy might be affected by an unexpected shortage of capital in the markets of equities and debt capital, or by an unexpected increase in the cost of new finance.

■ The profitability of a multinational company might be affected by changes in an important foreign exchange rate. For example, if a UK company sells its products in the US markets, and prices its goods in dollars, its profitability (measured in pounds sterling) would be affected by a fall in the value of the dollar against the pound.

1.5   The influence of fiscal policy and monetary policy

Fiscal policy refers to government policy on taxation, government spending and government borrowing. Monetary policy refers to government efforts to control the national economy by controlling interest rates or the exchange rate.

The strategic decisions of companies, and their performance, can be significantly affected by fiscal and monetary policy. For example:

- The profitability of companies is affected by taxation. Changes in tax rules and rates of taxation will have an impact on company profits.

- Increases in government spending will benefit companies that supply goods or services to the government.

- A government decision to increase interest rates will raise the cost of new borrowing and existing variable rate borrowing. It will also (possibly) reduce the willingness of customers to borrow and spend, which means that the total market demand for products might fall.

1.6   Environmental and ethical issues

Stakeholder groups

A stakeholder in an entity is a person who has an interest in what the entity does and how it performs. In a company, the main stakeholders are the equity shareholders, who have a direct interest in the profitability of the company, the dividends that it pays and the share price.

There are other stakeholders. The influence of these stakeholders on strategic planning and performance will vary between different entities. Some stakeholder groups are more influential than others. Stakeholder groups include:

- Employees, whose interests are jobs, job security, pay, working conditions, and so on.

- Suppliers, whose interests are maintaining a continuing profitable business relationship.

- Customers, whose interest arises because they buy goods or services from the company.

- The government, whose interests include revenues from taxation and the effect of company actions on employment (or unemployment), consumer interests and economic growth.

- Pressure groups. Some companies are strongly influenced by consumer groups and other pressure groups. In the UK for example, there are pressure groups for the protection of the environment, animal rights activists, groups opposed to genetically-modified foods, and so on.

Although the main objective of a company might be to increase the wealth of shareholders, strategy might also be influenced by the demands and expectations of other stakeholders.

- Senior management might agree to improve pay and working conditions for employees, even though this will affect profitability.

- A company might choose to develop long-term strategic relationships with key suppliers, even though this might result in higher material costs in the short term.

- Companies might sometimes be forced to agree to the demands of pressure groups, in order to avoid damage to their reputation and a loss of customer loyalty.

Ethical issues

Ethical issues can affect the choice of strategy and business performance in two basic ways.

- Senior management might promote a culture of ethical behaviour, and expect all its employees to act in an ethical manner. An entity will never behave in an ethical way unless senior management give the lead. This is often referred to as the 'tone at the top'.

- Unethical behaviour might damage a company's reputation, with the result that the company suffers a loss of customers and falling sales demand. Employees might also prefer to work for an ethical organisation than for an organisation with a reputation for unethical behaviour.

There are several aspects to ethical behaviour.

- For individuals, ethical business behaviour means dealing honestly and in an open manner with other people.

- For companies and other organisations, ethical behaviour can mean:

  - acting fairly as an employer and showing concern for the welfare of employees

  - contributing to the well-being of society, for example, providing financial support to local communities

  - refusing to deal with suppliers who use slave labour or child labour

  - showing concern for the environment and 'sustainable business'.

It might be argued that ethical behaviour can have an effect on business performance. There are two sides to this argument:

- Ethical behaviour might improve the reputation of a company and make customers more willing to buy goods from it (and make employees more willing to work for it).

- On the other hand, ethical behaviour might have a cost, in terms of higher employee costs, higher purchase costs from suppliers, higher expenditures on measures to protect the environment from pollution, and so on.

Pricing strategies

- Market position and pricing strategies
- Cost leadership
- Product differentiation
- Product differentiation and market segmentation
- Niche marketing
- Management information and pricing strategies

---

2 Pricing strategies

2.1 Market position and pricing strategies

A business entity that competes in its markets should develop a strategy that will enable it to compete successfully. It should 'position' itself in the market, and offer customers a combination of price and other product features (such as product quality) that will appeal to a sufficiently large part of the market.

In most competitive markets, it is important to be different, and to be seen by customers to be different.

Pricing is an important element in choosing a strategy for market position, and there are three broad categories of pricing strategy/market positioning strategy. These are:

- cost leadership
- product differentiation
- niche marketing.

2.2 Cost leadership

A cost leadership strategy is a strategy based on being the cheapest supplier of a product or service to the market, and to charge the lowest prices. The aim of low pricing is to gain the biggest share of the total market, and make profits by selling in large volumes.

For a cost leadership strategy to succeed, it is essential to minimise costs, so that the entity is able to supply the product or service at a lower price than competitors.

The main problem with this strategy is that only one company can be the cheapest producer. So if three companies, say, all have a cost leadership strategy, only one will succeed. The other two might be able to sell their products at the same low price as the cost leader, but their profits will be lower because their costs are higher.

A successful cost leadership strategy will reduce unit costs to a level where it is difficult for any other company to compete on the basis of price.

2.3   Product differentiation

A product differentiation strategy is an alternative to a cost leadership strategy. It is appropriate for business entities that cannot or do not want to be the cost leader in their market.

With a product differentiation strategy, a company seeks to offer customers a product that is different from the similar product offered by its competitors. A product or service can be made 'different' in several ways.

- It might be better in **quality and design**. The quality of a product or service can be reinforced by the use of **brand names**. Customers will often consider some brands to be better in quality than others.

- In the case of a service, a company might include **different features** in the service that it provides. For example, mobile telephone operators and providers of broadband services offer different 'packages' to customers.

- Similarly, a product might be offered with special features, such as a five-year guarantee.

- It might be provided to customers in a different way. For example, a bank might offer banking services by the internet. A small food store might compete with a large supermarket by opening later at night or earlier in the morning.

- It might offer faster delivery.

By offering products or services that are different, a company tries to appeal to some of the customers in the market. By offering something different, it can charge higher prices than the company that is the cost leader in the market. Through higher prices, it can achieve its strategic targets for profit and return on capital.

2.4   Product differentiation and market segmentation

A market segment is a section of the total market. A market might be divided into several large segments. For example, the total market for cars is divided into a market for family saloon cars, a market for two-seater sports cars, a market for low-cost town cars, a market for '4 × 4s' and so on. Similarly, the market for clothing is divided into markets for men's clothing, women's clothing, children's clothing and infant clothing, and so on.

Companies might concentrate on a particular segment of the total market. Within their chosen market segment (or segments) they might have a strategy of cost leadership for that segment, or product differentiation within the market segment.

2.5   Niche marketing

A niche in a room is a corner of the room, set aside from the main part of the room. In a market, a niche market is a small part of the total market, which is set aside and different from the main market. A niche could be described as a small market segment.

A niche market might have a sufficiently large number of potential customers to make it worthwhile for a company to develop products or services especially for that niche. For example, a food manufacturer might specialise in making pasta. A radio station might concentrate on attracting an audience in a particular age range such as under 20s, or in a particular local area.

A company that chooses to follow a niche market strategy should adopt a further strategy of either cost leadership or product differentiation within that niche. (This is the same as for companies that operate in a market segment, who should try to be cost leaders in their market segment or else differentiate their products from those of competitors.)

2.6 . Management information and pricing strategies

In order to decide on a suitable pricing strategy and market position strategy, a company needs information about the market, such as:

■ the total size of the market

■ expected changes in the future size of the market

■ the prices charged by the market leader

■ how products are services are differentiated by other competitors, and the prices they charge

■ the importance of price to customers in the market.

Pricing decisions: cost-based pricing methods

- Pricing decisions and pricing strategy
- Full cost plus pricing
- Marginal cost plus pricing (mark-up pricing)
- Return on investment (ROI) pricing
- Opportunity cost pricing (minimum pricing)
- Limitations of cost-based pricing

---

3 Pricing decisions: cost-based pricing methods

3.1 Pricing decisions and pricing strategy

Entities have to make decisions about pricing the goods they sell and the services they provide. Pricing decisions might be influenced by economic and market factors. Pricing strategies might be used as a way of achieving a competitive position in the market.

There are various methods of pricing, and the most suitable method of pricing depends on the circumstances. In your examination you might be required to discuss different approaches to making pricing decisions.

There are two approaches to making pricing decisions:

- calculating a price on the basis of **cost**
- deciding a price on the basis of **market factors**, such as prices charged by competitors for similar items, and the prices that customers are willing to pay.

3.2 Full cost plus pricing

With full cost plus pricing, a mark-up or profit margin is added to the fully-absorbed cost of the item to obtain a selling price.

Profit is expressed as either:

- a percentage of the full cost (a profit 'mark-up') or
- a percentage of the sales price (a 'profit margin').

	$
Variable production costs	600
Other variable costs	200
Absorbed overheads:	
Production overheads absorbed	800
Non-production overheads absorbed	300
Full cost	1,900
Profit (added to full cost)	380
Selling price	2,280

The profit therefore represents net profit from the sale.

When full cost plus pricing is used to calculate a selling price for standard units of a product, the selling price per unit may be calculated as:

$$\frac{[\text{Total budgeted production costs} + \text{Total budgeted non - production costs}] + \text{Pr}\mathit{ofit}}{\text{Budgeted sales units}}$$

The profit is the required percentage mark-up on total cost.

Notes on calculating the profit:

■ If the mark-up is x% of full cost, the selling price is Full cost + x%.

■ If the profit margin is y% of the sales price, the profit is [y/(100 – y)] × Full cost

Advantages of full cost plus pricing

A business entity might have an idea of the percentage profit margin it would like to earn. It might therefore decide the average profit mark-up on cost that it would like to earn from sales, as a general guideline for its pricing decisions. This can be useful for businesses that carry out a large amount of **contract work** or **jobbing work**, for which individual job or contract prices must be quoted regularly to prospective customers and there is no obvious 'fair market' price.

The percentage mark-up or profit margin does not have to be a fixed percentage figure. It can be varied to suit the circumstances, such as demand conditions in the market and what the customer is prepared to pay.

There are also other possible advantages in using full cost plus pricing:

■ If the budgeted sales volume is achieved, sales revenue will cover all costs and there will be a profit.

■ It is useful for justifying price rises to customers, when an increase in price occurs as a consequence of an increase in costs.

Disadvantages of full cost plus pricing

The main disadvantage of cost plus pricing is that it is calculated on the basis of cost, without any consideration of market conditions, such as competitors' prices.

■ Cost plus pricing fails to allow for the fact that when the sales demand for a product is affected by its selling price, there is a profit-maximising combination of price and demand. A cost plus based approach to pricing is unlikely to arrive at the profit-maximising price for the product.

■ In most markets, prices must be adjusted to market and demand conditions. The pricing decision cannot be made on a cost basis only.

There are also other disadvantages:

- The choice of profit margin or mark-up is arbitrary. How is it decided?
- When the entity makes and sells different types of products, the calculation of a full cost becomes a problem, due to the weaknesses of absorption costing. The method of apportioning costs between the different products in absorption costing is largely subjective. This affects the calculation of full cost and the selling price.

Example

Entity Q makes two products, product X and product Y. These products are both made by the same work force and in the same department. The budgeted fixed costs are $900,000. Variable costs per unit are as follows:

		Product X		Product Y
Direct costs		$		$
Materials		6		6
Labour	(2 hours)	12	(3 hours)	18
Expenses	(1 machine hour)	6	(1 machine hour)	6
		24		30

Budgeted production and sales are 15,000 units of product X and 10,000 units of product Y.

Required

Calculate the sale prices for each unit of product X and product Y which give a profit margin of 20% on the full cost, if overheads are absorbed on the following bases:

(a) on a direct labour hour basis

(b) on a machine hour basis.

Answer

(a) **Direct labour hour basis**

Budgeted direct labour hours = (15,000 × 2) + (10,000 × 3) = 60,000 hours.

Overhead absorption rate = $900,000/60,000 = $15 per direct labour hour.

	Product X	Product Y
Direct costs	$	$
Materials	6.00	6
Labour	12.00	18
Expenses	6.00	6
	24.00	30
Absorbed overhead	30.00	45
Full cost	54.00	75
Mark-up (20%)	10.80	15
Selling price/unit	64.80	90

The budgeted profit would be (15,000 × $10.80) + (10,000 × $15) = $312,000.

(b)   **Machine hour basis**

Budgeted machine hours = (15,000 × 1) + (10,000 × 1) = 25,000 hours.

Overhead absorption rate = $900,000/25,000 = $36 per machine hour.

	Product X	Product Y
Direct costs	$	$
Materials	6.00	6.00
Labour	12.00	18.00
Expenses	6.00	6.00
	24.00	30.00
Absorbed overhead	36.00	36.00
Full cost	60.00	66.00
Mark-up (20%)	12.00	13.20
Selling price/unit	72.00	79.20

The budgeted profit would be (15,000 × $12) + (10,000 × $13.20) = $312,000.

However, the different bases of absorbing overheads would give a significantly different full cost for each product, and a different selling price. It must be doubtful whether the entity can sell 15,000 units of product X and 10,000 units of product Y, no matter which prices are chosen.

3.3   Marginal cost plus pricing (mark-up pricing)

With marginal cost plus pricing, also called mark-up pricing, a mark-up or profit margin is added to the marginal cost in order to obtain a selling price.

	$
Variable production costs	600
Other variable costs	200
Marginal cost	800
Mark-up (added to marginal cost)	400
Selling price	1,200

The mark-up represents contribution.

When marginal cost plus pricing is used to calculate a selling price for standard units of a product, the selling price per unit may be calculated as:

$$\frac{\text{Budgeted total variable costs (production and non-production costs) + Mark-up}}{\text{Budgeted sales units}}$$

The total mark-up is the required percentage mark-up on total budgeted variable costs.

Advantages of marginal cost plus pricing

The advantages of a marginal cost plus approach are as follows:

■ It is useful in some industries such as retailing, where prices might be set by adding a mark-up to the purchase cost of items bought for resale. The size of the mark-up can be varied to reflect demand conditions. For example, in a competitive market, a lower mark-up might be added to high-volume items.

- It draws management attention to contribution and the effects of higher or lower sales volumes on profit. This can be particularly useful for short-term pricing decisions, such as pricing decisions for a market penetration policy (described later).

- It is more appropriate where fixed costs are low and variable costs are high.

Disadvantages of marginal cost plus pricing

A marginal cost plus approach to pricing also has disadvantages.

- Although the size of the mark-up can be varied according to demand conditions, marginal cost plus pricing is a cost-based pricing method, and does not properly take market conditions into consideration.

- It ignores fixed overheads in the pricing decision. Prices must be high enough to make a profit after covering all fixed costs. Cost-based pricing decisions therefore cannot ignore fixed costs altogether.

3.4   Return on investment (ROI) pricing

This method of pricing might be used in a decentralised environment where the investment centre is required to meet a target return on capital employed. Prices might be set to achieve a target percentage return on the capital invested.

With return on investment pricing, the selling price per unit may be calculated as:

$$\frac{\text{Budgeted total costs of the division} + [\text{Target ROI\%} \times \text{Capital employed}]}{\text{Budgeted volume}}$$

- When the investment centre makes and sells a single product, the budgeted volume is sales volume.

- When the investment centre makes and sells several different products, budgeted volume might be production volume in hours, and the mark-up added to cost is then a mark-up for the number of hours worked on the product item.

- Alternatively, the budgeted volume might be sales revenue, and the mark-up is then calculated as a percentage of the selling price (a form of full cost plus pricing).

Advantages of ROI pricing

The advantages of an ROI approach to pricing are as follows:

- ROI pricing is a method of deciding an appropriate profit margin for cost plus pricing.

- The target ROI can be varied to allow for differing levels of business risk.

Disadvantages of ROI pricing

An ROI approach to pricing also has disadvantages.

- Like all cost-based pricing methods, it does not take market conditions into sufficient consideration, and the prices that customers will be willing to pay.

- Since it is a form of full cost plus pricing, it shares most of the other disadvantages as full cost plus pricing.

Example

A manufacturer is about to launch a new product.

The non-current assets needed for production will cost $4,000,000 and working capital requirements are estimated at $800,000.

The expected annual sales volume is 40,000 units.

Variable production costs are $60 per unit.

Fixed production costs will be $600,000 each year and annual fixed non-production costs will be $200,000.

Required

(a) Calculate selling price using:

    (i) full cost plus 20%

    (ii) marginal cost plus 40%

    (iii) pricing based on a target return on investment of 10% per year.

(b) If actual sales are only 20,000 units and the selling price is set at full cost plus 20%, what will the profit be for the year?

Answer

(a)

(i) Full cost plus 20%	$ per unit
Variable cost	60
Fixed costs ($600,000 + $200,000)/40,000 units	20
Full cost	80
Mark-up: 20% on cost	16
Selling price	96

(ii) Marginal cost plus 40%	$ per unit
Variable cost	60
Mark-up: 40% on variable cost	24
Selling price	84

(iii) Target ROI pricing	$
Non-current assets	4,000,000
Working capital	800,000
Capital employed	4,800,000
Profit required ($4,800,000 × 10%)	480,000
Profit required per unit (40,000 units)	$12

	$
Variable cost	60
Fixed costs (see above)	20
Full cost	80
Profit	12
Selling price	92

(b)

Profit for the year	$
Sales (20,000 units × $96)	1,920,000
Variable costs (20,000 units × $60)	(1,200,000)
Fixed costs	(800,000)
Net loss	(80,000)

3.5 Opportunity cost pricing (minimum pricing)

Opportunity cost pricing might be used for pricing a product or a service in special circumstances. In some circumstances, an entity might be prepared to charge a price for an item that leaves it no worse off than if it were to choose the next most profitable course of action. This is the marginal price or **minimum price** of an item.

A minimum price of an item is the total of the **relevant costs** of making and selling it.

A profit margin can be added to the minimum price, to obtain an opportunity cost price. The profit margin added to the relevant costs is the additional profit the entity will earn from selling the item, instead of choosing the next most profitable course of action.

■ Minimum price = Relevant costs of making and selling the item

■ If a margin is added for incremental profit:

Price = Relevant costs + Profit margin.

If resources are in scarce supply (limiting factors), minimum prices must include an allowance for the opportunity cost of using the resources for making and selling the item.

 Example

Southampton is a shipbuilding company. It uses two materials, steel and fibreglass.

It needs to complete a shipping order using 500 tonnes of steel and 1,000 tonnes of fibreglass.

The work force will have to work 2,000 hours on making the boat: 1,200 hours will be in the assembly process and the remainder will be in the finishing (painting the boat and other finishing tasks).

Southampton will quote a price of relevant cost plus 50%.

Southampton has 200 tonnes of steel held in inventory. This originally cost $10 per tonne. It now has a current price of $12 and could be sold for $8 per tonne. Southampton no longer produces steel boats and has no other use for steel. It only produces fibreglass boats on a regular basis.

There are 400 tonnes of fibreglass held in inventory. This originally cost $20 per tonne. It currently has a purchase price of $23 per tonne and a selling price of $15 per tonne. (Selling price and net realisable value can be assumed to be the same figure).

All labour is paid $4 per hour. To complete the contract on time, labour for the finishing process will have to be transferred from other work which produces contribution at a rate of $3 per hour (after labour costs). There is currently surplus capacity for assembly labour amounting to 1,000 hours for the duration of the contract. Owing to other work requirements, however, any further assembly labour hours in excess of these 1,000 hours will have to be hired on a temporary basis at a rate of $5 per hour.

Required
Calculate the price Southampton will quote on the contract.

 Answer

		$
Steel	– lost net realisable value (200 × $8)	1,600
	– purchases (300 × $12)	3,600
Fibreglass	(1,000 × $23)	23,000
Finishing labour	– cost (800 × $4)	3,200
	– lost contribution (800 × $3)	2,400
Assembly labour	(200 × $5)	1,000
Relevant cost		34,800
Mark-up (50%)		17,400
Quoted price		52,200

3.6 Limitations of cost-based pricing

Cost-based approaches to pricing all ignore external market factors such as the prices that customers are prepared to pay and what competitors are charging for rival products or services.

Cost-based pricing does not ensure a profit, because sales volume must be sufficient to cover all fixed costs, and not even full cost plus pricing can ensure that sufficient sales volumes will be achieved to cover all fixed costs.

Pricing decisions: market-based approaches to pricing

- The economist's demand curve and profit-maximising model
- Using mathematical models to decide the profit-maximising price
- Using a demand curve to calculate break-even points
- The product life cycle and pricing
- Market skimming prices
- Market penetration prices
- Price discrimination (differential pricing)
- Loss leaders
- Going rate pricing
- Target pricing

4 Pricing decisions: market-based approaches to pricing

There are various methods of pricing based on market conditions and marketing strategies.

4.1 The economist's demand curve and profit-maximising model

The economist's model can be used to identify the profit-maximising selling price and sales volume. There are two sets of market conditions to consider:

- a market in which there is perfect competition
- a market in which there is imperfect competition.

Perfect competition

When there is perfect competition in the market, there are many different suppliers competing to sell identical products. In the real world, perfect competition is rare, but markets with features similar to those of perfect competition include foreign exchange markets and some commodities markets.

In perfect competition:

- an individual firm is unable to influence the price for its own goods, because identical products are obtainable from competitors
- the selling price in the market is determined by the forces of supply and demand
- the selling price in the market is the price that all suppliers in the market must accept to remain competitive: every supplier can produce and sell as much output as the want to and sell it at this price.

Suppliers in a perfectly competitive market are 'price takers', and they will maximise their profit by:

■ producing output up to the limit of their output capacity, provided that the marginal cost of producing extra units is less than the sales price for the units; or

■ producing output up to the point where its **marginal costs** of producing and selling more units is higher than the **marginal revenue** from selling them at the ruling market price.

Imperfect competition

When there is imperfect competition in the market, a supplier has more influence over the selling price that it charges for its products. Imperfect competition exists when there are relatively few suppliers in the market, and suppliers seek to differentiate their products from those of their competitors.

The effect of imperfect competition is that firms are able to decide their selling prices (they are 'price takers'). However, the higher the sales price, the lower the sales demand for their product. In microeconomics terms, firms in imperfectly-competitive markets face a 'downward-sloping demand curve'.

In the economist's model, a firm maximises its profits by setting the sales price at a level where:

[The marginal revenue from selling an extra unit] = [The marginal cost of making and selling the unit].

In other words, **profit is maximised where MR = MC**.

You might be expected to calculate the formula for MR, given a demand curve.

Calculating a demand curve

A demand curve is a graph showing the quantity demanded at different sales prices. A straight-line demand curve has the basic formula.

$P = a - bQ$

Where

P = the sales price
Q = the quantity demanded
a = the sales price when the quantity demanded is 0
b = a constant value.

Example

The sales demand curve for a product is straight-line. When the sales price is $0, the sales demand is 80,000 units. When the sales price is $40, sales demand is 0 units. For every $0.50 increase in price, the sales demand falls by 1,000 units.

The demand curve is therefore:

$P = 40 - (0.50/1,000)Q$
$P = 40 - 0.0005Q$

Note

For every $0.50 increase in price, sales demand changes by 1,000 units; therefore b in the formula is $0.50/1,000 = 0.0005$.

Calculating MR

The value of marginal revenue is found from the formula for total revenue.

- Total revenue = Price × Quantity
- The price is represented by the demand curve, $P = a - bQ$
- Total revenue = $(a - bQ) Q$, = $aQ - bQ^2$
- Marginal revenue MR is found using differential calculus.

However, if you are not familiar with differential calculus, whenever there is a total revenue formula:

- Total revenue (TR) = $aQ - bQ^2$
- Marginal revenue = $a - (2b)Q$

Example

Returning to the previous example:

- the demand curve is $P = 40 - 0.0005Q$
- TR = $(40 - 0.0005Q)Q = 40Q - 0.0005Q^2$
- MR = $40 - (2 \times 0.0005)Q = 40 - 0.001Q$.

Profit-maximisation, MR = MC

It is normally assumed that total costs consist of fixed and variable costs; therefore the formula for total costs is:

$TC = FC + vQ$

Where
FC = fixed costs
V = the variable cost per unit sold
Q = the number of units sold

Whenever the total cost line consists of fixed and variable costs, the marginal cost MC is the variable cost, so MC = v.

Example

Suppose that the monthly demand curve for a product is P = 40 – 0.0005Q. Fixed costs per month are $500,000 and the variable cost per unit is $2.

Required

Calculate the sales price and output quantity that maximise the profit each month, and calculate the amount of that profit.

Answer

MR = 40 – 0.001Q
MC = 2
Profit is maximised when MR = MC
40 – 0.001Q = 2
0.001Q = 38
Q = 38,000 units.
The sales price when Q = 38,000 is:
P = 40 – 0.0005(38,000) = $21.

	$
Sales (38,000 × $21)	798,000
Variable costs (38,000 × $2)	76,000
Contribution	722,000
Fixed costs	500,000
Profit	222,000

4.2 Using mathematical models to decide the profit-maximising price

In order to use a mathematical model to decide the profit-maximising selling price, at the price where MC = MR, the following conditions must be met:

■ There must be a reliable estimate of both the cost function and the sales revenue function. It is often possible to prepare an estimate of total cost as fixed costs plus variable costs (TC = F + Vx, where x is the number of units sold). However, it is much more difficult to obtain a reliable estimate of the demand function, and express the relationship between price and quantity demanded as a mathematical formula.

■ The purpose of using a mathematical model would be to decide the selling price for a product. This is only possible if the selling price is an 'endogenous' variable in the model.

  - An **endogenous variable** is a variable in the model that is under the control of management. It would normally be assumed, for example, that the variable costs are an endogenous variable, and that management can make sure that actual variable costs can be controlled at the level stated in the model.

  - An **exogenous variable**, in contrast, is a variable in a model that is outside the control of management. Exogenous variables might include variables such as long-term market trends or sales tax (value added tax) on the product. Changes in an exogenous variable can sometimes affect the value of an endogenous variable.

When using a mathematical model, management make decisions about the value of an endogenous variable, to maximise or optimise the value of the results from the model. For example, a mathematical model to determine the price where MC = MR would be used to decide the selling price. This assumes that the selling price is an endogenous variable in the model.

In reality, the selling price may be partly an endogenous variable and partly an exogenous variable. Management may be able to decide the selling price for its product (therefore selling price = endogenous variable), but the price they can charge may be restricted by considerations of the prices that competitors are charging for rival products (therefore selling price = exogenous variable). Since selling price may not be an entirely endogenous variable in the model, it is questionable whether using a mathematical model to decide the selling price for a product would be a useful exercise.

4.3 Using a demand curve to calculate break-even points

Problems involving marginal costs and marginal revenues can be fairly complex, particularly if you are unfamiliar with the mathematical techniques. Demand curves can be used to calculate a break-even selling price as well as a profit-maximising sales price. Study the following example carefully.

Example

The sales demand for Product X will depend on the price charged for the product. An estimate of the sales demand function is:

$$P = 80 - 0.0001Q$$

where P is the sales price per unit (in $) and Q is the annual sales quantity.

The variable cost of the product is $8 and annual fixed costs will be $11,520,000.

Required
(a)   Calculate the price at which product X should be sold in order to maximise profit for the year. Calculate the quantity of units that will be sold in the year.
(b)   Calculate the annual profit that will be made from selling product X.
(c)   There are two break-even points. One is below the profit-maximising output level and one is above the profit-maximising output level.
The total profit function can be expressed as a quadratic equation:

$$y = ax^2 + bx + c$$

The break-even points can be calculated as the values for x that solve the following equation:

$$x = \frac{-b +/ - \sqrt{b^2 - 4ac}}{2a}$$

Calculate the levels of output and the associated selling prices for product X at which the company would break even.

Answer

(a)

Total revenue = P × Q = (80 – 0.0001Q)Q = 80Q – 0.0001Q^2

Marginal revenue = 80 – (2 × 0.0001 × Q) = 80 – 0.0002Q.

Marginal cost = variable cost per unit = 8.

Profit is maximised where MR = MC:

80 – 0.0002Q = 8

0.0002Q = 72

Q = 360,000 units.

At this volume of sales, P = 80 – 0.0001 (360,000) = $44.

(b)

	$
Sales (360,000 × $44)	15,840,000
Variable costs (360,000 × $8)	2,880,000
Contribution	12,960,000
Fixed costs	11,520,000
Profit	1,440,000

The annual profit will be $1,440,000.

(c) Profit = Total revenue – Total costs

= (80Q – 0.0001Q^2) – (8Q + 11,520,000)

= – 0.0001Q^2 + 72Q – 11,520,000

At break-even point, profit = 0:

– 0.0001Q^2 + 72Q – 11,520,000 = 0

Re-arranging:

0.0001Q^2 – 72Q + 11,520,000 = 0

The break-even points can be calculated as the values for x that solve the following equation:

$$x = \frac{-b +/ - \sqrt{b^2 - 4ac}}{2a}$$

Remember that – (– 72) = + 72. (Minus a minus figure = 'plus'.)

$$Q = \frac{+72 +/ - \sqrt{(72)^2 - 4(0.0001)(11,520,000)}}{2(0.0001)}$$

$$Q = \frac{+72 +/ - \sqrt{5,184 - 4,608}}{0.0002}$$

The two break-even points are now calculated as follows:

(1) $Q = (+ 72 + 24)/0.0002 = 480,000$.

       $P = 80 - 0.0001(480,000) = \$32$.

or

(2) $Q = (+ 72 - 24)/0.0002 = 240,000$.

       $P = 80 - 0.0001(240,000) = \$56$.

Proof:

Break-even point 1 P = 32, Q = 480,000	$	Break-even point 2 P = 56, Q = 240,000	$
Sales	15,360,000	Sales	13,440,000
Variable costs (× $8)	3,840,000	Variable costs (× $8)	1,920,000
Contribution	11,520,000	Contribution	11,520,000
Fixed costs	11,520,000	Fixed costs	11,520,000
Profit	0	Profit	0

4.4   The product life cycle and pricing

As a product goes through the different stages of its life cycle, the pricing policy might be changed.

- **Introduction stage**. During the introduction stage, the product is introduced to the market. If the product is new, and there are no rival products on the market, there is a choice between a market skimming policy for pricing or a market penetration policy. These are explained below.

- **Growth stage**. During the growth stage of the life cycle, demand for the product increases rapidly, but more competitors enter the market. If the market is competitive, each firm might have to lower its prices to win a share of the growing market. However, because sales demand is strong, prices and profit margins are likely to be fairly high (although falling). Some companies might try to identify a specialist 'niche' of the market, where they have more control over pricing of their products. Similarly, companies might try to keep prices higher by differentiating their product from those of competitors on the basis of quality or other distinguishing features (such as design differences).

- **Maturity stage**. When a product reaches the maturity stage of its life cycle, total sales demand in the market becomes stable, but the product may become a 'commodity'. Firms must then compete for market share, often by cutting prices. Companies might use product differentiation strategies to keep the price of their product higher than it might otherwise be, but prices generally will be lower than during the growth stage of the life cycle.

- **Decline**. Eventually the market demand for a product declines. When sales demand falls, companies leave the market. Those that remain keep on selling the product as long as they can make a profit. Prices might remain very low. In some cases, however, a product might acquire 'rarity value', allowing companies to raise prices. However, since unit costs will also be higher, it is still difficult to make a profit.

When a business entity is trying to decide whether or not to develop and launch a new product, the **expected sales demand over its life cycle** should be taken into consideration in the DCF analysis.

4.5 Market skimming prices

When a company introduces a product to the market for the first time, it might choose a pricing policy based on 'skimming the market'.

When a new product is introduced to the market, a few customers might be prepared to pay a high price to obtain the product, in order to be one of the first people to have it. Buying the new product gives the buyer prestige, so the buyer will pay a high price to get it.

In order to increase sales demand, the price must be gradually reduced, but with a skimming policy, the price is reduced slowly and by small amounts each time. The contribution per unit with a skimming policy is very high.

To charge high prices, the firm might have to spend heavily on advertising and other marketing expenditure.

Market skimming will probably be more effective for new 'high technology' products, such as digital televisions and plasma screen televisions. Other examples in the past have been personal computers and laptop computers.

Firms using market skimming for a new product will have to reduce prices later as new competitors enter market with rival products.

Skimming prices and a product differentiation strategy

It is much more difficult to apply a market skimming pricing policy when competitors have already introduced a rival product to the market. Customers in the market will already have a view of the prices to expect, and might not be persuaded to buy a new version of a product in the market unless its price is lower than prices of existing versions.

However, it may be possible to have a policy of market skimming if it is possible to differentiate a product from its rivals, usually on the basis of quality. This is commonly found in the market for cars, for example, where some manufacturers succeed in keeping prices very high by producing and selling a high-quality product. High-quality cars cost more to produce, and sales demand may be fairly low: however, profits are obtained by charging high prices and earning a high contribution for each unit sold.

4.6 Market penetration prices

Market penetration prices is an alternative pricing policy to market skimming, when a new product is launched onto the market for the first time.

With market penetration pricing, the aim is to set a low selling price for the new product, in order to create a high sales demand as quickly as possible. With a successful penetration pricing strategy, a company might 'capture the market'.

A firm might also use market penetration prices to launch their own version of a product into an established market, with the intention that offering low prices will attract customers and win a substantial share of the market.

Penetration pricing and a cost leadership strategy

A cost leadership market strategy is a strategy of trying to become the lowest-cost producer of a product in the market. Low-cost production is usually achieved through economies of scale and large-scale production and sales volumes.

Penetration pricing is consistent with a cost leadership strategy, because low prices help a company to obtain a large market share, and a large market share means high volumes, economies of scale and lower costs.

4.7 Price discrimination (differential pricing)

With price discrimination (or differential pricing), a firm sells a single identical product in different segments of the market at different prices.

For price discrimination to work successfully, the different market segments must be kept separate. It might be possible to charge different prices for the same product:

- in different geographical areas – for example in the US and in China
- at different times of the day – for example, travel tickets might be priced differently at different times of the day or the week
- to customers in different age groups – for example offering special prices to individuals over a certain age, or to students or to children.

4.8 Loss leaders

Some products might be sold for a short time as 'loss leaders'. This type of pricing is used in retailing, where some products are offered at very low prices (below cost, or possibly below marginal cost) in order to attract customers into the store, where they will also buy other items as well as the low-priced items.

4.9 Going rate pricing

Many firms charge a price that is the 'going rate' in the market. This is a pricing policy for 'price followers'. Companies must often accept the going market price when they produce a fairly standard product (or service) and they are not in a particularly strong competitive position.

4.10   Target pricing

Target pricing has been described in an earlier chapter, in relation to target costing. When a company develops a new product, it might decide during the design stage of development what the price needs to be.

The decision about price may be based on a study of the existing market and prices for similar products. A target price is the price that a company thinks it will have to charge for a new product in order to be competitive in the market.

Having established a target price, the company can then establish a target cost. This is the maximum amount that the new product must cost to make and sell, so that the return on investment from the new product will be sufficient to justify its development.

The designers of the product are then required to design the product so that it costs no more than the target cost, and it can be sold for an appropriate return at the target price.

Target costing is explained in more detail in a later chapter.

CHAPTER

12

Performance measurement systems

Contents
1   Features of performance measurement systems
2   Information for performance measurement
3   Sources of information
4   Recording and processing methods. Management reports

Features of performance measurement systems
■ What is a performance measurement system?
■ The need for performance measurement
■ Management accounting and performance measurement
■ The analysis of costs

1 · Features of performance measurement systems

1.1 What is a performance measurement system?

A performance measurement system is an integral part of a system of planning and control.

■ Corporate objectives are converted into planning targets. Similarly, the objectives of strategic plans are converted into planning targets. A target should be a clear statement of what an entity wants to achieve within a specified period of time. Planning targets are usually quantified, but may be expressed in qualitative terms.

■ Planning targets are set at strategic, tactical and operational management levels.

■ In a well-designed performance management system, all planning targets are consistent with each other, at the strategic, tactical and operational levels.

■ When the business environment is changing, a performance measurement system should provide for the continual re-assessment of planning targets, so that targets can be altered as necessary to meet the changing circumstances.

■ Actual performance, at the strategic, tactical and operational levels should be measured and monitored. Comparing actual performance with targets provides useful control information. Differences between actual performance and targets can be analysed, to establish the causes. Where appropriate, action can be taken to improve performance by dealing with the causes of the poor performance.

■ A performance management system might be linked to a system of rewarding individuals for the successful achievement of planning targets.

1.2 The need for performance measurement

Every managed organisation needs a system of performance measurement.

■ Managers need to understand what they should be trying to achieve. A sense of purpose and direction is provided by plans (strategies, budgets, operational plans and so on), and for each plan there should be objectives and targets. Setting targets for achievement (performance targets) is an essential part of planning.

■ Managers also need to know whether they are successful. The information they need is provided by comparing:

  - their actual results or performance with the performance target, and

  - the performance target with the current forecast of what performance will be.

Targets, forecasts and actual performance should be measured, in order to compare them. Ideally measures of performance should be quantified values (financial or non-financial measures), because numerical measures of performance are easier to compare than non-quantified ('qualitative') measures.

The benefits of performance measurement systems

The advantages of having a formal system of performance measurement can be summarised as follows:

■ A well-structured system of performance measurement clarifies the objectives of the organisation, and shows how departments, work groups and individuals within the organisation contribute to the achievement of those objectives.

■ It establishes agreed measures of activity, based on key success factors.

■ It helps to provide a better understanding of the processes within the organisation, and what each should be trying to achieve.

■ It provides a system for comparing the performance of different organisations or departments.

■ The system establishes performance targets for the organisation's managers, over a suitable time period for achievement.

1.3   Management accounting and performance measurement

Management accounting is an important element in performance measurement systems. Many performance targets are financial in nature, such as achieving targets for return on capital, profits and sales revenue and targets for keeping expenditure under control.

However, a performance measurement system uses a wide range of targets at the strategic, tactical and operational level. Many of these are non-financial targets, and not all targets are quantifiable.

Clearly, a comprehensive management accounting system should therefore provide information for setting targets and measuring actual performance at all levels. It should also provide non-financial information as well as financial information.

If a management accounting system cannot provide all this information to management, managers will have to rely on other information systems in addition to the management accounting system. An entity might then have several different information systems, which is probably inefficient and less effective than a fully co-ordinated management information system.

1.4   The analysis of costs

The analysis of costs is a core feature of management accounting. A management accounting system must be capable of providing reliable and relevant information about costs for purposes of planning, setting targets, performance measurement and control.

- A management accounting system must be able to **analyse how costs should vary** with changes in activity. Understanding cost behaviour is important for planning decisions as well as for analysing actual performance.

- A management accounting system must also be able to report actual performance in a way that identifies the managers who are responsible for the costs or revenues. The **controllability** of costs and performance is also a key issue. Controllability is considered in more detail in the next section.

- A management accounting system should also provide information that enables managers to **assess performance**. Performance can be assessed by:
  - comparing actual performance with the targets
  - comparing current forecasts with the original targets
  - looking at trends and changes in performance over time
  - comparing performance with other entities (benchmarking).

- Information about performance should also make a distinction between what is significant (material) and what is unimportant (immaterial).

Assessing trends

Performance reports may show the changes in performance over a period of time, such as annual growth in sales and profits. The value of measuring changes in a measure of performance over time is that it helps managers to identify trends. When there is an upward or downward trend over time, it might be appropriate to assume that the trend is likely to continue unless action is taken to try changing it.

Materiality

Performance reports should help managers to identify the aspects of performance that appear significant or material. Reports may therefore highlight exceptional or material results. For example:

- Long reports usually begin with an executive summary, where the key aspects of performance are summarised.

- 'Reporting by exception' might be used to report results to management. This is a form of reporting in which only exceptional results are brought to management's attention.

Information for performance measurement

- Classification of costs by cost behaviour
- Classification of costs: controllability
- Responsibility accounting
- Performance reporting and responsibility accounting: problems with the principle of 'controllability'
- Practical difficulties with responsibility accounting
- Non-financial information for measuring performance

2 Information for performance measurement

2.1 Classification of costs by cost behaviour

Costs can be classified according to how they change ('behave') as the volume of activity increases or falls. Costs are classified as variable costs, fixed costs, stepped costs, or semi-fixed and semi-variable costs. Classifying costs in this way is useful for:

- forecasting and budgeting, including cost-volume-profit analysis
- budgetary control (flexible budgets and variance analysis)
- some decision-making.

It is often assumed that total costs of an activity or operation can be measured by a linear function:

$$y = a + bx$$

where:
y = total costs in a period of time
a = fixed costs in the period
b = variable cost per unit of activity (for example per units sold)
x = volume of activity in the period (for example the number of units sold in the period).

You might be required in your examination to estimate a variable cost per unit or a fixed cost per period of time, using a technique such as the high low method or linear regression analysis. Estimating costs using these techniques was described in a previous chapter.

2.2 Classification of costs: controllability

Revenues and costs might be classified as controllable or uncontrollable. A cost is controllable if a manager is able to take action that will alter its amount. Typically, a cost is controllable if action by a manager may result in a reduction in the cost.

However, a cost might be controllable by one manager in an organisation, but not by another. Management information should attribute costs to the managers who can control them

A performance management system should try to identify costs, revenues and investments that are:

■ directly attributable to a division or performance centre within the organisation, and

■ controllable by the manager responsible for the division or performance centre.

However, there are some problems with identifying and measuring controllable costs.

■ Costs that are directly attributable to a department or cost centre might not be controllable by the manager of the department or cost centre. For example, the rental costs of a building used by a department are a directly-attributable fixed cost of the department, but the manager of the department might have no control over the decision about whether the department remains in the building or not. The rental cost is therefore directly attributable, but non-controllable by the manager.

■ Some costs are partly-controllable, not fully controllable. For example, the quantity of materials used by a department might be controllable by its manager, but their purchase price is not controllable if the materials are purchased by a separate buying department. Total material costs depend on both the quantities used and their price. In this situation, quantities would be controllable by one manager and priced by another.

 Example

A business unit employs ten staff who are paid a fixed annual salary. The salary costs are directly attributable to the business unit, and salaries are decided centrally by head office. The manager of the unit has no control over salary levels. However, he should be able to influence the efficiency and effectiveness of the employees who work for him. It is therefore appropriate that the manager should be held accountable for the salary costs of the business unit, and the results achieved by incurring those costs, even though he does not have full control.

Terminology: endogenous variables and exogenous variables

You should note the following terms, which might be unfamiliar to you but might be used in an examination question.

■ **Endogenous variables**: these are factors under the control or influence of management

■ **Exogenous variables**: these are factors that are outside the control or influence of management.

2.3 Responsibility accounting

Responsibility accounting is a method of reporting based on measuring the performance of responsibility centres within an organisation. The manager of a responsibility centre is responsible and accountable for the performance of the centre.

Responsibility accounting is based on the principle that managers should be responsible – and so held accountable – for costs and other aspects of performance over which they have control. Managers should not be held accountable for costs and other matters over which they have no control.

The principle of 'controllability' is therefore a key issue in any system of responsibility accounting.

Cost centres, profit centres and investment centres

This is why, for example, reporting units within an organisation may be:

■ cost centres, where the manager is in a position to control costs, but not sales revenue

■ profit centres, where the manager is in a position to control costs and sales revenue, but is not in a position to control the amount of investment and other investment decisions

■ investment centres, where the manager is in a position to control costs and sales revenue, and also has control over investment decisions affecting the centre.

Within a system for reporting the costs of a centre, a system of responsibility accounting should also try to make a distinction between:

■ costs over which the manager should have short-term control: these are often reported as variable costs and directly-controllable fixed costs (or directly attributable fixed costs)

■ costs over which the manager has some control, but over the longer term rather than the short term

■ costs over which the manager has no control: in some systems of responsibility accounting, centres are not charged at all with any share of general overhead costs that the centre manager cannot control.

There might be a **hierarchy of responsibility centres**.

■ A business entity might be divided into several investment centres (strategic business units or operating subsidiaries).

■ Within each investment centre there might be several profit centres.

■ Within each profit centre there might be several cost centres and revenue centres.

Although the details of a responsibility accounting system may vary between different entities, the basic principle is consistent: the accounting system should identify performance that a manager should be able to control, and for which he or she should therefore be made responsible and held to account.

2.4 Performance reporting and responsibility accounting: problems with the principle of 'controllability'

Management information is provided to each responsibility centre manager, usually in the form of regular performance reports that the manager uses to:

- assess performance
- investigate any aspects of performance that seem poor (or very good), and
- take any appropriate control measures, depending on what the investigation reveals.

There are two ways in which the principle of 'controllability' may be applied in management performance reports.

- One approach is to include in a performance report only those matters over which the manager has control.
  - This means that many operational performance reports will include non-financial information, because the operational manager responsible does not have control over materials prices, or wage rates or salaries for employees.
  - Alternatively, performance reports might report variances by converting physical variance (materials usage variances in quantities and labour variances in hours) into a money value, using standard prices for materials and standard rates per hour for labour.
- Another approach is to include controllable costs and non-controllable costs in a performance report, but to distinguish clearly between these two types of cost. A profit centre report might therefore be presented as follows:

	$000
Profit centre sales revenue	2,000
Cost of sales	600
Gross profit/contribution	1,400
Other controllable costs	500
Controllable profit	900
Non-controllable costs	300
Net profit	600

Problems with the controllability principle

A problem with applying the principle of controllability is that it might be difficult to decide which costs are controllable and which are uncontrollable.

- In practice, many items of cost are partly controllable.
- Some costs that are uncontrollable in the short term (fixed costs) are controllable in the longer term.

■ A management information system for responsibility centres should identify revenues, costs and investment that are directly attributable to each centre, for which the centre manager is responsible and that the centre manager is in a position to control.

Type of responsibility centre	Performance information required
Cost centre	Controllable costs
Revenue centre (for example, a sales team)	Sales revenue
Profit centre	Controllable costs Revenues Profits
Investment centre	Controllable costs Revenues Profit Controllable investment Return on investment

An effective management accounting system must be able to supply the managers of responsibility centres with the information that they need, in a suitable form and with sufficient regularity. Managers must be able to use the information to help them with managing their centre, and taking appropriate control decisions so that actual performance meets (or exceeds) expectations or target.

Example

The manager of an operating division has received the following report about the performance of the division for the financial year that has just ended.

	Current year	Previous year
	$	$
Sales	800,000	500,000
Operating costs excluding depreciation	600,000	390,000
Depreciation	200,000	80,000
Interest charges	40,000	20,000
Profit/(loss)	(40,000)	10,000

The manager is responsible for operations within the division, but has no control over decisions relating to capital expenditure or borrowing to finance expenditure. These decisions are taken by senior executives within the company.

The manager has been asked to explain the deterioration in the performance of the division in the current year. The manager has replied that as far as he is concerned, there has been a significant improvement in performance.

What is the most appropriate method of assessing performance?

Answer

This performance report shows that although sales revenue has increased from $500,000 to $800,000 compared with the previous year, a $10,000 profit has turned into a $40,000 loss.

However, the division manager has no control over capital expenditure or borrowing. The decline in performance may be due to the increase in depreciation costs and interest charges since the previous year. If so, the decline in performance might be attributable wholly or partly to the buying and borrowing decisions of senior management.

A suitable measure of performance for the manager of the operating division might be operating profit, which is sales revenue minus operating costs. Operating profit may be referred to as:

- profit before interest and tax (PBIT), or possibly

- earnings before interest, tax, depreciation and amortisation (EBITDA).

Using this measure of performance, a performance report might be presented as follows:

	Current year	Previous year
	$	$
Sales	800,000	500,000
Operating costs excluding depreciation	600,000	390,000
Operating profit – manager's responsibility	200,000	110,000
Depreciation	200,000	80,000
Interest charges	40,000	20,000
Profit/(loss) for the division	(40,000)	10,000
Operating profit/sales ratio	25%	22%
Growth in annual sales revenue	60%	

This shows that sales revenue grew by 60% in the current year (presumably helped by new investment in non-current assets for the division) and the ratio of operating profit/sales went up from 22% to 25%. This lends support to the division manager's claim that performance has improved.

2.5 Practical difficulties with responsibility accounting

The principle of responsibility accounting is valid. In practice, however, it is often difficult to apply successfully. The main reason for this is that many costs are only partially controllable.

- A cost centre manager may be in a position to control the efficiency of resource utilisation (for example, materials usage, wastage rates, machine utilisation and labour efficiency).

- However, the centre manager may not be able to control purchase prices for materials, the effectiveness of machine repairs by maintenance staff or wage rates to employees under his or her management.

There is a risk that managers will be held responsible for costs or other aspects of poor performance over which they did not have effective control, and so were not in a position to deal with. For example, a production centre manager may be held responsible for a fall in production output during a month, when the reason for the fall was a mistake in the purchasing department which ordered the wrong materials and so caused a hold-up in production.

If managers are held responsible, within a system of responsibility accounting, for performance that they were unable to control, the reporting system will create problems of motivation. If so, the system may well have the opposite effect of what it was designed to achieve – better performance measurement as a means of giving managers an incentive to improve performance.

Controllability: long-term and short-term

Another serious limitation of responsibility accounting systems is the short-term nature of the performance that they measure. Managers are usually held accountable on a monthly, quarterly or annual basis for costs, revenues or return on investment. By concentrating on specific aspects of short-term performance, the reporting system encourages managers to ignore other aspects of performance – including long-term performance.

When a new manager is appointed to manage a responsibility centre, he will inherit the 'legacy' left by his predecessor. For a considerable time, the short-term performance of the centre will be affected by decisions made by the previous manager at some time in the past. As a result, the new manager's performance will be judged – praised or criticised – partly on the basis of another manager's decisions and efforts.

2.6   Non-financial information for measuring performance

Management information systems for planning and measuring performance will often focus on non-financial performance measures as well as on financial performance.

Some business organisations use a 'balanced scorecard' approach to setting planning targets and measuring performance. The main target is a financial performance target, but it is also recognised that non-financial performance is also vitally important for long-term financial success. In a balanced scorecard approach, targets and performance measurements are therefore established for:

■ a financial perspective

■ an internal business perspective

■ a customer perspective, and

■ an innovation and learning perspective.

The balanced scorecard approach is described in more detail in a later chapter.

Non-financial performance measurements might also focus on customer satisfaction, and whether the products or services sold by the organisation meet customer needs in terms of:

■ product quality

■ reliability of service

■ speed of service or delivery

■ selling price.

It is also possible to measure performance in terms of **'value added'**, which is the value of the additional benefits achieved, less the cost of creating these extra benefits.

Non-financial performance measurements will also be considered in more detail later.

> ## Sources of information
>
> - Control system theory
> - Feedback control system
> - Feed-forward and double loop feedback
> - Using control system theory
> - Information from internal sources
> - Information from external sources
> - Organising a system for providing external information
> - Limitations of external information

3 Sources of information

Performance measurement systems, both for planning and for monitoring actual performance, rely on the provision of relevant, reliable and timely information. Information comes from both inside and outside the organisation.

Traditionally, management accounting systems have been an information system providing financial information to managers from sources within the organisation. In large organisations, management accounting information might be extracted from a cost accounting system, which records and analyses costs.

With the development of IT systems, management information systems have become more sophisticated, using large databases to hold data, from external sources as well as internal sources. Both financial and non-financial data are held and analysed. The analysis of data has also become more sophisticated, particularly through the use of spreadsheets and other models for planning and cost analysis (for example, activity based costing).

3.1 Control system theory

Control system theory can be used to analyse information systems for planning, measuring performance and control. It is sometimes used to analyse a budgetary control system, but its general principles are relevant to any systems of planning and control, or systems of performance measurement.

An information system is a form of control system. It is used to establish planning targets, and to compare actual performance against targets. When actual performance is below target, control measures can be taken to improve performance and bring it up to the target level.

Open systems and closed systems

In control system theory, systems are either open or closed.

- An **open system** is one that interacts with its environment. It is affected by its environment, and accepts input from its environment. The system also produces output that goes into its environment.

- A **closed system** is one that does not interact with its environment. It is 'shut off' from its environment, and does not accept any input from the environment.

A business entity, for example is an open system. It interacts with its environment and is influenced by conditions in the environment. It accepts inputs from the environment (materials from suppliers, capital from investors, labour) and it produces output that affects its environment.

The distinction between open and closed systems might seem odd. However, there is some relevance in the context of management information systems and management accounting.

- A management information system that does not take in data from its environment can be described as a closed system.

- In contrast, a management information system that obtains data from external as well as internal sources can be described as an open system.

Ideally, management accounting systems should obtain data from external as well as internal sources. In practice, they might rely on data from internal sources, and exclude external sources of data.

3.2 Feedback control system

Using control system terminology, a control system might be described as a feedback control system. For a control system based on feedback, the basic concept of control system theory is as follows:

1   A plan or target is established.
2   A manager responsible for the plan or target puts the plan into action, and commits resources to operations
3   There is output from the process. Things happen as a result of the operations that take place. For example, output might be produced and sold.
4   The output (performance) should be measured.
5   These measures of actual performance are fed back to the manager concerned, as control information. (This information is called **'feedback'**.)
6   The manager compares actual performance with the target. Where appropriate, control action is taken to improve performance in the future.

A feedback control system consists of several inter-related elements. These are shown in the diagram below.

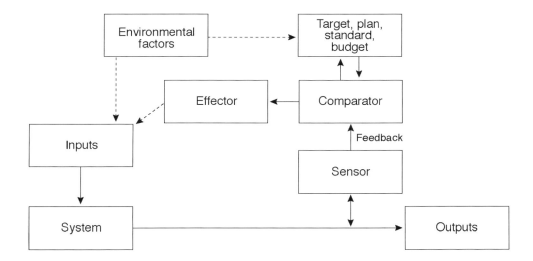

System

A system can be any operation or activity. It can be an entire business entity. A system can be anything that is subject to planning and control. In this diagram, the control information is measure output from the system itself. In this sense it is a closed system

Inputs

Every system has inputs. In a business operation, inputs include resources – materials, equipment, labour and cash. Inputs are used within a system to produce outputs. Some inputs are controllable by management. Other inputs are not controllable, and may be subject to influence from environmental factors.

For example, raw material prices are inputs to a production system. Materials prices might be controllable to some extent, by efficient purchasing. However, materials prices are often outside the control of management, and are affected by environmental factors such as inflation rates and materials supply shortages.

Outputs

Every system produces outputs. Some outputs are planned. For example, outputs from a business operation include the volume of production and sales. Some outputs can be quantified; others are more difficult to quantify. For example, the outputs from a business operation include the morale and satisfaction of the workforce, and customer satisfaction.

Sensor

Outputs from a system are measured. However, not all outputs are measured. Outputs are measured only if:

- they are measurable and
- if the control system has a procedure for measuring them.

For example, in the case of a business operation, measured outputs will include sales, costs and profit. Other measured outputs might include the efficiency of resource utilisation and capacity utilisation. Outputs that might or might not be measured include customer satisfaction, the quality of output and employee satisfaction. Management can decide what measurable outputs should be measured and fed back as information for the purpose of performance assessment.

Feedback

Feedback is measured information that is reported back to management for control purposes.

Comparator

A comparator compares measured outputs (feedback) with a target, plan or standard. Performance has to be measured against expected performance or target performance, to assess whether it is satisfactory. Where actual performance differs from the plan, it may be necessary to amend the plan or change the target. However, the comparison of actual performance with plan might suggest that action can be taken to improve future performance.

Effector

Control action is taken through an effector mechanism. An effector makes adjustments to the inputs to the system, so that future outputs will be changed.

An effector might take the form of management instructions to employees. For example, the quality of output is low and the rate of rejected units in a production process might be too high. On receiving feedback about the low quality of work, management might try to take measures to improve the situation – by employing more people in the work and instructing them to take more time and more care over their work.

It is important to recognise, however, that the effectors in a control system can only apply to controllable inputs to the system. Uncontrollable inputs, and inputs that are subject to environmental influence, cannot be controlled.

3.3 Feed-forward and double loop feedback

Strategic planning and control information is often:

- feed-forward control information, or
- double-loop feedback information.

Feed-forward

Feed-forward control information is forward-looking control information. It compares:

- the target performance and
- the latest forecast of what actual performance will be.

For example, the directors of a retail store company might obtain control information in September comparing the targeted sales for the company for the year to 31st December, and the latest forecast of what sales for the year will be. If the forecast is below the target, the directors will study the difference (the 'gap') between target and current forecast, and consider measures to close the gap.

A feed-forward system of control information is an alternative to a feedback system. In management accounting, feedback systems are often associated with budgetary control. Feed-forward systems are associated with decentralised decision-making, and techniques such as continuous budgeting.

Double-loop feedback

Feedback is control information reported to the manager responsible, comparing actual performance in a period with the target or budget for that period. In other words, feedback compares actual results with a plan for the benefit of the manager directly responsible for control. **Double-loop feedback** is control information comparing actual results with the plan that is reported to a higher level of management. Senior managers can use double-loop feedback to:

- assess the performance of the managers responsible and

- where appropriate, consider making changes to the budget or plan.

3.4 Using control system theory

Control system theory can be useful in providing a framework for the analysis of control systems and performance measurement systems. Each aspect of a control system can be reviewed, to decide whether it is appropriate or sufficient. For example, it provides a framework for asking questions such as:

- Are the targets or plans for the system suitable? Should there be different targets or more targets for achievement?

- Does the information system currently measure enough, or should it be measuring other outputs from the system. Are the sensors used to measure the outputs adequate? Is the feedback provided in an appropriate form?

- Is the feedback being sent to the most appropriate individuals?

- Are the effectors appropriate? Is enough control action being taken? To what extent is management able to control the inputs to the system?

3.5 Information from internal sources

A control system such as a management accounting system must obtain data from within the organisation (from internal sources) for the purposes of planning and control. The system should be designed so that it captures and measures all the data required for providing management with the information they need.

It is useful to remember the essential qualities of good information.

- It should be relevant to the needs of management. Information must help management to make decisions. Information that is not relevant to any decision-making (such as planning and control decisions) is of no value. An important factor in the design of information systems should be the purpose of the information. What decisions should be made, and what information will be needed to make those decisions.

■ It should be reliable. This means that the data should be sufficiently accurate for its purpose. It should also be complete.

■ It should be available in a timely manner. In other words, it should be available for when it is needed by management.

■ The cost of providing the information should not exceed the benefits that it provides. The key factor that limits the potential size of many information systems is that the cost of obtaining additional information is not justified by the additional benefits that the information will provide.

In designing a performance measurement system, and deciding what information is required from internal sources, these desirable qualities of good information should influence the design of the system.

Traditionally, management accounting systems have obtained internal data from the cost accounting system and costing records. In many organisations, IT systems now integrate costing data with other operational data. This means that data is available to the management accounting system from non-accounting sources.

Example

An information system might be required to provide information about the profitability of different types of customer.

The starting point for the design of this information system is the **purpose** of the information. Why is information about customer profitability needed? The answer might be that the company wants to know which of its customers contribute the most profits, and whether some customers are unprofitable. If some customers are unprofitable, the company will presumably consider ways of improving profitability (for example, by increasing prices charged to those customers) or will decide to stop selling to those customers.

The next consideration is: What data is needed to measure customer profitability? The answer might be that customers should first be divided into different categories, and each category of customer should have certain unique characteristics. Having established categories of customer, information is needed about costs that are directly attributable to each category of customers. This might be information relating to gross profits from sales, minus the directly attributable selling and distribution costs (and any directly attributable administration costs and financing costs).

Having established what information is required, the next step is to decide how the information should be 'captured' and measured. In this example, a system is needed for measuring each category of customer, sales revenues, costs of sales and other directly attributable costs.

The information should be available for when management intend to review customer profitability. This might be every three months, six months or even annually.

3.6 Information from external sources

Managers need information about customers, competitors and other elements in their business environment. The management information system must be able to provide this in the form that managers need, and at the time that they need it.

External information is needed for strategic planning and control. However, it is also often needed for tactical and operational management decisions.

Examples of the external information needed by companies are set out in the table below.

Information area	Examples of information needed
Customers	What are the needs and expectations of customers in the market?
	Are these needs and expectations changing?
	What is the potential for our products or services to meet these needs, or to meet them better?
Competitors	Who are they?
	What are they doing?
	Can we copy some of their ideas?
	How large are they, and what is their market share?
	How profitable are they?
	What is their pricing policy?
Legal environment	What are the regulations and laws that must be complied with?
Suppliers	What suppliers are there for key products or services?
	What is the quality of their products or services?
	What is the potential of new suppliers?
	What is the financial viability of each supplier?
Political/ environmental issues	Are there any relevant political developments or developments relating to environmental regulation or environmental conditions?
Economic/ financial environment	What is happening to interest rates?
	What is happening to exchange rates?
	What is happening in other financial markets?
	What is the predicted state of the economy

Sources of external information

Sources of external information, some accessible through the Internet, include:

- market research
- supplier price lists and brochures
- trade journals
- newspapers and other media
- government reports and statistics
- reports published by other organisations, such as trade bodies.

3.7 Organising a system for providing external information

If managers are to be provided with external information by a management information system (MIS), the system must be designed so that it is capable of providing it:

- There has to be a system of data capture. How should information be obtained from the environment and filed within the MIS? How should the data be held within the MIS?

- How should the information be provided to managers? Should it be e-mailed to them? Or should managers be expected to search for the information in the MIS when they need it?

- Should the external information be processed into a usable form for managers when it is captured, or should it be supplied to managers as 'raw unprocessed data'?

- The external information should be divided into strategic information and operational information. Which managers should be provided with the strategic information, and which ones need the operational information?

3.8 Limitations of external information

It is important to recognise the limitations of external information.

- It might not be accurate, and it might be difficult to assess how accurate it is.
- It might be incomplete.
- It might provide either too much or not enough detail.
- It might be difficult to obtain information in the form that is ideally required.
- It might not always be available when required.
- It might be difficult to find.

> **Recording and processing methods. Management reports**
>
> - Recording data
> - Processing methods
> - Management reports

4 Recording and processing methods. Management reports

4.1 Recording data

There are many different ways of 'capturing' data, and recording it in an information system. Methods of recording data will depend on circumstances, and also on the nature of the data required. For example:

- Records of labour time spent on particular tasks or jobs might be recorded on time sheets or job sheets.

- Records of materials used might be recorded in materials requisition notes.

- Data about customer satisfaction might be captured as records of customer complaints. Alternatively, data might be obtained from market research surveys.

The system of recording data should be made as convenient as possible for the individuals responsible for input of the data to the information system. Where possible, the information system should be designed to minimise the risk of errors.

Data should also be recorded in a form that will allow it to be processed. As a simple example, suppose that records of labour costs should provide for an analysis of these costs into production costs, administration costs and sales and distribution costs. The data about labour costs will have to be recorded in a way that will enable the costs to be divided into their different categories.

4.2 Processing methods

Performance measurement systems should be designed so that data can be processed in a way that meets the requirements of management. There are various ways of processing data, and IT systems enable managers to obtain large amounts of information for different purposes.

- Data might be needed for planning or forecasting. Many managers use spreadsheet models and other forecasting models.

- Accountancy software packages, including management accounting packages or modules, can be used to process accounting data.

- Data might be used to prepare regular, formal management reports.

- Alternatively, managers might want to obtain 'ad hoc' reports on demand.

E-mail allows managers to communicate information quickly between each other.

4.3 Management reports

Entities are able to produce large amounts of information, in formal reports or on demand. This raises problems of control and security.

There should be controls to ensure that reports are distributed only to individuals who are authorised to receive it. Much information is confidential, and access to it should be restricted.

- There should be distribution lists for routine reports, and a copy of the report should be available only to the individuals in the list.

- Access to online data files can be restricted by a system of identity codes and passwords.

- IT systems should have safeguards against unauthorised access by external users. For example, intranet systems should include firewalls (hardware and software). There should be physical controls over unauthorised access to computers and computer terminals (such as making sure that office doors are locked when the manager is away from his desk).

- There should be established procedures for preventing unauthorised access to confidential data. Managers should be required to keep all confidential information in a secure place. There should be restrictions over the type of information that can be sent by e-mail.

CHAPTER

13

Measuring performance

Contents

1	Performance hierarchy
2	Financial performance in the private sector
3	Non-financial performance indicators (NFPIs)
4	Performance measurement in not-for-profit organisations
5	Behavioural aspects of performance reporting: reward systems
6	Customer profitability

Performance hierarchy

- The nature of the performance hierarchy
- Mission statement
- Corporate vision
- High-level corporate objectives and strategic objectives
- Critical success factors (CSFs) and key performance indicators (KPIs)
- The planning gap
- The characteristics of operational performance
- Hard accountability and soft accountability

1 Performance hierarchy

1.1 The nature of the performance hierarchy

The targets for managers throughout an organisation should be consistent with each other. All managers and employees should be working towards the same goals.

Consistency in setting performance targets can be achieved through a performance hierarchy, linking the goals of the most senior management with the targets for operational managers.

- At the top of the hierarchy, an organisation might have a mission statement.
- The mission statement provides a framework for setting strategic objectives, and for strategic planning.
- Within the framework of a strategic plan, management at the 'tactical' level can prepare plans, such as annual budgets, capital expenditure budgets and marketing plans.
- Within the framework of tactical plans, operational managers can prepare operating plans and set operating targets.

Agency theory and the performance hierarchy

Agency theory considers the relationship between a principal (for example, the shareholders of a company) and an agent (for example, the directors and managers). The agent must be required to give an account of performance to the principal, and the principal must be able to hold the agent to account.

Within a company, there is a hierarchy of performance evaluation and accountability.

- Junior managers are accountable to senior managers, and their performance is measured and evaluated.
- Performance is also measured and evaluated in relation to time: short-term and long-term performance should be measured.

■ Performance should be measured and evaluated at strategic, tactical and operational levels.

1.2 Mission statement

Some organisations have a formal mission statement. The purpose of a mission statement is to provide a clear expression of the reason why the organisation is in existence and what it is seeking to achieve.

The content of mission statements varies between different organisations, but common elements are:

■ a statement of the purpose of the organisation

■ a statement of its broad strategy for achieving its purpose

■ a statement of the values and culture of the organisation.

The purpose of the organisation is usually expressed in terms of its business purpose, rather than its financial objectives (such as maximising the wealth of its shareholders). For example, the purpose of a company in the entertainment industry might be to provide audio-visual entertainment products to customers throughout the world.

The mission statement might also include a statement of the strategy for achieving the purpose. For example, the mission statement of company in the entertainment industry might include a strategy of providing audio-visual entertainment in all forms and through all media channels.

In contrast, the mission statement of another company in the entertainment industry might be to produce films for purposes of public entertainment and also education and training.

The usefulness of a mission statement

A mission statement can have several useful purposes.

■ It provides a guide to employees (and other stakeholders such as customers and suppliers) about what the organisation is in existence to achieve. It may help employees to identify more readily with their employer.

■ More significantly, it can help managers to formulate their business strategy. Business strategies should be consistent with the mission of the organisation. Managers should consider new strategies in the context of whether it is consistent with the organisation's purpose.

■ The mission statement can therefore be used as a screening device, for rejecting strategies that are inconsistent with the mission of the organisation. For example, suppose that the mission statement of a company in the entertainment industry is to produce films for purposes of public entertainment and also education and training. A proposed strategy to develop a chain of cinemas would be inconsistent with this mission, and either the strategy should be rejected or the mission statement should be amended.

- The mission statement can also be used to establish a corporate culture, such as a culture of encouraging all employees to develop to their full potential, or a culture of acting ethically in all dealings with customers and suppliers.

Limitations of mission statements

Mission statements can be of limited practical value, however, especially when they are worded in vague language that lacks real substance.

When the actual behaviour of an organisation contradicts what is said in its mission statement, the mission statement may be regarded as cynical and insincere. For example, a pharmaceuticals company might include in its mission statement the objective of promoting the improvement in the health of all people throughout the world. Its management might decide not to allow one of its drugs to be used to combat a serious epidemic in a developing country, because the country is unable to afford to pay for the drug. The actual decision of the company would be inconsistent with its mission statement, making a mockery of the mission statement.

Mission statements do not have a time scale for achievement. Strategies are needed to establish specific targets and time scales for achievement.

Mission statements may therefore be useful for formulating strategies, but they are of limited value for monitoring actual performance.

1.3   Corporate vision

Corporate vision is how a company sees itself, and how it wants to be seen by others, such as its customers, its employees and its shareholders. A corporate vision statement may set out the future direction that the company will take, and what it expects to achieve within the next few years. 'The vision process translates core values into actions and enables companies to design a desired future rather than simply letting fate happen' (PricewaterhouseCoopers).

Ideally a corporate vision:
- should be realistic, and not 'wishful thinking'.
- should be 'emotional', so that it can attract employees, customers and investors to the company
- should indicate a sense of direction, and what the company wants to achieve.

A corporate vision statement can be used instead of, or in addition to, a mission statement.

Examples

It might be useful to look at a few corporate vision statements, selected at random from the internet.

Translink, a transport company: 'To provide a transformed network of co-ordinated bus and rail services which attracts a growing number of passengers, enjoys public confidence and is recognised for its quality and innovation.'

Hitachi Chemical Company. 'Our vision is to contribute to society through the development of superior technologies and products. By combining and adapting our wide ranging advanced material and processing technologies, Hitachi Chemical aims to provide superior technologies, products and services that contribute to the betterment of human life and society.'

Colt Engineering. 'The corporate vision of the Colt companies is our primary objective and the overriding focus of Colt's activities: Being North America's contractor of choice for clients and staff.'

Tylö AB, manufacturer of bathroom equipment. 'To be perceived as the global market leader with the most inspiring, innovative bath, shower and sauna environments.'

1.4　High-level corporate objectives and strategic objectives

An organisation should have high level 'corporate' objectives that are consistent with its mission. For companies, the highest corporate objective is likely to be the aim of providing benefits to their shareholders. This objective may be expressed in general terms as 'maximising the wealth of shareholders over the long term'.

There may be social or ethical constraints or obligations that will be taken into consideration in the pursuit of the corporate objective. For example, companies may recognise the need to act in an ethical manner and in accordance with an ethical code of conduct. Some companies may recognise obligations for the protection of the environment. Others may recognise an obligation towards employees as well as shareholders.

High-level corporate objectives must be converted into more specific plans or strategies, each with its own strategic goal. Strategic objectives are high-level goals, usually with a long-term time horizon. Achieving the strategic goals should mean that the corporate objective will also be achieved.

There may be a hierarchy of strategies and strategic objectives. For example:

■ There may be a financial objective to achieve targets for growth in profitability, return on capital and shareholder wealth over a strategic planning period.

■ A company should develop strategies for achieving financial success in a competitive market. This calls for competitive strategies on how to position the business in its markets. There may be a strategy for growth in the business, through internal development or through mergers and acquisitions.

■ Strategies may be developed for marketing (meeting customer needs), product innovation and funding/capital expenditure and investment to enable the company to achieve the financial objective and objectives for competitive strategy.

■ Strategies may be developed for other aspects of the business, such as IT systems, human resource planning and the use of new technology. These would be designed to support the marketing, innovation and finance strategies.

As indicated earlier, strategic objectives should create a framework for subsidiary objectives, and for tactical and operational planning.

1.5 Critical success factors (CSFs) and key performance indicators (KPIs)

Critical success factors are factors that are critical to the success of an organisation and the achievement of its overall objectives. They are the key areas where targeted performance must be achieved. Failure to meet targets for any CSF will mean failure to achieve long-term targets and objectives. CSFs are therefore vitally important and an organisation cannot afford to fail in any of these areas.

At a strategic level, there are usually just a small number of CSFs. They might be expressed in terms of:

■ profitability

■ market share

■ product leadership

■ development of human resources

■ achieving a balance between long-term and short-term goals.

For each critical success factor, there should be a measure of performance. These performance measures might be called **key performance indicators** or KPIs. A target should be set for each KPI and actual performance can be measured against the target.

1.6 The planning gap

The concept of the planning gap can be useful for formulating strategies and other plans. The planning gap and gap analysis was described in an earlier chapter.

A planning gap is the difference between:

■ the target or objective that an organisation would like to achieve and

■ the forecast or expectation of what the actual achievement will be (on the assumption that there are no new initiatives to improve performance).

Normally, and particularly when objectives are challenging and ambitious, there will be a large gap between what an organisation wants to achieve and what it currently expects to achieve.

Having identified the planning gap over the planning period, management should then consider strategies, and then more detailed tactical and operational plans, for closing the gap. The planning gap may be closed either by:

■ developing strategies for improving performance, or

■ if new strategies will not be sufficient to close the gap, lowering the target.

1.7 The characteristics of operational performance

Although the main corporate objective may be expressed in financial terms, operational performance should be measured by a combination of financial and non-financial measures.

Performance measurement at an operational level also normally focuses more on providing information about actual performance for control purposes. Compared with strategic performance information, there is less emphasis on planning information at the operational level.

Performance targets should also be set for both the long-term and the short-term. The strategic aim should be directed towards long-term goals, but the long-term goals will not be achieved unless intermediate shorter-term goals are also achieved.

Each organisation should therefore develop its own hierarchy of financial and non-financial objectives, linked through the performance hierarchy and between the short-term and long-term.

1.8 Hard accountability and soft accountability

Performance measurement and evaluation systems are based on 'hard accountability'.

- **Hard accountability** means accountability to another person for performance, in the form of financial reports and other quantitative performance measurements.
- **Soft accountability** is self-accountability. An individual might be personally motivated to achieve performance targets, and will judge his or her own personal performance in relation to those targets. With soft accountability, control from above by senior management is not required.

Performance measurement systems are therefore based on setting targets and measuring actual performance, so that each manager is accountable to someone in a position of higher authority through performance reporting.

> ## Financial performance in the private sector
>
> - The primary performance objective
> - Differing primary measures of financial performance
> - Other financial measures of performance
> - Short-run and long-run financial performance
> - Setting financial targets: methods
> - Making comparisons of financial performance

2 Financial performance in the private sector

2.1 The primary performance objective

For companies, the primary performance objective should be concerned with the benefits of their owners, the shareholders. The aim should be to provide benefits to shareholders over the long term, in the form of dividends from profits and share price growth.

Share price growth comes mainly from growth in the business and earnings per share. However, growth should not be achieved if it exposes the company to excessive risks. The primary objective of financial performance targets should therefore be consistent with the long-term objectives of both:

- business growth and
- survival

2.2 Differing primary measures of financial performance

There are several measures of financial performance that could be used to assess success in achieving corporate objectives.

- It is inappropriate to use targets for share price growth and dividend growth as formal planning targets and measures of actual performance. Share prices can be volatile, and affected by stock market conditions outside the control of a company's management. Dividend policy, on the other hand, is under the control of the board of directors, but can be manipulated. Dividend payments do not have to move in line with changes in profitability or longer-term financial expectations of profit.

- It is therefore more appropriate to measure financial performance in terms of conditions that should lead to share price growth and dividend growth in the future.

Discounted cash flow measures of performance

Discounted cash flow is used to assess the value of proposed capital expenditure projects. (It can also be used to assess the value of companies and their shares.) In theory, if a company uses an appropriate cost of capital as the discount rate, projects that are expected to have a positive net present value (NPV) should add to the value of the company and its shares. Similarly, projects will add to the company's value if they are expected to have an internal rate of return (IRR) in excess of the company's cost of capital.

NPV and IRR are therefore used to assess the value of capital expenditure proposals.

However, although discounted cash flow techniques can be applied to evaluate forecasts of future cash flows from capital projects, they are not practical methods for analysing historical performance. This is because management accounting systems are not designed to identify specific cash flows arising from capital projects, and some relevant cash flows in DCF analysis, such as opportunity costs, would also be difficult to measure.

Financial measures of historical performance

Financial measures used to measure historical performance, and assess whether a company appears to be achieving its corporate objectives, may be:

- return on capital employed (ROCE)

- earnings per share and growth in earnings per share

- earnings before interest, tax, depreciation and amortisation (EBITDA)

- for investment centres, return on investment or residual income

None of these performance measures is ideal for assessing performance and progress towards achieving the corporate objective.

- **Return on capital employed (ROCE)** is a useful measure of performance, because it relates the amount of profit earned to the amount of capital employed in the business. However, the measurement of ROCE depends on accounting conventions for the measurement of profit and capital employed.

- **Earnings per share growth** is also commonly used to assess performance. On the assumption that in the long term, the ratio of the share price to EPS (the price/earnings ratio or P/E ratio) remains fairly constant, growth in EPS should result in a higher share price. However, the P/E ratio does not necessarily remain constant over the long term, and could change if the perception of investment risk in the company changed.

- **EBITDA** is a useful measure of performance only if it is assumed that management have no control over interest costs or depreciation and amortisation charges. This may be true for profit centre management, but is unlikely to be the case when managers have control over investment and financing decisions.

- The benefits and limitations of **ROI** and **residual income** are considered in the next chapter.

Measuring financial security: liquidity and gearing

A long-term objective of a company should be survival, as well as growth. It is therefore appropriate to measure financial risk. Measures of financial risk include:

- **liquidity** risk, measured by ratios such as the current ratio or quick ratio, or by cash flow analysis
- **gearing** or debt/equity ratios, which measure the potential risk to a company from its funding structure.

Liquidity can be important. Liquidity means having cash or access to cash to make payments when these are due. For example, a company must have cash to pay salaries and wages of its employees, and to pay suppliers and other creditors. In some cases, profitable companies might become insolvent because they cannot pay their debts.

A lack of liquidity also restricts flexibility of action. A company that is short of cash is often unable to take advantage of new opportunities that might arise, because they do not have the money to spend.

Gearing and debt levels can also be important. Highly-geared companies are exposed to the risk of a big fall in earnings per share whenever there is a fall in their operating profits. When they borrow at variable rates of interest, an increase in interest rates will also reduce profitability.

Historical profits and expected future profits

The main objective of a commercial company might be to maximise the wealth of shareholders. Wealth is increased by paying dividends and through increases in the share price. A common assumption in financial management is that the share price of a company depends on expectations of future profits and dividends.

During the late 1990s and early 2000s, the share prices of newly-formed 'new technology' companies reached very high levels, even though these companies were making heavy losses. The view of investors at the time was that high values for new technology companies were justified by the expectation of enormous future profits. The high share prices reached by these companies are now known as the '**dot.com bubble**', which collapsed in 2001. In 2000 and 2001 the share prices of these companies collapsed, and many went out of business.

It was eventually recognised that most of the new technology companies would never compete successfully against larger 'traditional' companies. Most never became profitable before they went out of business or were taken over at low prices.

A lesson from the 'dot.com bubble' is that future share prices (and shareholder wealth) will depend on future profits and dividends. However, it is important to convince investors that the company will be profitable in the future. Historical returns and profits, and trends in profitability, might provide some guide to what profits might be in the future.

2.3 Other financial measures of performance

Financial measures are used to set targets for performance and monitor actual performance throughout the management hierarchy. You should be familiar with many of these financial measures, such as:

- gross profit margin
- net profit margin
- cost/sales ratios
- growth in sales
- cost variances.

Another way of measuring the management of costs is to measure costs as a percentage of total sales revenue, and monitoring changes in this percentage figure over time. Cost ratios might include:

- production costs as a percentage of sales
- distribution and marketing costs as a percentage of sales
- administrative costs as a percentage of sales
- material costs as a percentage of total cost
- labour costs as a percentage of total costs.

Costs can also be monitored in terms of:

- cost per unit
- cost per machine hour
- cost per activity – for example the cost to process and despatch a customer's order, or the cost to rectify a defective unit
- comparison with a target cost.

2.4 Short-run and long-run financial performance

DCF methods of measuring financial performance are forward-looking and long-term in perspective. As stated already, DCF is not suitable for measuring historical performance.

A problem with other financial measures of performance is that they are mainly short-term in perspective, and focus in the current financial year. Trends can also be monitored (growth in EPS, sales, profits and so on), but it can be difficult to project historical trends into the future.

Rewards to individuals for performance are also often based on the achievement of targets for the current financial year, adding to the short-term focus.

The need to find a balance between short-term and long-term financial success has led to the development of differing views of performance measurement, such as the balanced scorecard and performance pyramid. These are described in a later chapter.

2.5 Setting financial targets: methods

There are several different ways of setting targets, such as financial targets, or making financial forecasts:

- engineering-based targets
- historical-based targets
- negotiated targets

Engineering-based targets

Engineering targets may be used when there is a stable and predictable relationship between inputs to the forecasting model and outputs. An example of this type of forecasting or targeting is standard costing. Standard costs assume a fixed relationship between the resources that go into making an item of product and the production of one finished unit. By setting a standard cost, it is possible to set a target total cost for the production of any given quantity of the items.

Historical-based targets

When it is not possible to identify stable and predictable relationships between inputs and outputs, it may be appropriate to establish targets on the basis of either:

- historical performance, and what has been accomplished in the past, or
- historical targets that have been used in the past, on the assumption that they are still based on valid assumptions

For example, a financial target may be set to achieve a gross profit to sales ratio of 40%, because this target has been used consistently for the past few years.

However, the past is not always a suitable basis for setting targets for the future:

- the circumstances that applied in the past may no longer apply for the future, and different assumptions might be appropriate for setting targets for the future
- the historical targets used in the past may allow for inefficiencies that ought to be eliminated for the future.

Negotiated targets

Financial targets may also be agreed as the outcome of negotiations between superiors and subordinates. Senior managers may try to impose financial targets on their subordinates, and the subordinates may argue that the targets are unrealistic and unfair. As a result of the discussions and negotiations that follow, 'compromise' targets may be agreed that are acceptable to both sides.

Advocates of negotiated financial targets argue that the negotiation process between superiors and subordinates helps to bridge the information gap between:

- senior managers, who can see the 'big picture' and what the entity should be trying to achieve (which subordinate managers may not be aware of)
- subordinate managers, who understand operational matters at a level of detail that their seniors do not.

Negotiating financial targets enables senior and subordinate managers to exchange information and views, each from their own perspective. As a result of the negotiations, the financial targets that are agreed should be achievable, striking a realistic balance between higher-level objectives and lower-level practical realities.

2.6 Making comparisons of financial performance

The performance of departments or divisions may be assessed through comparison. In other words, has one division performed better than the other? However, when making comparisons of performance between two divisions of the business, it is important to be aware of the reasons why their performance might be different. There could be very good reasons why one division has performed better than the other in the short-term. When there are good reasons for differences in performance, the comparison should take these reasons into consideration.

A simple example may help to illustrate this point.

Example

An international company has two operating divisions, one in Country X and the other in Country Y. The operating division in Country X has been in existence for many years. The operating division in country Y was established two years ago, when the company invested in country Y for the first time.

The financial results for the two divisions for the year just ended are as follows:

	Year 1 Country X	Year 1 Country Y	Total	Year 2 Country X	Year 2 Country Y	Total
	$ million	$ million	$ million	$ million	$ million	$ million
Sales	800	80	880	860	120	980
Direct costs						
Labour	280	15	295	302	22	324
Materials	160	20	180	182	28	210
	440	35	475	484	50	534
Other costs						
Marketing	70	40	110	80	80	160
Depreciation	100	8	108	100	16	116
	170	48	218	180	96	276
Total costs	610	83	693	664	146	810
Profit before interest	190	(3)	187	196	(26)	170
Interest			20			40
			165			130
Non-current assets (net book value)	90	25	115	100	55	155
Debt			300			650

These figures might suggest that operating performance was much better in Country X than in Country Y. Country Y made a loss in Year 1 and an even bigger loss in Year 2.

However, the operations in Country Y are fairly new, and the difference in the results between the two countries is probably due to the costs of starting up in Country Y. In particular, the marketing costs in Country Y are very high relative to sales. High marketing spending may be necessary to establish a foothold in the market and a suitable market share.

The ratio of total costs to sales can be compared. The ratio of material costs to sales is slightly higher in Country Y than in Country X, possibly due to difficulty in obtaining material supplies locally. However, the ratio of labour costs to sales is much lower in Country Y, suggesting that at some time in the future, it may be beneficial to switch production from country X to Country Y.

Sales are growing in Country X, but the profit/sales ratio has fallen slightly. Sales grew by 50% in Country Y in Year 2, suggesting that the greatest potential for growth in sales and profits might be in Country Y rather than Country X.

The data is by no means conclusive. The key point, however, is that comparisons should be made with care.

Non-financial performance indicators (NFPIs)

- The nature of non-financial measures of performance
- Strategic NFPIs
- Operational NFPIs
- Multiple measures of performance
- Measurements of quality
- Performance through quality
- Qualitative performance

---

3 Non-financial performance indicators (NFPIs)

3.1 The nature of non-financial measures of performance

Performance measures might be non-financial. Non-financial performance indicators (NFPIs) can be both quantitative and qualitative.

Non-financial measures of performance should focus on critical success factors of a non-financial nature. These will vary from one type of business entity to another, and they will also vary according to the 'level' of performance reporting – strategic or operational.

Typically, non-performance measures of performance will relate to a critical success factor in one of the following areas:

- quality
- speed (for example, speed of service or speed of delivery)
- reliability
- efficiency
- achieving a specific non-financial target
- meeting customer needs/customer satisfaction.

3.2 Strategic NFPIs

Non-financial performance measures are needed because success in achieving some strategic objectives cannot be measured in money terms alone, and in terms of financial performance measurements. Some strategic objectives are therefore set in terms of a non-financial performance target, and actual results are compared with this non-financial target.

Non-financial targets should be compatible with financial targets.

Examples of quantitative strategic non-financial performance measurements include:

- market share (as a target for competitive strategy and sales strategy)
- number of new products developed (as a target for innovation strategy)
- quality measures (where quality is a key strategic objective for meeting customer needs and expectations).

3.3 Operational NFPIs

Many operational targets are set and operational performance measured by NFPIs.

For example, measures of success in meeting customer needs include:

- customer service measures, such as average time to respond to customer calls, and average time to meet customer orders
- customer satisfaction reports
- measures of repeat business obtained or customer loyalty.

Measures of performance in relation to the management of employees would include:

- staff turnover rates
- absenteeism and sickness rates
- productivity ratios or similar productivity measurements.

Measures of performance in relation to the utilisation of resources include capacity utilisation ratios, such as:

- hotel room occupancy rates (hotels)
- machine utilisation rates
- proportion of seats filled (airlines, cinemas).

3.4 Multiple measures of performance

Performance can be assessed using several different measures or indicators. For example, performance can be measured by:

- A combination of financial measures, quantified non-financial measures and (possibly) non-quantified (qualitative) non-financial measures
- A balanced scorecard approach, with four different perspectives on performance targets
- Measures related to short-term financial and operating targets and measures related to longer-term strategic objectives.

3.5 Measurements of quality

Quality targets may be a major element in strategic planning. Quality is associated with meeting customer needs and expectations.

Quality performance can be measured and evaluated in relation to the key performance objectives of quality, speed, dependability (reliability), flexibility and cost. For example:

Performance objective	Performance measure
Quality	Percentage of items rejected or scrapped
	Average number of defects per unit produced
	Average time between machine breakdowns
	Number of customer complaints
	Number or cost of warranty claims
Speed	Average time between receiving an order and completing the work
	Throughput cycle time
	Transport times
Dependability	Percentage of customer orders met from inventory
	Percentage of orders or items delivered late
	Average delays
Flexibility	Average set-up time
	New product development time
	Range of products
Cost	Variances
	Cost per operating hour/per machine hour
	Labour productivity
	Throughput, contribution

Another approach to quality performance measurement is to use a combination of operational measures, financial measures and customer measures. For example:

■ **Operational measures**

- percentage of items rejected

- time lost in production

■ **Financial measures**

- the cost per unit produced

- quality costs

■ **Customer measures,** such as:

- number of customer complaints

- number of claims under warranty

- change in total market share.

3.6 Performance through quality

Cost and quality are inter-connected issues. Business entities provide goods or services to customers that combine a particular cost per unit (and sales price per unit) with a perceived level of quality. In a competitive business environment, companies should be trying either:

■ to provide customers with more quality for a given cost per unit or

■ to provide products of a given quality for a lower cost.

In the following diagram, the current position for a company in a competitive market is shown as point A. The company has six strategic options, A to F.

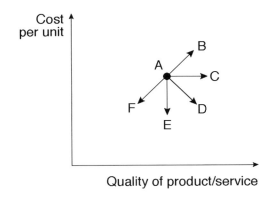

■ **Strategy A.** This is a do-nothing strategy. In a competitive business environment, it is the strategy most likely to result in eventual business failure. Companies cannot 'do nothing'. Like their competitors, they need to seek ways of providing more value to customers, by reducing costs or improving quality.

■ **Strategy B.** This strategy is to improve the quality of the product or service, and increasing the cost per unit to achieve the quality improvement.

■ **Strategy C.** This is a strategy of more quality for the same cost – improving the quality of the product or service without any change in the cost per unit.

■ **Strategy D.** This is a strategy of improving quality and at the same time reducing the cost per unit. This is the strategy most likely to succeed over the long term, but improving quality and reducing costs may be difficult to achieve.

■ **Strategy E.** This is a strategy of maintaining the same quality, but at a lower cost per unit.

■ **Strategy F.** This is a strategy of 'going down-market', and providing a cheaper product or service, but at a lower standard of quality.

Strategy A is the least likely to succeed and Strategy D the most likely to succeed. The likely success of the other strategies will depend on competitive conditions in the market (what competitors are doing) and on customer preferences.

3.7 Qualitative performance

Qualitative performance is performance that is not measured and expressed in quantitative terms. Qualitative performance targets may be expressed in general terms, such as:

- being the 'best' or 'better than competitors'
- 'meeting customer needs'
- 'high quality'.

Where possible, performance targets should be quantified. A quantified target provides a specific objective for achievement, and actual performance can be measured against it. With qualitative targets, assessing performance may be a matter of judgement and subjective opinion.

In many cases, it is possible to convert qualitative targets into quantitative targets. For example, an objective of achieving high quality can be expressed in quantitative quality targets. Similarly, 'being better than the competition' can be converted into quantitative targets, by identifying the ways in which the company wants to 'beat' the opposition. Even 'meeting customer needs' can be quantified, by identifying what customer needs are, or by measuring customer views in an attitude survey.

In some cases, however, it may be difficult to quantify critical performance targets. In particular, it may be difficult to set quantitative targets for:

- brand recognition, or
- reputation.

These can, however, be critical success factors.

- The commercial success of many companies is reinforced by a strong brand that the company reinforces through advertising and maintains through quality.

- The commercial success of a company may be put at risk by a 'bad' reputation. For example, a well-known footwear company suffered a decline in sales some years ago following media reports that its suppliers used child labour. Some oil companies promote an image of being environmentally-conscious, perhaps in the expectation that it will obtain longer-term benefits from a socially and environmentally-friendly image.

Performance measurement in not-for-profit organisations
■ The special characteristics of not-for-profit organisations
■ Identifying performance targets for not-for-profit organisations
■ Value for money (VFM)
■ Problems with performance measurement in not-for-profit entities

4 Performance measurement in not-for-profit organisations

4.1 The special characteristics of not-for-profit organisations

Not-for-profit organisations, such as government departments and charitable organisations, differ from commercial businesses because their main objective is not financial. The main objective of any such organisation depends on the purpose for which it exists: to administer the country (government departments), to provide education (schools and universities), provide medical care (hospitals), do charitable work, and so on.

A not-for-profit organisation will nevertheless have some financial objectives:

■ State-owned organisations must operate within their spending budget.

■ Charitable organisations may have an objective of keeping running costs within a certain limit, and of raising as much funding as possible for their charity work.

Because of this difference, a different approach is needed to setting performance targets and measuring performance in a not-for-profit organisation.

4.2 Identifying performance targets for not-for-profit organisations

You may be required in your examination to suggest quantitative targets for a not-for-profit organisation. The selection of appropriate targets will vary according to the nature and purpose of the organisation. The broad principle, however, is that any not-for-profit organisation should have:

■ strategic targets, mainly non-financial in nature

■ operational targets, which may be either financial (often related to costs and keeping costs under control) or non-financial (related to the nature of operations)

A useful approach to setting performance targets and performance measures in a not-for-profit entity is to group performance indicators into three groups:

■ **financial measurements**, which indicate the **efficiency** in using available financial resources and **economy** in spending

■ **non-financial measurements**, which indicate whether the entity has achieved its strategic objectives (measurements of **effectiveness**)

■ **qualitative indicators**, which also indicate effectiveness in achieving objectives, but which cannot be measured in quantifiable terms.

Example

The performance targets and performance measurements for a hospital might include the following items:

Financial measures (efficiency, economy)	Budgeted annual expenditure. Comparison of actual spending with the budget. Costs per selected units of activity, such as average costs per treatment, average costs per operation, average annual cost per hospital bed. Benchmarking costs against costs in other hospitals. Major items of cost as a percentage of total costs: for example, administration and management costs as a percentage of total running costs.
Non-financial measures (effectiveness)	Units of service delivered, such as the number of patients treated each year, and the number of operations performed. The speed of delivery of services, such as the speed of an ambulance service, average waiting time for treatment, average time between start and completion of treatment. Quality of service, measured in terms of successful treatments, number of serious errors in treatment. Utilisation of resources, such as 'bed occupancy rates' (percentage of beds occupied on average by patients each day).
Qualitative	Public confidence and satisfaction with the services provided. Morale of the work force. Standards of cleanliness in the hospital.

Example

Similarly, the performance measurements for a school might be as follows:

Financial measures (efficiency, economy)	Budgeted annual expenditure. Comparison of actual spending with the budget. Costs per selected units of activity, such as average costs per student per year. Benchmarking costs against costs in other schools. Major items of cost as a percentage of total costs: for example, cost of spending on books or IT systems as a percentage of total running costs.
Non-financial measures (effectiveness)	Examination results (compared with a government target or benchmarked against other schools). Number of students going on to university. Annual intake of new students. Utilisation of resources, such as the ratio of teachers to students.
Qualitative	Reputation of the school. Behaviour of students.

4.3   Value for money (VFM)

The performance of not-for-profit organisations may be assessed on the basis of value for money or VFM. Value for money is often referred to as the '3Es':

■ economy

■ efficiency

■ effectiveness.

Economy

Economy means keeping spending within limits, and avoiding wasteful spending. It also means achieving the same purpose at a lower expense. A simple example of economy is found in the purchase of supplies. Suppose that an administrative department buys items of stationery from a supplier, and pays $2 each for pens. It might be possible to buy pens of the same quality to fulfil exactly the same purpose for $1.50 each. Economy would be achieved by switching to buying the $1.50 pens, saving $0.50 per pen with no loss of operating efficiency or effectiveness.

Efficiency

Efficiency means getting more output from available resources. Applied to employees, efficiency is often called 'productivity'. Suppose that a sales order clerk processes 50 customer orders each day. Efficiency would be improved if a sales order clerk increases the rate of output, and processes 60 orders each day, without any loss of effectiveness.

Effectiveness

Effectiveness refers to success in achieving end results or success in achieving objectives. Whereas efficiency is concerned with getting more outputs from available resources, effectiveness is concerned with achieving outputs that meet the required aims and objectives. For example, the efficiency of sales representatives will be improved if they increase their calls to customers from eight to ten each day, but their effectiveness will not be increased if they do not achieve any more sales from the extra calls.

Management accounting systems and reporting systems may provide information to management about value for money. Has VFM been achieved, and if so, how much and in what ways?

Value for money audits may be carried out to establish how much value is being achieved within a particular department and whether there have been improvements to value for money. Internal audit departments may carry out occasional VFM audits, and report to senior management and the manager of the department they have audited.

VFM budgeting can be particularly useful in not-for-profit organisations, whose purpose is to achieve a stated objective as closely as possible, with the resources available.

Example

State-owned schools may be given a target that their pupils (of a specified age) must achieve a certain level of examination grades or 'passes' in a particular examination.

A VFM audit could be used to establish spending efficiency within a school.

- **Economy**. Was there any unnecessary spending? Could the same value have been obtained for lower spending?

- **Efficiency**. Have the school's resources been used efficiently? Could more output have been obtained from the available resources? Could the same results have been achieved with fewer resources? A study of efficiency might focus on matters such as teaching time per teacher per week, and the utilisation of resources such as science equipment and computer-based training materials.

- **Effectiveness**. The most obvious measurements of effectiveness are the number or percentage of pupils achieving the required examination 'passes', or the grades of pass mark that they have achieved. Effectiveness is improved by increasing the pass rate.

4.4 Problems with performance measurement in not-for profit entities

There are several problems commonly found with performance measurement in not-for-profit entities, particularly in entities that are controlled by the government.

The entity might have several different strategic targets, which may sometimes conflict with each other. For example, the strategic targets for a state-owned school might be to:

- raise the general standard of education, as measured by pass rates in examinations

- provide a broad education

- raise the standards of the most able students.

These targets conflict because it may be impossible to focus on examination results and also provide a broad education. Similarly, it might not be possible to raise education standards for all students but at the same time try to develop the most gifted students.

Multiple strategic targets might not be achievable within the limits of the available resources and expenditure budgets. For example, the strategic targets of a police force might be to:

- prevent crime and

- increase the detection rate for crimes that have been committed.

Given the limited resources available, a police force might be unable to prevent crime and also increase detection rates.

There are other problems with assessing performance of not-for-profit entities.

- There might be political interference that prevents strategic targets from being achieved. For example, the government might decide to change the strategic targets for the hospitals service, or introduce additional targets.

- It might be difficult to measure the output of a not-for-profit entity. For example, how might the output of a fire service be measured?

- The service may be organised on a regional basis. For example, there may be a regional fire service, a regional police force or a regional schools network. It is usual in these circumstances to compare the performance of each region or area. This is often unfair, since conditions and circumstances very widely between different areas of the country. (An extreme example in the UK in 2006 was the criticism by a government audit agency of the police force on Lundy Island: the agency criticised the police for failing to improve its road accident statistics, whereas many other police forces had succeeded in reducing road accidents in their area. There had not been any road accidents on Lundy Island since the car was invented, which made the criticism somewhat unfair!)

- There may be a tendency to measure performance by the amount of resources and money put into the entity, rather than measuring performance on the basis of outputs achieved. For example, it might be tempting to judge the health service on the basis of extra staff employed or extra money spent on hospitals, equipment and medicines.

Behavioural aspects of performance reporting: reward systems
■ Unintended consequences of performance measurement systems
■ Performance rewards
■ Designing reward schemes: factors to consider
■ Behavioural problems with reward systems

5 Behavioural aspects of performance reporting: reward systems

5.1 Unintended consequences of performance measurement systems

An aim of performance reporting systems should be to improve performance. In order to achieve this objective, it is often necessary to consider the behavioural implications of performance reports.

Performance reports should be used in the way intended. In practice, however, there may be unintended consequences, particularly when managers receive rewards for good performance.

Performance measurement systems can suffer from several problems that reduce their effectiveness.

■ **Tunnel vision**. Tunnel vision means focusing on performance measurement to the exclusion of other aspects of management.

■ **Sub-optimisation**. Sub-optimisation occurs when managers focus on achieving good performance in one area, but in doing so overlook other aspects of performance. As a result, overall performance is not as good as it should be. For example, management may be given performance targets for the sales of new products: they may focus on sales growth for new products, and in doing so overlook the need to maintain sales of established products. As a result total sales and profits might fall.

■ **Myopia**. Myopia is short-sightedness. In the context of performance measurement, it means concentrating on short-term performance measures to the exclusion of longer-term considerations.

■ **Measure fixation**. Measure fixation means taking action to ensure that specific performance targets are reached without considering the possible consequences. For example, a department might have a target for labour costs as a maximum proportion of its total operating costs. In order to meet this target, management might recruit and employ inexperienced and untrained staff who are paid less money than experienced employees. The labour cost target might be met, but the quality of work might deteriorate.

■ **Misrepresentation**. Misrepresentation describes the tendency to give a false but flattering picture of performance, by disguising actual results. For example, a sales manager might represent the sales performance for a period in a flattering light – with some growth in sales volume. However, this could be misleading:

sales volume growth might have been achieved only as a result of heavy price discounting and a big reduction in gross profit margins.

- **Misinterpretation**. Misinterpretation occurs when performance measures are interpreted in an incorrect or over-simplified way. Management might read something good or something bad in a set of performance figures, when the actual situation is more complex and the results are not so easy to interpret.

- **Gaming**. Gaming occurs when there is a deliberate distortion of a performance measure or a performance target, in order to make actual results subsequently appear much better than they really are. For example, a departmental manager might argue that productivity in the department has been poor, so that a low performance target is set for productivity in the department. If the target is set at a low level, it is relatively easy to achieve, and the department's performance will therefore appear better than it really is.

- **Ossification**. Performance measurement systems should be flexible, and new performance measures should be introduced as appropriate to replace measures that are no longer appropriate. Ossification refers to an unwillingness that may exist to change any parts of the measurement system, after it has been introduced.

- **Lack of consistency**. Within an organisation, the performance targets set for individuals or groups may be inconsistent with each other. For example, a production manager may be given performance targets relating to keeping costs under control, and a quality control manager may have performance targets for ensuring the quality of completed output. The targets of the production manager and the quality control manager may be inconsistent, if lower costs are achievable by reducing quality.

These problems need to be recognised and understood. Management should continually review the performance measurement system and the appropriateness of the performance targets and performance measurements that are used.

5.2 Performance rewards

Many organisations have systems for linking the achievement of performance targets with rewards for the successful individual. Rewards may take the form of higher pay (for example, a cash bonus or a higher salary) or promotion. Individuals may also feel rewarded by a sense of personal achievement (and possibly also by a formal recognition of their achievement by senior management). In some cases, there may be systems of 'punishment' for poor performance, such as withholding a bonus or even dismissal.

Advantages of reward systems

There are several advantages in having a system of rewards linked to performance:

- A well-designed reward scheme should link rewards to performance that supports strategic objectives. This should help the organisation to implement its strategies and achieve its strategic objectives.

- Rewards can motivate individuals to achieve their performance targets. They can also help to attract and retain talented individuals.

- The payment of rewards for achieving key targets helps to inform managers and employees about what the critical aspects of performance are.

- An effective reward system will encourage employees to focus on continuous improvement.

- Where rewards involve granting shares or share options in the company, employees who benefit from the rewards may be encouraged to think more about the long-term prospects of their company and its market value.

- Reward schemes might help to attract talented employees, and make them want to work for the entity.

5.3 Designing reward schemes: factors to consider

There are several factors to consider and questions to answer when designing a reward scheme.

- Should the rewards for performance be based on results (outputs) or on the effort that has been put in? A reward scheme for salesmen, for example, can be based fairly simply on results achieved (volume of sales). It is often much more difficult however to reward administrative staff for results achieved, because the results of their efforts might not be easily quantifiable, or measured against clear targets.

- Should rewards be given in a money form (a bonus or higher salary) or in non-monetary form (such as share options)?

- Should rewards be explicit or implicit? Explicit rewards are rewards that will definitely be given for meeting performance targets, such as a cash bonus. Implicit rewards are not specific promises, but there is a general understanding that the rewards will be available for good performance. For example, there is often an expectation of promotion or a higher salary for good performance, but these are not explicit promises, only an implicit understanding.

- How large should rewards be?

- Over what time period should performance be measured before rewards are given?

- Should rewards be given for individual performance, or should there be group rewards for team performance?

- Should the rewards involve equity participation – giving shares or share options to individuals?

- What are the tax implications of different reward schemes? Can a reward scheme be devised that limits the tax liabilities of the employees receiving the rewards, without breaching the tax laws?

5.4 Behavioural problems with reward systems

When individuals are rewarded for performance, some potential behavioural problems might occur.

It is often difficult to measure the performance of individuals, and the performance of groups or teams must be measured instead. When group performance is measured, there may be a problem in the following situations:

■ Some members of the group or team believe that they have been responsible for the successful performance of the group, whereas other team members have not contributed as much as they should have done. These individuals may be angered if rewards are paid to all members of the team, including the undeserving members.

■ The reward system provides rewards to some members of a group, but not to others: for example, a departmental manager may be rewarded, but none of the departmental staff.

When performance is rewarded, the individuals affected will be inclined to focus on the measures of performance that set the level of their reward – to the exclusion of all other aspects of performance. This can have unintended consequences.

Customer profitability

- Profitability: customers and channels of distribution
- Customer profitability analysis
- Using customer profitability analysis
- Improving customer profitability

---

6 Customer profitability

6.1 Profitability: customers and channels of distribution

In highly competitive markets, it is important that companies should remain profitable.

- They should avoid the risk of selling goods or services to customers at prices that are too low, and fail to cover the costs of selling to the customer.

- They should also avoid selling products through channels of distribution that are unprofitable.

For example, a book publisher might sell popular books to the general public through bookshops, and educational books to schools and universities by means of direct selling (with sales representatives visiting schools, universities and educational conferences). Selling to each type of customer, through different marketing channels, will involve different marketing and selling costs.

Companies should therefore measure the profitability of each of their customers, or each category of customers.

Traditional management accounting systems fail to do this.

- A traditional management accounting system reports gross profit for the period, and selling and distribution costs and administration costs are then treated as period costs (fixed costs). These are deducted from gross profit to arrive at the net profit for the period.

- Many costs associated with selling to customers are sales and distribution costs. For different types of customer, the costs of sales and distribution can differ. Traditional management accounting systems do not record these 'customer costs'.

 Example

A company has two customers X and Y. Customer X buys about 100 units per month and requires daily deliveries of five units on each working day of the month, to a location about 50 kilometres away. Customer Y also buys 100 units each month, but requires only one delivery each month, at the beginning of the month, to a location less than five kilometres away. The goods are delivered in the company's own transport vehicles.

It should be obvious that the costs of delivery to customer X will be much higher than costs of delivery to customer Y. There are more deliveries to customer X each month, and the goods have to be delivered a longer distance.

Because selling costs vary for different customers, the profitability of customers can also vary. Traditional management accounting systems would not record the differences in selling costs between customer X and customer Y. A system of customer profitability reporting, on the other hand, will recognise the different selling costs for each customer. The profitability of a customer can be measured as the gross profit from selling goods to the customer, minus other 'customer costs' – particularly selling and distribution costs associated with the customer.

6.2 Customer profitability analysis

Another approach to decision analysis involves assessing the profitability of particular channels of marketing or particular types of customer. A company might have several different types of customer, and it might sell to each type of customer in a different way.

Relevant cost analysis can be used to identify whether it is profitable to sell to particular types of customer:

	$
Sales revenue from category of customer	A
Variable/relevant production costs	B
Gross contribution from category of customer	(A – B)
Relevant marketing and selling costs	C
Contribution of customer category to profits	(A – B – C)

To analyse customer profitability, information is needed about the relevant costs of selling to each particular type of customer. This information might be obtained from activity based costing, where activities associated with different categories of customer can be identified and costed.

For example, some types of customer might buy in large volume orders, whereas another type of customer might buy in small size orders. The annual costs of processing and delivery per unit sold will probably be much lower for the customers who make large orders. These customers could therefore be much more profitable. Activity based costing might be useful by identifying the costs and cost drivers for order processing.

A potential benefit of **activity based costing** is the information it can provide to help managers with customer profitability analysis.

6.3 Using customer profitability analysis

Customer profitability analysis can be extremely useful in reaching pricing decisions.

- Prices charged to customers should be sufficiently high to cover all the 'customer costs' for that customer.

- In order to retain customers, or win new customers, prices should not be reduced to a level where they fail to cover customer costs – except perhaps as a short-term loss-making action to retain or win business.

- To improve profitability, it should be possible to consider ways of reducing the costs of selling to customers, as well as ways of improving the gross profit.

- If some types of customer are more profitable than others, a company might concentrate most of its marketing efforts on selling to the most profitable types of customer.

6.4 Improving customer profitability

An examination question on customer profitability analysis may also require you to suggest how the profitability of different categories of customer might be improved. There are three broad approaches to improving customer profitability.

- **Improvements can be made in the processes** used to supply customers, such as reducing production costs or distribution costs to the customer.

- Another important aspect of customer profitability is **pricing**. Large customers may be unprofitable if they are given large price discounts.

- **Managing customer relationships**. Companies spend money to develop customer relationships. For example, they may spend heavily on advertising to win new customers, or they may employ sales representatives to develop relationships with key clients. Customer profitability can be improved by making sure that the benefits from additional sales are more than the costs incurred in developing and maintaining the relationships. For example, it is not worth spending money on advertising for new customers, if the profits they provide are less than the cost of the advertising.

Customer profitability can be improved by making improvements in processes. In particular, improvements might be possible in the following processes:

- Order handling and production processes. It might be possible to persuade a customer to make fewer and larger orders, so that set-up costs and other batch costs can be reduced. (Alternatively, if a customer wants to have a just-in-time system of purchasing, he should be prepared to pay for the extra costs associated with producing in small batches.)

- Delivery processes. It might be possible to introduce improvements into delivery arrangements. For example, a customer might agree to accept delivery of goods at one location, instead of several different locations.

- Advertising. A company might reduce its spending on advertising and other forms of marketing (such as direct mail) to customers whose profitability is low.

It is important to look at the **total relationship with a customer**, and assess the overall profitability of the customer from all the different transactions. In banking, for example, a corporate customer of a bank will use many different services of the bank. The bank will charge for each different service that it provides, such as electronic payments, processing cheques, foreign exchange transactions, borrowing facilities and so on. The bank might be prepared to offer some of these services at a loss, in order to make profits on other types of transaction with the customer, provided that the customer contributes to the profitability of the bank taking the entire relationship into consideration.

Companies should also consider the relationship with a customer **in the longer term**, not just the short term. High initial costs might be incurred to establish a relationship with a new customer – for example, sales representatives might spend a long time in meetings or discussions with potential customers and new customers. In the short run, because of these high initial costs, the customer may be unprofitable. In the longer term, however, selling to the customer should become profitable. The high initial costs and early losses will be justified by the longer-term profits.

CHAPTER

14

Strategic models and performance measurement

Contents
1   Five Forces model
2   Boston Consulting Group (BCG) model
3   Ansoff's growth vector analysis

Five Forces model
■ Competitive strength and the five forces
■ Existing competitors and competitive rivalry
■ Threat from new entrants
■ Bargaining power of suppliers
■ Bargaining power of customers
■ Threat from substitute products

1 Five Forces model

Using strategic models to set targets and measure performance

Several strategic planning models have been developed that can be used to set strategic planning targets, and to measure and assess actual performance in relation to strategic targets. These include:

■ The Five Forces model of Michael Porter

■ The BCG matrix of the Boston Consulting Group

■ Ansoff's product/market growth strategies.

Each of these models considers strategies for achieving a competitive position for products in their markets, or for developing products and markets to grow the business.

1.1 Competitive strength and the five forces

Michael Porter (in *Competitive Strategy*) developed a model for analysing the competitive nature of markets and the competitive position of companies. It is also a model for assessing the problems that a company faces in establishing a strong competitive position in a market.

The model should be used to analyse a 'strategic business unit', rather than a company as a whole. A strategic business unit (or SBU) is a part of a company's operations for which there is a separate and distinct market.

The model is called the Five Forces model, because Porter suggests that there are five factors or 'forces' that affect the competitive position of a company in a market. These five forces are:

■ existing competitors and the rivalry between existing competitors

■ the threat from new entrants to the market

■ the bargaining power of suppliers

■ the bargaining power of customers

■ the threat from substitute products.

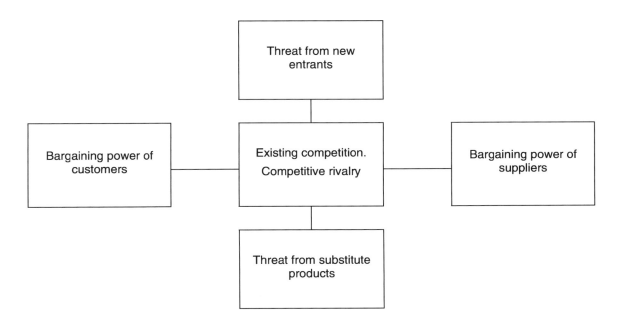

A management information system should be able to provide measures relating to each of these five forces, to assist management in making decisions about competitive strategy.

1.2 Existing competitors and competitive rivalry

The strength of competition varies between different markets. Some markets have several rival companies competing for customers. Other markets are dominated by a single company, although there may be some small and weak competitors.

When competition is strong, companies are likely to pursue active competitive strategies to retain existing customers and win new customers from their rivals. They might compete by offering lower prices, a wider range of products or products with a superior design or quality. For example, in the UK the retail market for food products is dominated by four large supermarket chains (Tesco, Sainsbury's, Asda and Wm Morrison), which compete with each other mainly on the basis of price, product range and location (convenience).

In a competitive market, an initiative by one company – such as a decision to the reduce prices of some goods – is often copied quickly by its rivals. Gains in market share might therefore be short-lived.

Companies in a competitive market try to retain or increase their share of the market, and important information for management is therefore information about:

■ growth in the total market, and

■ the market share of each competitor in the market.

If a company is losing market share, or if a competitor is gaining market share, this might indicate a weakness with the company's existing strategies.

Switching costs

Switching costs might affect the strength of competition in a market. Switching costs are the costs that a customer would incur by switching from one supplier to another. In some industries and markets, switching costs might be high. For example, it might be necessary to train employees in a different technology of the new supplier.

Switching costs might be high, for example, if a customer is considering a switch to a new supplier of software. All the existing data files would have to be converted to a format suitable for the new software and employees would have to be trained to use the new system.

1.3 Threat from new entrants

In some markets, it is difficult for new competitors to enter the market. (The 'barriers to entry' are high.) This may be because entry to the market would require a large capital investment, and any company entering the market would therefore be taking a big risk.

The strength of the threat from new entrants depends on the strength of the barriers to entry. Barriers to entry may not prevent competitors entering the market eventually, but they can delay the entry of new competitors.

The nature of barriers to entry

A variety of factors might create strong barriers to entry.

- **Economies of scale**. Economies of scale refer to the ability of an entity to reduce the average cost per unit of sales by producing and selling a larger quantity of the product. They occur for a variety of reasons:
  - By making and selling more units, fixed costs are spread over a larger quantity and fixed costs per unit fall.
  - An entity might be able to use larger machines that can produce larger quantities more efficiently than smaller machines.
  - An entity might be able to buy materials at a lower cost, by purchasing in larger quantities.
- **Capital investment**. Entering a new market might require a large capital investment. This might deter a new entrant, because the investment could be high-risk.
- **Customer loyalty**. Entities already operating in the market might have strong customer loyalty and a strong brand name. This would make it difficult for a new entrant to win market share.
- A barrier to entry might exist in the form of **legal or political protection**. For example, the products made by a company already in the market might be protected by patent. Government protection might be provided in the form of an import ban or by law. An example in 2006 was the failure of European online gambling firms to enter the US market, because of US legislation against online gambling. This legislation protected companies that operated casinos in the US.

Weak barriers to entry

In some markets, barriers to entry might be low, and it might be fairly easy for new competitors to enter the market. This is often the case with markets for services, where the service relies on the skill or expertise of the service provider. For example, it is often fairly easy for a professional person, such as an architect or a solicitor to set up in business.

Occasionally, technological changes might reduce barriers to entry and make it easier for new companies to enter. For example, the Internet has made it possible for some companies to enter a market by offering goods or services for sale on the Internet. Selling through a web site avoids the need for large investments in retail stores or office property.

Barriers to entry would be lowered the government offered a subsidy or grant to companies that invested in a particular industry.

A management information system should be able to provide information about any new entrants to the market, the type of product or service they are providing, the prices they are charging and the success they seem to be having in attracting customers.

1.4   Bargaining power of suppliers

The competitive position of a company in its market might be affected by the ability of one or more key suppliers to influence the market. Suppliers can have a very strong influence when:

■   there are very few suppliers to the market, and

■   there are a large number of companies in the market, buying from the same suppliers.

An example is the influence of producers of oil and natural gas over the energy markets.

Powerful suppliers might be able to increase prices or control the supply of their product to the market. Companies in the market are exposed to the risk that the cost or the supply of a key resource could be changed by their supplier's decision.

Companies in a market should try to:

■   avoid reliance on a single supplier, if possible, and try to use several different suppliers, or

■   develop close strategic relationships with key suppliers.

When suppliers have a strong influence over a market, a company's management information system should provide information about:

■   the number and identity of suppliers in the market

■   their prices

■ the proportion of total purchases of key products that are obtained from each supplier.

1.5 Bargaining power of customers

The competitive position of a company might also be affected by reliance on one or a small number of customers. An entire market might be dominated by a small number of potential customers. For example, the market for sophisticated weapons systems is influenced by the power of the rich governments that can afford to buy them. Similarly, the market for large passenger aircraft is strongly influenced by the bargaining power of the fairly small number of airline companies that might buy them.

The bargaining power of customers is particularly strong in markets where there is a large number of suppliers but only a few customers. The UK retail market for food was referred to earlier. In this market, there are only four major supermarket chains, which buy a large proportion of all food products sold in the UK, but there are large numbers of small suppliers. The powerful buyers are often able to dictate terms to the suppliers, and can threaten to switch to different suppliers if the do not get what they want.

When customers have a strong influence over a market, a company's management information system should provide information about:

■ the number and identity of the major customers in the market

■ what these customers are asking for, in terms of product or service quality and price

■ the proportion of the company's total sales that are made to each major customer.

1.6 Threat from substitute products

The competitive strength of a company might also be affected by the existence of substitute products. The company needs to be aware that its competitive strategy could result in a switch of customer demand to or from a substitute product.

For example, an increase in the worldwide price of tea could lead to a switch in demand from tea to coffee. Similarly, higher prices for travel by railway could lead to a switch by customers to alternative forms of transport, such as air or road.

When there are close substitutes for a company's products or services, management should be provided with market information about these substitutes. For example, a company that supplies tea should monitor the market for coffee and other drink products.

> ## Boston Consulting Group (BCG) model
>
> - The BCG matrix: market growth (potential) and market share (profitability)
> - Categories of product in the BCG matrix
> - Structure of the BCG matrix
> - Using the BCG matrix for planning and performance measurement
> - Weaknesses in BCG model analysis

2 Boston Consulting Group (BCG) model

2.1 The BCG matrix: market growth (potential) and market share (profitability)

In competitive markets, management need information to evaluate their products (or services) in terms of their:

- market potential, and
- ability to generate profits and cash flows for the business.

The Boston Consulting Group matrix (or BCG matrix) is a model that can be used to assess which products should be developed for future growth, and whether a business entity has an appropriate mix of products for achieving future growth. It incorporates the concept of the product life cycle. It is useful for companies that provide a number of different products (or services) for different markets.

The BCG matrix can be drawn as a 2 × 2 matrix, which 'maps' each product that a company sells, in terms of:

- the expected growth in the market as a whole, and
- the share of the total market that is currently held by the company's product.

2.2 Categories of product in the BCG matrix

Products are categorised into four types:

- stars
- cash cows
- dogs
- question marks.

Stars

Stars are products where the market is growing at a fast rate, and the product enjoys a large share of the total market. They are normally new products. Stars might not yet be profitable, but new investment in the product should provide high financial

---

returns in the future. Entities need 'stars' in order to succeed in the future, and so should invest in them.

Because the market is strong and growing, there are no problems with over-capacity in production and over-supply to the market. This means that the company has some control over prices that it can charge. (It may choose between a pricing strategy of 'market penetration' or 'market skimming'. These pricing strategies are explained in another chapter.)

A 'star' product has more potential for profits, and it is worthwhile to invest more money in the product, to increase sales.

Eventually when the growth in sales slows down, a star will become a cash cow. In other words, a product that is a star early in its life cycle will become a cash cow during the mature stage of the product's life.

Cash cows

Cash cows are products where the market is growing slowly, or is not growing at all, and the product enjoys a large share of the total market. These products are very profitable and provide large cash inflows for the entity. Every company needs cash cows to survive in the long-term. The cash from cash cows helps to finance investment in stars. Eventually, cash cows must be replaced when the product reaches the end of its economic life.

The strategy for a cash cow should be maintaining and protecting the position of the product in its market, and to keep costs under control (or reduce costs). The strategy should not be to seek more sales growth, because the product has no further growth potential (or very little further growth potential).

Dogs

Dogs are products where the market is growing slowly, or is not growing at all, and the product has only a small share of the total market. These products are often (but not always) losing money. The correct strategic decision is usually to withdraw the product from the market.

Question marks

Question marks (also called 'problem children') are products where the market is growing at a fast rate, but the company's product has only a small share of the total market. These products are currently losing money. New investment in 'dogs' (for example, more investment in research and development or marketing) might turn a 'question mark' into a 'star', but there is also a risk that it will become a 'dog' when the growth in the market slows down. Investing in these products will be a strategic gamble.

2.3   Structure of the BCG matrix

A BCG matrix is shown below. The individual products (or business units) can be plotted in the matrix as a circle. The size of the circle shows the relative money value of sales for the product. A large circle represents a product with large annual sales.

The position of the products in each quadrant also shows the relative rate of growth in the total market, and the relative share that the company's product has in the total market.

BCG matrix

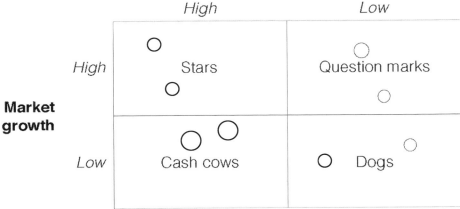

2.4   Using the BCG matrix for planning and performance measurement

Companies can use the BCG matrix to analyse the range of products that it sells, and to plan its future investment in products. The aim should be to ensure that there is a sufficient investment in 'stars', and that cash cows will generate enough cash flow to finance most or all of this investment.

To carry out an analysis, information is needed for each product about:

■   Total market size

■   Rate of growth in the total market

■   The company's share of the total market

■   Changes in the company's share of the total market.

 Example

A company produces five different products, and sells each product in a different market.

The management accountant has obtained the following information about market size and market share for each product. It consists of actual data for each of the last three years and forecasts for the next two years.

	Year - 2 Actual	Last year Year -1 Actual	Current year Actual	Next year Year + 1 Forecast	Year + 2 Forecast
Product 1					
Total market size ($ million)	50	58	65	75	84
Product 1 sales	2	2	2.5	3	3.5
Product 2					
Total market size ($ million)	150	152	149	153	154
Product 2 sales	78	77	80	82	82
Product 3					
Total market size ($ million)	40	50	60	70	80
Product 3 sales	3	5	8	10	12
Product 4					
Total market size ($ million)	60	61	61	61	60
Product 4 sales	2	2	2	2	2
Product 5					
Total market size ($ million)	100	112	125	140	150
Product 5 sales	4	5	5.5	6	6.5

In the current year, the market share of the market leader, or the nearest competitor to the company, has been estimated as follows:

Market for:	Market share of market leader or the company's nearest competitor %
Product 1	37
Product 2	26
Product 3	12
Product 4	29
Product 5	20

Required

(a) Using the Boston Consulting Group model, how should each of these products be classified?

(b) How might this analysis help the management of the company to make strategic decisions about its future products and markets ('product-market strategy')?

 Answer

A **star** is a product in a market that is growing quickly, where the company's product has a large market share or where the market share is increasing. **Product 3** appears to be a star. The total market is expected to double in size between Year – 2 and Year + 2. The expected market share in two years' time is 15%, compared with 7.5% in Year – 2. Its market share in the current year is over 13%, which makes it the current market leader.

A **cash cow** is a product in a market that has little or no growth. The market share, however, is normally quite high, and the product is therefore able to contribute substantially to operational cash flows. **Product 2** appears to be a cash cow. In the current year its market share was over 53%, and it is the market leader.

A **dog** is a product in a market with no growth, and where the product has a low share of the market. Dogs are likely to be loss-making and its cash flows are probably negative. **Product 4** appears to be a dog. The total market size is not changing, and the market share for product 4 is only about 3%. This is much less than the 29% market share of the market leader.

A **question mark** is a product with a fairly low market share in a market that is growing fairly quickly. **Product 1** appears to be a question mark. The total market is growing quite quickly, but the market share of Product 1 is about 4% and this is not expected to change. **Product 5** also appears to be a question mark, for the same reason.

The company should decide on its strategy for the products it will sell.

- It should benefit from the cash flows generated by its only cash cow, Product 2.
- It should invest in its star, Product 3, with the objective that this will eventually become a cash cow.
- It should give serious consideration to abandoning its dog, Product 4, and withdrawing from the market.
- It has to make a decision about its two question marks, Product 1 and Product 5. The main question is whether either of these products can become a star and cash cow. Additional investment and a change of strategy for these products might be necessary, in order to increase market share.

For all the products (with the exception of Product 4, if this is abandoned) the company should also consider ways of making the products more profitable. Techniques such as **value chain analysis** might help to identify cost savings.

2.5 Weaknesses in BCG model analysis

There are several criticisms of the BCG model.

- The BCG model assumes that the competitive strength of a product in its market depends on its market share, and the attractiveness of a market for new investment depends only on the rate of sales growth in the market. Unless a product can achieve a large share of the market, it is not sufficiently competitive. Unless a market is growing quickly enough, it is not worthwhile to invest more money in it. It can be argued that these assumptions are incorrect.
  - A product can have a strong competitive position in its market, even with a low market share. Competitive strength can be provided by factors such as product quality, brand name or brand reputation, or low costs.
  - A company might benefit from investing in an industry or market where sales growth is low.
- It might be difficult to define the market.
  - There might be problems with defining the geographical area of the market. A market might be defined in terms of a single country, a region of a country or as an international or global market.

- It might also be difficult to identify which products are competing with each other. For example, the total market for cars may be divided into different categories of car, but there may be problems in deciding which models of car belong to each category.

■ It might be that the BCG matrix is better for analysing the performance of strategic business units (SBUs) and market segments. It is not so useful for analysing entire markets, which might consist of many different market segments.

■ It might be difficult to define what is meant by 'high rate' and 'low rate' of growth in the market. Similarly, it might be difficult to define what is meant by 'high' market share and 'low' market share.

Ansoff's growth vector analysis

- Four product market strategies for growth
- Market penetration strategy
- Product development strategy (innovation strategy)
- Market development strategy
- Diversification strategy
- The growth vector
- Ansoff's growth vector and gap analysis

---

3   Ansoff's growth vector analysis

3.1   Four product market strategies for growth

Ansoff's growth vector analysis is another model for strategic development and growth. The model identifies four strategies for developing products and markets in order to grow the business.

The four strategies are as follows:

- Market penetration
- Product development (innovation)
- Market development
- Diversification

3.2   Market penetration strategy

This is a strategy of trying to gain higher sales in the entity's current markets with its existing products. Market penetration is achievable:

- when the total market is growing, or
- by increasing market share.

For example, a company providing mobile telephone services might pursue a market penetration strategy, by trying to sell to more customers. This is possible if the total demand for mobile telephone services is increasing, or by taking market share from competitors.

A market penetration strategy is a low-risk strategy, and is unlikely to result in a high rate of sales growth. The product is not altered and there is no attempt to find new markets for the product.

3.3 Product development strategy (innovation strategy)

This is a strategy for growth that involves developing new products for existing markets and customers. For example, a software company might develop a new product or enhanced product that it tries to sell to its existing customers. Similarly, a car manufacturer might develop a new model of car, which it then tries to sell to its existing customers.

3.4 Market development strategy

This is a strategy of trying to enter new markets for the entity's existing products. In other words, it is a strategy of selling current products to new customers by finding a new market, or a new market segment. For example:

■ a supermarkets company might try to increase its sales by entering the market for Internet shopping and home delivery

■ a company might grow by trying to enter markets in other countries.

3.5 Diversification strategy

This is a strategy of developing new products for new markets. A diversification strategy is a high-risk strategy, because the company needs to develop a new product that will meet customer needs successfully, but it does not yet have much knowledge or understanding of customers in the market and what their needs might be.

There are two types of diversification:

■ **Related diversification**, where the business entity develops new products and markets that are in a related industry. For example, a manufacturer of ice cream might diversify into producing soft drinks.

■ **Unrelated diversification**, where the business entity develops new products and markets that are in an industry where it has no previous experience. For example, a manufacturer of ice cream might diversify into making and selling shoes.

Unrelated diversification is usually a much higher-risk strategy than related diversification. However, even a strategy of related diversification can be a high risk.

3.6 The growth vector

The Ansoff growth vector might be presented as follows:

		Product	
		Current	**New**
Market	**Current**	Market penetration	Product development
	New	Market development	Diversification

Management should be provided with information that helps them to monitor the success of their growth strategy. The items of information that might be provided include:

■ Potential market demand

■ Market size

■ Market share

■ Information about competitors and their products

■ Pricing information

■ Information about costs

■ Information about required investment and financing

■ Estimated returns from a chosen strategy

■ The risks in the chosen strategy.

3.7 Ansoff's growth vector and gap analysis

Ansoff's growth vector can be used together with gap analysis. Gap analysis is the analysis of the difference between a strategic target and the expected performance that will be achieved without any new strategies.

For example, a company might measure the gap between the profits it would like to make in five years' time and the profits it would expect to make if it did not undertake any new growth strategy.

Having estimated the size of the profit gap, the company can then consider growth strategies to increase profitability. The contribution of each growth strategy to profits can be estimated. Together, a combination of growth strategies might enable a company to close the profit gap and pursue strategies that will enable it to meet its targets.

Strategies to fill the profit gap

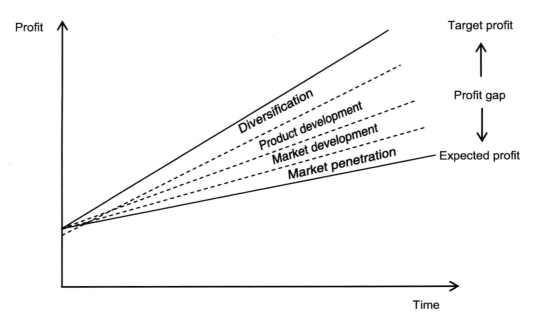

CHAPTER

15

Decentralisation and divisional performance

Contents
1   Divisional performance evaluation
2   Return on Investment (ROI)
3   Residual income (RI)
4   Divisional performance and depreciation
5   Economic Value Added (EVA)

> ## Divisional performance evaluation
>
> - Decentralisation of authority
> - Benefits of decentralisation
> - Disadvantages of decentralisation
> - Controllable profit and traceable profit

1 Divisional performance evaluation

1.1 Decentralisation of authority

Decentralisation involves the delegation of authority within an organisation. Within a large organisation, authority is delegated to the managers of cost centres, revenue centres, profit centres and investment centres.

The term 'decentralised divisionalised structure' means an organisation structure in which authority has been delegated to the centre's manager to decide selling prices, choose suppliers, make output decisions, and so on. A divisionalised structure therefore usually means a structure in which there are investment centres and profit centres.

1.2 Benefits of decentralisation

Decentralisation should provide several benefits for an organisation.

- Decision-making should improve, because the divisional managers make the tactical and operational decisions, and top management is free to concentrate on strategy and strategic planning.
- Decision-making at a tactical and operational level should improve, because the divisional managers have better 'local' knowledge.
- Decision-making should improve because decisions will be made faster. Divisional managers can make decisions 'on the spot' without referring them to senior management.
- Divisions provide useful experience for managers who will one day become top managers in the organisation.
- Within a large multinational group, there can be tax advantages in creating a divisional structure, by locating some divisions in countries where tax advantages or subsidies can be obtained.

1.3 Disadvantages of decentralisation

The divisional managers might put the interests of their division before the interests of the organisation as a whole. Taking decisions that benefit a division might have adverse consequences for the organisation as a whole. When this happens, there is a lack of 'goal congruence'.

Top management may lose control over the organisation if they allow decentralisation without accountability. It may be necessary to monitor divisional performance closely. The cost of such a monitoring system might be high.

It is difficult to find a satisfactory measure of historical performance for an investment centre that will motivate divisional managers to take the best decisions. For example, measuring divisional performance by Return on Investment (ROI) might encourage managers to make inappropriate long-term investment decisions. Economies of scale might be lost. For example, a company might operate with one finance director. If it divides itself into three investment centres, there might be a need for four finance directors – one at head office and one in each of the investment centres. Similarly there might be a duplication of other systems, such as accounting system and other IT systems.

1.4   Controllable profit and traceable profit

Profit is a key measure of the financial performance of a division. However, in measuring performance, it is desirable to identify:

■ Costs that are controllable by the manager of the division

■ Costs that are traceable to the division. These are controllable costs plus other costs directly attributable to the division over which the manager does not have control.

There may also be an allocation of general overheads, such as a share of head office costs.

In a divisionalised system, profit centres and investment centres often trade with each other, buying and selling goods and services. These are internal sales, priced at an internal selling price (a 'transfer price'). Reporting systems should identify external sales of the division and internal sales as two elements of the total revenue of the division.

	$
External sales	600,000
Internal sales	150,000
Total sales	750,000
Costs controllable by the divisional manager:	
Variable costs	230,000
Contribution	420,000
Controllable fixed costs	140,000
Profit attributable to the manager (controllable profit)	280,000
Costs traceable to the division but outside the manager's control	160,000
Profit traceable to the division	120,000
Share of general overheads	30,000
Net profit	90,000

Notes

■ **Controllable profit** is used to assess the manager and is therefore sometimes called the **managerial evaluation**.

■ **Traceable profit** is used to assess the performance of the division and is sometimes called the **economic evaluation**.

■ The apportionment of general head office costs should be excluded from the analysis of the manager's performance and the division's performance.

These profit measures can be used with variance analysis, ratio analysis, return on investment, residual income and non-financial performance measurements to evaluate performance.

> ## Return on Investment (ROI)
>
> - Measuring ROI
> - ROI and investment decisions
> - Advantages and disadvantages of ROI for measuring performance
> - ROI and incentive schemes

2 Return on Investment (ROI)

Return on investment (ROI) is a measure of the return on capital employed for an investment centre. It is also called the accounting rate of return (ARR).

It is often used as a measure of divisional performance for investment centres because:

- the manager of an investment centre is responsible for the profits of the centre and also the assets invested in the centre, and
- ROI is a performance measure that relates profit to the size of the investment.
- Profit is not a suitable measure of performance for an investment centre. It does not make the manager accountable for his or her use of the net assets employed (the investment in the investment centre).

2.1 Measuring ROI

ROI is the profit of the division as a percentage of capital employed.
However, performance measurement systems should use ROI to evaluate the performance of both the manager and the division.

Although ROI can be measured in different ways, the recommended measures are as follows:

- Managerial evaluation

$$ROI = \frac{Controllab\ le\ profit}{Division'\ s\ capital\ employed} \times 100\%$$

- Divisional/economic evaluation

$$ROI = \frac{Traceable\ profit}{Division'\ s\ capital\ employed} \times 100\%$$

Where possible, the capital employed by the division should be analysed into:

- capital (assets less liabilities) controllable by the manager, and
- capital (assets and liabilities) traceable to the division.

Profit is usually measured as an accounting profit, after deduction of any depreciation charges on non-current assets.

2.2 ROI and investment decisions

When an investment centre manager's performance is evaluated by ROI, the manager will probably be motivated to make investment decisions that increase the division's ROI, and reject investments that would reduce ROI.

Example

A divisional manager is considering an investment in a new item of equipment that would cost $80,000.

The estimated life of the equipment is four years and the expected residual value is $0.

The estimated profit before depreciation is as follows:

Year	$
1	20,000
2	25,000
3	35,000
4	25,000

The asset will be depreciated on a straight-line basis.

What would be the ROI on this investment? Would the investment centre manager decide to undertake this investment or not?

Answer

	$
Total four-year profits before depreciation	105,000
Depreciation over four years	80,000
Total profit over four years	25,000
Average annual profit	6,250

Average asset carrying value over four years: $\dfrac{80,000+0}{2} = \$40,000$

$$\text{ROI (or investment ARR)} = \frac{6,250}{40,000} \times 100\% = 15.63\%$$

The manager might decide to undertake this investment if the average ROI of the division in less than 15.63%. By undertaking the investment, the average ROI over the next four years should increase, and the measured performance of the division would improve.

However, the manager is unlikely to undertake the investment if the average ROI of the investment centre is already higher than 15.63%. This is because over the life of the investment, the average ROI of the investment centre would fall.

The disadvantage of ROI for investment decisions

In practice, ROI (ARR) is an inappropriate basis for making investment decisions. Investment decisions should be based on DCF analysis.

 Example

The managers of investment centres A and B are considering new investments for their division. The following estimates have been prepared;

	Division A	Division B
Average investment (controllable investment)	$100,000	$100,000
Average annual profit after depreciation	$16,000	$11,000
Current controllable ROI of the division	18%	9%
Cost of capital of the company	13%	13%

Division A decision

Using ROI as a basis for the investment decision, Division A would reject their project.

- The project ROI is 16%
- The current ROI of the division is 18%. Investing in the project would reduce the division's ROI.
- However, the ROI of the project is higher than the company's cost of capital.

Division B decision

Using ROI as a basis for the investment decision, Division B would invest in their project.

- The project ROI is 11%.
- The current ROI of the division is 9%. Investing in the project would increase the division's ROI.
- However, the ROI of the project is lower than the company's cost of capital, and investing would almost certainly be undesirable because it would have a negative NPV.

The decision by Division A whether or not to invest should be based on a DCF evaluation. There is insufficient information to calculate the project NPV.
Decisions using ROI are inappropriate because they do not make reference to the company's cost of capital.

2.3   Advantages and disadvantages of ROI for measuring performance

Advantages of using ROI

There are several advantages in using ROI as a measure of the performance of an investment centre.

- It relates the profit of the division to the capital employed, and the division manager is responsible for both profit and capital employed.

- ROI is a percentage measure and can be used to compare the performance of divisions of different sizes.

- It is an easily understood measure of financial performance.

- It focuses attention on capital as well as profit, and encourages managers to sell off unused assets and avoid excessive working capital (inventory and receivables).

Disadvantages of using ROI

There are also disadvantages in using ROI as a measure of the performance of an investment centre.

- As explained above, investment decisions might be affected by the effect they would have on ROI, and this is inappropriate for making investment decisions.

- There are different ways of measuring capital employed. ROI might be based on the net book value (carrying value) of the division at the beginning of the year, or at the end of the year, or the average for the year. Comparison of performance between different organisations is therefore difficult.

- When assets are depreciated, ROI will increase each year provided that annual profits are constant. There is a risk from high accounting returns on assets that are fully depreciated or nearly fully depreciated. This is the risk that the division's manager might not want to get rid of ageing assets, because ROI will fall if new (replacement) assets are purchased.

- ROI is an accounting measure of performance. An alternative system of performance measurement, such as a balanced scorecard approach, might be more appropriate.

2.4 ROI and incentive schemes

Some companies reward managers by paying them an annual bonus if they achieve or exceed a specified target. For divisional managers, an annual bonus might be calculated on the basis of ROI, and whether they succeed in achieving a target ROI each year, or improving the ROI of their division each year.

If divisional managers are rewarded on the basis of ROI performance, this could lead to 'wrong' investment decisions. The following example illustrates this point.

 Example

XYZ Company has a divisionalised structure. The manager of North Division has the authority to invest in capital projects, but only if the board of directors have given their permission. When permission is given by the board, the divisional manager can then decide whether or not to undertake the investment project.

There is an incentive scheme for divisional managers. This scheme provides for annual bonus payments to divisional managers. This cash bonus is paid by reference to the ROI that new investment projects achieve in the first two years. ROI is calculated on the basis of average investment in the project each year.

The manager of North Division has been given permission to spend $30 million on an investment, but there are three mutually exclusive ways in which this investment can be made. These have been called Option 1, Option 2 and Option 3.

XYZ Company has a cost of capital of 10% which it applies to all investment projects. The cash flows and NPV for each Option would be as follows:

	Option 1		Option 2		Option 3	
	Cash flow	Present value at 10%	Cash flow	Present value at 10%	Cash flow	Present value at 10%
Year	$000	$000	$000	$000	$000	$000
0	(30,000)	(30,000)	(30,000)	(30,000.0)	(30,000)	(30,000)
1	8,000	7,272	12,500	11,362.5	15,000	13,635
2	10,000	8,260	12,500	10,325.0	12,000	9,912
3	15,000	11,265	12,500	9,387.5	8,000	6,008
4	12,000	12,000			2,000	1,366
NPV		+ 4,993		+ 1,075.0		+ 921

The assets purchased with the $30 million would be depreciated over the life of the project, using the straight-line method, and would have no residual value.

Required

(a) Calculate the ROI for each Option in each of the first two years of the project.

(b) Comment on the effect that the incentive scheme might have on the choice of Option by the manager of North Division.

Answer

	Option 1	Option 2	Option 3
	$000	$000	$000
Annual depreciation	7,500	10,000	7,500
Investment, beginning of Year 1	30,000	30,000	30,000
Investment, end of Year 1	22,500	20,000	22,500
Average investment, Year 1	26,250	25,000	26,250
Investment, beginning of Year 2	22,500	20,000	22,500
Investment, end of Year 2	15,000	10,000	15,000
Average investment, Year 2	18,750	15,000	18,750

	Option 1	Option 2	Option 3
Year 1	$000	$000	$000
Cash profit	8,000	12,500	15,000
Annual depreciation	7,500	10,000	7,500
Net profit	500	2,500	7,500
ROI, Year 1	**1.9%**	**10.0%**	**28.6%**
Year 2			
Cash profit	10,000	12,500	12,000
Annual depreciation	7,500	10,000	7,500
Net profit	2,500	2,500	4,500
ROI, Year 2	**13.3%**	**16.7%**	**24.0%**

If the manager wants to maximise his bonus, he will choose the Option that gives the highest ROI in Year 1 and Year 2. His decision will be based on the short-term (years 1 – 2) instead of the longer term (the full life of each project).

He will therefore choose Option 3.

However, Option 3 has the lowest NPV of the three options, and from the company's point of view, the preferred option should be Option 1, because this has the highest NPV.

This is therefore an example of how the payment of a bonus on the basis of ROI could result in 'wrong' investment decisions.

Residual income (RI)
■ Measuring residual income
■ Imputed interest (notional interest)
■ Residual income and investment decisions
■ Advantages and disadvantages of residual income

3   Residual income (RI)

Residual income (RI) is another way of measuring the performance of an investment centre.

Residual income = Divisional profit minus Imputed interest charge.

Notes

Divisional profit is an accounting measurement of profit, after depreciation charges are subtracted.

The interest charge is calculated by applying a cost of capital to the division's net investment (net assets). The appropriate measure of net investment is the average investment during the period.

3.1   Measuring residual income

Residual income is measured in either of the following ways:

Managerial evaluation

	$
Controllable profit	A
Less notional interest on average controllable investment	B
Controllable residual income	A – B

Divisional/economic evaluation

	$
Traceable profit	A
Less notional interest on average traceable investment	B
Divisional residual income	A – B

3.2   Imputed interest (notional interest)

Residual income is calculated by deducting an amount for imputed interest (also called notional interest) from the accounting profit for the division.

Imputed interest (notional interest) is the division's capital employed, multiplied by:

- the organisation's cost of borrowing, or
- the weighted average cost of capital of the organisation, or
- a special risk-weighted cost of capital to allow for the special business risk characteristics of the division. A higher interest rate would be applied to divisions with higher business risk.

3.3 Residual income and investment decisions

If investment centres are evaluated on the basis of residual income, their managers will be motivated to undertake new investments that increase residual income and to avoid new investments that would reduce residual income.

However, the investment decisions will often be different to what the decision would be if ROI is used. Residual income increases if the annual profit exceeds the notional interest charge.

- Investments with an average annual profit higher than the cost of capital are undertaken.
- Investments with an average annual profit lower than the cost of capital are rejected.

Example

The difference between the ROI and residual income can be illustrated by returning to the previous example.

	Division A	Division B
Average investment (controllable investment)	$100,000	$100,000
Average annual profit after depreciation	$16,000	$11,000
Current controllable ROI of the division	18%	9%
Cost of capital of the company	13%	13%

Division A decision

Using RI as a basis for the investment decision, Division A would invest in their project, because RI would increase.

	Division A
	$
Average annual profit after depreciation	16,000
Notional interest (13% × $100,000)	13,000
Increase in average annual RI	3,000

Average annual return on capital from the project (16%) is higher than the company's cost of capital. This is why the average annual residual income increases.

Division B decision

Using RI as a basis for the investment decision, Division B would not invest in their project, because RI would fall.

	Division B
	$
Average annual profit after depreciation	11,000
Notional interest (13% × $100,000)	13,000
Fall in average annual RI	(2,000)

Average annual return on capital from the project (11%) is less than the company's cost of capital. This is why the average annual residual income falls.

The decisions by Division A and Division B whether or not to invest should be based on a DCF evaluation. There is insufficient information to calculate the project NPV. However, using residual income for investment decisions is more likely than using ROI to result in a decision that agrees with the decision based on DCF analysis.

In the above example, it is almost certain that a DCF analysis would show that the Division B investment has a negative NPV. The decision using DCF would be to reject the investment, and the decision based on RI is consistent with this.

3.4 Advantages and disadvantages of residual income

Advantages of RI

There are several advantages in using RI as a measure of the performance of an investment centre.

■ It relates the profit of the division to the capital employed, by charging an amount of notional interest on capital employed, and the division manager is responsible for both profit and capital employed.

■ Divisional managers are made aware, through the charge for imputed interest, that investments have a financing cost.

■ RI is a flexible measure of performance, because a different cost of capital can be applied to investments with different risk characteristics.

■ As explained above, measuring performance with RI is more likely to encourage managers to make investment decisions that are consistent with DCF-based investment decisions.

Disadvantages of RI

There are also disadvantages in using RI as a measure of the performance of an investment centre.

■ RI is an accounting-based measure, and suffers from the same problem as ROI in defining capital employed.

■ Its main weakness is that it is difficult to compare the performance of different divisions using RI. Larger divisions should earn a bigger RI. A small division making RI of $50,000 might actually perform much better than a much larger division whose RI is $100,000.

■ RI is not easily understood by management, especially managers with little accounting knowledge.

■ There may be problems in deciding a suitable rate of interest for the imputed interest charge.

Example

The performance of a divisional manager is evaluated by RI. The company's cost of capital is 10%.

The manager is considering whether to invest in a project to buy an asset costing $600,000. The asset would have a three-year life and no residual value. Cash flows from the investment would be $500,000 in each year.

Required

(a)   Calculate the RI for each of the three years of the project, using net book value (NBV) at the start of the year as capital employed.

(b)   Calculate the NPV of the project. Assume that cash flows occur at the end of each year.

Answer

(a)   Residual income

	Year 1	Year 2	Year 3
	$	$	$
Opening net book value	600,000	400,000	200,000
Annual depreciation	200,000	200,000	200,000
	$	$	$
Profit	300,000	300,000	300,000
Notional interest (10%)	60,000	40,000	20,000
Residual income	240,000	260,000	280,000

(b)   NPV

Year	Cash flow	Discount factor at 10%	Present value
	$		$
0	(600,000)	1.000	(600,000)
1 – 3	500,000	2.487	1,243,500
			+ 643,500

> **Divisional performance and depreciation**
>
> - ROI or RI: the problem with depreciation
> - Annuity-based depreciation

4 Divisional performance and depreciation

4.1 ROI or RI: the problem with depreciation

If straight-line depreciation is used and capital employed is based on carrying values (net book values) ROI and RI will rise over time if:

- annual profits are constant and
- assets are not replaced, and existing assets remain in use as they get older.

In the early years of an investment project, the ROI or RI might be very low. If a divisional manager is concerned about the effect that this would have on the division's ROI or RI for the next year or two, the manager might refuse to invest in the project. This is because performance in the next year or so might be much worse, even though the project might be expected to earn a high return over its full economic life.

 Example

Palace Division is a part of the Crystal Group. Its manager has the authority to invest in new capital expenditure, within limits set by head office. The senior management team of the division is considering an investment of $4.2 million. This would have a residual value of zero after four years. Net cash inflows from the investment would be $1.4million for each of the next four years.

The cost of capital for the Palace Division is 10%. It is the group's policy to use straight-line depreciation when measuring divisional profit.

For measurement purposes and reporting purposes, 'capital' is defined as the opening net book value at the start of each year.

Required

For this particular investment:

(a) Calculate residual income each year

(b) Calculate the Return on Investment each year

(c) Calculate the NPV of the investment

(d) State whether the decision would be in the best interests of the company if the manager makes the decision on the basis of the effect of the investment on:

    (i) RI or

    (ii) ROI.

Ignore taxation.

Answer

(a) Residual income

	Year 1	Year 2	Year 3	Year 4
	$000	$000	$000	$000
Opening net book value	4,200	3,150	2,100	1,050
Annual depreciation	1,050	1,050	1,050	1,050
	$	$	$	
Profit before depreciation	1,400	1,400	1,400	1,400
	1,050	1,050	1,050	1,050
	350	350	350	350
Notional interest (10%)	420	315	210	105
Residual income	(70)	35	140	245

The total residual income over the four years is $350,000 (profit of $1,400,000 minus notional interest charges of $1,050,000).

(b) Return on Investment

Capital is defined here as the value of the net assets at the beginning of the year.

	Year 1	Year 2	Year 3	Year 4
	$000	$000	$000	$000
Opening net book value	4,200	3,150	2,100	1,050
Annual depreciation	1,050	1,050	1,050	1,050
	$	$	$	
Profit before depreciation	1,400	1,400	1,400	1,400
	1,050	1,050	1,050	1,050
Profit	350	350	350	350
Return on investment (ROI)	8.3%	11.1%	16.7%	33.3%

The average return on investment = average annual profit/average investment = $350,000/$2,100,000 = 16.7%.

(c) NPV

Year		Cash flow	Discount factor at 10%	Present value
		$		$
0	Capital expenditure	4,200,000	1.000	4,200,000
1 - 4	Net cash flow	1,400,000	3.170	4,438,000
	Net present value			+ 238,000

(d)

Ignoring risk and uncertainty in the forecast cash flows, the decision should be to undertake the capital investment, because the NPV is positive. In theory, undertaking the project will add to shareholders' wealth by this amount.

If the management of Palace Division are concerned about the short-term performance of the division, they might decide not to undertake the investment. This is because the ROI will be less than 10% in Year 1 and the residual income would be negative.

However, if the management team takes a longer-term view, and considers performance over the full four years, they would undertake the investment, because the average annual ROI on the new investment would be 16.7% and the average annual increase in residual income for the division would be $87,500.

Unfortunately, decision-making often focuses on the short term, and there is a possibility that the investment will not be undertaken in order to prevent a fall in ROI or residual income.

Conflicts with NPV

This previous example should demonstrate that on occasions there may be a conflict between NPV and ROI/RI.

NPV gives the correct decision under the assumption that we want to maximise shareholder wealth.

NPV cannot be used to assess historical performance, but ROI and residual income do not always indicate the most appropriate investment decision. This raises the question: Is there any way in which ROI or residual income could be made more consistent with NPV in the assessment of new capital investments?

4.2   Annuity-based depreciation

The problem might sometimes be overcome if annuity-based depreciation is used to measure ROI and RI, instead of straight-line depreciation. However, this approach is only valid if the annual cash flows from an investment project are expected to be a constant amount each year (and are not low in the early years of the investment project).

An annual depreciation charge is calculated as follows:

- Assume that the investment is purchased using a bank loan at the company's cost of capital.
- Convert this loan into an annuity (constant annual cash flow). To do this, divide the cost by the DCF annuity factor for the number of years of the project.
- This annuity or equivalent annual cash flow consists of an interest charge and a loan repayment. The loan repayment element is assumed to be the depreciation charge for the year.
- This depreciation charge, which increases each year over the life of the project, is used to calculate the division's profit for the year.

Annual equivalent cash flow (annuity) = Depreciation + Interest

Annuity depreciation = Annual equivalent cash flow – Notional interest on capital employed.

Example 1

An investment centre invests $3,170,000 in capital equipment that is expected to have a four-year life. The DCF cost of capital is 10%. The investment centre's performance is measured by ROI, but annuity depreciation is used for the centre's capital assets.

For the new equipment annual depreciation will be calculated as follows:

- The DCF annuity factor for four years at 10% is about 3.170 (from DCF tables).
- The annuity cost of the new equipment is therefore $3,170,000/3.170 = $1,000,000.
- This annuity cost consists of an interest charge and depreciation.

The depreciation charge is calculated as the difference between the total annuity cost ($1,000,000) and the annual interest, as follows.

Year	Opening balance	Interest at 10%	Annuity	Balance at end of year
	$	$	$	$
1	(3,170,000)	(317,000)	1,000,000	(2,487,000)
2	(2,487,000)	(248,700)	1,000,000	(1,735,700)
3	(1,735,700)	(173,570)	1,000,000	(909,270)
4	(909,270)	(90,927)	1,000,000	(197)

The closing balance at the end of the four years should be $0. The $197 arises from rounding errors in the annuity discount factor.

The annual depreciation charge is the difference between the annuity cost of $1,000,000 and the interest charge each year. So it is $683,000 in Year 1, rising to $751,300 in Year 2, $816,430 in Year 3 and $909,073 in Year 4.

Example 2

Palace Division is a part of the Crystal Group. Its manager has the authority to invest in new capital expenditure, within limits set by head office. The senior management team of the division is considering an investment of $4.2 million. This would have a residual value of zero after four years. Net cash inflows from the investment would be $1.4million for each of the next four years.

The cost of capital for the Palace Division is 10%. It is the group's policy to use annuity depreciation when measuring divisional profit.

For measurement purposes and reporting purposes, 'capital' is defined as the opening net book value at the start of each year.
The equivalent annual charge or annuity =

$$\frac{\text{Cost of investment}}{\text{DCF factor for years } 1-4 \text{ at } 10\%} = \frac{\$4.2 \text{ million}}{3.170} = \$1,324,921 \text{ (say, } \$1,325,000).$$

Residual income

	Year 1	Year 2	Year 3	Year 4
	$000	$000	$000	$000
Cash flow	1,400	1,400	1,400	1,400
Depreciation + notional interest	1,325	1,325	1,325	1,325
Residual income	75	75	75	75

The residual income is now constant in every year, and a positive value. The investment adds to RI each year.

The decision, based on residual income and using annuity depreciation, would be to undertake the investment project. This is consistent with the NPV assessment.

ROI

For an ROI calculation, we must separate the equivalent annual charge into the interest charge and the depreciation element (the balance).

Year	Investment at the start of the year	Interest at 10%	Equivalent annual charge	Depreciation charge (=total annual charge minus interest)
	$	$	$	$
1	4,200,000	420,000	1,324,921	904,921
2	3,295,079	329,508	1,324,921	995,413
3	2,299,666	229,967	1,324,921	1,094,954
4	1,204,712	120,471	1,324,921	1,204,450
5	0**			

** *Allowing for rounding errors in the discount factor.*

	Year 1	Year 2	Year 3	Year 4
	$	$	$	$
Cash flow	1,400,000	1,400,000	1,400,000	1,400,000
Depreciation	904,921	995,413	1,094,954	1,204,450
Profit	495,079	404,587	305,046	195,550
Investment	4,200,000	3,295,079	2,299,666	1,204,450
ROI	11.8%	12.3%	13.3%	16.2%

The ROI exceeds the cost of capital (10%) in each year. The decision by the divisional manager, based on ROI, would therefore be to undertake the investment. This decision would be consistent with the NPV assessment.

The project, which has a positive NPV, will therefore be accepted under both ROI and RI when depreciation is charged by the annuity method. It is important to recognise, however, that this conclusion is valid only if:

■ the cash flows in each year of the project are constant (and are not fairly low in the first year or early years of the project), and

■ the investment does not have any residual value at the end of its life.

Economic Value Added (EVA)
■ Profits and adding value to a business
■ Measuring economic value added (EVA)
■ Using EVA

5 Economic Value Added (EVA)

5.1 Profits and adding value to a business

In theory, if a company makes a profit, the value of its shares ought to increase by the amount of the profit (less any dividends paid to shareholders). In practice, this does not happen.

One reason for this is that in order to make a profit, capital is invested. Capital is a resource which has a cost. The actual creation of extra value should therefore be the profit less the cost of capital invested.

Residual income is the accounting profit earned by a division less a notional charge for capital employed. In theory, there is a connection between residual income and the expected increase in the value of a business.

However, there is a second – and more important – reason why profits are not a good measure of the expected increase in the value of a business. This is that profit measured by accounting conventions is not a proper measure of 'real' economic profit.

It can be argued that if **economic profit** is measured, instead of accounting profit, we will arrive at a better measurement of the increase in the value of a business during a given period of time.

A management consultancy firm, Stern Stewart, devised a method of measuring economic profit, which they have called economic value added or EVA.

5.2 Measuring economic value added (EVA)

Economic value added (EVA) for a financial period is the economic profit after deducting a cost for the value of capital employed.

The formula for EVA is as follows:

EVA = Net operating profit after tax – (Capital employed × Cost of capital)

or

EVA = NOPAT – (Capital employed × WACC)

NOPAT

The net operating profit after tax is calculated by making adjustments to the accounting profit in order to arrive at an estimate of economic profit. NOPAT is similar to 'free cash flow' and is an estimate of economic profit before deducting a cost for the capital employed. In practice, the calculation of NOPAT is fairly complex and requires a number of different adjustments to the figure for accounting profit.

A few of the problems are as follows:

(1)   In calculating NOPAT, interest costs of debt capital should not be deducted from profit. This is because debt capital is included in the capital employed. NOPAT should be the profit before deducting interest costs but after deducting tax. There is tax relief on interest, so to reach a figure for NOPAT the amount of interest charges in the period less relief on the interest cost should be added back to the figure for profit after tax.

NOPAT = Profit after tax + Interest costs less tax relief on the interest

(2)   Non-cash expenses should not be deducted from profit. The main item of non-cash expense is usually depreciation of non-current assets. However, there should be a charge for non-current assets, to allow for the economic consumption of value that occurs when the assets are used.

NOPAT = Profit after tax + Post-tax interest cost + Accounting depreciation – Economic depreciation

If it can be assumed that accounting depreciation charges are similar to the loss of economic value in non-current assets, the two items cancel out, and:

NOPAT = Profit after tax + Interest costs less tax relief on the interest

These are just two of the adjustments to convert accounting profit after tax into NOPAT. Other adjustments are more complex.

Charge for capital

EVA is NOPAT minus a charge to represent the cost of capital employed. However, the valuation of capital should be based on economic values of the capital employed. In most cases, this means that non-current assets should be valued close to their current value, rather than at a value based on historical cost.

The capital charge is calculated by applying the weighted average cost of capital (WACC) to the value of capital employed. WACC is the weighted average of equity capital and debt capital.

5.3 Using EVA

If it is measured with reasonable accuracy, EVA should be a measure, in economic terms, of how much extra value or wealth has been created by a business operation during a period.

It can therefore be argued that EVA would be a much more useful measure of divisional performance – and company performance – than traditional accounting measures of ROCE and profit.

The problem with EVA however is its complexity. To arrive at an estimate of EVA, it is necessary to make many adjustments to accounting values for profit and asset values, and there might be some uncertainty about the reliability of the figure that is calculated as EVA. It might also be questioned whether the extra cost of calculating EVA (compared with ROCE or ROI/residual income) is justified.

Example

A company reported the following results in Year 8:

	$000
Profit before interest and tax	26,000
Interest	6,000
Profit before tax	20,000
Tax at 25%	5,000
Profit after tax	15,000
Dividends paid	7,000
Retained profit	8,000

The profit is after charging $3,000,000 for depreciation. However, it has been estimated that the economic cost of depreciation was $3,500,000.

The value of capital employed has been estimated as $120 million and the weighted average cost of capital is 9%.

Using this information, make the best estimate possible of economic value added in Year 8.

Answer

	$000	$000
Profit after tax		15,000
Add back: Interest	6,000	
Less tax relief (25%)	(1,500)	
		4,500
Adjustment for higher cost of economic depreciation		(500)
NOPAT		19,000
Capital cost (9% × $120 million)		(10,800)
EVA		8,200

EVA and measuring the performance of divisions

EVA can be used as an alternative to ROI or residual income as a method of measuring the performance of operating divisions. However, using EVA for performance measurement of operating divisions might make little sense unless the company as a whole also measured its total performance in terms of EVA.

CHAPTER

16

Transfer pricing

Contents

> ### Transfer pricing: purpose and objectives
>
> - Purpose of transfer pricing
> - Definition of a transfer price
> - The objectives of transfer pricing
> - The motivation of divisional managers
> - Goal congruence
> - Divisional autonomy

1 Transfer pricing: purpose and objectives

1.1 Purpose of transfer pricing

When an entity has a divisionalised structure, some of the divisions might supply goods or services to other divisions in the same entity.

- One division sells the goods or services. This will be referred to as the 'selling division'.
- Another division buys the goods or services. This will be referred to as the 'buying division'.

For accounting purposes, these internal transfers of goods or services are given a value. Transfers could be recorded at cost. However, when the selling division is a profit centre or investment centre, it will expect to make some profit on the sale.

1.2 Definition of a transfer price

A transfer price is the price at which goods or services are sold by one division within an entity to another division in the same entity. Internal sales are referred to as transfers, so the internal selling and buying price is the transfer price.

1.3 The objectives of transfer pricing

A decision has to be made about what the transfer price should be.

For the purpose of performance measurement and performance evaluation in a divisionalised organisation, it is appropriate that:

- the selling division should earn some profit or return on sales to other divisions and
- the buying division should pay a fair price for the goods or services that it buys from other divisions.

Transfer prices are decided by management. The objectives of transfer pricing should be to:

- achieve goal congruence for the entity as a whole, and

■ give autonomy (freedom to make decisions) to the managers of the profit centres or investment centres.

These two objectives are often in conflict with each other, and unless the transfer prices are set at a suitable level, it might be impossible to achieve both objectives.

1.4 The motivation of divisional managers

An assumption is that the managers of every profit centre will take decisions that maximise the profits of the division.

If every division maximises its profits, the profits of the entity as a whole will also be maximised.

However, a division might take action that maximises its own profit, but reduces the profits of another division. As a result, the profits of the entity as a whole might also be reduced.

1.5 Goal congruence

Every divisional manager should work towards the maximisation of the profits and returns of the entity as a whole. When every divisional manager has the same aim or goal, there is goal congruence.

■ Transfer prices should therefore encourage divisional managers to take decisions that are in the best interests of the entity as a whole.

■ Transfer prices should not encourage a divisional manager to take decisions that are against the interests of the entity as a whole and would reduce the profits of the entity.

1.6 Divisional autonomy

Autonomy is freedom of action and freedom to make decisions. Divisional managers should be free to make their own decisions. Autonomy should improve motivation of divisional managers.

For example, when transfer prices have been decided, the managers of all divisions within the entity should be free to decide:

■ whether to sell their output to other divisions (internal transfers) or whether to sell them to external customers, if an external market exists for the output

■ whether to buy their goods from another division (internal transfers) or whether to buy them from external suppliers, if an external market exists.

Divisional managers should be allowed to make their own choices. They should not have to be told what to do by senior management at head office.

If there is a conflict between the objectives of goal congruence and divisional autonomy, goal congruence should have priority. If divisional managers cannot agree to do what is best for the entity as a whole, they should be instructed about what to do by senior management. However, this situation would be undesirable.

Ideally, transfer prices should be set so that divisional managers can agree on selling and buying between each other in a way that is in the best interests of all the divisions and the entity as a whole.

The ideal transfer price

- Assumptions
- Market-based and cost-based transfer prices
- The opportunity cost of transfers
- Identifying the ideal transfer price

---

2 The ideal transfer price

The ideal transfer price is a price that will result in goal congruence and also allow the divisional managers autonomy to make their own decisions, without having to be told by head office what they must do.

The main problems arise when there is an external market for the goods (or services) that one division transfers to another. When an external market exists for goods or services that are also transferred internally, the market might be called an **external intermediate market**.

- The selling division can sell its goods into this market, instead of transferring them internally.
- Similarly the buying division can buy its goods from other suppliers in this market, instead of buying them internally from another division.

2.1 Assumptions

The following assumptions will be made:

- When there is an external intermediate market, divisional managers will decide between internal transfers and using the external market in a way that maximises the profits of their division.
- When there is no difference in profitability between internal transfers and selling or buying externally, the divisional managers should agree to transfer the goods internally.
- If the performance of the divisions and the divisional managers is based on divisional profitability, it is reasonable to expect that:
  - the selling division will earn some profit on internal transfers, and
  - the buying division will pay a fair price for internal transfers.

2.2 Market-based and cost-based transfer prices

As a general rule:

- when an external intermediate market does not exist for transferred goods, the transfer price will be based on cost
- when an external intermediate market does exist for transferred goods, the transfer price will be based on the external market price.

However, the situation is more complicated when:

- there is a limit to production capacity in the selling division, or
- there is a limit to sales demand in the external intermediate market.

In these circumstances, we need to consider the **opportunity costs** for the selling division of transferring goods internally instead of selling them externally.

2.3 The opportunity cost of transfers

The selling division and the buying division have opportunity costs of transferring goods internally.

- For the selling division, the opportunity cost of transferring goods internally to another division might include a loss of contribution and profit from not being able to sell goods externally in the intermediate market.
- For the buying division, the opportunity cost of buying internally from another division is the price that it would have to pay for purchasing the items from external suppliers in the intermediate market.

Goal congruence is achieved when the transfer price is at a level where both the selling division and the buying division will want to do what is in the best interests of the entity as a whole, because it is also in the best interests of their divisions.

Ideal transfer prices must therefore take opportunity costs into consideration.

2.4 Identifying the ideal transfer price

The following rules should help you to identify the ideal transfer price in any situation:

- **Step 1**. Begin by identifying the plan that maximises the profits of the entity as a whole. In other words, what is the goal congruence that we are trying to achieve?
- **Step 2**. Having identified the plan that is in the best interests of the entity as a whole, identify the transfer price, or range of transfer prices, that will make the manager of the buying division want to work towards this plan. The transfer price must ensure that, given this transfer price, the profits of the division will be maximised by doing what is in the best interests of the entity as a whole.
- **Step 3**. In the same way, having identified the plan that is in the best interests of the entity as a whole, identify the transfer price, or range of transfer prices, that will make the manager of the selling division want to work towards the same plan. Again, the transfer price must ensure that, given the transfer price, the profits of the division will be maximised by doing what is in the best interests of the entity as a whole.

These rules will be illustrated with a number of different examples and different situations.

> ### Finding the ideal transfer price
>
> ■ No external intermediate market
>
> ■ An external intermediate market and no production limitations
>
> ■ An external intermediate market and production limitations
>
> ■ Transfer pricing and more than one limiting factors

3 Finding the ideal transfer price

The ideal transfer price depends on circumstances.

3.1 No external intermediate market

When there is no external intermediate market, the ideal transfer price is at cost or cost plus a contribution margin or profit margin for the selling division.

 Example

An entity has two divisions, Division A and Division B. Division A makes a component X which is transferred to Division B. Division B uses component X to make end-product Y. Details of costs and selling price are as follows:

Division A	$
Cost of component X	
Variable cost	10
Fixed cost	8
Total cost	18
Division B	
Further processing costs	
Variable cost	4
Fixed cost	7
	11
Selling price per unit of product Y	40

The further processing costs of Division B do not include the cost of buying component X from Division A. One unit of component X goes into the production of one unit of Product Y.

Fixed costs in both divisions will be the same, regardless of the volume of production and sales.

Required

What is the ideal transfer price, or what is a range of prices that would be ideal for the transfer price?

Answer

Step 1

What is in the best interests of the entity as a whole?

The total variable cost of one unit of the end product, product Y, is $14 ($10 + $4). The sales price of product Y is $26. The entity therefore makes additional contribution of $26 for every unit of product Y that it sells.

It is in the best interests of the entity to maximise production and sales of product Y.

Step 2

What will motivate the buying division to buy as many units of component X as possible?

Division B will want to buy more units of component X provided that the division earns additional contribution from every unit of the component that it buys.

Division B	$
Selling price of Product Y	40
Variable further processing costs	4
	36

The opportunity cost of not buying units of component X, ignoring the transfer price, is $36 per unit. Division B should therefore be willing to pay up to $36 per unit for component X.

Step 3

What will motivate the selling division to make and transfer as many units of component X as possible?

Division A will want to make and sell more units of component X provided that the division earns additional contribution from every unit of the component that it sells.

The marginal cost of making and transferring a unit of component X is $10. Division A should therefore be willing to transfer as many units of component X as it can make (or Division B has the capacity to buy) if the transfer price is at least $10.

Ideal transfer price

The ideal transfer price is anywhere in the range $10 to $36.

3.2 An external intermediate market and no production limitations

When there is an external intermediate market for the transferred item, a different situation applies, and if there are no production limitations in the selling division, the ideal transfer price is usually the external market price.

Example

An entity has two divisions P and Q. Division P makes a component X which it either transfers to division Q or sells in an external market. The costs of making one unit of component X are:

Component X	$
Variable cost	60
Fixed cost	30
Total cost	90

Division Q uses one unit of component X to make one unit of product Y, which it sells for $200 after incurring variable further processing costs of $25 per unit.

Required

What is the ideal transfer price or range of transfer prices, if the price of component X in the external intermediate market is:

(a) $140

(b) $58?

Answer

Step 1

What is in the best interests of the entity as a whole?

The entity will benefit by maximising the total contribution from external sales of component X and product Y.

If component X is not transferred by division P to Division Q, Division Q will have to buy units of component X in the external market. Every unit of component X transferred therefore reduces the need to purchase a unit externally.

Since the additional contribution from making and selling a unit of product Y is $175 (S200 – $25), a profit-maximising plan is to maximise the sales of division Q, and transfer component X from Division P to Division Q rather than sell component X externally.

Step 2

What will motivate the buying division to buy as many units of component X as possible from Division P?

Division Q will be prepared to buy component X from Division P as long as it is not more expensive than buying in the external market from another supplier. Division Q will be willing to buy internally if the transfer price is:

(a)   not more than $140 when the external market price is $140

(b)   not more than $58 when the external market price is $58.

However, the external market price is less than the variable cost of internal manufacture.

This suggests that component X should be brought from the external market and not manufactured internally.

Step 3

What will motivate the selling division to make and transfer as many units of component X as possible?

Division P should be prepared to transfer as many units of component X as possible to Division Q provided that its profit is no less than it would be if it sold component X externally.

Units transferred to division Q are lost sales to the external market; therefore there is an opportunity cost of transfer that division P will wish to include in the transfer price.

Component X: market price $140	$
Variable cost	60
Opportunity cost of lost external sale (140 – 60)	80
Total cost = minimum transfer price	140

Component X: market price $58	$
Variable cost	60
Opportunity cost of lost external sale (58 – 60)	(2)
Total cost = minimum transfer price	58

Ideal transfer price

The ideal transfer price is the maximum that the buying division is prepared to pay and the minimum that the selling division will want to receive. In both situations, the ideal transfer price is therefore the price in the external intermediate market.

When the external market price is $58, Division P is losing contribution by selling component X externally. It would also be cheaper for the entity as a whole to buy the component externally for $58 rather than make internally for a marginal cost of $60. Division P should consider ending its operations to produce component X.

3.3 An external intermediate market and production limitations

When there is an external intermediate market for the transferred item, and the selling division has a limitation on the number of units it can produce, the ideal transfer price should allow for the opportunity cost of the selling division. Every unit transferred means one less external sale.

Example

An entity consists of two divisions, Division A and Division B. Division A is working at full capacity on its machines, and can make either Product Y or Product Z, up to its capacity limitation. Both of these products have an external market.

The costs and selling prices of Product Y and Product Z are:

	Product Y	Product Z
	$	$
Selling price	15	17
Variable cost of production	10	7
Variable cost of sale	1	2
Contribution per unit	4	8

The variable cost of sale is incurred on external sales of the division's products. This cost is not incurred for internal sales/transfers from Division A to Division B.

To make one unit of Product Y takes exactly the same machine time as one unit of Product Z.

Division B buys Product Y, which it uses to make an end product.

The profit of the entity will be maximised by making and selling as many units as possible of Division B's end product.

Required

What is the ideal transfer price or range of transfer prices?

Answer

Step 1

What is in the best interests of the entity as a whole?

This is stated in the example. The entity wants to make and sell as many units of the end product of Division B as follows. It is not clear, however, whether it is better for Division B to buy Product Y externally or to buy internally from Division A.

If division A does not make Product Y, it can make and sell Product Z instead. Product Z earns a higher contribution per unit of machine time, the limiting factor in Division A.

Step 2

What would motivate the buying division to buy as many units of Product Y as possible from Division A?

Division B will be prepared to buy Product Y from Division A as long as it is not more expensive than buying in the external market from another supplier.

Division B will be willing to buy Product Y internally if the transfer price is $15 or less.

Step 3

What would motivate the selling division to make and transfer as many units of Product Y as possible?

The selling division will only be willing to make Product Y instead of Product Z if it earns at least as much contribution as it would from making Z and selling it externally. (In this situation, the division can make as many units of Z as it can make of Y, and Product Z earns a higher contribution).

Product Y	$
Variable cost	10
Opportunity cost of lost external sale (17 − 7 − 2)	8
Total cost = minimum transfer price	18

Ideal transfer price/ideal production and selling plan

Division B will not want to pay more than $15 for transfers of Product Y; otherwise it will buy Product Y externally.

Division A will want to receive at least $18 for transfers of Product Y; otherwise it will prefer to make and sell Product Z, not Product Y.

The ideal solution is for Division B to buy Product Y externally at $15 and for Division A to make and sell Product Z.

Example

An entity consists of two divisions, Division A and Division B. Division A is operating at full capacity making Product X, for which there is an external market. The variable cost of making one unit of Product X is $70, and the sale price of Product X in the external market is $100 per unit.

Division B needs one unit of Product X to manufacture another product, Product Y. The variable conversion costs and further processing costs in Division B are $29 per unit of Product Y, and one unit of Product Y requires one unit of Product X as a component. The external selling price of Product Y is $140 per unit.

An external supplier has offered to sell units of Product Y to Division B for $103 per unit.

Required

(a) Identify the ideal transfer price.

(b) Calculate the contribution per unit for each Division and for the entity as a whole if this transfer price is used.

(c) Suggest with reasons whether this transfer price provides a fair measure of divisional performance.

Answer

Step 1

What is in the best interests of the entity as a whole?

For each additional unit of Product Y that division B makes and sells, the additional contribution for the entity is $41 ($140 – $29 – 70). The entity makes more contribution from making and selling Product Y than it makes from selling Product X externally.

The production plan that will optimise the profit for the entity as a whole is for Division A to make units of Product X and transfer them to Division B.

Step 2

What would motivate the buying division to buy as many units of Product X as possible from Division A?

Division B will not want to pay more to Division A for Product X than the price it has been offered by an external supplier, $103. However, Division B can presumably find another supplier who is willing to offer the current market price of $100, and the maximum price that Division B should pay ought to be $100.

Step 3

What would motivate the selling division to make and transfer as many units of Product X as possible?

Product Y	$
Variable cost	70
Opportunity cost of lost external sale (100 – 70)	30
Total cost = minimum transfer price	100

Ideal transfer price

The ideal transfer price is $100 per unit of Product X.

Contribution per unit

	Division A	Division B	Entity as a whole
	$/unit	$/unit	$/unit
External sale	-	140	140
Internal sale	100	-	-
Sales revenue	100	140	140
Transfer: purchase cost	-	100	-
Other variable costs	70	29	99
Total variable costs	70	129	99
Contribution per unit	30	11	41

Comment

The contribution per unit for each division is a fair representation of the economic contribution of each division to the profitability of the entity as a whole.

The transfer price will achieve goal congruence and provides an appropriate measurement of divisional performance.

3.4   Transfer pricing and more than one limiting factors

The selling division might have more than one limiting factor that restricts its output capacity. When this happens, it might be necessary to use a linear programming model to identify the shadow price (also called the dual price) of each of the limiting factors.

A shadow price is the amount of contribution that will be lost for each reduction of one unit in the available scarce resource. (It is also the extra contribution that could be earned for each extra unit of the scarce resource that is available).

For example, suppose that direct labour is a scarce resource. There are only 2,000 hours available each week, and the shadow price of direct labour is $5 per hour. This means that the maximum possible contribution will be reduced by $5 if there are only 1,999 hours available, and will be reduced by $500 if there are only 1,900 hours available each week, and so on.

The ideal transfer price should include the shadow prices of any scarce resources used in the transferred product.

Example

An entity consists of two divisions, Division A and Division B. Division A can make three products, Product P, Product Q and Product R.

Product P and Product Q are sold in an external market. Their variable cost and selling price are:

	Product P	Product Q
	$/unit	$/unit
Selling price	20	28
Variable cost	10	16
Contribution	10	12

There is a limited supply of labour and machine time each week in Division A. Labour hours are restricted to 3,000 each week and machine hours are restricted to 1,000 hours each week.

Product R does not have an external market. Units of Product R are needed by Division B to go into the manufacture of one of its products.

One unit of Product R requires:

■   one labour hour

■   two machine hours.

The variable costs of one unit of Product R, including the direct labour cost, is $16 per unit.

A linear programming model has been used to calculate that if Division A makes only Product P and Product Q, and does not make any units of Product R, it would make 500 units of P and 500 units of Q each week. Total contribution would be $13,000. The shadow price of labour would be $3 per hour and the shadow price of machine time would be $4 per hour.

Required

What should be the transfer price for each unit of Product R?

 Answer

From the point of view of the entity as a whole, it is only worth making and transferring units of Product R if it is more profitable for Division B to use Product R than for Division A to make and sell Products P and Q.

The ideal transfer price should therefore include the shadow price of the labour and machine hours that units of Product R would require.

Transfer price of Product R	$/unit
Variable cost of making R in Division A	16
Shadow price of labour (1 hour x $3)	3
Shadow price of machine time (2 hours x $4)	8
Transfer price	27

Transfer pricing in practice

- Transfer price at market price
- Transfer price at full cost plus
- Transfer price at variable cost plus or incremental cost plus
- Two-part transfer prices
- Negotiated transfer prices
- Dual pricing
- Transfer pricing in multinational groups

---

4 Transfer pricing in practice

Transfer prices might be decided by head office and imposed on each division. Alternatively, the managers of each division might have the autonomy to negotiate transfer prices with each other.

Ideally, the transfer prices that are decided with meet the two objectives of goal congruence and divisional autonomy.

In practice, transfer prices might be agreed and expressed in one of the following ways.

4.1 Transfer price at market price

A transfer price might be the external selling/buying price for the item in an external intermediate market. This price is only possible when an external market exists.

If the selling division would incur some extra costs if it sold its output externally rather than transferred it internally to another division, the transfer price might be reduced below market price, to allow for the variable costs that would be saved by the selling division.

Advantages of market price as the transfer price

Market price is the ideal transfer price when there is an external market. A transfer price below this amount will make the manager of the selling division want to sell externally, and a price above this amount will make the manager of the buying division want to buy externally.

Transferring at market price also encourages efficiency in the supplying division, which must compete with the external competition.

Disadvantages of market price as the transfer price

The current market price is not appropriate as a transfer price when:

- the current market price is only temporary, and caused by short-term conditions in the market, or

- there is imperfect competition in the external market, and the selling division faces a downward-sloping demand curve when it sells its output into the market. The opportunity cost of transferring output internally is not the market price, because the selling price would have to be reduced in order to sell the extra units.

4.2   Transfer price at full cost plus

A transfer price might be expressed as the full cost of production plus a margin for profit for the selling division.

Standard full costs should be used, **not actual full costs**. This will prevent the selling division from increasing its profit by incurring higher costs per unit.

Full cost plus might be suitable when there is no external intermediate market.

However, there are disadvantages in using full cost rather than variable cost to decide a transfer price.

- The fixed costs of the selling division become variable costs in the transfer price of the buying division. This might lead to decisions by the buying division manager that are against the best interests of the entity as a whole.

- The size of the profit margin or mark-up is likely to be arbitrary.

4.3   Transfer price at variable cost plus or incremental cost plus

A transfer price might be expressed as the variable cost of production plus a margin for profit for the selling division.

Standard variable costs should be used, **not actual variable costs**. This will prevent the selling division from increasing its profit by incurring higher variable costs per unit.

Variable cost plus might be suitable when there is no external intermediate market. It is probably more suitable in these circumstances than full cost plus, because variable cost is a better measure of opportunity cost.

Another type of cost plus transfer price is **incremental cost plus**. This might be used when making and transferring units results in an increase in total fixed costs (the fixed costs are stepped costs).

Incremental cost =

Variable cost + Share of incremental fixed costs + Profit margin

4.4 Two-part transfer prices

With two-part transfer prices, the selling division charges the buying division for units transferred in two ways:

- a standard variable cost per unit transferred, plus
- a fixed charge in each period.

The fixed charge is a lump sum charge at the end of each period. The fixed charge would represent a share of the contribution from selling the end product, which the supplying division has helped to earn. Alternatively, the charge could be seen as a charge to the buying division for a share of the fixed costs of the selling division in the period.

4.5 Negotiated transfer prices

A negotiated transfer price is a price that is negotiated between the managers of the profit centres.

The divisional managers are given the autonomy to agree on transfer prices. Negotiation might be a method of identifying the ideal transfer price in situations where an external intermediate market does not exist.

An **advantage** of negotiation is that if the negotiations are honest and fair, the divisions should be willing to trade with each other on the basis of the transfer price they have agreed.

Disadvantages of negotiation are as follows:

- The divisional managers might be unable to reach agreement. When this happens, management from head office will have to act as judge or arbitrator in the case.
- The transfer prices that are negotiated might not be fair, but a reflection of the bargaining strength or bargaining skills of each divisional manager.

4.6 Dual pricing

In some situations, two divisions might be unable to agree a transfer price, because there is no transfer price at which the selling division will want to transfer internally or the buying division will want to buy internally. However, the profits of the entity as a whole would be increased if transfers did occur.

These situations are rare.

However, when they occur, head office might find a solution to the problem by agreeing to dual transfer prices.

- the selling division sells at one transfer price, and
- the buying division buys at a lower transfer price.

There are two different transfer prices. The transfer price for the selling division should be high enough to motivate the divisional manager to transfer more units to the buying division. Similarly, the transfer price for the buying division should be low enough to motivate the divisional manager to buy more units from the selling division.

In the accounts of the entity, the transferred goods are:

- sold by the selling division to head office and

- bought by the buying division from head office.

The loss from the dual pricing is a cost for head office, and treated as a head office overhead expense.

However, dual pricing can be complicated and confusing.

4.7 Transfer pricing in multinational groups

Multinational companies have subsidiaries in different countries for many reasons. Each subsidiary will be treated as a profit centre or an investment centre within the group. These subsidiaries may trade with each other, exchanging goods and services. When they do, a transfer price must be agreed.

The same broad principles already described in this chapter should apply to transfer pricing within multinationals. When deciding a transfer price for transfers between subsidiaries in different countries, the following additional factors may be relevant:

- taxation

- import duties

- currency fluctuations

- repatriation of funds

Taxation

The taxation rules in each country, and tax rules relating to the pricing of transfers between group companies, may affect the choice of transfer prices. There may be a transfer price that will minimise the tax cost for the group as a whole, when there are differing rates of tax in the different countries.

- A multinational might choose to locate a selling division in a country with a low marginal rate of tax and a buying division in a country with a high marginal rate of tax.

- If the transfer price is high, the selling division will make high profits and the buying division will make low profits.

- The total tax charge for the group as a whole can be reduced, because the high profits are taxed at a low rate and the high tax rate is applied only to low profits.

However, anti-avoidance legislation exists to prevent companies from using transfer pricing to move profits from subsidiaries in high-tax countries to subsidiaries in low-tax countries.

Import duties

A transfer price may be kept low in order to minimise the import duty or tariff payable on transfers to another country. However, there may be anti-avoidance legislation to prevent international companies from using transfer prices to minimise their payments of import duties.

Currency fluctuations

Transfers will be priced in one currency, and this will expose the investment centres to the risk of losses from adverse currency movements. A group should give careful consideration to the currency or currencies for pricing transfers. The problem of currency exposures is particularly severe when the exchange rate between the domestic currencies of the two investment centres is volatile and subject to large movements. Adverse movements in an exchange rate could wipe out an investment centre's trading profit on transfers.

Repatriation of funds

Decisions about transfer prices may also need to take account of foreign exchange restrictions in the country of one of its investment centres. The aim should be to avoid having surplus funds tied up in a country from which cannot be repatriated.

 Example

The marginal rate of tax in country A is 30% and the marginal rate of tax in country B is 50%. A multinational company locates a supplying division in country A and the buying division in country B.

If the transfer price is made higher, the total tax charge for the group will be reduced by 20% for each $1 of goods transferred.

However the taxation authorities in many countries are aware of the possibilities for tax avoidance. The Organisation for Economic and Social Development in 1995 produced guidelines stating that transfers should be at 'arm's length' and the transfer prices used should be prices that would be negotiated between two unrelated parties.

CHAPTER

17

Alternative views of performance measurement

Contents

1	The balanced scorecard approach
2	The performance pyramid
3	Performance measurement in service industries
4	Predicting corporate failure

> ## The balanced scorecard approach
>
> - The balanced scorecard: four perspectives of performance
> - Using the balanced scorecard
> - Conflicting targets for the four perspectives

1 The balanced scorecard approach

1.1 The balanced scorecard: four perspectives of performance

The balanced scorecard approach is an approach to measuring performance in relation to long-term objectives. This approach to target setting and performance measurement was developed by Kaplan and Norton in the 1990s. The most important objective for business entities is a financial objective, but to achieve long-term financial objectives, it is important to achieve goals or targets that are non-financial in nature as well as financial.

The reason for having a balanced scorecard is that by setting targets for several key factors, managers will take a more balanced and long-term view about what they should be trying to achieve. A balanced scorecard approach should remove the emphasis on financial targets and short-term results.

In a balanced scorecard, critical success factors are identified for four aspects of performance, or four 'perspectives':

- customer perspective
- internal perspective
- innovation and learning perspective
- financial perspective.

Perspective	The key question
Customer perspective	**What do customers value?** By recognising what customers value most from the organisation, the organisation can focus performance on satisfying the customer more effectively. Targets might be developed for performance such as cost (value for money), quality or place of delivery.
Internal perspective	**To achieve its financial and customer objectives, what processes must the organisation perform with excellence?** Management should identify the key aspects of operational performance and seek to achieve or maintain excellence in this area.
Innovation and learning perspective	**How can the organisation continue to improve and create value?** The focus here is on the ability of the organisation to maintain its competitive position, through the skills and knowledge of its work force and through developing new products and services.
Financial perspective	**How does the organisation create value for its owners?** Financial measures of performance in a balanced scorecard system might include share price growth, profitability and return on investment.

1.2 Using the balanced scorecard

The focus is on strategic objectives and the critical success factors necessary for achieving them. In a balanced scorecard approach, targets are set for a range of critical financial and non-financial areas covering these four perspectives. The main performance report for management each month is a balanced scorecard report, not budgetary control reports and variance reports.

Examples of measures of performance for each of the four perspectives are as follows:

Perspective	Outcome measures
Critical financial measures	Return on investment
	Profitability
	Economic value added (EVA)
	Revenue growth
	Productivity and cost control
	Cash flow
Critical customer measures	Market share
	Customer profitability
	Attracting new customers
	Retaining existing customers
	Customer satisfaction
	On-time delivery
Critical internal measures	Success rate in winning contract orders
	Production cycle time/throughput time
	Amount of re-working of defective units
Critical innovation and learning measures	Revenue per employee
	Employee productivity
	Employee satisfaction
	Employee retention
	Percentage of total revenue earned from sales of new products
	Time to develop new products

Example: balanced scorecard

Kaplan and Norton described the example of Mobil in the early 1990s, in their book *The Strategy-focussed Organisation*. Mobil, a major supplier of petrol, was competing with other suppliers on the basis of price and the location of petrol stations. Its strategic focus was on cost reduction and productivity, but its return on capital was low.

The company's management re-assessed their strategy, with the aim of increasing market share and obtaining stronger brand recognition of the Mobil brand name. They decided that the company needed to attract high-spending customers who would buy other goods from the petrol station stores, in addition to petrol.

As its high-level financial objective, the company set a target of increasing return on capital employed from its current level of about 6% to 12% within three years.

- From a **financial perspective**, it identified key success factors as productivity and sales growth. Targets were set for productivity (reducing operating costs per gallon of petrol sold) and 'asset intensity' (ratio of operational cash flow to assets employed).

- From a **customer perspective**, Mobil carried out market research into who its customers were and what factors influenced their buying decisions. Targets were set for providing petrol to customers in a way that would satisfy the customer and differentiate Mobil's products from rival petrol suppliers. Key issues were found to be having petrol stations that were clean and safe, and offering a good quality branded product and a trusted brand. Targets were set for cleanliness and safety, speedy service at petrol stations, helpful customer service and rewarding customer loyalty.

- From an **internal perspective**, Mobil set targets for improving the delivery of its products and services to customers, and making sure that customers could always buy the petrol and other products that they wanted, whenever they visited a Mobil station.

1.3 Conflicting targets for the four perspectives

A criticism that has been made against the balanced scorecard approach is that the targets for each of the four perspectives might often conflict with each other. When this happens, there might be disagreement about what the priorities should be.

This problem should not be serious, however, if it is remembered that the financial is the most important of the four perspectives for a commercial business entity.

A useful sporting analogy was provided in an article in *Financial Management* magazine (Gering and Mntambo, November 2001). They compared the balanced scorecard to the judgements of a football team manager during a football match. The objective is to win the match and the key performance measure is the score.

However, as the match progresses, the manager will look at other important aspects of performance, such as the number of shots at the goal by each side, the number of corner kicks, the number of tackles and the percentage of possession of the ball enjoyed by the team.

Shots on goal corner kicks, tackles and possession of the ball are all necessary factors in scoring goals, not conceding goals, and winning the match. The manager will therefore use them as indicators of how well or badly the match is progressing. However, the score is ultimately the only thing that matters.

In the same way, targets for four perspectives are useful in helping management to judge progress towards the company's objectives, but ultimately, success in achieving those objectives is measured in financial terms. The financial objective is the most important.

The performance pyramid

- The pyramid structure: linking performance targets throughout an organisation
- Interpreting the pyramid

2 The performance pyramid

Another approach to structuring the performance evaluation system is the performance pyramid. The concept of a performance pyramid is based on the idea that an organisation operates at different levels. Each level has different concerns, but these should support each other in achieving the overall business objectives.

Performance can therefore be seen as a pyramid structure, with a large number of operational performance targets supporting higher-level targets, leading to targets for the achievement of overall corporate objectives at the top.

2.1 The pyramid structure: linking performance targets throughout an organisation

The performance pyramid was developed by Lynch and Cross (1991). They argued that traditional performance measurement systems were not as effective as they should be, because they had a narrow financial focus – concentrating on measures such as return on capital employed, profitability, cash flow and so on. They argued that in a dynamic business environment, achieving strategic business objectives depends on good performance with regard to:

- **Customer satisfaction** (a 'marketing' objective: here, the focus is on external/market effectiveness)
- **Flexibility** (the flexibility objective relates to both external effectiveness and internal efficiency within the organisation)
- **Productivity** (resource utilisation: here, the focus is on internal efficiency, much of which can be measured by financial performance)

These key 'driving forces' can be monitored at the operational level with performance measures relating to quality, delivery, cycle time and waste.

Lynch and Cross argued that within an organisation, there are different levels of management and each has its own focus. However, there must be consistency between performance measurement at each management level, so that performance measures at the operational level support the corporate strategy.

They presented these ideas in the form of a pyramid of targets and performance that links operations to corporate strategy.

A performance pyramid can be presented as follows:

Performance pyramid

2.2   Interpreting the pyramid

The performance pyramid links strategic objectives with operational targets, and internally-focused with externally-focused objectives.

- Objectives and targets are set from the top level (corporate vision) down to the operational level. Performance is measured from an operational level upwards. If performance targets are achieved at the operational level, targets should be achieved at the operating systems level. Achieving targets for operating systems should help to ensure the achievement of marketing and financial strategy objectives, which in turn should enable the organisation to achieve its corporate objectives.

- A key level of performance measurement is at the operating systems level – achieving targets for customer satisfaction, flexibility and productivity. To achieve performance targets at this level, operational targets must be achieved - for quality, delivery, cycle time and waste.

- With the exception of flexibility, which has both an internal and an external aspect, performance measures within the pyramid (and below the corporate vision level) can be divided between:

    - market measures, or measures of external effectiveness, and

    - financial measures, or measures of internal efficiency.

- The measures of performance are inter-related, both at the same level within the pyramid and vertically, between different levels in the pyramid. For example:

    - New product development in a business operating system. When a new product is introduced to the market, success depends on meeting customer needs (customer satisfaction), adapting customer attitudes and production systems in order to make the changes (flexibility) and delivering the product to the customer at the lowest cost for the required quality (productivity).

- Achieving improvements in productivity depends on reducing the cycle time (from order to delivery) or reducing waste.

Lynch and Cross argued that the performance measures that are chosen should link operations to strategic goals.

■ All operational departments need to be aware of how they are contributing to the achievement of strategic goals.

■ Performance measures should be a combination of financial and non-financial measures that are of practical value to managers. Reliable information about performance should be readily available to managers whenever it is needed.

> ## Performance measurement in service industries
>
> - The characteristics of services and service industries
> - Controllable performance in service industries: Fitzgerald and Moon
> - Fitzgerald and Moon: Performance measurement in service industries
> - Applying the Fitzgerald and Moon framework

3 Performance measurement in service industries

3.1 The characteristics of services and service industries

Many organisations provide services rather than products. There are many examples of service industries: hotels, entertainment, the holiday and travel industries, professional services, banking, recruitment services, cleaning services, and so on.

Performance measurement for services may differ from performance measurement in manufacturing in several ways:

- **Simultaneity**. With a service, providing the service ('production') and receiving the service ('consumption' by the customer) happen at the same time. With production, the product is sold to the customer after it has been manufactured.

- **Perishability**. It is impossible to store a service for future consumption: unlike manufacturing and retailing, there is no stock or inventory of unused services. The service must be provided when the customer wants it.

- **Heterogeneity**. A product can be made to a standard specification. With a service provided by humans, there is variability in the standard of performance. Each provision of the service is different. For example, even if they perform the same songs at several concerts, the performance of a rock band at a series of concerts will be different each time. Similarly, a call centre operator answering telephone calls from customers will be unable to deal with each call in exactly the same way.

- **Intangibility**. With a service, there are many intangible elements of service that the customer is given, and that individual customers might value. For example, a high quality of service in a restaurant is often intangible, but noticed and valued by the customer.

Since services differ to some extent from products, should performance setting and performance measurement be different in service companies, compared with manufacturing companies?

3.2 Controllable performance in service industries: Fitzgerald and Moon

A starting point for analysing performance measurement in service industries is that companies in a service industry should be able to link their competitive strategy to their operations, to make sure that the services that they are providing will enable the company to achieve its strategic objectives. Performance management systems have an important role, because they can:

- show how well or how badly the organisation has performed in achieving its strategic objectives, and
- identify where improvements are needed.

Performance management systems have been developed in many organisations that:

- link performance measures to objectives
- include external as well as internal measures of performance, and
- include non-financial as well as financial performance measures, and also
- recognise that a compromise is often necessary between different performance targets, such as targets for service quality and targets for the cost or the speed of providing the service.

The performance measures that are used can vary widely between different service industries, and there is no standard set of performance measurements that apply to all services.

There have been various suggestions about how to provide a framework for performance management linked to strategic objectives. A framework can be used to analyse the strengths or weaknesses of an existing performance management system, and can be used to suggest improvements in a performance management system.

A framework for analysing performance management systems in service industries has been provided by Fitzgerald and Moon.

3.3 Fitzgerald and Moon: performance measurement in service industries

Fitzgerald and Moon (1996) suggested that a performance management system in a service organisation can be analysed as a combination of three building blocks:

- dimensions
- standards, and
- rewards.

These are shown in the following diagram.

Building blocks for performance measurement systems
(Fitzgerald and Moon 1996)

Dimensions	
Profit Competitiveness Quality Resource utilisation Flexibility Innovation	
Standards	**Rewards**
Ownership Achievability Equity	Clarity Motivation Controllability

Dimensions of performance

Dimensions of performance are the aspects of performance that are measured. A critical question is: What are the dimensions of performance that should be measured in order to assess performance?

Research by Fitzgerald and others (1993) and by Fitzgerald and Moon (1996) concluded that there are six aspects to performance measurement that link performance to corporate strategy. These are:

- profit (financial performance)
- competitiveness
- quality
- resource utilisation
- flexibility
- innovation.

Some performance measures that might be used for each dimension are set out in the following table:

Dimension of performance	Possible measure of performance
Financial performance	Profitability Growth in profits Profit/sales margins Note: Return on capital employed is possibly not so relevant in a service industry, where the company employs fairly small amounts of capital.
Competitiveness	Growth in sales Retention rate for customers (or percentage of customers who buy regularly: 'repeat sales') Success rate in converting enquiries into sales Possibly market share, although this may be difficult to measure

Service quality	Number of complaints
	Whether the rate of complaints is increasing or decreasing
	Customer satisfaction, as revealed by customer opinion surveys
	Number of errors discovered
Flexibility	Possibly the mix of different types of work done by employees
	Possibly the speed in responding to customer requests
Resource utilisation	Efficiency/productivity measures
	Utilisation rates: percentage of available time utilised in 'productive' activities
Innovation	Number of new services offered
	Percentage of sales income that comes from services introduced in the last one or two years

Other measures of performance might be appropriate for each dimension, depending on the nature of the service industry. However, this framework of six dimensions provides a structure for considering what measures of performance might be suitable.

The dimensions of performance should also distinguish between:

■ 'results' of actions taken in the past, and

■ 'determinants' of future performance.

Some dimensions of performance measure the results of decisions that were taken in the past, that have now had an effect. Fitzgerald and Moon suggested that results of past actions are measured by:

■ financial performance and

■ competitiveness.

Other dimensions of performance will not have an immediate effect, and do not measure the effects of decisions taken in the past. Instead they measure progress towards achieving strategic objectives in the future. The 'drivers' or 'determinants' of future performance are:

■ quality

■ flexibility

■ resource utilisation

■ innovation.

These are dimensions of competitive success now and in the future, and so are appropriate for measuring the performance of current management. Measuring performance in these dimensions 'is an attempt to address the short-termism criticism frequently levelled at financially-focused reports' (Fitzgerald). This is because they recognise that by achieving targets now, future performance will benefit. Improvements in quality, say, might not affect profitability in the current financial period, but if these quality improvements are valued by customers, this will affect profits in the future.

Standards

The second part of the framework for performance measurement suggested by Fitzgerald and Moon relates to setting expected standards of performance, once the dimensions of performance have been selected.

There are three aspects to setting standards of performance:

- To what extent do individuals feel that they **own** the standards that will be used to assess their performance? Do they accept the standards as their own, or do they feel that the standards have been imposed on them by senior management?

- Do the individuals held responsible for achieving the standards of performance consider that these standards are **achievable**, or not?

- Are the standards **fair ('equitable')** for all managers in all business units of the entity?

It is recognised that individuals should 'own' the standards that will be used to assess their performance, and managers are **more likely to own the standards when they have been involved in the process of setting the standards**.

It has also been argued that if an individual accepts or 'owns' the standards of performance, better performance will be achieved when the standard is more demanding and difficult to achieve than when the standard is easy to achieve. This means that the standards of performance that are likely to motivate individuals the most are standards that will not be achieved successfully all the time. Budget targets should therefore be challenging, but not impossible to achieve.

Finding a balance between standards that the company thinks are achievable and standards that the individual thinks are achievable can be a source of conflict between senior management and their subordinates.

Standards should also be fair for everyone in all business units, and should not be easier to achieve for some managers than others. To achieve fairness or equity, when local conditions for the individual business units can vary, it is often necessary to assess performance by relying on subjective judgement rather than objective financial measurements.

Rewards

The third aspect of the performance measurement framework of Fitzgerald and Moon is rewards. This refers to the structure of the rewards system, and how individuals will be rewarded for the successful achievement of performance targets.

One of the main roles of a performance measurement system should be to ensure that strategic objectives are achieved successfully, by linking operational performance with strategic objectives.

According to Fitzgerald, there are three aspects to consider in the reward system.

- The system of setting performance targets and rewarding individuals for achieving those targets must be clear to everyone involved. Provided that managers accept their performance targets, **motivation** to achieve the targets will be greater when the targets are **clear** (and when the managers have participated in the target-setting process).

- Employees may be motivated to work harder to achieve performance targets when they are **rewarded for successful achievements**, for example with the payment of a bonus.

- Individuals should only be held **responsible for aspects of financial performance that they can control**. This is a basic principle of responsibility accounting. A common problem, however, is that some costs are incurred for the benefit of several divisions or departments of the organisation. The **costs of these shared services** have to be allocated between the divisions or departments that use them. The principle that costs should be controllable therefore means that the allocation of shared costs between divisions must be fair. In practice, arguments between divisional managers often arise because of disagreements as to how the shared costs should be shared.

3.4 Applying the Fitzgerald and Moon framework

The actual measures of performance used by companies in service industries will vary according to the nature of the service. Fitzgerald and Moon have used case studies, however, to show how their framework can be used to assess performance management systems.

One successful (and large) organisation reported as a case study by Fitzgerald was a food retailing business with a large number of stores. Applying the Fitzgerald and Moon framework, the performance management system was analysed as follows:

(a) **Dimensions of performance**

The company used four of the six dimensions of performance to assess the performance of individual stores and the performance of each region.

Dimension of performance	Measures used	Comments
Profit	Profit by store and by region.	Profit is seen as a very important measure of performance. The performance of each store and region is publicised within the company, by means of 'league tables', so that each store manager knows how his store has performed in comparison with others.
Competitiveness	Market share (at company level). Prices of competitors for each local store.	Market share is assessed from published market share statistics. The company places great importance on monitoring the prices charged by competitors. Prices are monitored for each store, at the 'local' level.

	Observation.	Managers of local stores may visit the stores of competitors to see how full their car park is, and compare this with the number of cars in the car park of his own store.
Quality of service on specific transactions	Letters and other messages from customers. Observation	The quality of service is monitored by 'mystery shoppers' – individuals hired by the company to visit stores disguised' as a customer, to observe the quality of service provided.
Quality of service overall	A range of measures for each store and warehouse/depot	A number of different aspects of service quality are monitored and measured, and a performance league table for stores and warehouses is published internally.
Resource utilisation	Sales per square metre. Wastage rates	
Flexibility	No formal performance measurement	However, managers are aware of the need for flexibility. For example, when there are staff shortages due to absenteeism, store managers will telephone part-time staff and ask them to fill the vacancies at short notice.
Innovation	No formal performance measurement	The need to innovate continually is recognised, however, and innovation is discussed regularly at business planning meetings.

(b)   **Standards of performance**

The research found a significant difference between the level of ownership for:

■   profit, and

■   quality of service.

Managers participated in the process of setting profit targets for their store or region, through the formal business planning process. However, standards for quality of service were imposed by central management (head office). The view of senior management was that quality standards must be the same at every store in the country; therefore standards must be decided at head office for the company as a whole.

'Standards' of performance were assessed for both profitability and quality of service.

Standard		**Comments**
Profit	**Ownership**	Managers were involved in setting profit targets, as part of the discussions with head office about annual targets and business planning.

	Achievability	The standards/targets were considered achievable by the managers responsible for achieving them.
	Equity	In setting profit targets for each store, allowance was made for the effect of competition from local competitors to each individual store.
Quality of service	Ownership	Standards were imposed by head office.
	Achievability	However, they were seen as achievable. An aspect of standard-setting was the use of internal benchmarks, and comparisons of quality standards at different stores within the company.
	Equity	No allowances were made for different local conditions. All stores throughout the country were expected to achieve the same standards.

(c) Reward mechanisms for achieving standards

The three elements of reward systems within the Fitzgerald and Moon framework are:

- clarity of goals and targets
- how managers are motivated to achieve targets, and
- whether there are any problems about shared costs and controllability of costs.

The research findings were as follows:

Clarity of goals	Managers were aware of company strategy, and clearly understood how their performance would contribute to the achievement of strategic objectives.
Motivation: short-term financial motivation	Store managers received a bonus for achieving targets. In addition, there were 'team' bonus payments.
Motivation: non-financial aspects	Managers had pride in their position in the league tables of stores, and were motivated to improve or maintain their position in the league.
Controllability	There were no problems with controllability of costs or allocation of shared costs.

(d)   Conclusions

Conclusions drawn from this case study, based on the Fitzgerald and Moon framework, were as follows:

- The company was highly successful.

- It had a clear statement of strategy that was well understood by management in regions and local stores.

- Performance measures were consistent with that strategy.

- Performance measures were reported regularly, covering a range of financial and non-financial aspects of performance.

- The performance measurements were clearly defined and communicated to employees at all levels in the company, and there were regular reports on actual achievements.

- The driving force for performance targets was the satisfaction of customer needs.

- The performance measurement system was reinforced by a rewards system to motivate managers and by a pride in performance.

> **Predicting corporate failure**
>
> ■ Causes of corporate failure: two differing views
> ■ Financial ratio analysis
> ■ Quantitative corporate failure prediction models: the Z score model
> ■ Altman: Z score model
> ■ Predicting corporate failure: qualitative measures
> ■ Using failure prediction models to prevent corporate failure

4 Predicting corporate failure

4.1 Causes of corporate failure: two differing views

Corporate failure occurs when a company becomes insolvent and goes out of business. Companies that fail have obviously performed badly. After a company has failed, it should be possible to analyse the reasons why failure happened and what went wrong.

Corporate failure prediction is concerned with trying to identify companies that are at risk of failure, before the failure actually happens. If management can identify the signs of failure in advance, they might be able to take action to deal with the problems and prevent failure from happening.

There are two differing views about predicting corporate failure.

■ One view is that corporate failure is caused by financial problems, such as losses or an inability to pay creditors (liquidity problems).

■ Another view is that the causes of failure are not financial. Financial problems are the consequences of other problems, and failure is caused by these other non-financial reasons.

If failure can be predicted by the existence of financial problems, it should be possible to use financial ratios and quantitative analysis to predict the failure. On the other hand, if the causes of failure are non-financial, it might be necessary to use qualitative measures of performance – and judgement – to predict failure.

4.2 Financial ratio analysis

Financial ratio analysis is widely used to assess financial performance. For example:

■ ROCE is used to assess profitability in relation to the amount of capital invested. A low ROCE or losses are an indication of a poor financial performance.

■ Financial gearing is used to assess the size of a company's long-term debts in relation to equity capital. A high gearing ratio might indicate that the company could have difficulty in meeting its interest payment obligations.

■ Liquidity ratios (the current ratio and quick ratio) can be used to assess the liquidity of a company, and whether it might be at risk from a shortage of liquidity (cash).

However, individual financial ratios are not sufficient to predict corporate failure.

■ It is difficult to assess when an individual financial ratio is at a dangerous level.

■ The ratios of a company change over time.

■ Financial ratios might also give contradictory signals: for example, if a company has poor liquidity (a low current ratio) but good profitability (a high ROCE), what is the probability of corporate failure?

4.3 Quantitative corporate failure prediction models: the Z score model

A quantitative corporate failure prediction model is a formula that can be used to predict corporate failure. The formula consists of a number of key financial ratios and each ratio is given a weighting. It produces a 'score' from the ratios, and this score can be used to decide whether the company is at risk of corporate failure.

Creating a failure prediction model

A quantitative corporate failure prediction model is based on an objective statistical analysis of historical financial data. There are several statistical methods that might be used to construct a model, but the most commonly-used method is called Multiple Discriminant Analysis or MDA.

Researchers have developed different MDA models for different industries, and for different countries. The key financial ratios for predicting failure have been found to differ between industries, countries and size of company.

MDA models are constructed in the following way:

■ A sample is taken of a number of different companies of the same type. These are grouped into two different categories: those that have failed and those that have not failed (and continue in business).

■ Historical financial data is gathered for all the companies in the sample, and a variety of financial ratios are calculated for each company.

■ Statistical analysis is used to identify the ratios that appear to discriminate most between the two different groups or categories of company (failed companies and successful companies).

■ Weightings are given to these key financial ratios according to how significant they appear to be in discriminating between failed and successful companies.

■ A 'Z score' model is established. This is the score obtained from the model.

A Z score can be calculated for any company. Statistical analysis is used to establish three categories of Z score.

■ A Z score above a certain value indicates that the company is 'safe' and is not at risk of failure.

- A Z score below a certain value indicates that the company has a high risk of failure within a given period of time, such as within the next one or two years.

- A Z score between these two values (safe and high risk) indicates that the company is in a 'grey area'. There is some risk of corporate failure, but the risk is not (yet) high.

4.4 Altman: Z score model

Altman was the first person to develop a corporate failure prediction model using the MDA method. This model was developed in the 1970s, from a study of 22 US companies.

His first Z score model used five key accounting ratios. The model was as follows:

$$Z \text{ score} = 1.2X_1 + 1.4X_2 + 3.3X_3 + 0.6X_4 + 1.0X_5$$

where X_1, X_2, X_3, X_4 and X_5 are the five financial ratios in the model.

X_1 = working capital/total assets
X_2 = retained earnings/total assets
X_3 = earnings before interest and tax/total assets
X_4 = market value of equity/book value of total debt
X_5 = sales/total assets.

(You do not need to learn this formula. It is included here to illustrate the nature of Z score models.)

With this model, Altman predicted that:

- a Z score of 2.7 or higher indicated that the company was not at risk of failure

- a Z score below 1.8 indicated a high risk of failure

- a Z score between 1.8 and 2.7 was in the 'grey area' where failure was a possibility but not a high risk.

In 1982, Gritta applied the Altman model to the airline industry and successfully predicted the failure of the Braniff airline company.

Other Z score models

Other researchers have developed corporate failure prediction models. In 1991, the first industry-specific Z score model was developed for the airline industry. This is called the AIRSCORE model but is based on the Altman Z score model. In the UK, failure prediction models have been developed by Taffler.

Researchers generally agree that their models are good for predicting corporate failure up to two years in the future, but are not reliable for longer-term predictions.

4.5 Predicting corporate failure: qualitative measures

A criticism of Z score models is that they focus on financial performance. It can be argued that poor financial ratios are a symptom of corporate failure, but they are not the cause of failure. Analysing financial ratios does not help management to understand the nature of the problems that create the risk of corporate failure.

John Argenti (1976) commented: 'Whilst these (financial) ratios may show that there is something wrong … I doubt whether one would dare to predict collapse or failure on the evidence of these ratios alone.'

The factors that could be the real cause of corporate failure might be:

- poor management for example, inexperienced management or autocratic management)
- an inability to retain key staff
- ownership of the company in the hands of a small number of individuals
- poor management information systems
- the loss of a big client
- a large increase in interest rates
- the launch of a big project (that does not go to plan).

Argenti: 'A score' model

Argenti developed a model for predicting corporate failure based on qualitative factors. His model produced a score that he called an 'A score'. Like a Z score, an A score could be used to predict corporate failure, particularly in small and medium-sized companies.

Argenti assigned scores to qualitative factors under three main headings:

- **Defects**. These are weaknesses within the organisation and management structure, such as:
  - an autocratic or inexperienced managing director/CEO
  - poor management information and control systems, such as a lack of any budgetary control system
- **Mistakes** or 'errors in action'. These are mistakes that the company makes that could have been avoided such as:
  - expanding the business too quickly without the cash resources/capital to finance the expansion: (this is 'overtrading')
  - excessive borrowing from banks
  - undertaking a large and risky project, which subsequently fails
- **Symptoms**. Symptoms are evidence of a position that is getting worse, but they are not the actual cause of the company's problems. Symptoms include:
  - financial ratios getting worse
  - the morale of employees being low and getting lower

- possibly, the use of 'window dressing' in the financial statements, to make the financial position appear better than it really is.

4.6 Using failure prediction models to prevent corporate failure

Corporate failure prediction models might be used 'after the event' to explain why companies failed. However, there is no practical value in analysing the problem after it is too late and corporate failure has already happened.

The value of corporate failure prediction models, if there is any at all, must lie in using a model to identify whether a particular company is at risk of failure, and if so:

■ how serious the risk is: the size of the risk can be judged according to the value of the Z score

■ what are the main causes of the problem.

Z score models can be criticised because they identify symptoms of the problem, but not the causes. 'A score' models can be criticised because they rely on subjective judgements of qualitative factors.

A company might also be unaware that it is at risk of failure, and so might not consider hiring a firm of specialist consultants to analyse their position using a failure prediction model.

CHAPTER

18

Developments in management accounting and performance management

Contents
1   Management accountants as 'change agents': Burns and Scapens
2   Just-in-time (JIT)
3   Quality management and quality costs
4   Target costing and Kaizen costing
5   Environmental management accounting
6   Six Sigma
7   Performance prism

> **Management accountants as 'change agents': Burns and Scapens**
>
> ■ Resistance to change in management accounting
> ■ Management accountants as agents of change

1 Management accountants as 'change agents': Burns and Scapens

This chapter describes a variety of developments in management accounting and performance management that are identified in the Study Guide for the examination syllabus.

1.1 Resistance to change in management accounting

Burns and Scapens (*Conceptualising Management Accounting Change*, 2000) have carried out research into resistance to change within organisations generally, and more particularly within management accounting practices. In many organisations, management accountants have been reluctant to adopt new techniques and methods.

Resistance to change has three separate causes.

■ There may be formal and clearly-expressed resistance to change, due to a competing interest.

■ Resistance to change might be caused by an inability to cope with the change.

■ Resistance to change might also be caused by a 'mental allegiance' to established ways of thinking, and existing routines and institutions.

The arguments of Burns and Scapens are based on 'institutional theory'. Institutions are ways of thinking and acting that make it difficult for individuals to consider change and the possibility that change might bring improvements. There are both formal and informal institutions.

■ Formal institutions are settled patterns of thought and actions. These are expressed in established formal rules and procedures.

■ Informal institutions are actions that people take because 'things have always been done this way.'

 Example

The directors of a company wanted to introduce an Enterprise Resource Planning (ERP) system into the company, and instructed their key managers, including senior accountants, that the system had to be introduced. The managers resisted the implementation of the new system, and through their control over resources and systems were successful in making the project fail. The ERP system was abandoned.

Changes in routines and institutions can happen, but there will be much less resistance to change when the change can be accommodated within existing ways of thinking.

Burns and Scapens argue that this is the reason why change in management accounting practices is often very slow. Existing management accounting systems are both formal and informal institutions that create resistance to change.

1.2 Management accountants as agents of change

Burns and Scapens argue, however, management accountants should be in a position to encourage change and act as 'change agents'. This requires a different outlook and attitude.

■ Management accountants should recognise that most companies and other entities must accept change as inevitable. In order to survive and succeed in a changing environment, it is necessary to recognise changes when they occur.

■ Entities must change internally in order to respond to the changes in the business environment.

■ To help entities to change, management must be provided with relevant information.

■ Management accounting systems must therefore respond to change, and adapt so that they provide the required (relevant) information.

Just-in-time (JIT)

- JIT production and JIT purchasing
- Practical implications of JIT
- Eliminating waste
- JIT techniques
- JIT in service operations
- Problems with JIT
- Information requirements and JIT

2 Just-in-time (JIT)

JIT originated in Japan in the 1970s. It is based on concepts that have close similarities to continuous improvement ('kaizen'), lean manufacturing and total quality management (TQM).

2.1 JIT production and JIT purchasing

Just-in-time is a concept that can be applied to both manufacturing and service operations, although it is usually associated with manufacturing.

The principle of JIT is that producing items for inventory is wasteful, because inventory adds no value, and holding inventory is therefore an expense for which there is no benefit.

If there is no immediate demand for output from any part of the system, the production system should not produce output for holding as inventory. There is no value in achieving higher volumes of output if the extra output goes into inventory that has no immediate use.

It follows that in an ideal production system:
- there should be no inventory of finished goods: items should be produced just in time to meet customer orders, and not before (**just in time production**)
- there should be no inventories of purchased materials and components: purchases should be delivered by external suppliers just in time for when they are needed in production (**just in time purchasing**).

JIT has also been called 'stockless production' and 'fast throughput manufacturing'.
- 'Just-in-time production is a production system which is driven by demand for finished products, whereby each component on a production line is produced only when needed for the next stage.
- Just-in-time purchasing is a purchasing system in which material purchases are contracted so that the receipt and usage of the materials, to the maximum extent, coincide' (CIMA *Official Terminology*).

2.2 Practical implications of JIT

It is important that items should be available when required. Finished goods must be available when customers order them, and raw materials and components must be supplied when they are needed for production.

In practice, this means that:

■ Production times must be very fast. If there is no inventory of finished goods, production has to be fast in order to meet new customer orders quickly.

■ Production must be reliable, and there must be no hold-ups, stoppages or bottlenecks. Poor quality production, leading to rejected items and scrap, is unacceptable.

■ Deliveries from suppliers must be reliable: suppliers must deliver quickly and purchased materials and components must be of a high quality (so that there will be no scrapped items or rejected items in production).

JIT therefore depends for its success on highly efficient and high-quality production, and efficient and reliable supply arrangements with key suppliers. For successful JIT purchasing, there must be an excellent relationship with key suppliers. Collaborative long-term relationships should be established with major suppliers, and purchasing should not be based on selecting the lowest price offered by competing suppliers.

Flexibility in production. The production system must be flexible, so that it can be switched immediately to making products that are ordered by customers, as soon as the order is received. Batch sizes should be small (to avoid inventory), and the ideal batch size is 1. A flexible production system requires a skilled and flexible work force.

Lower costs. Another aim of JIT is to reduce costs. Costs can be reduced by:

■ eliminating waste in production

■ speeding up production times and

■ reducing inventory levels to zero.

2.3 Eliminating waste

Waste is any activity that does not add value. In the Toyota car manufacturing system in Japan, where JIT originated, seven causes of waste were identified.

■ **Over-production**. Producing items is wasteful if the items go into inventory or are held in production as part-finished work in progress.

■ **Waiting time**. Time spent waiting for work is wasteful, and creates inefficiency in both labour and machine usage.

■ **Transport (movement of materials)**. It costs money and uses up time to move items from one place to another, but moving items adds no value. The layout of the factory floor should therefore be designed in a way that minimises movement of materials from one stage in production to the next.

■ **Waste in the process**. Waste in the process results in lost materials.

405

- **Inventory**. As explained already, holding inventory is wasteful. It does not add value but it creates a cost and ties up cash. The aim is to reduce inventory to zero.

- **Motion**. When individuals move from one place to another in their work, they might not be adding value. The aim should be to simplify work procedures by eliminating unnecessary movements by people.

- **Defective goods** are 'quality waste'.

2.4 JIT techniques

Various techniques and methods are associated with JIT:

- **Work flow and the layout of the factory floor**. The layout of the factory floor should be designed in a way that minimises waste of transportation and waste of motion. One way of doing this is to organise the work around 'dedicated work cells'. A work cell is a small group of employees with all the equipment and skills necessary to produce a finished item.

- **Reducing setup time**. 'Setup' activities are the activities that have to be carried out to get ready for the next job, for example tidying up the work place and cleaning machinery, and getting the materials for the next job. Setup activities do not add value. The aim should therefore be to reduce setup times.

- **Total productive maintenance**. (TPM). The aim of Total Productive Maintenance is to prevent breakdowns in equipment that cause an unscheduled hold-up in production, by improving maintenance systems.

- **'Kanban' systems and visibility in the work place**. To improve production flow, and avoid production of items that are not yet wanted, there should be clear signs in the workplace that indicate when more production is required. In a JIT system, 'kanban' cards might be used as a signalling system. These are signals – similar to flags – that send messages to other parts of the production system.

  For example, a card can be used by one stage in the production process to signal to the previous stage in production that more output is now required. Details of the output required can be written on the card. Kanban cards can therefore be used to authorise a movement of materials within the production system. Without the authorisation, there should be no movement.

2.5 JIT in service operations

JIT can be applied to service operations. In particular, JIT regards queuing as wasteful, because it wastes the time of the individuals waiting in the queue.
It might also be expensive to provide a system for holding customers in a queue (such as a system for making people wait in a telephone answering system).

2.6 Problems with JIT

There might be several problems with using JIT in practice.

- Zero inventories cannot be achieved in some industries, where customer demand cannot be predicted with certainty and the production cycle is quite long. In these situations, it is necessary to hold some inventories of finished goods.

■ It might be difficult to arrange a reliable supply system with key suppliers.

2.7 Information requirements and JIT

In a JIT production and purchasing system, managers have information requirements that are different from those of managers in traditional manufacturing systems. In particular:

■ When inventory levels are small and insignificant, inventory costs are immaterial. Costing systems such as absorption costing, whose main purpose is to value inventory, are too complex for management information needs.

■ If inventories are always kept close to zero, they will always have a relatively small value. If inventories are small and of no material value, there is no value in trying to keep continuous accounting records for inventory. The cost of production and sales in any period should be very close to the material purchases, labour costs and other expenses of the organisation. JIT systems may therefore encourage the use of either **throughput accounting** or **backflush accounting**.

■ Managers need information about bottlenecks in production that create delays for just-in-time production.

■ If employees are 'empowered' to take more decisions themselves, the information system must be capable of providing these employees – probably through an online and on-demand information system – with the information they need to take decisions about their work.

> ## Quality management and quality costs
>
> - The importance of quality
> - Quality-related costs
> - Managing quality-related costs
> - Total Quality Management (TQM)
> - Continuous improvement (Kaizen)
> - Quality circles
> - Potential benefits from TQM
> - Performance measurement for TQM
> - TQM and JIT compared

3 Quality management and quality costs

3.1 The importance of quality

Success in business depends on satisfying the needs of customers and meeting the requirements of customers. An essential part of meeting customer needs is to provide the quality that customers require. Quality is therefore an important aspect of product design and marketing.

Quality is also important in the control of production processes. Poor quality in production will result in losses due to rejected items and wastage rates, sales returns by customers, repairing products sold to customers (under warranty agreements) and the damaging effect on sales of a loss of reputation.

3.2 Quality-related costs

CIMA's *Official Terminology* defines quality-related costs as: 'the expenditure incurred in defect prevention and appraisal activities and the losses due to internal and external failure of a product or service, through failure to meet agreed specification'.

An organisation must incur costs to deal with quality.

- It might incur costs to prevent poor quality, or detect poor quality items when they occur.
- It might incur costs in correcting the problem when poor quality does occur.

Quality costs can be classified as:

- prevention costs
- appraisal costs
- internal failure costs
- external failure costs.

Prevention costs

Prevention costs are the costs of action to prevent defects (or reduce the number of defects). They are costs incurred to prevent a quality problem from arising. Prevention costs include:

- designing products and services with in-built quality
- designing production processes of a high quality
- training employees to do their jobs to a high standard.

Appraisal costs

Appraisal costs are the costs of checking the quality of work that has been done. Appraisal costs include inspection and testing costs.

Internal failure costs

Internal failure costs are costs incurred when defective production occurs. They include:

- the cost of scrapped items
- the cost of re-working items to bring them to the required quality standard
- the cost of production time lost due to failures and defects.

External failure costs

External failure costs are costs incurred when the quality problem arises after the goods have been delivered to the customer. They include the costs of:

- dealing with customers' complaints
- the costs of carrying out repair work under a guarantee or warranty
- the costs of recalling all items from customers in order to correct a design fault
- legal costs, when a customer takes the organisation to court
- the cost of lost reputation: when an organisation gets a reputation for poor quality, customers will stop buying from it.

It is commonly argued that the biggest quality costs that an entity incurs are its 'external failure costs': these are the quality costs incurred after goods have been delivered to the customer.

The aim should be to reduce quality costs. Ideally this can be done by improving product design and production systems. If necessary, more should be invested in identifying quality problems before they leave the factory, for example through improved inspection and testing systems.

3.3 Managing quality-related costs

The traditional view of managing quality costs is that the total of all quality costs should be minimised. An organisation should spend more money on prevention and detection costs, if this reduces internal and external failure costs by a larger amount. On the other hand, there is no reason to spend more on preventing poor quality if the benefits do not justify the extra cost.

This traditional view is rejected by supporters of the Total Quality Management (TQM) principle. The TQM view is that it is impossible to identify and measure all quality costs. In particular, it is impossible to measure the costs of lost reputation, which will lead to a decline in sales over time. The aim should therefore always be to work towards zero defects. To achieve zero defects, it will be necessary to spend more money on prevention costs.

The TQM approach to quality costs is to 'get things right the first time'.

Example

You are presented with the following list of performance measurements before the implementation of a Total Quality Management Programme (Pre-TQM) and after its implementation (Post-TQM).

	Pre-TQM performance	Post-TQM performance
	%	%
Returns by customers due to packaging defects	5	2
Rejections on final inspection	6	4
Losses in production	3	1

Required

Calculate how many units must be input to the process to achieve final sales of 1,000 units:

(a)   before the TQM programme

(b)   after the TQM programme.

Answer

	Performance	
	Pre-TQM	Post-TQM
	units	units
Sales	1,000	1,000
Packaging failures	50	20
	1,050	1,020
Rejected units	67	43
	1,117	1,063
Process losses	35	11
Units to be input	1,152	1,074

The TQM improvements have led to a reduction of about 7% (78/1,152) in the quantity of units that need to be input to produce 1,000 units of output.

3.4 Total Quality Management (TQM)

It is now widely accepted that in order to succeed in business in highly competitive markets, companies must adopt strategies aimed at satisfying the customer. Customer needs can be satisfied to some extent by cutting costs and selling at lower prices. However, strategies to achieve customer satisfaction must also focus on three other critical success factors:

- quality
- time, and
- innovation.

One approach to achieving improvements in these critical success factors is a Total Quality Management programme.

Total Quality Management is a philosophy of quality management with its origins in Japan in the 1950s. CIMA *Official Terminology* defines Total Quality Management (TQM) as 'the continuous improvement in quality, productivity and effectiveness obtained by establishing management responsibility for processes as well as outputs. In this, every process has an identified process owner and every person in an entity operates within a process and contributes to its improvement'.

It is important to understand that TQM is a philosophy or culture.

- For a TQM programme to succeed, it must have the full support of everyone in the organisation, from senior management to lowest-paid employees.

- Everyone in the organisation is actively involved in trying to achieve improvements in processes, systems and products. Each individual accepts personal responsibility for his or her own standards of quality.

- Employees are encouraged to be involved actively in the TQM process. This is achieved partly through the use of quality circles.

TQM has several different aspects, including:

- statistical quality control systems and
- a 'zero defects' policy – similar to the approach in JIT
- continuous improvement
- quality circles.

3.5 Continuous improvement (Kaizen)

TQM applies the concept of continuous improvement (or 'Kaizen'). Kaizen means 'improvement in small steps'. In a continual improvement programme, the aim is to keep on finding ways of improving performance. It is not important that each new improvement is small. What is important, however, is that improvements should continue all the time, and that everyone should be constantly looking for ways of making improvements.

The ISO 9004 international quality standard describes continuous improvement as an eight-step method:

- Involve the entire organisation

- Initiate quality improvement projects or activities
- Investigate possible causes of quality problems
- Establish cause-and-effect relationships
- Take preventative or corrective action to improve quality
- Confirm the improvement
- Sustain the gains
- Continue the improvement.

Kaizen: quality improvements and cost reductions

Kaizen has two aims. One is to improve quality without adding to cost. The other is to reduce costs without reducing quality. The process of continuous improvement therefore takes place within a framework of **quality assurance**. Checks are made to ensure that changes do not reduce quality, because reductions in quality create a loss in value. Loss in value reduces customer satisfaction, and this will be damaging to the company in the long term.

Kaizen costing, which is a costing system to support Kaizen, is described later.

3.6   Quality circles

Quality circles might be used as a part of a continuous improvement programme. A quality circle is a small group of employees, usually five to eight people, who meet regularly to discuss work-related problems and possible solutions to them. The main focus for discussion is on the quality of processes and work systems.

With quality circles, ordinary workers are encouraged to contribute ideas for improvement, and so participate in the continuous improvement programme.

Quality circles cannot replace other quality management processes and methods, such as statistical quality control systems.

Quality circles are not used in all companies that use TQM. However, a system of continuous improvement (Kaizen) does depend on **work by teams** of individuals representing different functions and skills. For example, a team might be established consisting of an engineer, an accountant, a person from manufacturing and a person from the buying department. The team members then combine their knowledge and skills to devise methods of achieving improvements in a particular aspect of operations for which they have been given responsibility for improvement.

3.7   Potential benefits from TQM

There are several potential benefits that might be obtained from introducing a TQM approach:

- Formally establishing a TQM system will establish the importance of 'quality' in a way that all employees and managers should recognise.
- The commitment to quality should also establish 'customer satisfaction' as a prime business objective.

- A successful introduction of a TQM approach should result in continuous improvements in all processes and operations.

However, the successful application of TQM will depend on the provision of relevant and useful quality-related information, and in particular, information about quality-related costs.

3.8   Performance measurement for TQM

A system of TQM and continuous improvement needs the support of an information system that provides relevant information.

- Management accounting information can be provided by the Kaizen costing system.

- There is extensive use of non-financial performance indicators, such as production setup times, the number of times materials are moved, and the number of units scrapped or wastage levels.

A report in the US (1993) on the use of Kaizen by Japanese manufacturing companies commented: 'These quantitative, non-financial measures allow employees to monitor their performance and interpret the results of their efforts. With relevant training and frequent reports on the company's financial health, companies ensure employees understand how their work directly affects the company's performance.'

3.9   TQM and JIT compared

Many of the concepts applied by total quality management are similar to those in a just-in-time management philosophy.

- The aim in both should be to have zero inventory. Raw materials should be delivered from suppliers only when they are needed, and items should be produced only when they are required for sale to a customer. In practice, this ideal is usually impossible to achieve, and the aim should therefore be to minimise inventory of raw materials and finished goods.

- A 'pull system' should therefore operate, with items being manufactured only when they are required by customers. This is different from the traditional 'push' system of manufacture, when the aim was to maximise the use of production capacity in order to minimise fully absorbed production costs per unit.

- The aim should be to create a uniform factory load and continual rate of production, so that the speed of manufacture matches the rate of customer demand.

- The key aim should be to provide a level of quality that satisfies customers and meets their needs.

- Employees should be encouraged to participate in the TQM/JIT process. Successful implementation of both TQM and JIT requires a flexible work force, capable of switching from one task to another as requirements dictate.

- Many JIT manufacturing systems use a factory layout that minimises the need to move materials. Movement of materials does not add value, and should be avoided. This is consistent with the TQM view that movement is waste.

- Setup times between jobs should be minimised, because setting up does not add value.

- There should be a focus on simplification of products and processes, in order to maximise the utilisation of available resources.

Target costing and Kaizen costing

- The purpose of target costing
- The target costing method
- Techniques for achieving the target cost
- Kaizen costing

---

4 Target costing and Kaizen costing

4.1 The purpose of target costing

Target costing is a method of strategic profit management. **It is used for new product development.**

- An idea for a new product is proposed. The features and functions of the product are specified – what it will do, what it should be made of, what it should look like and so on. These features and functions may be altered later in the process.

- The company carries out market research to decide what price customers would be willing to pay for the product. It then decides the price that it would like to charge for the new product, in order to win a target share of the market.

- The company then decides on the level of profitability that it wants to achieve for the product, in order to make the required return on investment. This target profit margin should reflect the company's strategic planning objectives.

- Having identified a target price and a target profit, the company then establishes a target cost for the product. The target cost is the target selling price minus the target profit margin. This is the cost at which the product must be manufactured and sold in order to achieve the target profits and return at the strategic market price.

- The target cost is usually less than the cost that could reasonably be achieved with current manufacturing methods and materials.

- Achieving this cost is a target towards which everyone involved in the project then works.

Since there is 'gap' between the target cost and the expected cost, the gap must be closed by finding ways of making the product more cheaply – for example, by simplifying the design or using a different material. However, the reductions in cost should be achieved without reducing the quality or value of the product, because if quality is reduced, customers will not pay the target price.

4.2 The target costing method

Target costing is based on the idea that when a new product is developed, a company will have a reasonable idea about:

- the price at which it will be able to sell the product, and

---

■ the sales volumes that it will be able to achieve for the product over its expected life.

There may also be estimates of the capital investment required, and any incremental fixed costs (such as marketing costs or costs of additional salaried staff).

Taking estimates of sales volumes, capital investment requirements and incremental fixed costs over the life cycle of the product, it should be possible to calculate a target cost. The target cost for the product is the maximum variable cost for the product, that will provide at least the minimum required return on investment.

There will be a gap between the cost at which the product can be made now and the target cost. The aim should be to close the gap, and reduce the cost of making the product to the target cost level. The most effective way of closing the gap is to re-design the product, so that it can be produced at less cost.

The steps in a target costing exercise are therefore as follows:

■ Decide the type of product required

■ Decide what the required sales volume should be (and market share)

■ Decide what price the product must have in order to achieve the target sales volume

■ Estimate the amount of investment required to develop and market the product

■ Estimate the required profit, measured as a return on the investment (ROI, NPV or IRR measurements are possible)

■ Measure the target cost for the product: the target cost per unit of product is estimated total revenue minus target profit, divided by the expected sales volume in unit.

The target cost should be compared with the estimated cost of making the product to the current specification. The current cost of the product is likely to be much higher than the target cost, and the challenge is therefore to reduce costs from the current estimated level to the target cost level. Usually, this will require a re-design of the product, to new (and cheaper) specifications.

The elements in the target costing process are shown in the diagram below.

Target costing

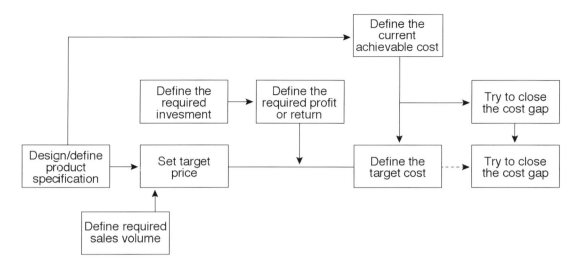

Example

A company has designed a new product. It currently estimates that to make the product, an investment of $1,000,000 in machinery would be required. The residual value of this investment would be $300,000 at the end of year 4, when the product is expected to reach the end of its marketable life.

After studying potential demand in the market, the company has set a target selling price of $20. It has been estimated that at this price, the annual sales volume in units would be:

Year	Sales volume
	units
1	20,000
2	30,000
3	40,000
4	10,000

The current estimate of costs is that it would cost $14 to make each unit of the product, but that there would be no incremental fixed costs. The company has a cost of capital of 10% for this type of project.

This data can be used to calculate a target cost for the new product, and to identify the current size of the cost gap.

In the table below, the variable cost per unit of product is shown as V.

Year	Capital cost/ residual value	Revenue	Variable costs	Discount factor at 10%	PV of variable costs	PV of other cash flows
	$	$	$		$	$
0	(1,000,000)			1.000		(1,000,000)
1		400,000	20,000V	0.909	18,180V	363,600
2		600,000	30,000V	0.826	24,780V	495,600
3		800,000	40,000V	0.751	30,040V	600,800
4	300,000	200,000	10,000V	0.683	6,810V	340,500
					79,810V	800,500

In order to make a return of at least 10% on the investment in the project, the maximum variable cost per unit that can be permitted is $800,500/79,810 = $10.03.

The target cost for the product should therefore be $10.03, say $10 per unit. The current estimated cost is $14 per unit; therefore the cost gap is $4.

The company needs to identify ways of closing this cost gap.

4.3 Techniques for achieving the target cost

Techniques used by project teams to achieve the target cost include **value engineering (VE)** and **functional analysis**.

Value engineering (VE)

Value engineering is an approach to designing new products in a way that achieves the target amount of value. The target cost is analysed into:

- **cost elements** for each department (such as direct material costs, direct labour costs and depreciation costs), and
- **functional components** (for example, in a motor car functional components include the engine, the transmission system, the braking system, the chassis and so on).

Value engineering then begins with an investigation into the functions of the materials and parts purchased, with a view to either reducing costs or improving the product's performance and quality. For each material or component, the VE team might ask questions such as:

- What is the function of this material or component?
- Is it necessary?
- Can it be simplified?
- Are all the features of the product or component necessary?
- Can a standard part or component be used, instead of the part or component that is currently in the product specification. Using standard components will reduce costs, because standard components are purchased in larger quantities at lower costs.

A VE project makes extensive use of **cost tables**. These provide a detailed analysis of the costs of the product, and help the VE project team to identify the major factors that drive the costs of the product. The team can identify areas of product design where cost reductions of the required magnitude can be made.

The cost tables can be used to provide information about how the costs of the product would be affected by:

- using different production resources
- using different materials, different manufacturing methods
- changing the functions of the product, and
- changing the product design.

Functional analysis

Functional analysis looks at each function of a product, with the aim of deciding:

- whether the functions performed by the product can be modified
- whether the product functions can be reduced
- whether the product functions can be increased (increasing the functions of a product may increase the cost of the product, but add to its value to the customer by even more), or
- whether two or more functions can be combined.

To carry out functional analysis, cost tables are needed. These should provide detailed costs of each product function, so that the implications for cost of altering the product's functions can be considered.

4.4   Kaizen costing

For companies that practice TQM and continuous improvement methods, Kaizen costing takes over where target costing ends.

- Target costing is used in the design and development stage for a new product.
- Kaizen costing is applied from the time that a product goes into full production until the end of the product's life.

Taken together, target costing and Kaizen costing are systems for life cycle costing.

The philosophy of continuous improvement (Kaizen) is based on the view that markets are highly competitive and industry must try to keep reducing costs in order to reduce selling prices in order to maintain a competitive advantage. Kaizen costing is a management accounting system that provides cost information to help with achieving improvements without loss of product quality or value.

Most of the costs of a product over its entire life cycle are committed during the design and development stage. This is why target costing is a valuable technique for the control of costs (without loss of value). However, there is still some scope for further cost reduction after commercial production and marketing of the product has begun.

A Kaizen costing system is therefore a costing system that is designed to help a company to reduce product costs.

- A target for cost reductions is set. This target is below the current cost. The cost reduction must be achieved without any loss of value for the customer. For example, a target might be set to reduce unit costs of production by 5% within two years.
- Teams are established to identify methods of making improvements.
- Kaizen focuses on making small improvements, and it is unlikely that a single improvement will be sufficient to achieve the target cost reductions. Many different improvements might be needed, over a period of time.
- Actual costs are continually compared with the target costs, and progress towards achieving the target cost is monitored through regular reporting.

- The project teams must continually review production conditions to find ways of making more improvements and more cost reductions.

- Normally, teams are rewarded with bonuses if they achieve their cost reduction targets.

- When one cost reduction target is met, another cost reduction target takes its place. With Kaizen, the process of seeking improvements never ends.

Techniques for continuous improvement

Teams that are given the responsibility for making improvements might use **value analysis (VA)** methods. VA is similar to value engineering, except that VA is applied to existing products and VE to products during their design and development stage.

The types of questions that might be asked are as follows:

- Can common materials and parts be used? The same part might be used in two or more parts of the product, or the same part might be used for several different products that the company manufactures.

- How much of the cost consists of purchased materials and components? Can major suppliers be persuaded to reduce their own costs and prices?

- Can improvements be made in logistics (distribution) or packaging?

- Can the investment in the product (for example, working capital) be reduced?

- Can improvements be made in production systems or maintenance methods?

- Can the work be organised in a different way?

A system of value analysis must be supported by a management accounting system that provides relevant cost data.

Kaizen costing compared with standard costing

It is useful to compare Kaizen costing with traditional standard costing.

- With standard costing, expected costs are established based on current production methods. Variances between actual and standard costs are calculated, and variance reports focus on significant variations between actual costs and the current standard. There is no motivation to make improvements and reduce costs below the existing standard.

- With Kaizen costing, actual costs are compared with the target, not an existing standard. The variance reporting system is used to monitor progress towards the target cost.

- With standard costing, managers are encouraged to prevent adverse variances. For example, if there is an adverse material price variance, the manager responsible might decide to buy materials at a lower price from a different supplier. The result could be a loss of quality, a fall in value and a reduction in customer satisfaction. With Kaizen costing, reductions in cost must be achieved without any loss of value.

Target costing and Kaizen costing are examples of management techniques that call for a different management accounting system. In particular, project teams need cost tables to assist them with identifying ways in which cost reductions might be achieved and they need information to monitor progress towards targets.

A 1993 article on Kaizen and Kaizen costing concluded: 'In the US, changes in the focus and methods of production need to be accompanied by changes in management accounting systems. The Japanese have provided guidance on how management accounting can play a significant role in creating sustainable competitive advantage for a firm. The more organisations rid themselves of traditional management accounting practices, the better is the chance that the new ideas about manufacturing can take over and really show their worth. Old ways of product costing blunt a firm's ability to compete effectively and hinder their ability to focus on world-class performance.'

('New product costing, Japanese style': Margaret Lgagne and Richard Discenza. CPA Journal May 1993).

> ## Environmental management accounting
>
> - The purpose of environmental management accounting
> - A framework for environmental management accounting
> - EMA techniques

5 Environmental management accounting

5.1 The purpose of environmental management accounting

For some companies, environmental issues are significant, in terms of both strategy and cost.

- Poor environmental behaviour can result in significant costs or losses, such as fines for excessive pollution, environmental taxes, loss of land values, the cost of law suits, and so on.
- Environmental behaviour can affect the perception of customers, and their attitudes to a company and its products. Increasingly, consumers take environmental factors into consideration when they make their buying decisions.

Environmental management accounting can be used to provide information to management to help with the management of environmental issues. Traditional management accounting techniques:

- Under-estimate or even ignore the cost of poor environmental behaviour
- over-estimate the costs of improving environmental practices, and
- under-estimate the benefits of improving environmental practices.

Environmental management accounting (EMA) provides managers with financial and non-financial information to support their environmental management decision-making. EMA complements other 'conventional' management accounting methods, and does not replace them.

The main applications of EMA are for:

- estimating annual environmental costs (for example, costs of waste control)
- budgeting
- product pricing
- investment appraisal (for example, estimating clean-up costs at the end of a project life and assessing the environmental costs of a project)
- estimating savings from environmental projects.

5.2   A framework for environmental management accounting

Burritt et al (2001) suggested a framework for EMA based on providing information to management:

■   from internal or external sources

■   as monetary or physical measurements

■   as historical or forward-looking information

■   where the focus is short-term or longer-term

■   that consists of routine reports or ad hoc information.

Four of these elements of EMA are shown in the following table:

Environmental management accounting (EMA)

| | Monetary EMA | | Physical EMA | |
	Short-term focus	Long-term focus	Short-term focus	Long-term focus
Historical orientation				
Routine reporting	Environmental cost accounting	Analysis of environmentally-induced capital expenditures	Material and energy flow accounting	Accounting for environmental capital impacts
Ad hoc (one-off) information	Historical assessment of environmental decisions	Environmental life cycle costing, environmental target costing	Historical assessment of short-term environmental impacts, e.g. of a site or product	Post-investment assessment of environmental impacts of capital expenditures
Future orientation				
Routine reporting	Environmental operational budgets and capital budgets (monetary reporting)	Environmental long-term financial planning		Environmental long-term physical planning
Ad hoc (one-off) information	Relevant environmental costing (e.g. special orders)	Environmental life cycle budgeting and target costing	Assessment of environmental impacts	Physical environmental investment appraisal. Specific project life cycle analysis

5.3   EMA techniques

Environmental management accounting techniques include:

- re-defining costs
- input-output analysis
- environmental activity based accounting
- environmental life cycle costing

Re-defining costs

The US Environmental Protection Agency (1998) suggested terminology for environmental costing that distinguishes between:

- conventional costs: these are environmental costs of materials and energy that have environmental relevance and that can be 'captured' in costing systems

- potentially hidden costs: these are environmental costs that might get lost within the general heading of 'overheads'

- contingent costs: these are costs that might be incurred at a future date, such as clean-up costs

- image and relationship costs: these are costs associated with promoting an environmental image, such as the cost of producing environmental reports. There are also costs of behaving in an environmentally irresponsible way, such as the costs of lost sales as a result of causing a major environmental disaster.

In traditional management accounting systems, environmental costs (and benefits) are often hidden. EMA attempts to identify these costs and bring them to the attention of management.

Input-output analysis

Input-output analysis is a method of analysing what goes into a process and what comes out. It is based on the concept that what goes into a process must come out or be stored. Any difference is residual, which is regarded as waste.

Inputs and outputs are measured initially in physical quantities, including quantities of energy and water. They are then given a monetary value.

Environmental activity based accounting

Environmental activity based accounting is the application of environmental costs to activity based accounting. A distinction is made between:

- environmental-related costs: these are costs that are attributable to cost centres involved in environmental-related activities, such as an incinerator or a waste recycling plant

- environmental-driven costs: these are overhead costs resulting from environment-related factors, such as higher costs of labour or depreciation.

The cost drivers for environment-related costs may be:

- the volume of emissions or waste

- the toxicity of emissions or waste

- 'environmental impact added' (units multiplied by environmental impact per unit)

- the volume of emissions or waste treated.

Environmental life cycle costing

Life cycle costing is a method of costing that looks at the costs of a product over its entire life cycle. Life cycle costing can help a company to establish how costs are likely to change as a product goes through the stages of its life (introduction, growth, maturity, decline and withdrawal from the market). This analysis of costs should include environmental costs.

Xerox provides a good example of the environmental aspect of life cycle costing. Xerox manufactures photocopiers, which it leases rather than sells. At the end of a lease period, the photocopiers are returned from the customer to Xerox. At one time, photocopiers were delivered to customers in packaging that could not be re-used for sending the machines back at the end of the lease period. Customers disposed of the old packaging and had to provide their own new packaging to return the machines to Xerox. Xerox then disposed of this packaging. The company therefore incurred two costs: the cost of packaging to deliver machines and the cost of disposal of the packaging for returned machines.

By looking at the costs of photocopiers over their full life cycle, Xerox found that money could be saved by manufacturing standard re-usable packaging. The same packaging could be used to deliver and return machines, and could also be re-used. At the same time, the company created benefits for the environment by reducing disposals of packaging materials.

> ## Six Sigma
>
> - Seeking 'near perfection'
> - The basic approach in Six Sigma
> - Process improvement and process design
> - Process improvement: DMAIC
> - New process design or radical improvement: DMADV

6 Six Sigma

6.1 Seeking 'near perfection'

Six Sigma is an approach to eliminating defects from products and operations, and achieving near perfection. Although it was originally applied to manufacturing operations and defects in products, it can also be applied to any product, process or transaction.

The term 'Six Sigma' comes from statistical analysis, but it is now generally accepted as meaning that there should be no more than 3.4 defects in every 1 million items, for any product or process to which the Six Sigma methodology is applied. The limit of 3.4 defects per 1 million items can be seen as a target, and improvements in existing products and processes and designs of new products and processes should aim towards this target.

Six Sigma was originated in the US in the 1980s, by Motorola. (Although the term 'Six Sigma' is widely used, it is a registered trademark of Motorola.) Modern technology was becoming more complex, and it was becoming apparent in some manufacturing industries that old ideas about quality standards and quality control no longer applied. Unless quality standards could be improved in component production, for example, the quality of complex end-products would be much lower than customers had a right to expect. In 1989, having experimented for several years with its approach to quality by improvements, Motorola announced that within five years it intended to achieve a defect rate of no more than 3.4 parts per million in its products.

 Examples

A company might establish target specifications for the manufacture of a product, and products should be manufactured to this exact specification, or within acceptable tolerance limits. A Six Sigma approach should be to ensure that no more than 3.4 items per 1 million produced will fail to meet the specification, or will be manufactured outside the acceptable tolerance limits.

The IT department of a company that writes software for other departments might set a target for the programs that it writes of no more than 3.4 coding errors per 1 million lines of software code.

6.2 The basic approach in Six Sigma

A definition of Six Sigma will help to explain its key features. Six Sigma has been defined as 'a data-driven method for achieving near-perfect quality. Six Sigma analysis can focus on any element of production or service, and has a strong emphasis on statistical analysis in design, manufacturing and customer-oriented activities' (UK Department of Trade and Industry).

The basic objective with Six Sigma is to focus on improvements in processes and a reduction in variations. **Perfection is achieved by reducing the amount of variations in processes.** For example, if a product is designed with a length of exactly one metre, Six Sigma improvements might be aimed at reducing the variation in the length of products actually manufactured to acceptable tolerance limits of, say, plus or minus one millimetre.

The aim of Six Sigma is to improve customer satisfaction. Its approach is to apply a standard approach (a structured methodology) to reduce and control the causes of variation in a process, and to focus on reducing the standard deviation of actual performance from the target specification.

The Six Sigma approach relies heavily on **statistical measurements**. Actual performance is measured and compared with the target, and the number of 'defects' – products or processes that fail to meet acceptable standards – can be established, to see whether the required quality standards have been achieved.

Another feature of Six Sigma is that **project teams** are established to achieve the required improvements in processes or products. These project teams should consist of representatives from every department or aspect of operations that might contribute towards making the required improvements. The projects teams should be led by individuals who are specially trained in Six Sigma methods, who are commonly called Master Black Belts, Black Belts and Green Belts, according to their level of skill and knowledge of Six Sigma.

General Electric Company, another US company that adopted Six Sigma methods, has stated that Six Sigma is based on the following key concepts:

- **'Critical to quality'**. These are attributes or characteristics of a product or service that are the most important to customers.
- **Defect**. This is failing to deliver what the customer wants.
- **Process capability**. This is the level of quality or performance that a process is capable of achieving.
- **Variation**. This refers to variations in quality that the customer can see or feel in a product or service.
- **Stable operations**. This means consistent and predictable processes and operations that improve what customers see and feel.
- **Design for Six Sigma**. This refers to designing a product or process that meets customer needs and achieves the level of process capability for doing this.

6.3　Process improvement and process design

The Six Sigma approach differs slightly between:

■ making improvements in existing processes, where the required changes in the process are fairly small ('incremental improvements'), and

■ the design of a new process, or major re-design of an existing process.

Process improvements

The Six Sigma approach to making incremental improvements in existing processes is in five steps, known as DMAIC.

■ **Define** an opportunity

■ **Measure** performance

■ **Analyse** the opportunity

■ **Improve** performance

■ **Control** performance.

New process design/process re-design

The Six Sigma approach to designing a new process or the major re-design of an existing process is also in five steps, known as DMADV.

■ **Define** the goals for the new process

■ **Match** performance requirements with these goals

■ **Analyse** these performance requirements and produce an outline design (a design, but not in detail) of a new process that will meet these requirements

■ **Design** and implement the process

■ **Verify** performance.

6.4　Process improvement: DMAIC

The five steps in process improvement using the Six Sigma method are explained in more detail below.

Define

A serious problem with quality is identified.

■ A **problem statement** is prepared. This describes the nature of the problem, which must be defined specific, measurable terms. What is the visible evidence of the problem? What are the **symptoms** of the problem? (A 'symptom' is something that is going wrong in the process, expressed as a quantified measurement of **output** from the process).

■ A **'mission statement'** is then prepared. This is a statement of what will be done to deal with the problem. The mission statement should also be expressed as a quantified measurement, using the same units of measurement or symptoms that are used in the problem statement. For example, the problem statement may be that the number of defects in a particular process is 1 in 1,000. The mission statement may then be that the aim should be to reduce the number of defects to no more than 1 in 100,000

- A **project team is set up**. This team is given the responsibility and the resources to solve the problem and make an improvement. It should be a 'cross-functional' team consisting of members from all the departments or functions that will be affected by the improvement project.

Measure

Data is obtained about the current process, and the 'symptoms' of the problem are measured in detail. At this stage in the project, the project team should measure how the process is working, and obtain data that can be analysed in order to identify what seems to be causing the problem. Where there are several causes of a 'symptom', the project team should concentrate on those problems that are the main causes.

This is a preliminary analysis. The project team will not make a final decision about the main causes of the problem until it has carried out a more extensive analysis.

The mission statement should be verified, and if necessary amended.

Analyse

The preliminary ideas about what might be causing the problem are investigated in more detail. Different theories are tested, until the project team believes that it has discovered the main cause (or causes) of the problem.

- The project team formulate different theories about the main causes of the problem, and documents these theories.
- Each theory is then tested, to establish whether it might be correct. Theories are rejected when it is decided that they cannot be correct.
- The 'root' cause (or causes) of the problem is identified when the testing of the theories has been completed.

Improve

The cause (or causes) of the problem are removed by means of re-designing and improving the process that is causing the problem.

- Several different alternative methods of improving the process should be evaluated, to decide which will be the most effective in achieving the 'mission statement' for the project.
- The chosen improvement is then designed in detail.
- If the improvements are likely to meet resistance to change from some employees, plans should be developed for overcoming the expected resistance.
- Before the improvement is implemented, it should be tested to prove that it will be effective.
- The improvement is then implemented.

Control

New controls are designed and implemented to prevent the problem from returning and to make sure that the improvements are sustained.

Controls will include regular measurements of output from the process, and a comparison of actual performance with the target.

The controls should be audited from time to time, to make sure that they are effective.

6.5   New process design or radical improvement: DMADV

Sometimes, making improvements in existing processes is not sufficient to achieve the required quality standard, and a completely different process must be designed. The five steps in new process design using the Six Sigma method are explained in more detail below.

- **Define**. The goals and target quality standards of the new process must be defined. Customer requirements and expectations should be taken into consideration when defining these goals.

- **Match**. The next step is to develop a set of performance measurements (quantified performance targets) that will enable the goals for the process to be achieved.

- **Analyse**. These performance standards for the new process must be analysed. Based on this analysis, a preliminary design for a new process is developed.

- **Design**. The preliminary design for the new process is developed into a more detailed design, and the new process is then implemented.

- **Verify**. After the new process has been implemented, controls and checks should be introduced to confirm that the required performance targets are met, and that the goals of the process are successfully achieved.

> ### Performance prism
>
> - Origins of the performance prism
> - Five sides to the performance prism
> - Stakeholder satisfaction
> - Strategies
> - Processes and capabilities
> - Stakeholder contribution
> - Performance prism: a summary

7 Performance prism

7.1 Origins of the performance prism

The performance prism is a model of performance management that has been developed by the Centre for Performance at Cranfield Business School. It is an attempt to overcome the limitations of earlier models or frameworks of performance measurement, such as the balanced scorecard, shareholder value added, activity based costing and competitive benchmarking.

These other performance management models have a variety of limitations.

- The balanced scorecard is used to set targets on four key areas: financial performance, the customer, internal processes and innovation and learning. In doing so, it fails to recognise the potential importance of other stakeholders in the business, particularly suppliers and employees.

- Shareholder value added also focuses on returns and value for shareholders, and gives no consideration to any other stakeholders in the business.

- Activity based costing is concerned with analysing business processes, to identify cost drivers and eliminate activities that fail to add value. This focus on improving the efficiency of processes ignores the opinions of all stakeholders – such as shareholders, customers and employees.

- Competitive benchmarking is often used as a 'one off' exercise to identify improvements that can be made in processes, and it is normally used to introduce short-term improvement measures. It does not provide a long-term and formal system of performance measurement.

Note: The term 'stakeholder' may not be familiar to you. Every company or other entity has a number of different stakeholders. 'Stakeholder' is a term for any individual, entity or group of similar individuals or entities that has an interest (or 'stake') in what the company does. The stakeholder groups for a company include its shareholders, lenders (banks and bondholders), suppliers, customers, the government and the general public (or sections of the general public).

Each of the performance measurement models listed above looks at a different aspect of performance and each model can be very useful in particular circumstances. However, none of them provide a performance measurement framework that considers all aspects of performance and the full significance of all stakeholders. The performance prism has been developed as a framework for performance measurement that considers all aspects of performance and all significant stakeholders.

7.2   Five sides to the performance prism

The performance prism can be shown in diagram form as a solid block of glass with five sides, a top, a bottom and three vertical sides. The five sides of the prism represent:

- stakeholder satisfaction
- strategies
- processes
- capabilities
- stakeholder contribution.

Performance prism

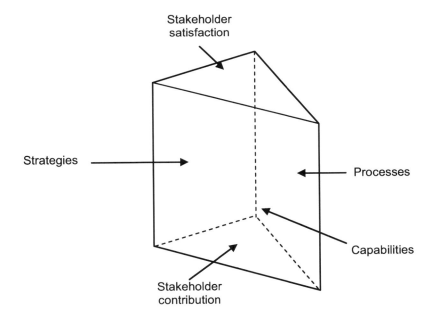

There are five aspects to successful performance in the long term.

- The entity must have a very clear picture of who its key stakeholders are, and what they want. The key stakeholders of a company will include the shareholders, but other stakeholders might also be significant. (Stakeholder satisfaction)
- The entity must have defined the strategies it will select and pursue in order to ensure that 'value' is given to all the key stakeholders. (Strategies)

- They must understand the processes that will be necessary in order to achieve the strategic targets. (Processes)

- They must have defined the resources that they need to perform these processes effectively, and must be capable of providing these required resources. (Capabilities)

- The most successful entities will also have identified what they want to obtain from their stakeholders, such as loyalty from their employees and profitability from their customers. (Stakeholder contribution).

7.3 Stakeholder satisfaction

An entity must satisfy the needs and expectations of its key stakeholders. According to the performance prism framework, the starting point for a performance management system should be the satisfaction of key stakeholders.

- Who are the most influential stakeholders?

- What do they need and want?

The starting point should **not** be to establish **performance targets for strategies**.

'Performance measures are designed to help people track whether they are moving in the direction they want to. They help managers establish whether they are going to reach the destination they set out to reach. Strategy, however, is not about destination. Instead, it is about the route you choose to take – **how** to reach the desired destination' (Neely and Adams).

A criticism of the **balanced scorecard** model for performance measurement is that it begins by establishing strategic targets, on the assumption that the aim should be to satisfy shareholders and maximise shareholder value. The approach in the performance prism framework is that although shareholders are key stakeholders for a company, other stakeholders might be just as important.

- Some manufacturing companies rely heavily on suppliers, and should not establish a performance management system without considering the needs and expectations of those suppliers. In an article of the performance prism, Neely and Adams mention the example of Boeing, which manufactures only three of the components in a 777 aircraft. All the other components are manufactured by external suppliers.

- Some entities rely heavily on key employees, and the performance targets they set cannot ignore their needs and expectations. An extreme example is a professional football club, which must consider the needs and expectations of its star players.

- The government or government agencies can be powerful stakeholders in companies. In some countries, services such as the supply of water, gas and electricity are provided by commercial companies, but because of their monopoly position (and because of public concern about these services) companies are subject to regulation by a government-appointed regulatory body. This 'stakeholder' might have the power to instruct companies to reduce prices or improve the quality of their service, and companies failing to comply with the regulator's demands might have to pay heavy fines. In many other industries, companies might have to consider the risk of punishment (often in the form of fines or legal settlements) for failing to comply with various government regulations.

- In some industries, pressure groups might have a significant influence on the activities of companies. Pressure groups are sometimes able to organise action against a company, using the internet as their method of communication. For example, a few years ago, public pressure in some European countries successfully forced Monsanto to remove its genetically-modified food products from the market.

7.4   Strategies

When an entity has identified its key stakeholders, and their needs and wants, the next step is to select strategies that will satisfy these needs and wants. For each strategy, performance measures are needed. Performance measures are needed for four reasons.

- Managers need performance measures for strategic targets so that they can monitor whether the strategies are being implemented.

- Performance measures can also be used to communicate strategies to others within the organisation, so that they have a clear understanding of strategic objectives.

- Performance measures are used to encourage the achievement of strategic objectives, for example by paying bonuses for the successful achievement of targets.

- Actual data about performance can be used to assess whether strategic objectives are being achieved (and if they are not being achieved, to find out why not).

However, it is essential that performance targets should be consistent with the entity's strategies. Individuals respond to performance measures, and will often do anything to succeed in meeting their targets, even if their actions are damaging and harmful. An example used by Neely and Adams is a telephone call centre that had a target of dealing with customer calls within one minute. In order to achieve this target, staff at the call centre would often cut off a customer in the middle of a call, to make it appear that the call had been dealt with on time. In this example, the objective of answering calls within one minute was not properly aligned with the company's strategic objectives.

Neely and Adams comment: 'Measures send people messages about what matters and how they should behave. When the measures are consistent with organisation's strategies, they encourage behaviour that is consistent with strategy. The right measures then not only offer a means of tracking whether strategy is being implemented, but also a means of communicating strategy and encouraging implementation.'

7.5   Processes and capabilities

In practice, managers often fail to achieve the strategic objectives of their company. One reason is that the performance targets that have been selected are inappropriate.

Another important reason for 'strategic failure' is that the processes of the entity are not consistent with its strategies. The processes that the entity uses do not allow the strategies to be implemented.

Neely and Adams refer to the view of Michael Hammer, advocate of Business Process Re-engineering. Hammer argues that processes should be analysed from the point of view of the customer. A customer usually wants a product or service:

- with quick delivery ('quick')
- to the required quality standard ('right')
- at a good price ('cheap'), and
- in a way that is easy to organise and arrange ('easy').

Providing products or services that are 'quick, right, cheap and easy' should be a strategic objective, but in many cases a company's products or services are 'slow, wrong, expensive and unfriendly', because its processes are inappropriate for delivering what the customer wants.

Neely and Adams argue that it is necessary to identify suitable performance measures for processes, as well as for strategies.

In addition, an entity must have the resources and capabilities to operate the processes. Capabilities are the combination of the entity's people, policies and procedures, technology and physical infrastructure that create value for the stakeholder 'Even the most brilliantly designed process needs people with certain skills, some policies and procedures about the way things are done, some physical infrastructure for it to happen and ... some technology to enable or enhance it' (Neely and Adams).

Taken together, the processes and capabilities of an entity are able to create a competitive advantage. Neely and Adams make a distinction between:

- 'winners': these are processes and capabilities that make the entity distinctive and give it a competitive advantage, and
- 'qualifiers': these are processes and capabilities that need to be improved or maintained at standard levels that are expected within the industry.

7.6   Stakeholder contribution

The fifth side of the performance prism is stakeholder contribution. It is important to consider not only satisfaction for key stakeholders, but also what the entity expects to obtain from its stakeholders.

Customers are stakeholders of a business entity, and the entity should expect its customers to be profitable. Customer profitability should be an important aspect of performance measurement. However, research has shown that entities often ignore this aspect of performance.

■ Some types of customer might not be profitable. This should raise the question: do we want to keep these customers? Or, how can we make these customers profitable? Research in retail banking, for example, has suggested that 20% of customers generate 130% of the profits of a bank, and the remaining 80% of customers contribute a loss.

■ Creating an improvement in customer satisfaction might cost more than the benefits are worth.

A business entity wants its customers to be loyal and profitable, but its customers want high quality products for a low price. An entity's ideas about stakeholder contribution are therefore different from stakeholder satisfaction.

A difference also exists between:

■ what a business expects from its suppliers (prompt and reliable delivery, low prices, high quality), and

■ what is required to provide supplier satisfaction (prompt payment, a forward schedule of orders).

The performance prism includes stakeholder contribution as an element of performance measurement. 'Gaining a clear understanding of the "dynamic tension" that exists between what stakeholders want and need from the organisation and what the organisation wants and needs from its stakeholders, can be an extremely valuable learning exercise for the vast majority of corporations and, especially, their ... business units' (Neely and Adams).

7.7 Performance prism: a summary

To provide a complete system of performance measurement, entities should consider five inter-related aspects of performance:

■ Who are the key stakeholders and what do they want?

■ What strategies must be implemented in order to satisfy the key stakeholders?

■ What are the critical processes needed to execute these strategies successfully?

■ What capabilities are needed to operate and improve these critical processes?

■ What contributions are required from stakeholders in order to maintain and develop these capabilities?

Practice questions

Contents		
		Page

Decentralisation and divisional performance

Transfer pricing

Alternative views of performance measurement

Developments in management accounting and performance management

1   Lard Company

Lard Company is a warehousing and distribution company. It receives and stores products from customers, and then re-packs them for distribution as required. There are three customers for whom the service is provided – Customer A, Customer B and Customer C. The products stored and re-packaged for all three customers are similar in nature and size, but some are more fragile than others and break more easily. These have to be packaged more carefully.

Basic budget information has been gathered for the year to 31st December 20X6 and is shown in the following table:

	Products handled
	units
Customer A	30,000
Customer B	45,000
Customer C	25,000
	Costs
	$000
Packaging materials (See note)	1,950
Labour:	
Basic pay	350
Overtime pay	30
Occupancy costs	500
Administration and management costs	60

Note

Packaging materials are used in re-packing each unit of product for Customer A, Customer B and Customer C in the ratio 1:2:3 respectively. This ratio is linked to the relative fragility of the goods for each customer. It applies to the cost of packaging materials but not to the costs of labour and overheads.

Additional information has been obtained so that unit costs can be prepared for each of the three customers using an activity based costing approach. The additional information for the year to 31st December 20X6 has been estimated as follows:

(1)   Labour and overhead costs have been identified as attributable to each of three work centres: receipt and inspection, storage, and packing as follows:

(2)

	Cost allocation proportions		
	Receipt and inspection	Storage	Packing
	%	%	%
Labour:			
Basic pay	20	10	70
Occupancy cost	20	60	20
Administration cost	40	10	50
Labour: overtime pay	$15,000	$6,250	$8,750

(3)   A study has shown that the fragility of different goods affects the receipt and inspection time needed for the products for each customer. Storage required is related to the average size of the basic incoming product units from each customer. The re-packing of goods for distribution is related to the complexity

of packaging required by each customer. The relevant requirements per unit of product for each customer have been evaluated as follows:

	Customer A	Customer B	Customer C
Receipt and inspection (minutes)	6	9	15
Storage (square metres)	0.3	0.3	0.3
Packing (minutes)	36	45	60

Required

(a) Calculate the average cost per unit of packaged products for each customer using each of the following methods:

   (i) Ignoring the ABC study, calculate a cost per unit using traditional absorption costing.

   (ii) Taking an activity based costing approach, using the information provided.

(b) Suggest ways in which activity based costing might improve product costing and cost control for Lard Company.

2   LC Company

LC Company has total budgeted production overheads for next year of $816,000 and has traditionally absorbed overheads on a machine hour basis. It makes two products, Product V and Product W.

	Product V	Product W
Direct material cost per unit	$20	$60
Direct labour cost per unit	$50	$40
Machine time per unit	3 hours	4 hours
Annual production	6,000 units	4,000 units

Required

(a) Calculate the product cost for each of the two products on the assumption the firm continues to absorb overhead costs on a machine hour basis.

(b) The firm is considering changing to an activity based costing (ABC) system and has identified the following information:

	Product V	Product W
Number of set-ups	18	32
Number of purchase orders	48	112
Overhead cost analysis	$	
Machine-related overhead costs	204,000	
Set up related overhead costs	280,000	
Purchasing-related overhead costs	332,000	
Total production overheads	816,000	

You are required to calculate the unit cost for each of the two products on the assumption that the firm changes to an ABC system, using whatever assumptions you consider appropriate.

(c) Suggest how ABC analysis could be useful for measuring performance and improving profitability.

3 Throughput

A company manufactures two products, product X and product Y, on the same machines. Sales demand for the products exceeds the machine capacity of the company's production department. The potential sales demand in each period is for 8,000 units of Product X and 12,000 units of Product Y. Sales prices cannot be increased due to competition from other firms in the market. The maximum machine capacity in the production department is 32,000 hours in each period.

The following cost and profitability estimates have been prepared:

	Product X	Product Y
	$	$
Sales price	22	27
Direct materials	10	9
Direct labour and variable overhead	6	11
Contribution per unit	6	7
Machine hours per unit	1.5 hours	2 hours

Fixed costs in each period are $90,000.

Required

(a) Using marginal costing principles, calculate the profit-maximising output in each period, and calculate the amount of profit.
(b) Explain how throughput accounting differs from marginal costing in its approach to maximising profit.
(c) Use throughput accounting to calculate the throughput accounting ratio for Product X and for Product Y. You should assume that the direct labour cost and variable overhead cost in your answer to part (a) is fixed in the short-term.
(d) Using throughput accounting principles, calculate the profit-maximising output in each period, and calculate the amount of profit.

4 Throughput ratio

Dust Company exports cases to Spain. Each pallet of cases costs $2,000 in material costs and are sold for $3,000. Production and sales are limited by a shortage of highly trained quality control inspectors. Only 200 inspection hours are available per week. Every pallet is inspected and an inspection takes 30 minutes.
Other factory costs are $300,000 per week.

Required

Calculate the throughput accounting ratio.

5 Backflush

Transactions for the year for AYZ are as follows:

Purchases of raw materials	$5,000,000
Conversion costs	$3,000,000
Finished goods manufactured	100,000 units
Sales	98,000 units at $100 per unit

There was no inventory at the beginning of the year. The cost per unit is $80, consisting of $50 per unit for materials and $30 per unit for conversion costs.

Required

Show the book-keeping entries in the cost accounting system using backflush accounting, with two trigger points.

6 Villaco

Villaco produces two products with the following costs and revenue per unit.

	Product A	Product B
	$	$
Sales price	20	10
Variable cost	8	6
Fixed cost	4	3
	units	units
Sales demand	2,000	3,000

There are only 7,000 machine hours available, and Product A requires four machine hours per unit and Product B requires one machine hour per unit

Required

(a) Calculate the profit-maximising production and sales mix.

(b) Assume that all the data is the same, except that we are able to sub-contract the products for an additional variable cost of $1 per unit for A and $0.50 per unit for B.

What is the profit-maximising decision?

7 Shortages

An engineering company has been experiencing problems with restricted availability of resources. The company manufactures a variety of casings. It makes four types of casing. Each casing requires the same bought-in component and some high-grade steel. The standard costs for the four types of casing are as follows:

Casing	A	B	C	D
	$	$	$	$
Steel	250	500	190	390
Bought-in component	50	50	50	50
Direct labour	60	60	50	100
Variable production costs	40	50	40	50
Fixed production costs	180	240	150	270
Selling and administration costs	145	225	120	215
Profit	35	55	30	55
Selling price	760	1,180	630	1,130

All the selling and administration costs are fixed and the same single component is used for each of the four products. Direct labour is paid $8 per standard hour and each member of the workforce is capable of producing any of the casings.

The company's main customer has ordered 30 units of Casing A, 20 units of B, 30 units of C and 20 units of D for production and delivery in the next month. Senior management have agreed that this order should be treated as a priority order and that these casings must be manufactured and delivered to the customer next month. This is necessary to maintain the goodwill of the customer. It is estimated that this order represents 10% of the total demand next month for each type of casing.

The company operates a just in time system, and has no inventories of steel, components or finished goods.

Required

If the aim is to maximise profit for the month, establish the production and selling plan for the company next month in each of the following situations:

(a)   **Situation 1**. Supplies of steel are limited to $250,000.

(b)   **Situation 2**. Only 400 bought-in components are available from suppliers.

(c)   **Situation 3**. A labour dispute restricts available productive labour hours in the month to 2,125.

(d)   **Situation 4**. A labour dispute restricts available productive labour hours in the month to 2,125; but the manufacture of any quantities of the four casings could be sub-contracted to an outside supplier. The cost of buying the casings externally would be $475, $705, $380 and $640 for Casing A, Casing B, Casing C and Casing D respectively. In addition, it should be assumed that a major customer insists that its order is completed by the company itself and the manufacture should not be sub-contracted.

Each of the restrictions on production should be treated independently, as four different situations.

8 Product B22

BB Company has received an enquiry from a customer for the supply of 500 units of a new product, product B22. Negotiations on the final price to charge the customer are in progress and the sales manager has asked you to supply relevant cost information.

The following information is available:

(1) Each unit of product B22 requires the following raw materials:

Raw material type

X   4 kg

Y   6 kg

(2) The company has 5,000 kg of material X currently in stock. This was purchased last year at a cost of $7 per kg. If not used to make product B22, this stock of X could either be sold for $7.50 per kg or converted at a cost of $1.50 per kg, so that it could be used as a substitute for another raw material, material Z, which the company requires for other production. The current purchase price per kilogram for materials is $9.50 for material Z and $8.25 per kg for material X.

(3) There are 10,000 kilograms of raw material Y in stock, valued on a FIFO basis at a total cost of $142,750. Of this current stock, 3,000 kilograms were purchased six months ago at a cost of $13.75 per kg. The rest of the stock was purchased last month. Material Y is used regularly in normal production work. Since the last purchase of material Y a month ago, the company has been advised by the supplier that the price per kilogram has been increased by 4%.

(4) Each unit of product B22 requires the following number of labour hours in its manufacture:

Type of labour

Skilled five hours

Unskilled three hours

Skilled labour is paid $8 per hour and unskilled labour $6 per hour.

(5) There is a shortage of skilled labour, so that if production of B22 goes ahead it will be necessary to transfer skilled workers from other work to undertake it. The other work on which skilled workers are engaged at present is the manufacture of product B16. The selling price and variable cost information for B16 are as follows:

	$/unit	$/unit
Selling price		100
Less: variable costs of production		
Skilled labour (three hours)	24	
Other variable costs	31	
		55
		45

(6) The company has a surplus of unskilled workers who are paid a fixed wage for a 37-hour week. It is estimated that there are 900 hours of unused unskilled

labour time available during the period of the contract. The balance of the unskilled labour requirements could be met by working overtime, which is paid at time and a half.

(7) The company absorbs production overheads by a machine hour rate. This absorption rate is $22.50 per hour, of which $8.75 is for variable overheads and the balance is for fixed overheads. If production of product B22 is undertaken, it is estimated that an extra $4,000 will be spent on fixed costs. Spare machining capacity is available and each unit of B22 will require two hours of machining time in its manufacture using the existing equipment. In addition, special finishing machines will be required for two weeks to complete the B22. These machines will be hired at a cost of $2,650 per week, and there will be no overhead costs associated with their use.

(8) Cash spending of $3,250 has been incurred already on development work for the production of B22. It is estimated that before production of the B22 begins, another $1,750 will have to be spent on development, making a total development cost of $5,000.

Required

Calculate the minimum price that the company should be prepared to accept for the 500 units of product B22. Explain briefly but clearly how each figure in the minimum price calculation has been obtained.

(Note: the minimum price is the price equals the total relevant costs of producing the items. Any price in excess of the minimum price will add to total profit).

9 Payoff table

A baker pays $0.10 for buns and sells them for $0.30. At the end of a day, any pastries that have not been sold must be thrown away. On any particular day, the probability distribution of sales demand is as follows:

Number of pastries demanded by customers	20	40	60
Probability	0.3	0.5	0.2

Required

(a) Construct a payoff matrix to show all the possible outcomes

(b) What is the maximum amount the baker should be willing to pay for perfect information (in advance) about sales demand each day.

10 Grab Company

Grab Company engages in site clearance and site preparation work. Information about its operations is as follows:

(1) It is Grab Company's policy to hire all the plant and machinery it needs, rather than to purchase its own plant and machinery.

(2)   Grab Company will enter into an advance hire agreement contract for the coming year at one of three levels – high, medium or low – which correspond to the requirements of a high, medium or low level of orders obtained.

(3)   The level of orders obtained will not be known when the advance hire agreement contract is entered into. Probabilities have been estimated by management as to the likelihood of the orders being at a high, medium or low level.

(4)   Where the advance hire agreement entered into is lower than that required for the level of orders actually obtained, a premium rate must be paid to obtain the additional plant and machinery required.

(5)   No refund is obtainable where the advance hire agreement for plant and machinery is at a level in excess of that required to satisfy the site clearance and preparation orders actually obtained.

A summary of the information relating to the above points is as follows:

| Level of orders | Sales revenue | Probability | Plant and machinery hire costs | |
			Advance hire	Conversion premium
	$000		$000	$000
High	15,000	0.25	2,300	
Medium	8,500	0.45	1,500	
Low	4,000	0.30	1,000	
Low to medium				850
Medium to high				1,300
Low to high				2,150

Variable cost (as a percentage of turnover) 70%

Required

(a)   Prepare a summary which shows the forecast net margin earned by Grab Company for the coming year for each possible outcome.

(b)   On the basis of maximising expected value, advise Grab Company whether the advance contract for the hire of plant and machinery should be at the low, medium or high level.

(c)   Explain how the risk preferences of the management members responsible for the choice of advance plant and machinery hire contract may alter the decision reached in (b) above.

(d)   Grab Company is considering employing a market research consultant who will be able to say with certainty in advance of the placing of the plant and machinery hire contract, which level of site clearance and preparation orders will be obtained. On the basis of expected value, determine the maximum sum that Grab Company should be willing to pay the consultant for this information.

11 Learning

A company has developed a design for a new product, the Widgette. It intends to sell the product at full production cost plus a profit margin of 40%. The estimated production cost and selling price for the first unit of the Widgette are as follows:

	$
Direct materials	2,000
Direct labour (200 hours at $15 per hour)	3,000
Fixed production overhead ($20 per direct labour hour)	4,000
Full production cost	9,000
Profit margin (40%)	3,600
Selling price	12,600

The company's management expects reductions in the time to produce subsequent units of the Widgette, and an 80% learning curve is expected.

A customer has expressed an interest in buying units of the Widgette, and has asked the following questions:

(1) If we bought the first Widgette for $12,600 and immediately ordered another one, what would be the selling price for the second Widgette?

(2) If we waited until you have sold the first two Widgettes to another customer, and then ordered the third and the fourth units that you produce, what will be the average price for the third and fourth units?

(3) If we decided to buy eight Widgettes immediately, and asked you to quote a single price for all eight units, what price would you charge?

Required

(a) Answer each of these questions, assuming that the policy of the company remains to make a profit margin of 40% on every unit that it makes and sells.

(b) List three limitations of learning curve theory.

12 Greenears

Greenears is a new business producing woollen hats, which it makes in small batches of a standard size. It estimates that the first batch of a new design of hand-made hats will have a labour cost of $2,000. There will be an 85% learning curve effect for subsequent batches.

In month 1 production is five batches, and in month 2 production is seven batches.

Required

Estimate the total labour cost in month 2 for making the hats.

13   Regression

A company has achieved the following total sales in each year for the past five years:

Year	Total sales
	$ million
20X2 = Year 1	12
20X3 = Year 2	15
20X4 = Year 3	15
20X5 = Year 4	18
20X6 = Year 5	19

Required

(a)   Use linear regression analysis to establish a formula for the trend line in sales, and use this formula to estimate what total sales should be in 20X7 and 20X8.

(b)   Calculate the correlation coefficient to decide how much reliance you can place in your forecasts.

To produce your answer, you can make use of the following calculations:

Year	Total sales			
x	y	xy	x·	y·
1	12	12	1	144
2	15	30	4	225
3	15	45	9	225
4	18	72	16	324
5	19	95	25	361
15	79	254	55	1,279

14   Replacement product

A well-established company manufactures engines. One of its current products is Product T, for which sales will be 150,000 units in the year just ending (Year 1). However, after four more years, at the end of Year 5, Product T will no longer be permitted, when new government environmental regulations come into force. On or before that time, the company needs to introduce a new product to replace Product T.

A replacement product has already been developed. This is Product V. A market research report has estimated that, if Product V is introduced to the market now to replace Product T, annual sales of Product V at a unit price of $350 would be:

Annual sales	Probability
units	
100,000	0.2
80,000	0.5
50,000	0.3

The current selling price of Product T is $250 per unit, and its variable cost of sales is $180. There is no possibility of increasing the selling price.

The annual sales demand for Product T is expected to fall each year if it is kept on the market. The best estimate is that annual sales in Year 2 will be 10,000 units less than in Year 1, with a further fall in sales by 10,000 units each year until Year 5.

To prepare a production facility for manufacturing Product V instead of Product T, an initial capital outlay of $2,000,000 would be required. Annual fixed costs would increase by $160,000. The variable cost of making and selling Product V would be $230 per unit.

The company's cost of capital is 8%. Ignore inflation and taxation.

Required

(a)   Using DCF analysis, calculate the NPV of a proposal to replace Product T with Product V from Year 2 onwards.

(b)   Estimate the minimum annual sales for Product V that would be required to justify the immediate replacement of Product T with Product V. Assume that the estimates of annual sales of Product T are correct.

(c)   Calculate the minimum reduction in the annual sales of Product T, in Year 2 and in each subsequent year that would be necessary before you recommended the immediate replacement of Product T with Product V. Assume that the estimates of annual sales of Product V are correct.

(d)   List briefly the weaknesses or limitations in the financial analysis in part (a) to (c) above.

15   Probabilities

A company is considering whether or not to invest in a project where the initial cash investment would be $6,250,000. The project would have a five-year life, and the estimated annual cash flows are as follows:

Year	Cash inflows	Cash outflows
	$	$
1	3,000,000	1,500,000
2	4,000,000	1,800,000
3	5,000,000	2,400,000
4	4,000,000	1,700,000
5	3,000,000	1,000,000

The cost of capital is 10%.

The estimates of cash outflows are considered fairly reliable. However, the estimates of cash inflows are much more uncertain. Several factors could make the annual cash flows higher or lower than expected.

■   Factor 1: There is a 20% probability that government measures to control the industry will reduce annual cash inflows by 20%.

■   Factor 2: There is a 30% probability that another competitor will also enter the market: this would reduce the estimated cash inflows by 10%.

■   Factor 3: There is a 40% probability that demand will be stronger than expected. The company would not be able to supply more products to the market, but it would be able to sell at higher prices and cash inflows would be 5% higher than estimated.

Required

Calculated the expected net present value of the project.

16   Sensitivity

A company is considering an investment in a new project to make and sell a new product that will have a five-year life. The project will require an investment of $3 million in equipment. The residual value of this equipment after five years will be 30% of its original cost.

The estimates of net cash flows from operations in each year of the project are as follows:

Year	Net cash flow
	$
1	400,000
2	800,000
3	800,000
4	700,000
5	400,000

These cash flows are based on estimates that the annual increase in cash spending on fixed costs will be $200,000, and the contribution/sales ratio from transactions will be 40%. The company's cost of capital is 8%.

The management of the company are aware that actual cash flows could be higher or lower than those expected, and sensitivity analysis should be carried out to establish the extent to which costs or revenues could differ from the estimate before the project ceased to have a positive NPV.

The investment in working capital will be minimal. Inflation and taxation should be ignored.

Required

(a)   Calculate the net present value of the project.

(b)   Carry out sensitivity analysis on the following items:

    (i)   the cost of the equipment, assuming that the residual value will be 30% of cost

    (ii)   the residual value of the equipment

    (iii)   sales revenue

    (iv)   variable costs

    (v)   annual fixed costs.

    By how much could each of these items vary in amount before the project ceased to have a positive NPV?

(c)   Comment on the risk in undertaking this project.

17   The Jin Company

The directors of the Jin Company are meeting to decide about the replacement of a machine. The existing machine has to be replaced soon, and there is a choice of two machines that could be purchased to replace it. These are Machine A and a larger Machine, B. The following information is available about each machine:

	Machine A	Machine B
Expected working life	4 years	5 years
Initial cost	$600,000	$750,000
Residual value	$0	$0
Working capital requirement	$100,000	$200,000

The forecast pre-tax cash flows that will be earned using each machine are as follows:

	Year 1	Year 2	Year 3	Year 4	Year 5
	$000	$000	$000	$000	$000
Machine A	470	520	490	450	
Machine B	580	640	500	500	400

The Jin Company uses 10% as its cost of capital for capital expenditure evaluation.

Taxation at 30% is payable one year in arrears. Capital allowances are available at the rate of 25% each year on the reducing balance method. Inflation should be ignored.

Required

(a)   Calculate the NPV with each of the machines.
(b)   Calculate the payback period for each machine.
(c)   Recommend with reasons which machine should be purchased.

18   Growth objective

A company has an objective in its long-term business plan of achieving significant growth in its business in the period Year 1 to Year 5. It is now the end of Year 2.

Its results for the years to 31st December Year 1 and Year 2 are summarised below.

Income statement for the year ended 31 December

	Year 2	Year 1
	$	$
Sales	31,200,000	26,000,000
Cost of sales	18,720,000	15,600,000
	12,480,000	10,400,000
Operating expenses	6,780,000	5,200,000
Interest charges	500,000	0
Depreciation	3,000,000	3,000,000
Net profit	2,200,000	2,200,000

Balance sheet as at 31st December

	Year 2	Year 1
	$	$
Non-current assets	27,300,000	26,000,000
Net current assets	15,600,000	7,800,000
	42,900,000	33,800,000
Loan	9,000,000	0
	33,900,000	33,800,000
Share capital	19,500,000	19,500,000
Accumulated profit	14,400,000	14,300,000
	33,900,000	33,800,000

Sales are seasonal, and are much higher in the first six months of the year than in the second six months. The half-yearly sales figures in the past two years have been as follows:

Sales

	Year 2	Year 1
	$	$
1st January – 30th June	21,645,000	16,900,000
1st July – 31st December	9,555,000	9,100,000
	31,200,000	26,000,000

The company employs part-time workers during the first six-months of each year. Part-time workers operate for a full working week during the weeks that they are employed. Employee numbers have been as follows:

Employee numbers

	Year 2	Year 1
Full time employees	318	260
Part time (seasonal) employees	494	310

The company introduced four new products to the market in Year 1 and another five new products in Year 2.

Required

Explain with reasons whether the company appears to be on course for achieving its objective of growing the business.

In particular, you should consider growth in sales, profits, investment and product range.

19 Gap analysis

Blank Company manufactures and sells a single product. Its budget for the next financial year is as follows:

	$000	$000
Sales (80,000 units at $600 per unit)		48,000
Production costs: materials and labour	16,000	
Other production costs	8,000	
Marketing and distribution costs	12,000	
Administration costs	10,000	
Total costs		46,000
Profit		2,000

Materials and labour costs in production are 100% variable, and 25% of other production costs are variable. All administration costs are fixed costs and two-thirds of marketing and distribution costs are also fixed.

The directors of Blank Company are dissatisfied with the budgeted profit, and believe that annual profits should be at least double the size of the budgeted profit.

Three strategies have been proposed to improve profitability.

(1) **Strategy 1.** Increase sales by opening a new sales office in a neighbouring country. It is expected that this would increase annual sales by 5,000 units, but would add $1.2 million to annual fixed costs.

(2) **Strategy 2.** Re-design the product by adding several additional features that should add value for the customer. This would have no effect on annual sales volume in units, but the company would be able to raise the sales price to $625. The additional costs of producing the new product design would be $1.5 million each year (all fixed costs).

(3) **Strategy 3.** Implement a cost reduction exercise throughout the company. It is expected that the planned exercise would reduce all variable costs by 20%, but would add to annual fixed costs by $3.5 million.

Required

(a) Calculate the effect of each individual strategy on annual profit, assuming that the strategy is implemented on its own, without the other two strategies.

(b) Show whether the three strategies, if they are all introduced together, will close the profit gap between the budgeted profit and the target profit that the directors would like to achieve.

20 Zero based budgeting

State briefly where zero based budgeting is likely to be of the greatest value and suggest how often ZBB should be used.

21 Marginal

The marketing director of a company selling home entertainment products has estimated that at a sales price of $250, a new product (the Blaze) will sell 400,000 units in the next year. He also estimates that for every $10 increase or reduction in price, annual sales will fall or increase by 20,000 units below or above this 400,000 units level.

The production engineer has estimated that the costs of making the Blaze will be a variable cost of $210 per unit sold and annual fixed costs of $20 million.

(a) You are given the following formulae:

Price function: $P_q = P_0 - bq$

Total revenue function (TR): $P_0q - bq^2$

Marginal revenue function (MR): $P_0 - 2bq$

where

P_0 = Price at zero units of demand

P_q = Price at q units of demand

b = relationship between price and demand

q = units of annual demand

Required

(i)   Calculate the price at which the Blaze should be sold in order to maximise profit for the year.

(ii) Calculate the quantity of units that will be sold in the year, if the marketing director's forecast is correct.

(iii) Calculate the annual profit that will be made from selling the Blaze.

(b)   Since the total cost function is a curved line, there are two break-even points. One is below the profit-maximising output level and one is above the profit-maximising output level.

The total profit function can be expressed as a quadratic equation:

$y = ax^2 + bx + c$

The break-even points can be calculated as the values for x that solve the following equation:

$$x = \frac{-b +/ - \sqrt{b^2 - 4ac}}{2a}$$

Required

Calculate the levels of output and the associated selling prices for Blaze at which the company would break even.

22   MC = MR

A business entity has estimated that it faces the following price/quantity relationship.

Sales price	Quantity demanded
$	Units
50	1,000
30	2,000
10	3,000

Required

(a)   Calculate a formula for the demand curve, assuming that the demand curve can be drawn as a straight line on a graph.

(b)   Find the formula for total revenue.

(c)   If the marginal cost per unit is $8, calculate price at which contribution is maximised.

23   Snap Company

Snap Company makes product SP8 in department C. For the year commencing 1st January 20X7 the following budget has been formulated for department C:

	$000
Direct costs	
Materials	60
Labour	40
	100
Production overheads	100
Full production cost	200
Administrative and marketing overheads	50
Full cost of sale	250
Profit	50
Revenue (see note)	300

Note: From budgeted sales of 20,000 units.

Production overheads are absorbed on the basis of 100% of direct costs. However, half of these costs are fixed, and the other half are variable. It is assumed that they vary with the cost of materials.

The administrative and marketing overheads are based on 25% of factory costs and do not vary within wide ranges of activity. A profit margin of 20% is applied to the full cost of sale. This also results in a price that appears to be fair to customers.

Halfway through the year to 31st December 20X7, it became clear that actual sales of SP8 would be 25% below budget. At about the same time that this shortfall in sales became evident, a customer asked about buying 5,000 units of a simplified version of product SP8. If Snap Company were to produce this simplified model for the customer, the direct material and labour costs would be lower. It is estimated that materials costing $12,000 and direct labour of $8,000 would be required to produce the 5,000 units. As the production could take place within the firm's existing capacity, fixed costs would not be affected.

Required

(a)   Calculate the prices that Snap Company should quote to the customer for each unit of the simplified product, assuming that the following pricing policies are applied:

(i)   Full cost plus pricing, on the current basis.

(ii)   A price that would enable the company to achieve its original budgeted profit.

(b)   Give your advice on the price that should be quoted to the customer.

24   Bridge Company

The following costs per unit relate to the production and sale of 20,000 of a product by Bridge Company, for the financial year that has just ended.

	$ per unit
Direct material	30
Direct labour	10
Overheads:	
Variable	10
Fixed	10
	60

It has been estimated that major cost increases will apply to the following year, assuming that production and sales volumes are still 20,000 units.

	Increase
Direct material	20%
Direct labour	5%
Variable overhead	5%
Fixed overhead	10%

It would be possible to substitute a cheaper grade of direct material allowing the cost of direct materials to be $31.25 per unit. However, a rejection rate of 5% will arise. (There are currently no rejected units.) This would require an additional annual inspection costs of $30,000.

In the past, the selling price has been set using a mark-up of 50% on full cost and a price of $90 per unit was charged in the current year. However, the sales manager has estimated the price/demand relationships as follows:

Price	$80	$84	$88	$90	$92	$96	$100
Demand (000s units)	25	23	21	20	19	17	15

Required

(a)   Decide whether the product should use the regular or the cheaper grade of material.

(b)   Calculate the price that should be charged for the product to maximise the annual profit, and the profit that should be expected.

25   Responsibility

A multinational company established a new operating division in Fenland four years ago. The operating division has been established as a profit centre. Decisions relating to the purchase of capital equipment for the division, and borrowing to finance the capital, have been taken at head office.

The results for the first four years of operation have been as follows:

	Year 1	Year 2	Year 3	Year 4
	$000	$000	$000	$000
Sales revenue	172	646	810	1,792
Operating costs	167	620	718	1,490
Depreciation	25	104	187	530
Interest charges	0	132	240	462
Profit/(loss)	(20)	(210)	(335)	(690)

The managing director of the division has been asked to explain its poor performance and the escalating losses. In response, the managing director has argued that the performance of the division has improved, and is not getting worse.

Required

(a) Identify a measure of performance that would suggest that the performance of the division has been improving over the four-year period.

(b) Suggest how the performance of the division should be assessed, and state whether you agree or disagree with the view of the managing director that performance has improved.

26 Crosstreets Hotel

Crosstreets Hotel owns five hotels in the same country, providing accommodation mainly to business people and tourists. Each hotel has a bar and restaurant open to residents and non-residents.

The directors of the company work in two offices in the oldest hotel in the southern region of the country, where the small finance office is also located. Until now the company has only produced statutory financial accounts, and has not produced management accounts.

The directors disagree with each other about the profitability of each of the individual hotels owned and operated by the company. The head of the finance office has proposed that performance reports should be produced, based on a system of responsibility accounting for each of the hotels. The performance of all five hotels should also be amalgamated to prepare performance reports at company level.

Required

Suggest:

(a) What periodic reports this management information system should produce, and,

(b) what information the reports should contain.

27 Three services

A company provides three types of delivery service to customers: service A, service B and service C. Customers are a mix of firms with a contract for service with the company, and non-contract customers.

The following information relates to performance in the year to 31st December Year 1:

	Service A	Service B	Service C
Number of deliveries made	350,000	250,000	20,000
% of deliveries to contract customers	60%	60%	80%
Price charged per delivery:			
Contract customers	$9	$15	$300
Premium for non-contract customers	+ 30%	+ 50%	+ 20%

The premium for non-contract customers is in addition to the rate charged to contract customers.

All employees in the company were paid $45,000 per year and sundry operating costs, excluding salaries and fuel costs, were $4,000,000 for the year.

The following operational data for the year relates to deliveries:

	Services A and B	Service C
Average kilometres per vehicle/day	400	600
Number of vehicles	50	18
Operating days in the year	300	300

For Year 2, the company has agreed a fixed price contract for fuel. As a result of this contract, fuel prices will be:

(a) $0.40 per kilometre for Services A and B

(b) $0.80 per kilometre for Service C.

Sales prices will be 3% higher in Year 2 than in Year 1, and salaries and operational expenses will be 5% higher. Sales volume will be exactly the same as in Year 1.

The number of employees will also be the same as in Year 1: 60 employees working full-time on Services A and B and 25 employees working full-time on Service C.

Required

(a)   Prepare a budgeted income statement for the year to 31st December Year 2.

(b)   Comment on vehicle utilisation.

28 Private medical practice

A private medical practice has five full-time doctors, five full-time assistants and two administrators.

Each doctor treats 18 patients each day on average. The medical centre is open for five days each week, 46 weeks each year.

Charges for patients vary according to the age of the patient and the nature of the treatment provided.

Charges	Adults below 65 year of age	Children and individuals aged 65 years old and over
	$	$
No treatment: consultation only	50	30
Minor treatment	200	120
Major treatment	600	280

The patient mix and the treatment mix are as follows:

Patients:		Treatment	
Adults	45%	No treatment	20%
Children	25%	Minor treatment	70%
Over 65 years old	30%	Major treatment	10%

The salary of each doctor is $240,000, assistants earn $100,000 and administrators earn $80,000. In addition, everyone receives a 5% bonus at the end of the year.

The medical practice expects to pay $414,300 for materials next year and other (fixed) costs will be $733,600.

Required

Using the information provided, present an income statement for the medical practice for next year. (Ignore the effects of inflation.)

29   Train times

A railway company has two operating divisions, Northern Region and Southern Region. Each division runs inter-city train services and suburban ('commuter') train services. Performance figures for the most recent reporting period are as follows:

	Northern Region		Southern Region	
	Inter-city services	Suburban services	Inter-city services	Suburban services
Journeys	1,500	34,000	1,800	42,000
Completed on schedule	1,240	25,100	1,590	38,600
Completed within five minutes of schedule	1,350	29,500	1,690	40,300
Completed within ten minutes of schedule	1,440	33,100	1,730	41,500
Cancelled journeys	16	405	2	220
Target for on-time completion of journeys	90%	95%	90%	95%

The chief executive officer of the railway company is trying to improve standards of service, and targets have been set for the number of train journeys that should end with the train arriving at its destination on schedule. It is his intention to raise the standards still further in the future.

Required

Assess the service performance of the two regions.

30 Non-financial performance measurements

Suggest **three** non-financial measures of performance that might be helpful to management in assessing the following aspects of operations in a commercial bank:

(1)   service quality

(2)   marketing effectiveness

(3)   personnel

31 Mission

The managing director of Branded Company, a listed company, has recently returned from a conference entitled 'Strategic planning and its context within the global business environment'. Whilst at the conference she attended a session on 'corporation mission statements'. She found the session very interesting but it was rather short. She now has some questions for you.

(1)   'What does "corporate mission" mean? I don't see how it fits in with our strategic planning process'.

(2)   'Where does our mission come from and what areas of corporate life should it cover'?

(3)   'Even if we were to develop one of these mission statements, what benefits would the company get from it'?

Required

Prepare brief answers to the managing director's questions.

32 Customer profitability

PQR Company sells a range of five products. Budgeted annual data for sales and costs are as follows:

Product	Selling price	Variable cost
	$	$
A	3.60	2.40
B	2.50	2.00
C	4.00	2.80
D	2.40	1.50
E	6.00	4.00

Budgeted total annual sales are:

Product	Annual sales
	units
A	100,000
B	150,000
C	120,000
D	180,000
E	80,000

The products are sold to four different types or category of customer, as follows:

% of annual sales

	Category of customer			
Product	C1	C2	C3	C4
A	10%	20%	20%	50%
B	40%	-	30%	30%
C	10%	20%	10%	60%
D	30%	10%	20%	40%
E	20%	-	20%	60%

Rebates on sales

At the end of each year, the company will pay rebates to Category 3 and Category 4 customers, as follows:

(c) Category 3 customers: rebate = 5% of annual sales

(d) Category 4 customers: rebate = 10% of annual sales.

Fixed costs

Budgeted total fixed costs for the year are $465,000, analysed as follows:

	$
Delivery costs	250,000
Order processing costs	105,000
Cost of promotion events	30,000
	385,000
Other fixed costs	80,000
	465,000

The company operates an activity based costing system. Relevant budgeted data relating to activities is as follows:

	Category of customer			
	C1	C2	C3	C4
Number of deliveries	40	80	50	100
Number of orders	30	70	50	60
Number of promotion events	0	0	2	10
Average km per delivery	100	200	300	150

The cost drivers for each activity are:

- Delivery: kilometres (km)

- Order processing: number of orders

- Promotion events: number of promotion events

- The other fixed costs are general fixed costs, and are not allocated to activities, products or customers.

Required

Using activity based costing, prepare a statement of budgeted customer profitability, for each category of customer.

33   RTC

Round Table Conferences (RTC) organises scientific conferences. It began trading in Hereland in Year 1, and in Year 3 it opened a similar operation in a neighbouring country, Thereland. The divisional managers in Hereland and Thereland have the authority to make most operational decisions, but decisions relating to acquisitions and financing are reserved for the board of directors of RTC.

Financial data is shown below for both divisions, for the years ending 31st December Year 4 and Year 5.

Actual results		Year 4			Year 5	
	Hereland	Thereland	Total	Hereland	Thereland	Total
	$000	$000	$000	$000	$000	$000
Revenues	4,300	950	5,250	4,500	1,200	5,700
Salaries and fees	1,400	580	1,980	1,500	600	2,100
Other direct costs	1,450	430	1,880	1,480	430	1,910
	2,850	1,010	3,860	2,980	1,030	4,010
Marketing	240	70	310	290	95	385
Depreciation/ amortisation	330	45	380	330	95	425
Interest cost			110			95
	570	115	800	620	190	905
Total costs	3,420	1,125	4,660	3,600	1,220	4,915
Profit/(loss)	880	(175)	590	900	(20)	785

Summary balance sheets		Year 4			Year 5	
Non-current assets	2,610	240	2,850	2,600	480	3,080
Net current assets	710	140	850	1,250	190	1,440
	3,320	380	3,700	3,850	670	4,520
Loan stock			1,400			1,200
			2,300			3,320
Capital and reserves			2,300			3,320

Required

(a)   Assess the financial performance of RTC in Year 4 and Year 5, and the contribution of the operations in Hereland and Thereland to the overall performance.

(b)   Suggest, with reasons, four additional items of information that you would require in order to provide a more comprehensive financial analysis of performance.

(c)   Suggest, with reasons four factors that should be taken into consideration when comparing performance in Hereland and Thereland.

34 Value for money

A school teaches children from the age of 11 to the age of 18. The governors of the school have been concerned that in recent years, the performance of the school has deteriorated. The chairman of the board of governors has stated his view that parents of the children at the school have a right to expect more value for money, and he proposes that a value for money exercise should be carried out.

Required

(i) What aspects of the school and its operations would a value for money exercise investigate?

(ii) What might be the benefits of a value for money exercise?

35 Decentralisation

(a) Define the following concepts:

(i) Responsibility accounting

(ii) An investment centre

(iii) Return on investment (for a division)

(iv) Residual income (for a division).

(b) The following information available about Divisions M and W, which are investment centres in LK Group.

	Division M	Division W
Divisional investment	$200,000	$5,000,000
Division profit	$20,000	$410,000

The weighted average cost of capital for LK Group is 8%.

Ignore taxation.

Required

(a) Evaluate the performance of Division M and Division W.

(b) Re-evaluate the situation given that the weighted cost of capital is

(1) 6%

(2) 10%.

36 West Division

Large Group has several separate divisions, each operating as an investment centre within the group. West Division makes and sells three products, A, B and C. All three products are sold under the Titan brand label, but Product A and Product B are also sold through a supermarket group as unbranded products.

Budgeted data for the year to 31st December Year 7 is as follows:

Product sales

	Product A	Product B	Product C
	units	units	units
Titan brand	160,000	120,000	50,000
Unbranded	450,000	600,000	-

Selling prices

	Product A	Product B	Product C
	$ per unit	$ per unit	$ per unit
Titan brand	2.50	3.20	5.00
Unbranded	1.50	2.00	-

Variable costs

	Production	Packaging
	$ per unit	$ per unit
Product A:		
Titan brand	1.20	0.30
Unbranded	1.20	0.10
Product B:		
Titan brand	1.60	0.40
Unbranded	1.60	0.20
Product C:		
Titan brand	2.50	0.50

Budgeted marketing expenditure is $180,000 for the year, and other budgeted expenditure for other fixed costs is $375,000. The average capital employed in West Division in Year 7 is expected to be $400,000 and the division's cost of capital is 10%.

Required

(a) Calculate the budgeted ROI for West Division for the year to 31st December Year 7.

(b) Calculate the budgeted residual income for West Division for the year to 31st December Year 7.

37   Annuity method

An investment centre is considering an investment in new machinery that would cost $600,000. The machines would have a life of three years and no residual value. The introduction of the machines will reduce annual operating costs (cash expenditures) by $300,000. The cost of capital for the investment centre is 12%.

Required

Calculate the change in the residual income of the investment centre in each of the three years of the investment, if:

(a) depreciation is charged by the straight-line method and notional interest is charged in the mid-year book value of investment

(b) the annuity method of depreciation is used.

38   Residual

A company is organised into several investment centres. In the past, investment centres have been required to achieve a DCF return of at least 12% on all new investment projects. The annual performance of each investment centre is measured on the basis of ROI. ROI is measured each year as the profit before interest as a percentage of the average investment/average capital employed in the investment centre.

One of the investment centres has achieved a ROI in excess of 35% in each of the past four years. Its managers are considering a new investment project that will have the following cash flows:

Year	Cash flow
	$
0	(42,000)
1 – 3	19,000 each year

The Year 0 investment will be in an item of machinery that will have no residual value at the end of Year 3. Assume that depreciation is charged on a straight-line basis.

Required

(a)   Calculate the NPV of the project, using a cost of capital of 12%.

(b)   Calculate the ROI for the project, each year and on average for the three-year period.

(c)   Suggest whether the managers of the investment centre are likely to invest in the project.

(d)   Calculate the residual income for the project, assuming that a cost of capital of 12% is applied. Suggest how the decision by the centre's managers about investing in the project might be changed if residual income rather than ROI were used to measure divisional performance.

(e)   Calculate the residual income from the project if the annuity depreciation method is used, instead of the straight-line method of depreciation. (When the annuity method of depreciation is used, there is no separate charge for notional interest.)

(f)   Explain the connection between residual income using the annuity method of depreciation and the NPV of the project.

39   Uncertain

A company is considering whether or not to undertake an investment in a project to acquire an item of equipment. The equipment would cost $7,200,000 and would have a three-year operating life. At the end of that time, its residual value would be zero.

The following estimates have been made of the cash flows from the investment:

Year	Cash flow benefits	Cash outflows
	$	$
1	6,000,000	3,000,000
2	8,000,000	4,000,000
3	5,000,000	3,000,000

However, there is some uncertainty in these cash flow figures, and it is estimated that:

(e) annual cash flow benefits could be up to 6% higher or 6% lower

(f) annual cash outflows could be up to 10% higher or lower.

The equipment would be depreciated by the straight-line method.

The appropriate cost of capital for the project is 9%, but there is some uncertainty about the risk in the project and the appropriate cost of capital could be anywhere in the range 7% to 11%.

Required

(a) Assuming that the most optimistic estimates should be applied, calculate:

   (i) the NPV of the project

   (ii) the residual income each year from the project, assuming that notional interest is calculated on the net book value of the equipment at the beginning of the year.

(b) Assuming that the most pessimistic estimates should be applied, calculate:

   (i) the NPV of the project

   (ii) the residual income each year from the project, assuming that notional interest is calculated on the net book value of the equipment at the beginning of the year.

(c) Suggest whether the company is likely to undertake the project.

40   Two divisions

A company has two operating divisions, X and Y, that are treated as profit centres for the purpose of performance reporting.

Division X makes two products, Product A and Product B. Product A is sold to external customers for $62 per unit. Product B is a part-finished item that is sold only to Division Y.

Division Y can obtain the part-finished item from either Division X or from an external supplier. The external supplier charges a price of $55 per unit.

The production capacity of Division X is measured in total units of output for Products A and B. Each unit requires the same direct labour time. The costs of production in Division X are as follows:

	Product A	Product B
	$	$
Variable cost	46	48
Fixed cost	19	19
Full cost	65	67

Required

You have been asked to recommend the optimal transfer price, or range of transfer prices, for Product B.

(a)   What is an optimal transfer price?

(b)   What would be the optimal transfer price for Product B if there is spare production capacity in Division X?

(c)   What would be the optimal transfer price for Product B if Division X is operating at full capacity due to a limited availability of direct labour, and there is unsatisfied external demand for Product A?

41   Training company

A training company has two training centres, each treated as a profit centre for the purpose of transfer pricing.

Each training centre hires its training staff to client organisations, and charges a fixed rate for each 'trainer day'. Trainers are either full-time staff of the company, or are hired externally. Externally-hired trainers are all vetted for quality, and are used when client demand for training exceeds the ability of the division to meet from its full-time staff.

The London centre is very busy and charges its client £2,000 per trainer day. It pays £1,200 per day to external trainers. The variable cost of using its own full-time trainers is £200 per day.

The other training centre is in Liverpool. The manager of the Liverpool centre is meeting with the manager of the London centre to discuss the possibility of the London centre using trainers from the Liverpool centre instead of external trainers. They have agreed this arrangement in principle, but need to agree a daily fee that the London centre should pay the Liverpool centre for these of its trainers.

It has been estimated that if trainers from the Liverpool centre are used in London, the variable costs incurred will be £200 per day, plus £250 per day for travel and accommodation costs. These costs will be paid by the Liverpool centre.

Required

Identify the optimal charge per day for the use of Liverpool trainers by the London training centre, in each of the following circumstances:

(a)   assuming that the Liverpool centre has spare consulting capacity

(b)   assuming that the Liverpool training centre is fully occupied charging clients £750 per trainer day

(c)   assuming that the Liverpool training centre is fully occupied charging clients £1,100 per trainer day.

42 Shadow price

Division A supplies a special chemical to Division B, another profit centre in the same group. The output capacity for making the special chemical in Division A is limited.

(g) The variable cost of making the chemical is $500 per kilo.

(h) There is no external intermediate market for the chemical.

(i) Division B uses the chemical to manufacture a tablet. Each tablet uses ten grams of the chemical.

Sales demand for the tablet exceeds the production capacity of Divisions A and B.

The selling price for each tablet is $10. Further variable processing costs in Division B to make the tablet from the special chemical are $2 per tablet.

Required

(a) Calculate the shadow price of each kilo of the special chemical.

(b) Identify the ideal transfer price.

(c) Suggest whether this transfer price will provide a suitable basis for performance evaluation of the two divisions.

43 Bricks

ABC Company is organised into two trading groups. Group X makes materials that are used to manufacture special bricks. It transfers some of these materials to Group Y and sells some of the materials externally to other brick manufacturers. Group Y makes special bricks from the materials and sells them to traders in building materials.

The production capacity of Group X is 2,000 tonnes per month. At present sales are limited to 1,000 tonnes to external customers and 600 tonnes to Group Y.
The transfer price was agreed at $200 per tonne in line with the external sales trade price at 1st July which was the beginning of the budget year. From 1st December, however, strong competition in the market has reduced the market price for the materials to $180 per tonne.

The manager of Group Y is now saying that the transfer price for the materials from Group X should be the same as for external customers. The manager of Group X rejects this argument on the basis that the original budget established the transfer price for the entire financial year.

From each tonne of materials, Group Y produces 1,000 bricks, which it sells at $0.40 per brick. It would sell a further 40,000 bricks if the price were reduced to $0.32 per brick.

Other data relevant are given below.

	Group X	Group Y
	$	$
Variable cost per tonne	70	60
Fixed cost per month	100,000	40,000

The variable costs of Group Y exclude the transfer price of materials from Group X.

Required

(a) Prepare estimated profit statements for the month of December for each group and for ABC Company as a whole, based on transfer prices of $200 per tonne and of $180 per tonne, when producing at

(i) 80% capacity

(ii) 100% capacity, on the assumption that Group Y reduces the selling price to $0.32.

(b) Comment on the effect that might result from a change in the transfer price from $200 to $180.

(c) Suggest an alternative transfer price that would provide an incentive for Division Y to reduce the selling price and increase sales by 40,000 bricks a month.

44 International transfers

An international company has two operating subsidiaries, one in Country X and one in Country Y. The subsidiaries operate independently, and report to head office as investment centres. Each investment centre manager has the freedom to make his own decisions about what products they should sell, who to sell them to, and the prices at which they should be sold. Each investment centre is required to maximise its annual profit

The main subsidiary (X Division) is in Country X. It makes and sells two products, Product P and Product Q.

Sales and cost data for X Division is as follows:

	Product P	Product Q
Annual sales demand	150,000 units	600,000 units
	$	$
Selling price	9.00	
Variable cost of production	3.40	
Contribution per unit	5.60	0.50

Products P and Q are made on the same machines and with the same work force, at a production centre in Country X. Each product requires exactly the same amount of machine time and labour time, and production can be switched easily from one product to another. Total production capacity is 800,000 units each year, for Product P and Product Q in total.

The investment centre in Country Y (Y Division) is considering a decision to sell Product P. It would not manufacture the product itself, but would buy units of Product P either from Division X or from an external supplier. The external supplier would be willing to sell units of Product P to Division Y at a price of $5 per unit.

The manager of Division Y has asked the manager of Division X to quote a price for supplying Product P. Division X has replied by saying that they would be willing to supply units of Product P at its normal selling price less 40%.
Division Y is not yet sure whether it will want to buy 50,000 units of Product P each year, or 120,000 units.

Required

(a)   If Division X offers to sell units of Product P at the normal selling price in Country X less 40%, what will be the decision of the manager of Division Y if annual purchase requirements are:

(i)   50,000 units of Product P

(ii)   120,000 units of Product P?

(b)   Recommend a transfer price, or a range of transfer prices, at which Division X should offer to sell units of Product P to Division Y, **if the annual profits of the company as a whole are to be maximised** and annual purchase requirements are:

(i)   50,000 units of Product P

(ii)   120,000 units of Product P?

Ignore taxation.

(c)   Suppose that the rate of taxation on company profits is 50% in Country X and 30% in Country Y.

Recommend, with reasons, whether Division Y should obtain units of Product P from Division X or from the external supplier, if its annual purchase requirements are 120,000 units and if the transfer price is the market price in Country X less 40%.

45   Long and Short

Long and Short are two divisions in the Range Group of companies. Both require components S and M for their operations. Component S is available from Division A and component M is available from Division B.

Long Division converts the components S and M into a final product, RDZ. Short Division converts the components S and M into another final product, BL.

The market demand for RDZ and BL exceeds the production capacity of Range Group, because of the limited availability of components S and M. There is no external intermediate market for S or M. No other intermediate product market is available to the Long and Short Divisions.

Other data

Long Division

RDZ	Selling price per unit	$45
	Processing cost per unit	$12
	Components required per unit of RDZ	
	Component S	3 units
	Component M	2 units

Short Division

BL	Selling price per unit	$54
	Processing cost per unit	$14
	Components required per unit of BL	
	Component S	2 units
	Component M	4 units

Division A

Component S	Variable cost per unit	$6
	Maximum production capacity	1,200 units

Division B

Component M	Variable cost per unit	$4
	Maximum production capacity	1,600 units

The solution to a linear programming model for production planning in Range Group shows that the imputed scarcity value (shadow price) of product S is $0.50 and the imputed scarcity value of product M is $2.75 per unit. The model also indicates that the components S and M should be transferred to Long and Short Divisions such that 200 units of RDZ and 300 units of BL are produced and sold.

Required

(a) Calculate the contribution earned by the Range Group if the production and sales plan indicated by the linear programming model is implemented.

(b) If the transfer prices are set on the basis of variable cost plus shadow price, show detailed calculations for the following:

   (i) the contribution per unit of intermediate product earned by divisions A and B.

   (ii) the contribution per unit of products RDZ and BL.

(c) Comment on the results in (b) above and on the possible attitude of management of the various divisions to the proposed transfer pricing and the production and sales plan.

(d) In the following year, the capacities of Divisions A and B have each doubled and the following changes have taken place:

   (i) Component S – There is still no external market for this product, but Division A has a large demand for other products which could use its spare capacity and earn a contribution of 5% over cost. The variable cost per unit for the other products would be the same as for Component S and these products would use capacity in Division A at the same rate as Component S.

   (ii) Component M – An intermediate market for this product now exists and Component M can be bought and sold in unlimited amounts at $7.50 per unit. External sales of Component M would incur additional transport costs of $0.50 per unit which are not incurred in inter-divisional transfers.

The sales demand for units of RDZ and BL will still exceed the production capacity of Divisions A and B to make component S and M for Long and Short Divisions.

Calculate the transfer prices at which Components S and M should now be offered to Long and Short Divisions, in order that the transfer policy implemented will lead to the maximisation of group profit.

Determine the production and sales pattern for Component S, Component M, product RDZ and product BL that will now maximise contribution for the Range Group, and calculate the amount of this total contribution.

You should assume that all the divisions will make decisions that are consistent with the financial data available.

46   Balanced

A balanced scorecard approach may be used to set performance targets and monitor performance.

(a) List the four aspects of performance in a balanced scorecard approach.

(b) Suggest how a professional football club might use a balanced scorecard approach. Indicate what key aspects of performance might be identified and suggest performance targets that a football club might use in a balanced scorecard approach.

47   Pyramid

(a)   Describe briefly the performance pyramid.

(b)   List the dimensions of performance for a service industry, as suggested by Fitzgerald and others.

48   The Vet Centre

The Vet Centre is a company that specialises in the medical treatment of animals. The services provided by the Centre are grouped into three categories:

(1)   domestic animals
(2)   farm animals
(3)   'exotic' animals.

There are several other local centres for treating sick animals, and the owner of the Vet Centre is very aware of the threat from competitors. The system used by the Centre to deal with customers is as follows. Customers are required to telephone the Centre when they suspect that there might be a problem with their animal. The Centre Controller then:

(1)   in the case of domestic and exotic animals, suggests to the customer whether or not the animal should be brought into the Centre for examination and treatment

(2)   in the case of farm animals, suggests whether a vet should go out to visit the farmer to examine the animal (or animals), and

(3)   gives an indicative price that the customer might have to pay.

Customers cannot bring their animal into the Centre without first making an appointment with the Controller.

The Centre has a policy of employing no more than ten full-time veterinary surgeons ('vets'), who work full time on either domestic animals or farm animals. 'Exotic' animals are treated by specialists. These are not full-time employees, but work for the Centre when required in response to telephone requests for assistance from the Centre.

Full time vets are paid $60,000 each per year in salary. In addition, they receive a bonus of 50% of the amount by which actual fee income exceeds the budgeted fee income for the year. The total bonus is shared equally between the full-time vets.

The full-time vets are also required to deal with complaints from customers about poor treatment or unsuccessful treatments.

The owner of the Vet Centre is committed to keeping his staff fully up-to-date with current developments in the treatment of sick and injured animals. Each vet has a personal development programme, and is allowed to attend external training courses and seminars on up to eight days each year.

The Vet Centre: statistics for the year ended 31st December Year 8

	Budget	Actual
Number of vets:		
Dealing with domestic animals	6	5
Dealing with farm animals	4	5
Customer enquiries by telephone		
New business	5,000	9,000
Repeat business	18,000	15,000
Number of examinations/treatments		
New business	3,000	4,000
Repeat business	16,000	14,000
Mix of examinations/treatments		
Domestic animals	14,880	11,800
Farm animals	4,000	5,800
'Exotic' animals	120	400
Other statistics:		
Fee income	$2,520,000	$2,820,000
Training costs	$75,000	$100,000
Fess for part-time vets (exotic animals)	$18,000	$60,000
Other operating costs	$1,400,000	$1,610,000
Number of complaints	380	540

'Repeat business' refers to customers who have used the services of the Vet Centre before.

Required

Fitzgerald and Moon suggested a framework for the analysis of performance systems.

(a) Select a performance indicator for each of the six dimensions of performance in the Fitzgerald and Moon framework, and use this to measure the performance of the Vet Centre in Year 8.

(b) State three factors that should be considered when setting standards of performance.

(c) State three factors that should be considered when linking rewards to the achievement of performance standards.

49 Total quality

(a) List the key aspects of Total Quality Management (TQM).

(b) What are quality-related costs? What is the TQM approach to quality-related costs, and how does this differ from the more traditional approach to these costs?

(c) List the key aspects of just-in-time (JIT) management

(d) Briefly explain the nature of activity based management (ABM).

50 Poole Company

Poole Company makes and sells a single product. The existing product specifications are as follows:

Material X	8 square metres at $4 per square metre
Machine time	0.6 running hours
Other machine costs	$40/hour
Selling price	$100

Poole Company needs to fulfil orders for 5,000 units per period. There will be no change in inventory level during the period.

The following Information is available about performance before the introduction of a TQM programme:

(1) 5% of incoming material from suppliers is scrapped due to poor receipt and storage.

(2) 4% of material input to the machine process is wasted in process.

(3) Inspection and storage of material cost $0.10 per metre.

(4) Inspection during the cycle costs $25,000 per period.

(5) Production is increased to allow for the downgrading of 12.5% of units at the final inspection phase. Downgraded units are sold as 'second quality' units at a discount of 30% of the final selling price.

(6) Production is increased to allow for returns from customers. These are replaced free of charge. Returns are due to specification failure and account for 5% of units initially delivered to customers. Replacement units incur a delivery cost of $8 per unit. 80% of the returns from customers are rectified using 0.2 hours of machine running time and are resold as 'third quality' products at a discount of 50% on the standard selling price. The remaining returned units are sold as scrap for $5 per unit.

(7) Product liability claims are estimated at 3% of sales revenue from standard product sales.

(8) Machine idle time is 20% of gross machine hours used.

(9) Sundry costs of administration, selling and distribution total $60,000 per period.

(10) Poole Company is aware of these excess costs and currently spends $20,000 per period to prevent them from happening.

Poole Company is planning a quality management programme that will increase its cost prevention expenditure from $20,000 to $60,000 per period. The estimates of performance levels after the TQM programme are as follows:

(1)   A reduction in stores losses of material to 3%.

(2)   A reduction in the downgrading of products inspected to 7.5%.

(3)   A reduction in material losses in the process to 2.5% of input to the machine process.

(4)   A reduction in returns of products from customers to 2.5% delivered.

(5)   A reduction in machine idle time to 12.5% of gross hours used.

(6)   A reduction in product liability claims to 1% of sales revenue.

(7)   A reduction in inspection checks by 40% of the existing figure.

(8)   A reduction in sundry administration, selling and distribution costs by 10% of the existing figure.

(9)   A reduction in machine running time per unit of product to 0.5 hours.

Required

(a)   Prepare summaries showing total units, purchases of material and gross machine hours:

(i)   before implementation of the TQM programme, and

(ii)   after implementation of the TQM programme.

(b)   Prepare income statements for the period both before and after implementation of the TQM programme.

51   Target cost

A company has designed a new product that it would like to introduce to the market. It has spent $250,000 on the design work so far. A market research report has indicated that the product will have a life of four years, and at a selling price of $35 per unit, annual sales would be as follows:

Year	Sales
	units
1	40,000
2	60,000
3	50,000
4	20,000

It has been estimated that to produce the new product, annual fixed production costs (all cash flows) will increase by $200,000, and the variable cost per unit will be $10.

Other cash flows for the project will be:

■   Capital expenditure of $1,400,000 at the beginning of the project. There will be a residual value of $600,000 from this investment at the end of Year 4.

- An investment of $400,000 will be required in working capital. This will be recovered at the end of Year 4.

- Expenditure on advertising will be required, as follows:

Year	Advertising costs
	$
0	800,000
1	600,000
2	400,000
3	200,000

Required

(a) Calculate the expected NPV of the project to launch the new product, if the company's cost of capital is 12%.

(b) Calculate the target cost for the product that is needed to achieve a return of 12% on investment, and calculate the size of the current cost gap.

52   Cost and quality

Explain briefly how each of the following management accounting techniques can be used to analyse the relationship between cost and quality:

(1)   Total Quality Management (TQM)

(2)   Activity Based Costing (ABC)

(3)   Balanced scorecard

(4)   Just in Time management (JIT)

(5)   Value analysis

Answers

Contents		
		Page

Discounted cash flow (DCF) and long-term decisions

Introduction to strategic management accounting

Budgets and alternative budgeting models

Economic, fiscal and environmental factors. Pricing strategy

Performance measurement systems

Measuring performance

1 Lard Company

(a) (i) Budgeted cost: traditional absorption costing

It is assumed that the weighting of 1:2:3 applies to packaging materials, but not to labour and overhead costs.

Packaging material

	Output		Material usage		
Customer A	30,000	×	1 =		30,000
Customer B	45,000	×	2 =		90,000
Customer C	25,000	×	3 =		75,000
Weighted units of material					195,000

Therefore, packaging material per weighted unit = $1,950,000/195,000 = $10.

Labour and overheads

Total cost of labour and overheads (000s) = 350 + 30 + 500 + 60 = 940

Total units = (30,000 + 45,000 + 25,000) = 100,000.

Labour and overhead cost per unit = $940,000/100,000 = $9.40.

Budgeted average cost/unit

	Customer A	Customer B	Customer C
	$	$	$
Material	10.0	20.0	30.0
Labour/overhead	9.4	9.4	9.4
Product cost/metre	19.4	29.4	39.4

(ii) Activity based costing analysis of labour and overhead costs

	Receipts and inspection	Storage	Packaging
	$	$	$
Labour			
Basic pay (20:10:70)	70,000	35,000	245,000
Overtime	15,000	6,250	8,750
Occupancy cost (20: 60: 20)	100,000	300,000	100,000
Administration cost (40: 10: 50)	24,000	6,000	30,000
	209,000	347,250	383,750

Activity levels (cost drivers)

Customer	Units		Receipts and inspection (hours)		Storage (metres^2)		Packaging (hours)
A	30,000	(× 6/60)	3,000	(× 0.3)	9,000	(× 36/60)	18,000
B	45,000	(× 9/60)	6,750	(× 0.3)	13,500	(× 45/60)	33,750
C	25,000	(× 15/60)	6,250	(× 0.3)	7,500	(× 60/60)	25,000
			16,000		30,000		76,750

Cost	$209,000	$347,250	383,750
Cost/unit of activity	$13.0625 per hour	$11.575 per m·	$5 per hour

ABC-based costs

	Customer A	Customer B	Customer C
	$	$	$
Material	10.00	20.00	30.00
Receipts ($13.0625/hour)	1.31	1.96	3.27
Storage ($11.575/m·)	3.47	3.47	3.47
Packing ($5/hour)	3.00	3.75	5.00
Product cost/unit	17.78	29.18	41.74

(b)   Total costs per unit for Lard Company are not much different using activity based costing than they are with traditional absorption costing. However, ABC analysis allows management to look at the costs of overhead-related activities. This may help them to control these costs, through better management of these activities and the resources they use.

2   LC Company

(a)

Budgeted machine hours	hours
Product V: 6,000 × 3	18,000
Product W: 4,000 × 4	16,000
Total budgeted machine hours	34,000
Budgeted production overheads	$816,000
Absorption rate per machine hour	$24

	Product V	Product W
	$	$
Direct materials	20	60
Direct labour	50	40
Production overhead (3 hours/4 hours × $24)	72	96
Full production cost per unit	142	196

(b)   **Machine-related overhead costs:**
Overhead cost per machine hour = $204,000/34,000 hours = $6 per machine hour

Set-up related overhead costs:
Overhead cost per set-up = $280,000/(18 + 32) = $5,600 per set-up.

Purchasing-related overhead costs:
Cost per purchase order = $332,000/(48 + 112) = $2,075 per order.

Overhead cost analysis		Product V			Product W	
		Total cost	Cost/ unit		Total cost	Cost/ unit
		$	$		$	$
Overheads:						
Machine-related	(18,000 × 6)	108,000	18.0	(16,000 × 6)	96,000	24.0
Set-up related	(18 × 5,600)	100,800	16.8	(32 × 5,600)	179,200	44.8
Purchasing-related	(48 × 2,075)	99,600	16.6	(112 × 2,075)	232,400	58.1
		308,400	51.4		507,600	126.9

Unit costs	V	W
	$	$
Direct materials	20.0	60.0
Direct labour	50.0	40.0
Production overhead	51.4	126.9
Full production cost per unit	121.4	226.9

(c) ABC analysis could be used by LC Company to analyse the profitability of Products V and W. Using ABC, the overhead cost per unit of W is much higher than with traditional absorption costing, and the cost per unit of V is less. This is because Product W has a relatively large amount of setup activity and purchasing-related activity.

Management could look at the reasons why Product W needs so many setups and purchase orders, and by trying to reduce the resources used up by these activities, it might be possible to reduce the costs (and increase the profitability) of Product W.

3 Throughput

(a) Marginal costing approach

Profit will be maximised by producing output to maximise the contribution per machine hour (contribution per unit of limiting factor).

	Product X	Product Y
Contribution per unit	$6	$7
Machine hours per unit	1.5 hours	2 hours
Contribution per machine hour	$4	$3.50
Priority for manufacture	1·	2·

Profit will be maximised by making and selling 8,000 units of Product X in each period (maximum sales demand). This will require 12,00 machine hours. The remaining 20,000 machine hours should be used to make and sell 10,000 units of Product Y.

	$
Contribution from Product X: 8,000 × $6	48,000
Contribution from Product Y: 10,000 × $7	70,000
Total contribution	118,000
Fixed costs	90,000
Profit	28,000

(b) Throughput accounting is based on the view that value is not added to a product until the product is eventually sold. There is no value in inventory. When there is a limiting factor restricting production, all costs except for the cost of bought-in materials (raw materials, purchased components) are fixed costs in the short term, including direct labour costs and associated 'variable' overheads.

The aim should be to maximise throughput in a period, where throughput is defined as sales minus the cost of bought-in materials.

The main difference between throughput accounting and marginal costing is in the treatment of direct labour and variable overhead costs as a 'fixed cost' in the short term. In throughput accounting, fixed costs are referred to as 'factory cost'.

(c) Throughput accounting ratio =

Return per bottleneck unit / Factory cost per bottleneck unit

Here, the bottleneck resource is machine time.

	Product X	Product Y
	$	$
Sales price	22	27
Materials cost	10	9
Throughput	12	18
Machine hours per unit	1.5 hours	2 hours
Throughput/return per machine hour	$8	$9

To calculate the cost per factory hour, we need to make an assumption about direct labour cost and variable overhead costs. It is assumed that the direct labour cost and variable overhead cost in the answer to part (a) is fixed in the short term.

	$
Direct labour and variable overhead costs:	
Product X: 8,000 × $6	48,000
Product Y: 10,000 × $11	110,000
Total contribution	158,000
Fixed costs	90,000
Factory cost in each period	248,000

Factory cost per machine hour = $248,000/32,000 hours = $7.75.

	Product X	Product Y
Return per machine hour	$8	$9
Factory cost per machine hour	$7.75	$7.75
Machine hours per unit	1.5 hours	2 hours
Throughput accounting ratio	1.03	1.16
Priority for manufacture	2-	1-

Tutorial note: The aim should be to maximise the throughput accounting ratio, and to ensure that the ratio is higher than 1.0. The throughput accounting ratio for both Product X and Product Y is low, close to the minimum acceptable level.

(d) Profit will be maximised by making and selling 12,000 units of Product Y (maximum sales demand). This will use up 24,000 machine hours. The remaining 8,000 machine hours should be used to make 5,333.33 units of Product X.

	$
Return from Product Y: 12,000 × $18	216,000
Return from Product Y: 5,333.33 × $12	64,000
Total return/throughput	280,000
Fixed costs	248,000
Profit	32,000

4 Throughput ratio

Throughput per pallet = $3,000 − $2,000 = $1,000.

Throughput per inspection hour = $1,000/0.5 hours = $2,000.

Operating expenses per inspection hour = $300,000/200 = $1,500.

Throughput accounting ratio = $2,000/$1,500 = 1.33.

5 Backflush

Backflush accounting, with two trigger points

Raw materials inventory account

	$		$
Creditors	5,000,000	Finished goods inventory	5,000,000

Finished goods inventory account

		$		$
Raw materials	(100,000 × 50)	5,000,000	Income statement (98,000 × 80)	7,840,000
Conversion costs	(100,000 × 30)	3,000,000	Balance c/f (2,000 × 80)	160,000
		8,000,000		8,000,000

Conversion costs account

	$		$
Creditors (overheads)	3,000,000	Finished goods inventory	3,000,000
	3,000,000		3,000,000

Sales

	$		$
Income statement (98,000 × 100)	9,800,000	Receivables (98,000 × 100)	9,800,000

Income statement

	$		$
Finished goods	7,840,000	Sales	9,800,000
Profit	1,960,000		
	9,800,000		9,800,000

6 Villaco

(a) Total machine hours required to meet sales demand = (2,000 × 4) + (3,000 × 1) = 11,000. Since only 7,000 hours are available, machine hours are a limiting factor.

	Product A	Product B
	$	$
Sales price	20	10
Variable cost	8	6
Contribution	12	4
Machine hours per unit	4	1
Contribution per hour	$3	$4
Priority for manufacture	2	1

Decision: produce and sell the following products

Product	Units	Machine hours	Contribution per unit	Total contribution
			$	$
B	3,000	3,000	4	12,000
A (balance)	1,000	4,000	12	12,000
		7,000		24,000

(b)

	Product A	Product B
	$	$
Extra cost of external purchase	1	0.50
Machine hours saved by external purchase	4	1
Extra cost per machine hour saved	$0.25	$0.50
Priority for manufacture	2nd	1st

Item	Number of units	Machine hours	Contribution per unit	Contribution
Make			$	$
A	1,750	7,000	12	21,000
Buy				
A (balance)	250	(12 − 1)	11	2,750
B	3,000	(4 − 0.5)	3.5	10,500
Total contribution				34,250

7   Shortages

Working: contribution per unit

	A	B	C	D
	$/unit	$/unit	$/unit	$/unit
Profit	35	55	30	55
Fixed costs:				
Production	180	240	150	270
Selling	145	225	120	215
Contribution	360	520	300	540

Resources required for the priority order for the major customer

Casing	Units required	Steel per unit $	Total $	Direct labour per unit hours	Total hours
A	30	250	7,500	7.5	225.0
B	20	500	10,000	7.5	150.0
C	30	190	5,700	6.25	187.5
D	20	390	7,800	12.5	250.0
Total			31,000		812.5

(a) Steel in short supply and restricted to $250,000

Casing	A	B	C	D
	$	$	$	$
Contribution/unit	360	520	300	540
Steel costs/unit	250	500	190	390
Contribution/$1 steel cost	1.44	1.04	1.58	1.38
Ranking for manufacture	2-	4-	1-	3-

It is assumed that the sales forecasts for the month are correct.

Profit-maximising production schedule

	Steel used $	A units	B units	C units	D units
Priority order	31,000	30	20	30	20
Sales of C	51,300			270	
Sales of A	67,500	270			
Sales of D	70,200				180
	220,000				
Balance: Sales of B	30,000		60		
Total steel available	250,000				
Total production/sales		300	80	300	200

(b) Components are in short supply and restricted to 400 units

	A	B	C	D
Contribution/unit	$360	£520	$300	$540
Components/unit	1	1	1	1
Contribution/component	£360	$520	$300	$540
Ranking for manufacture	3-	2-	4-	1-

Profit-maximising production schedule

Components used		A	B	C	D
	units	units	units	units	units
Priority order	100	30	20	30	20
Sales of D	180				180
	280				
Balance: Sales of B	120		120		
Total available	400				
Total production/sales		30	140	30	200

(c) Labour is in short supply and restricted to 2,125 hours

Casing	A	B	C	D
Contribution/unit	$360	$520	$300	$540
Labour hours/unit	7.5	7.5	6.25	12.5
Contribution per hour	$48.00	$69.33	$48.00	$43.20
Ranking for manufacture	2· =	1·	2· =	4·

Profit-maximising production schedule

	Labour hours	A	B	C	D
		units	units	units	units
Special order	812.5	30	20	30	20
Remaining hours	1,312.5		175		
Total hours	2,125.0				
Total production/sales		30	195	30	20

(d) Make or buy decision

	A	B	C	D
	$	$	$	$
Contribution if made	360	520	300	540
Contribution if bought in	285	475	250	490
Extra contribution if made	75	45	50	50
Labour hours	7.5	7.5	6.25	12.5
Extra contribution per hour	$10	$6	$8	$4
Ranking/priority for making	1·	3·	2·	4·

Profit-maximising production schedule

Casing	Hours	A	B	C	D
Special order	1,625	30	20	30	20
Remaining hours	2,625	175			
Total hours	4,250				
Made internally		205	20	30	20
Purchased externally		95	180	270	180
Total sales		300	200	300	200

8 Product B22

Workings for relevant costs

Material X

The company has enough kilograms of material X in stock for the contract. When it is used, the stocks of material X will not be replaced. The relevant cost of the material is therefore its opportunity cost, not its replacement cost. The opportunity cost is the higher of its current sale value ($7.50 per kg) or the net saving obtained if it is used as a substitute for material Z ($9.50 – $1.50 = $8 per kg). The relevant cost of material X is therefore $8 per kg.

Material Y

Material Y is in regular use, so its relevant cost is its current replacement cost.

	kg		$
Total inventory	10,000		142,750
Purchased six months ago	3,000	(× $13.75)	41,250
Purchased last month	7,000		101,500

Purchase price last month = $101,500/7,000 kg = $14.50 per kg.

Current purchase price = 4% higher = $14.50 × 1.04 = $15.08.

Skilled labour

Skilled labour is in short supply. If it is used to make product B22, workers will have to be taken off other work. The relevant cost of skilled labour is the wages for the skilled workers for the time spent on B22, plus the lost contribution (net of skilled labour cost) from not being able to make units of product B16.

Opportunity cost of skilled labour

Skilled labour cost per unit of Product B16 = $24
Number of hours per unit = 3 hours
Contribution per unit of B16 = $45
Contribution per skilled labour hour from B16 = $15
Opportunity cost of skilled labour if it is used to make B22 = (500×5) × $15 = $37,500

Unskilled labour

900 unskilled labour will be available at no incremental cost to the company (as it is already being paid and is not fully employed). There is no relevant cost for these hours. The additional 600 hours required will involve extra wage payments, including overtime payments. The relevant cost of these 600 hours is $6 per hour × 150% = $9 per hour, including the overtime premium.

Overheads

Variable overheads are included as relevant costs because they will be additional costs if the units of B22 are made. The only incremental fixed costs, however, are the extra cash costs of $4,000. The fixed overhead absorption rate is ignored. The additional costs of hiring special finishing machinery are also included as a relevant cost.

Development costs

Those costs already incurred are past costs (sunk costs) and are not relevant. The future development costs involve additional expenditure and are included as relevant costs.

Minimum price for making 500 units of B22

Materials:		£
X	(500 units × 4kg) × $8	16,000
Y	(500 units × 6kg) × $15.08	45,240
Labour:		
Skilled wages	(500 units × 5 hours) × $8	20,000
Opportunity cost	(500 units × 5 hours) × $15	37,500
Unskilled	[(500 × 3) − 900] x 6 × 1.5	5,400
Overheads:		
Variable	(500 units × 2 hours) × 8.75	8,750
Fixed	Incremental spending	4,000
Machine hire	(2 weeks × $2,650)	5,300
Development costs		1,750
Minimum price		143,940

9   Payoff table

(a)

Cost of buying		Revenue from selling	
Quantity	$	Quantity	$
20	2	20	6
40	4	40	12
60	6	60	18

Pay-off table, without perfect information

	Sales demand per day		
	20	40	60
Purchases per day	$	$	$
20	4	4	4
	(6 − 2)	(6 − 2)	(6 − 2)
40	2	8	8
	(6 − 4)	(12 − 4)	(12 − 4)
60	0	6	12
	(6 − 6)	(12 − 6)	(18 − 6)

EV of buying decision, without perfect information

	Sales demand			EV of daily profit
	20	40	60	$
Probability	0.3	0.5	0.2	
Purchases per day	$	$	$	
20	4	4	4	
EV	1.2	2.0	0.8	4.0
40	2	8	8	
EV	0.6	4.0	1.6	6.2
60	0	6	12	
EV	0	3.0	2.4	5.4

On the basis of EV, and without perfect information about daily sales demand, the decision should be to buy 40 buns per day, and the EV of daily profit will be $6.20.

(b)

With perfect information

With perfect information about daily sales demand, the baker will purchase the exact number of buns to meet demand. Profit will be $4 when sales demand is 20, $8 when sales demand is 40 and $12 when sales demand is 60.

Sales and purchases	Profit	Probability	EV
	$		$
20	4	0.3	1.2
40	8	0.5	4.0
60	12	0.2	2.4
EV of profit with perfect information			7.6
EV of profit with perfect information			6.2
Value of perfect information			1.4

The value of having perfect information about sales demand each day is $1.40 per day.

10   Grab Company

(a)   Outcomes

Decision	Outcome	Turnover	Variable cost	Advance hire	Conversion premium	Profit
Low	Low	4,000	2,800	1,000	0	200
	Medium	8,500	5,950	1,000	850	700
	High	15,000	10,500	1,000	2,150	1,350
Medium	Low	4,000	2,800	1,500	0	(300)
	Medium	8,500	5,950	1,500	0	1,050
	High	15,000	10,500	1,500	1,300	1,700
High	Low	4,000	2,800	2,300	0	(1,100)
	Medium	8,500	5,950	2,300	0	250
	High	15,000	10,500	2,300	0	2,200

(b)   Pay-off matrix

	Low	Medium	High	Expected value
Probability (p)	0.30	0.45	0.25	Σpx
Decision	x =	x =	x =	
Low	200	700	1,350	712.5
Medium	(300)	1,050	1,700	807.5
High	(1,100)	250	2,200	332.5

The highest expected value is earned if the medium advance hire usage contract is signed.

(c)   Risk preferences

The above decision assumes a neutral risk preference. It is possible the organisation may adopt a different decision criterion than expected value. Other decision criteria may be based on a risk-seeking approach or a risk-averse approach.

Risk-seeking managers would prefer a maximax approach. This is to maximise the highest possible outcome. In this example this would require a high advance hire contract.

Risk-averse managers would prefer a maximin approach. This is to maximise the lowest possible outcome of a course of action. This would require a low advance hire contract.

(d)   Value of perfect information

The maximum value to be paid for perfect information will be

EV(perfect information) – EV(no information)

EV(perfect information) will ensure that the decision will always maximise the EV of a given outcome.

	Net profit	Probability	Expected value
	$000		$000
High outcome – High advance hire	2,200	0.25	550.0
Medium outcome – Medium advance hire	1,050	0.45	472.5
Low outcome – Low advance hire	200	0.30	60.0
			1,082.5

Value of perfect information = $1,082,500 – $807,500 = $275,000.

11   Learning

(a)   (1)

	hours
Average time for 1st 2 units (200 hours × 80%)	160
Total time for 1st 2 units (160 × 2)	320
Time for first unit	200
Time for second unit	120

Selling price for the second unit:	$
Direct materials	2,000
Direct labour (120 hours × $15)	1,800
Fixed production overhead (120 hours × $20)	2,400
Full production cost	6,200
Profit margin (40%)	2,480
Selling price	8,680

(2)

	hours
Average time for 1st 4 units (200 hours × 80% × 80%)	128
Total time for 1st 4 units (128 × 4)	512
Time for 1st 2 units	320
Time for 3rd and 4th units	192
Average time per unit for 3rd and 4th units	96

Average price for the 3rd and 4th units:	$
Direct materials	2,000
Direct labour (96 hours × $15)	1,440
Fixed production overhead (96 hours × $20)	1,920
Full production cost	5,360
Profit margin (40%)	2,144
Average selling price	7,504

(3)

	hours
Average time for 1- 8 units (200 hours × 80% × 80%× 80%)	102.4
Total time for 1- 8 units (102.4 × 8)	819.2

Selling price for the first 8 units	$
Direct materials ($2,000 × 8)	16,000.0
Direct labour (819.2 hours × $15)	12,288.0
Fixed production overhead (819.2 hours × $20)	16,384.0
Full production cost	44,672.0
Profit margin (40%)	17,868.8
Selling price	62,540.8

This gives an average selling price of $7,817.6 per unit.

(b) (1) It may be difficult to establish an expected learning rate. Reliable statistical evidence of a constant learning rate (for example, as in the aircraft manufacturing industry) is required.

(2) Learning curve theory is of little value for the development of low-cost items where direct labour input is small. The benefits from the learning curve would be small and fairly insignificant.

(3) Learning curve theory assumes that when the first unit has been made, every other unit will be similar. It does not allow for changes in design or other factors that could disrupt the learning effect and change the learning rate.

12 Greenears

The cost of producing batches 6 – 12 is the difference between:

■ the cost of producing batches 1 – 5, and

■ the cost of producing batches 1 – 12.

(1) **Learning factor**

$$\frac{\text{Logarithm } 0.85}{\text{Logarithm } 2} = \frac{-0.07058}{0.30103} = -0.23446$$

(2)   **Average labour cost of producing the first five batches**

$$y = \$2,000 \times \frac{1}{5^{0.23446}}$$

$$= \$2,000\,(0.68568)$$

$$= \$1,371 \text{ per batch}$$

(3)   **Average labour cost of producing the first 12 batches**

$$y - \$2,000 \times \frac{1}{12^{0.23446}}$$

$$= \$2,000\,(0.55844)$$

$$= \$1,117 \text{ per batch}$$

(4)   **Labour cost of producing batches 6 – 12**

	$
Total cost for the first 12 batches (12 × $1,117)	13,404
Total cost for the first 5 batches (5 × $1,371)	6,855
Labour cost for batches 6 – 12	6,549

13   Regression

(a)

$$b = \frac{5(254) - (15)(79)}{5(55) - (15)(15)}$$

$$= \frac{1,270 - 1,185}{275 - 225}$$

$$b = 85/50 = 1.7$$

$$a = \frac{79}{5} - \frac{1.7(15)}{5}$$

$$a = 10.7$$

Forecast: Sales in $millions = 10.7 + 1.7x

(b)

Forecast for Year 6 (20X7) = 10.7 + 1.7(6) = 20.9 ($20.9 million)

Forecast for Year 7 (20X8) = 10.7 + 1.7(7) = 22.6 ($22.6 million).

$$r = \frac{85}{\sqrt{(50)[5(1,279) - (79)(79)}}$$

$r = 85/87.75 = + 0.97$

This is very close to + 1, suggesting that the forecast will be very reliable.

14 Replacement product

(a) Workings

If Product T is kept on the market for four more years:

Year	Unit sales	Unit contribution	Annual contribution
		£	£
1	140,000	70	9,800,000
2	130,000	70	9,100,000
3	120,000	70	8,400,000
4	110,000	70	7,700,000

If Product V is introduced:

- EV of annual sales = $(0.2 \times 100,000) + (0.5 \times 80,000) + (0.3 \times 50,000) = 75,000$ units.

- Unit contribution = $350 - $230 = $120.

- EV of annual contribution = 75,000 units × $120 = $9,000,000.

Solution

Year	Extra costs	Lost contribution from T	Contribution from V	Net cash flow	Discount factor 8%	PV
	$000	$000	$000	$000		$000
0	(2,000)			(2,000)	1.000	(2,000)
1	(160)	(9,800)	9,000	(960)	0.926	(889)
2	(160)	(9,100)	9,000	(260)	0.857	(223)
3	(160)	(8,400)	9,000	440	0.794	349
4	(160)	(7,700)	9,000	1,140	0.735	838
					NPV	(1,925)

The NPV is – $1925,000, indicating that the immediate replacement of Product T with Product V is not justified.

(b)

The discount factor for Year 1- 4 at a cost of capital of 8% = 3.312.

To justify the immediate replacement of Product T with Product V, the annual contribution from Product V would need to be higher by at least: $1,925,000/3.312 = $581,220.

The annual contribution per unit from Product V is currently estimated to be $120.

Annual sales in units from Product V would therefore need to be higher by at least: $581,220/$120 per unit = 4,843.5 units – say 5,000 units.

(c)

Tutorial note: Annual sales of Product T are expected to fall by an additional amount each year. It is therefore not possible to devise a simple computation for the minimum fall in annual sales that would be required to justify immediate replacement by Product V. The method used in the solution below is therefore based on an interpolation method. The NPV is estimated assuming a fall of 15,000 units in sales each year, rather than 10,000 units. A net present value is calculated, and this is used together with the answer in (a) to obtain a 'break-even' point.

Solution

If annual sales of Product T were to fall by 15,000 units in each subsequent year from Year 2 onwards, the contribution lost by replacing Product T with Product V would be as follows:

Year	Unit sales	Unit contribution	Annual contribution
		£	£
1	135,000	70	9,450,000
2	120,000	70	8,400,000
3	105,000	70	7,350,000
4	90,000	70	6,300,000

The NPV of a decision to introduce Product V immediately would be:

Year	Extra costs	Lost contribution from T	Contribution from V	Net cash flow	Discount factor 8%	PV
	$000	$000	$000	$000		$000
0	(2,000)			(2,000)	1.000	(2,000)
1	(160)	(9,450)	9,000	(610)	0.926	(565)
2	(160)	(8,400)	9,000	440	0.857	377
3	(160)	(7,350)	9,000	1,490	0.794	1,183
4	(160)	(6,300)	9,000	2,540	0.735	1,867
					NPV	+ 862

If annual sales of Product T fall by 10,000 units each year, the NPV would be $(1,925,000).

If annual sales of Product T fall by 15,000 units each year, the NPV would be $862,000.

The minimum fall in annual sales of Product T needed to justify its immediate replacement by Product V is therefore approximately:

$$10,000 + \left[\frac{1,925}{(862+1,925)}\right] \times (15,000 - 10,000) \text{ units}$$

= 13,453 units = about 13,500 units.

(d) Limitations of analysis:

(1) Expected value used for sales of Product V. Actual sales could be higher or lower than 75,000 each year.

(2) Estimates of falls in sales of Product T cannot be predicted accurately.

(3) The calculations have ignored taxation and inflation, which is inappropriate in practice.

(4) A cost of capital of 8% has been assumed. This may be inappropriate.

(5) There has been no consideration of the options to introduce Product V at the beginning of Year 3, or Year 4 or Year 5.

(6) The option to reduce the selling price of Product T to increase annual sales has not been considered. Similarly an option to sell Product V at a lower price to increase annual sales has not been considered.

(7)   Non-financial factors have been ignored: for example, there could be a longer-term marketing advantage to be gained from introducing Product V as soon as possible.

15   Probabilities

Cash inflows for the project can be calculated as an EV of expected annual cash inflows.

The first step is to establish a probability distribution of possible outcomes.

	Factor 1	Factor 2	Factor 3	Joint probability
Yes, No, No	0.2	0.7	0.6	0.084
Yes, Yes, Yes	0.2	0.3	0.4	0.024
Yes, No, Yes	0.2	0.7	0.4	0.056
Yes, Yes, No	0.2	0.3	0.6	0.036
No, No, No	0.8	0.7	0.6	0.336
No, Yes, Yes	0.8	0.3	0.4	0.096
No, No, Yes	0.8	0.7	0.4	0.224
No, Yes, No	0.8	0.3	0.6	0.1440

Probability of outcome		Cash inflows as a proportion of expectation	EV
0.084	(- 25%)	0.75	0.0630
0.024	(- 25% − 10% + 5%)	0.70	0.0168
0.056	(- 25% + 5%)	0.80	0.0448
0.036	(- 25% − 10%)	0.65	0.0234
0.336		1.00	0.3360
0.096	(- 10% + 5%)	0.95	0.0912
0.224	(+ 5%)	1.05	0.2352
0.144	(- 10%)	0.90	0.1296
1.000			0.9400

The EV of cash inflows, allowing for the three additional factors, will be 94% of the original estimates.

Year	Cash inflows (0.94 of original estimate)	Cash outflows	Net cash flow	Discount factor at 10%	PV
	$m	$m	$m		$m
0	(6.25)		(6.25)	1.000	(6.25)
1	2.82	1.50	1.32	0.909	1.20
2	3.76	1.80	1.96	0.826	1.62
3	4.70	2.40	2.30	0.751	1.73
4	3.76	1.70	2.06	0.683	1.41
5	1.88	1.00	1.88	0.621	1.17
				NPV	+ 0.88

16 Sensitivity

(a) The residual value of the equipment at the end of year 5 will be 30% × $3 million = $900,000.

Year	Cash flow	Discount factor at 8%	Present value
	$		$
0	(3,000,000)	1.000	(3,000,000)
1	400,000	0.926	370,400
2	800,000	0.857	685,600
3	800,000	0.794	635,200
4	700,000	0.735	514,500
5	400,000	0.681	272,400
5	900,000	0.681	612,900
Net present value			+ 91,000

(b) **Sensitivity analysis**

(i) *Cost of equipment*

The estimated PV of the cost of the equipment, allowing for a residual value of 30% of cost after five years, is:

3,000,000 − (0.681 × 0.30 × 3,000,000) = 2,387,100.

This estimate can be wrong by $105,400 before the project ceases to have a positive NPV. The cost of the equipment can therefore be higher by (91,000/2,387,100) = 3.8%.

(ii) *Residual value of equipment*

The estimated PV of the residual value is $612,900. This estimate can be wrong by $105,400 before the project ceases to have a positive NPV. The PV of the residual value could therefore be (612,900 − 105,400) = $521,900.

The residual value (without discounting) could therefore be $507,500/0.681 = $745,228. This is 24.8% of the original cost of $3,000,000.

The residual value could therefore be as low as about 25% of cost before the project ceased to have a positive NPV.

((iii),(iv) and (v)) Sales revenue and annual costs

Workings

The estimated contribution/sales ratio is 40%, therefore sales revenue will be 100/40 = 2.5 times annual contribution. Variable costs will be 60/40 = 1.5 times annual contribution. Fixed costs are $200,000 each year; therefore total contribution is $200,000 more than the annual net cash flow.

Year	Contribution	PV factor at 8%	Total	Revenue PV	Total	Variable costs PV
	$000		$000	$	$000	$000
1	600	0.926	1,500	1,389,000	900	833,400
2	1,000	0.857	3,500	2,142,500	1,500	1,285,500
3	1,000	0.794	2,500	1,985,000	1,500	1,191,000
4	900	0.735	2,250	1,653,750	1,350	992,250
5	600	0.681	1,500	1,021,500	900	612,900
				8,191,750		4,915,050

The PV of annual fixed costs = $200,000 × discount factor for years 1 – 5 at 8%

= $200,000 × 3.993 = $798,600.

Sales revenue: The PV of sales revenue could be lower by $91,000 before the project ceases to have a positive NPV. Sales revenue could therefore be lower by 91,000/8,245,750 = about 1.3%.

Similarly, **variable costs** could be higher by (91,000/4,947,450) 2.1% before the project ceases to have a positive NPV.

Similarly, **fixed costs** could be higher by (91,000/798,600) 13.2% before the project ceases to have a positive NPV.

(c)   The positive NPV of the project appears to depend on the accuracy of the cash flows. If these are only a small amount worse than estimated, the NPV will be negative. The project is particularly sensitive to estimates of sales revenue, variable costs (and the contribution/sales ratio), the cost of the equipment and its residual value.

This suggests that the project could be high-risk.

17   The Jin Company

(a)

Tutorial note. There are two ways of calculating the taxation cash flows. One approach is to calculate the tax on the cash profits ignoring capital allowances, and then to calculate the savings in tax payments because of the capital allowances separately. The second approach is to calculate the profit liable to tax in each year and the tax on that profit. Both methods should produce the same net cash flows. The second approach is used here.

Machine A

Workings

	Year 1	Year 2	Year 3	Year 4
Cost $600,000	$	$	$	$
Capital allowance (25%)	150,000	112,500	84,375	253,125
Written down value (WDV)	450,000	337,500	253,125	0
Operating cash flow	470,000	520,000	490,000	450,000
Capital allowance	150,000	112,500	84,375	253,125
Profit liable for tax	320,000	407,500	405,625	196,875
Tax at 30% on the profit	96,000	122,250	121,688	59,063

	Year 0	Year 1	Year 2	Year 3	Year 4	Year 5
	$	$	$	$	$	
Machine	(600,000)					
Working capital	(100,000)				100,000	
Operating cash flow		470,000	520,000	490,000	450,000	
Tax (one year in arrears)			(96,000)	(122,250)	(121,688)	(59,063)
Net cash flow	(700,000)	470,000	424,000	367,750	428,312	(59,063)
Discount factor 10%	1.000	0.909	0.826	0.751	0.683	0.621
Present value	(700,000)	427,230	350,224	276,180	292,537	(36,678)

NPV = + $609,493

Machine B

Workings

	Year 1	Year 2	Year 3	Year 4	Year 5
	$	$	$	$	$
Cost $750,000					
Capital allowance (25%)	187,500	140,625	105,469	79,102	237,304
Written down value (WDV)	562,500	421,875	316,406	237,304	0
Operating cash flow	580,000	640,000	500,000	500,000	400,000
Capital allowance	(187,500)	(140,625)	(105,469)	(79,102)	(237,304)
Profit liable to tax	392,500	499,375	394,531	420,898	162,696
Tax at 30% on the profit	117,750	149,813	118,359	126,269	48,809

	Year 0	Year 1	Year 2	Year 3	Year 4	Year 5	Year 6
	$	$	$	$	$	$	$
Machine	(750,000)						
Working capital	(200,000)					200,000	
Operating cash flow		580,000	640,000	500,000	500,000	400,000	
Tax (one year in arrears)			(117,750)	(149,813)	(118,359)	(126,269)	(48,809)
Net cash flow	(950,000)	580,000	522,250	350,187	381,641	473,731	(48,809)
Discount factor 10%	1.000	0.909	0.826	0.751	0.683	0.621	0.564
Present value	(950,000)	527,220	431,379	262,990	260,661	294,187	(27,528)

NPV = + $798,909

(b)

	Machine A	Machine B
	$	$
Year 0 spending	(700,000)	(950,000)
Year 1 net cash flow	470,000	580,000
	(230,000)	(370,000)
Year 2 net cash flow	424,000	522,250
	194,000	152,250

Payback will be during year 2 for both machines.

Machine A. Payback = 1 year + (230,000/424,000) years = 1.54 years.
Machine B. Payback = 1 year + (370,000/522,250) years = 1.71 years.

(c)
Here is no information to assess whether strategic factors and non-financial factors might affect the choice between Machine A and Machine B.

On purely financial grounds, Machine B has the higher NPV, but this is for a five-year project whereas the Machine A project would be only four years. Machine A has the slightly earlier payback period.

The recommendation on financial grounds should be to select the machine that will provide the higher equivalent annual value.

	Machine A		Machine B
NPV	$609,493	NPV	$798,909
Annuity factor at 10%, Years 1 - 4	3.170	Annuity factor at 10%, Years 1 - 5	3.791
Equivalent annual value	$192,269		$210,738

Machine B will provide the higher equivalent annual value of benefits, and should therefore be chosen in preference to Machine A.

18   Growth objective

Sales

Sales growth: Year 2 compared with Year 1	20.0%
Sales growth: 1st six months of Year 2 compared with 1st six months of Year 1	28.1%
Sales growth: 2nd six months of Year 2 compared with 2nd six months of Year 1	5.0%

Sales increased by 20% in Year 2 compared with Year 1. However, the strong growth in sales occurred in the first six months of the year (28% compared with the same period in Year 1). In the second half of the year, sales growth compared with the same period in Year 1 was down to 5%. There is insufficient information to judge whether the growth in sales revenue is slowing down or coming to an end.

Net profit

There was no increase in net profit between Year 1 and Year 2. The increase in sales (20%) is offset by an increase of 30.4% in operating costs and some interest charges. In terms of annual net profit, the business is therefore not growing.

If a part-time employee is the equivalent of 50% of a full-time employee, there were 415 equivalent full time employees in Year 1 (260 + 50% × 310). There were 565 equivalent full time employees in Year 2 (318 + 50% × 494). Sales revenue per equivalent full-time employee was therefore $62,651 in Year 1 and $55,221 in Year 2. This fall in employee productivity is one reason for the failure to achieve growth in the annual net profit.

Investment

The investment in non-current assets has risen by just 5%, but the investment in working capital has doubled. The increase in net assets has been almost entirely financed by borrowing. (Presumably, this means that most of the profits earned in Year 1 have been paid in taxation or distributed as dividends to shareholders.)

It is difficult to draw definite conclusions from the limited amount of data, but management should be concerned about a 100% increase in working capital, when the increase in annual sales is only 20%. Could there be large quantities of unsold inventory as a result of the decline in sales growth in the second half of the year?

It is not clear why it was considered necessary to borrow $9,000,000 when increases in non-current assets have been only $1,300,000. It would appear that the new borrowing might be financing unnecessary working capital investment, and not investment in non-current assets for longer-term development.

On the other hand, investment in non-current assets will probably need to exceed 5% per year (by a large amount) if the company is to achieve significant long-term growth in its business.

Product range/new product sales

The data about new products is difficult to interpret, because there is no information about the total size of the product portfolio and no information about whether the new products sold well or badly.

19   Gap analysis

(a) Workings

Budgeted variable costs per unit	$000
Material and labour costs	16,000
Variable other production costs (25% × 8,000)	2,000
Variable marketing and distribution costs (1/3 × 12,000)	4,000
Total variable costs	22,000

Volume of production and sales	$80,000
Budgeted variable cost per unit	275
Budgeted contribution per unit (600 – 275)	325

Budgeted annual fixed costs	$000
Fixed other production costs (75% × 8,000)	6,000
Fixed marketing and distribution costs (2/3 × 12,000)	8,000
Administration costs	10,000
Total annual fixed costs	24,000

Strategy 1	
Increase in sales (units)	5,000
	$000
Increase in total annual contribution ($325 × 5,000)	1,625
Increase in annual fixed costs	1,200
Increase in annual profit	425

Strategy 2

	$25
Increase in sales price and unit contribution	
	$000
Increase in total annual contribution ($25 × 80,000 units)	2,000
Increase in annual fixed costs	1,500
Increase in annual profit	500

Strategy 2

Reduction in variable cost per unit (20% × $275)	$55
Therefore increase in unit contribution	$55
	$000
Increase in total annual contribution ($55 × 80,000 units)	4,400
Increase in annual fixed costs	3,500
Increase in annual profit	900

(b)

Taking all three strategies together	$000	$000
Sales (85,000 units at $625 per unit)		53,125
Variable costs (85,000 × $220 per unit)		18,700
Total contribution		
Fixed costs		34,425
In the original budget	24,000	
Extra fixed costs of strategies 1, 2 and 3	6,200	
		30,200
Profit		4,225

	$000	$000
Profit taking all three strategies together		4,225
Original budget profit		2,000
Difference		2,225
Extra profit from Strategy 1 only	425	
Extra profit from Strategy 2 only	500	
Extra profit from Strategy 3 only	900	
		1,825
Balancing figure		400

The balancing figure comes from the combination of the three strategies. The company will sell 5,000 units more than in the original budget, and the contribution per unit will be $80 per unit higher ($25 per unit from strategy 2 and $55 per unit from strategy 3).

5,000 extra units of sale × $80 extra contribution per unit = Extra total contribution of $400,000.

Gap analysis

	$000	$000
Target profit		4,000
Original budget profit		2,000
Profit gap		2,000
Extra profit from Strategy 1 only	425	
Extra profit from Strategy 2 only	500	
Extra profit from Strategy 3 only	900	
Extra profit from combination of three strategies	400	
		2,225
Profit in excess of the 'gap'		225

Conclusion: Strategies 1, 2 and 3 together will successfully close the profit gap, if the targets for each of the strategies can be achieved.

20 Zero based budgeting

Zero based budgeting is most useful when:

■ There is a lot of budget slack, and wasteful spending. Zero based budgeting can be much more effective than incremental budgeting in identifying and eliminating unnecessary expenditure in a budget.

■ There is a shortage of resources for 'overhead' spending, and decisions have to be made about priorities for spending.

Zero based budgeting is more effective for the planning and control of overhead spending on overhead activities than for controlling direct costs of production.

A zero based budgeting operation can be time-consuming and expensive. It should not be needed every year. A ZBB approach to the budget might be sufficient, say, every three or four years.

21 Marginal

(a) When p = 250, q = 400,000.

The quantity sold will fall by 20,000 for every $10 increase in price.

Therefore the price when q = 0 will be 250 + [(400,000/20,000) × $10] = 450

The price function can be stated as:

$P_q = 450 - (10/20,000)q = 450 - 0.0005q$.

Total revenue = pq = $(450 - 0.0005q)q = 450q - 0.0005q^2$

Marginal revenue = $450 - (2 \times 0.0005 \times q) = 450 - 0.001q$

Marginal cost = variable cost per unit = 210.

Profit is maximised where MR = MC:

$450 - 0.001q = 210$

$0.001q = 240$

q = 240,000 units.

At this volume of sales, p = 450 – 0.0005 (240,000) = 330.

Profit is maximised at a price of $330 per unit, and annual sales will be 240,000 units.

	$000
Sales (240,000 × 330)	79,200
Variable costs (240,000 × 210)	50,400
Contribution	28,800
Fixed costs	20,000
Profit	8,800

The annual profit will be $8,800,000.

(b)   Profit = Total revenue – Total costs

= $(450q – 0.0005q^2) – (210q + 20,000,000)$

= $– 0.0005q^2 + 240q – 20,000,000$

At break-even point, profit = 0:

$– 0.0005q^2 + 240q – 20,000,000 = 0$

Re-arranging:

$0.0005q^2 - 240q + 20,000,000 = 0$

The break-even points can be calculated as the values for x that solve the following equation:

$$x = \frac{-b +/ - \sqrt{b^2 - 4ac}}{2a}$$

$$q = \frac{+240 +/ - \sqrt{(240)^2 - 4(0.0005)(20,000,000)}}{2(0.0005)}$$

The two break-even points

(1)   q = (+ 240 + 132.67)/0.0010 = 372,670 [and p = 450 – 0.0005(372,670) = $263.67]

or

(2)   q = (+ 240 – 132.67)/0.0010 = 107,330 [and p = 450 – 0.0005(107,030) = $396.34]

22   MC = MR

(a)   The demand falls by 1,000 units for every $20 increase in price.

Demand will be 0 when the sales price is $50 + $20 × (1,000/1,000) = $70. The quantity demanded rises by 20/1,000 = 0.02 for every unit of demand.

The **demand curve** can therefore be expressed as:

P = 70 – 0.02Q

(b)   **Total revenue** = PQ = (70 – 0.02Q)Q
= 70Q – 0.02Q²

(c)   Marginal revenue = 70 – 0.04Q
Marginal cost = 8

Profit is maximised where MC = MR
8 = 70 – 0.04Q
Q = 62/0.04 = 1,550

P = 70 – 0.02Q = 70 – 0.02 (1,550) = 39.

The profit is maximised at a price of $39, when demand will be 1,550 units.
Contribution per unit will be $31 ($39 – $8).
Total contribution will be $48,050 ($31 × 1,550).

23   Snap Company

(a)   (i)   **Full cost pricing plus, on the current basis**

	$000
Direct materials	12
Direct labour	8
Direct cost	20
Production overheads (100% of direct cost)	20
Full production cost	40
Administrative and marketing overheads (25%)	10
Full cost of sale	50
Profit (20% of full cost of sale)	10
Selling price for order (5,000 units)	60

Sales price per unit = $12.

(ii)   **Price to maintain budgeted profit of $50,000**

If sales of SP8 falls are 25% below budget, the expected profit will be as follows:

		$000
Direct costs	75% × 100,000	75.0
Variable overheads	75% × 50,000	37.5
Total variable costs		112.5
Fixed production overhead		50.0
Other fixed overheads		50.0
Total costs		212.5
Sales	75% × 300,000	225.0
Profit		12.5

In order to make a profit of $50,000 for the year, the simplified units of SP8 must make $37,500 contribution to profit. The price for the order should be as follows:

	$000
Materials	12.0
Labour	8.0
Direct cost	20.0
Variable overhead (see note)	10.0
Variable cost	30.0
Contribution	37.5
Selling price	67.5

Note: Variable overheads are assumed to vary with direct materials cost. In the original budget variable overheads, are $50,000 and direct material costs are $60,000. Variable overheads are therefore 50/60 × material costs. For the simplified units, variable overheads will be $12,000 × 50/60 = $10,000.

The selling price per unit would need to be $67,500/5,000 units = $13.50.

(b) Advice

The price of SP8 is currently $15 ($300,000/20,000 units). The price for the simplified units of SP8 must be lower than this; otherwise the customer will not buy them.

A price of $13.50 is needed to achieve the budgeted profit, but the customer may be unwilling to pay this amount. A price of $12 will give a profit of 20% on full cost, using the budgeted absorption rates for overhead, but there will be some under-absorbed overheads.

Any price in excess of the minimum price of $30,000 ($6 per unit) will make profit higher than it will be if the simplified units are not sold to the customer.

However, the company must think of the longer term. Will the customer want to buy more units of the simplified product next year? If so, the company will want to charge a price at which it will make satisfactory profits.

The recommendation should therefore be to negotiate with the customer. If the agreed price is lower than $13.50, Snap Co might want to warn the customer than more units of the simplified SP8 might not be available in the future, except at a higher price.

24 Bridge Company

(a) Budgeted variable production costs

	Cost in current year	Inflation	Cost next year Current material	New material
	$	%		
Direct material	30	20	36.0	31.25
Direct labour	10	5	10.5	10.50
Variable o'hd	10	5	10.5	10.50
	50		57.0	52.25
Cost of rejected units (5%)				2.75
				55.00

Using the cheaper substitute material will reduce the variable unit cost by $2, but fixed costs will increase by $30,000. Since annual sales at the current price will be 20,000 units, it will be more profitable to use the cheaper material.

The unit variable cost will be $55.

Annual fixed costs will be:

	$
Costs in the current year ($10 × 20,000 units)	200,000
Add inflation (10%)	20,000
Inspection costs	30,000
Total fixed costs for the year	250,000

(b) Optimal selling price

Method 1

It is assumed that the only sales prices to be considered are those in the sales manager's estimates of sales demand.

The variable cost will be $55 per unit.

Price	Contribution/unit	Sales	Total contribution
$	$	000 units	$000
80	25	25	625
84	29	23	667
88	33	21	693
90	35	20	700
92	37	19	703
96	41	17	697
100	45	15	675

Contribution will be maximised at a price of $92, and sales will be 19,00 units.

	$
Total contribution	703,000
Fixed costs	250,000
Profit	453,000

Method 2

It is assumed that the sales manager has identified a straight-line demand curve, and any sales price on this curve may be selected.

Sales demand falls by 1,000 units for every $2 increase in the sales price.

Sales demand will be 0 when the sales price is $130 [$100 + (15 × $2)]

Demand curve:

$P = 130 - 2Q$, where Q is sales demand in 000s units

Total revenue $TR = (130 - 2Q)Q = 130Q - 2Q^2$

Marginal revenue $MR = 130 - 4Q$

Marginal cost MC = variable cost per unit = 55.

Profit is maximised when $MR = MC$

$130 - 4Q = 55$

$Q = 18.75$

Price $= 130 - 2(18.75) = \$92.50$.

Profit will be maximised at a price of $92.50, and the contribution per unit will be $37.50.

	$
Total contribution (18,750 × $37.50)	703,125
Fixed costs	250,000
Profit	453,125

25 Responsibility

(a) We are told that decisions about capital investment and borrowing are taken at head office. It would therefore be appropriate to look at the performance of the division over which the managing director has control – sales revenue and operating costs, but not depreciation or interest.

Sales revenue minus operating costs provides a measure of **profit or earnings before interest, depreciation and amortisation (EBITDA).**

	Year 1	Year 2	Year 3	Year 4
	$000	$000	$000	$000
Sales revenue	172	646	810	1,792
Operating costs	167	620	718	1,490
EBITDA	5	26	92	302

This indicates improving performance over each year of the four-year period.

(b) Controllable performance has been improving each year. There has also been a continuing improvement in the ratio of EBITDA to sales revenue.

On the basis of the information available, the managing director's view is justified.

However, senior management should assess the return that the company is obtaining on its investment in the Fenland Division. Presumably, there was an investment plan for the project, containing an estimate of the profits that the division should be expected to make.

■ If sales are lower than expected, or if costs are higher than expected, the managing director of the division might be asked to give reasons why performance has not been better.

■ If the size of the investment or the cost of borrowing has been more than expected, the poor performance should be attributed to the managers responsible for the investment and borrowing decisions.

26 Crosstreets Hotel

A well-designed management information system should provide relevant, accurate and timely information to all levels of management. Hence the introduction of a new system should not only allow the directors to monitor performance, but may actively help to address the issue of declining profits by providing greater feedback to tactical and operational managers. There should be an online link between each hotel and head office so that data and information can be transmitted quickly in both directions.

(a) and (b)   Periodic reports

The computerisation of hotel records and an online link to head office allow the head office to acquire and assimilate large volumes of data rapidly. This would permit monthly financial statements to be produced for each hotel in time for directors to review them and action their findings whilst the implications are still relevant.

The statements should comprise balance sheet, cash flow and income statement, and would enable directors to gain an overview of the effects of local management decisions and the effectiveness of corporate policy on a regional basis.

These periodic reports should include comparative data in addition to actual data. Figures could be included for budget/previous periods/industry data. Variances could be reported.

Demand reports

The new system should also be capable of producing a range of reports on demand, so that senior management can assess high-risk aspects of the business by obtaining information whenever they need it.

(i)   Room occupancy report

This report gives details of the proportion or percentage of a hotel's available rooms that were occupied. By using information from registration cards, it should be possible to split this figure between business and non-business users.

The incorporation of room charge-out rates into the same report would enable management to:

- assess the accuracy of revenues from room-letting

- identify whether variations in regional rates have a significant impact on occupancy rates and overall profitability

- identify any trends in business/non-business usage and the opportunity for differential pricing and attracting more guests.

Room rates should also be compared to a centralised master file of approved rates and discounts to ensure hotel managers are not offering rooms at below cost in an attempt to attract business.

To ensure all income from rooms is recorded, the room occupancy report should compare rooms for which income has been recorded to a housekeeper's report giving details of the rooms cleaned.

(ii)   Late payments report

It is assumed that some regular business customers are given credit. A late payments report should highlight all receivables that are more than, say, 60 days overdue.

Bad debts could be a major contributor to declining profits, particularly if the hotels catering for business travellers are taking block corporate bookings.

As an additional control to ensure that all reported bookings are genuine, this report should also include a comparison of revenues with a direct room cost such as laundry bills.

(iii) Restaurant sales report

This report should compare total revenues from the restaurant to the room occupancy rate and also the number of restaurant table bookings, thereby allowing the directors to ascertain if unduly preferential arrangements are being allowed by some of their hotels.

Differentiation should also be made between billings to residents and non-residents, as this will enable attention to be focused on this separate revenue source. This is important if the restaurant is not being operated at capacity such that non-residents could be a useful source of income.

(iv) Bar sales report

Total bar sales should be compared for restaurant sales, but without the division between residents and non-residents (because reliable information about this division would be difficult to obtain in view of the large number of cash transactions).

(v) Restaurant and bar inventories report

Physical control over bar and restaurant inventories is difficult to maintain and yet losses could have a potentially significant effect on profits.

An official from head office should attend a physical count at each hotel, and this figure should then act as the benchmark for subsequent movements and be "enforced" by random spot checks.

The inventories report should compare the verified figure as adjusted for subsequent purchases and sales to occupancy rate and highlight any significant percentage variation from preceding months (indicating pilferage and misappropriation). The overall holding of inventory in each hotel should be compared to inventory turnover to ensure the former does not represent an excessive usage of working capital.

(vi) Cash availability report

Many of the bar and restaurant takings of each hotel will be in cash; as with inventories, cash is easily susceptible to misappropriation.

The head office directors will require a report that summarises the cash takings and receipts, and makes a comparison between hotels making allowances for differences in the number and type of resident (for example, business users may utilise corporate client cards rather than their own cash).

(vii) Wages report

Given that wages, often casual wages, represent a significant item of cash expenditure for hotels and one which can be directly related to revenue, a report should be produced detailing the number of wage-earning staff per week and their wages.

This could then be compared to revenue reports to identify any significant departures from the expected relationship. This may indicate general inefficiency capable of improvement or fraud.

Error/exception reports

A unique feature of computerised systems is their ability to search through large volumes of data and extract only those figures of significance to users.

These exception reports should be produced automatically to highlight matters such as:

- hotel revenue falling below budget (for example, by more than 10%)
- group cash reserves/funding requirements exceeding available limits
- hotels selling room accommodation below the approved room rate.

27 Three services

(a) Workings

Revenue:

Service A: contract customers – 350,000 × 60% × \$9 × 1.03 = \$1,946,700

Service A: non-contract customers – 350,000 × 40% × \$9 × 1.30 × 1.03 = \$1,687,140

Service B: contract customers – 250,000 × 60% × \$15 × 1.03 = \$2,317,500

Service B: non-contract customers – 250,000 × 40% × \$15 × 1.50 × 1.03 = \$2,317,500

Service C: contract customers – 20,000 × 80% × \$300 × 1.03 = \$4,944,000

Service C: non-contract customers 20,000 × 20% × \$300 × 1.20 × 1.03 = \$1,483,200

Salaries: \$45,000 × 85 employees × 1.05 = \$4,016,250

Sundry operational costs: \$4,000,000 × 1.05 = \$4,200,000

Fuel

Services A and B – 400 km × 50 vehicles × 300 days × \$0.40 = \$2,400,000

Service C – 600 km × 18 vehicles × 300 days × \$0.80 = \$2,592,000

Budgeted income statement for the year to 31 December Year 2

	Service A	Service B	Service C	Total
Revenue:	$	$	$	$
Contract customers	1,946,700	2,317,500	4,944,000	9,208,200
Non-contract customers	1,687,140	2,317,500	1,483,200	5,487,840
Total revenue	3,633,840	4,635,000	6,427,200	14,696,040
Costs:				
Salaries			4,016,250	
Fuel:				
Services A and B		2,400,000		
Service C		2,592,000		
			4,992,000	
Sundry operational costs			4,200,000	
Total costs				13,208,250
Net profit				1,487,790

(b) Vehicle utilisation

There is no information about weight carried, only about distance travelled.

All vehicles were used for 300 days in the year. Presumably, vehicles might be used for 365 days per year, indicating an overall utilisation ratio for all vehicles of 82.2%.

Other utilisation measure: a revenue measure might be used as an indication of the utilisation of vehicles.

	Services A and B	Service C
Revenue per vehicle	($8,268,840/50) $165,377	($6,427,200/18) $357,067

Kilometres travelled each year might also be a measure of utilisation:

- Service A and B vehicles travel on average $(400 \times 300) = 120{,}000$ kilometres each year.

- Service C vehicles travel on average $(600 \times 300) = 180{,}000$ kilometres each year.

28   Private medical practice

Workings

Total number of patients per year = 5 doctors × 18 patients per day × 5 days per week × 46 weeks per year = 20,700.

		Patients		
	Total	Adults	Children	65 years and over
	20,700	(45%) = 9,315	(25%) = 5,175	(30%) = 6,210
Treatment				
None: 20%		1,863.0	1,035.0	1,242
Minor: 70%		6,520.5	3,622.5	4,347
Major: 10%		931.5	517.5	621

Revenue:

Adults, no treatment: $1{,}863 \times \$50 = \$93{,}150$

Adults, minor treatment: $6{,}520.5 \times \$200 = \$1{,}304{,}100$

Adults, major treatment: $931.5 \times \$600 = \$558{,}900$

Children, no treatment: $1{,}035 \times \$30 = \$31{,}050$

Children, minor treatment: $3{,}622.5 \times \$120 = \$434{,}700$

Children, major treatment: $517.5 \times \$280 = \$144{,}900$

65 years and over, no treatment: $1{,}242 \times \$30 = \$37{,}260$

65 years and over, minor treatment: $4{,}347 \times \$120 = \$521{,}640$

65 years and over, major treatment: $621 \times \$280 = \$173{,}880$.

Budgeted income statement for the year to [...]

	Adults	Children	Aged 65 years and over	Total
Revenue:	$	$	$	$
No treatment	93,150	31,050	37,260	161,460
Minor treatment	1,304,100	434,700	521,640	2,260,440
Major treatment	558,900	144,900	173,880	877,680
Total revenue	1,956,150	610,650	732,780	3,299,580
Costs:				
Salaries				
Doctors (5 × $240,000)		1,200,000		
Assistants (5 × $100,000)		500,000		
Administrators (2 × $80,000)		160,000		
		1,860,000		
Bonus		93,000		
			1,953,000	
Materials costs			414,300	
Other costs			733,600	
Total costs				3,100,900
Net profit				198,680

29   Train times

	Northern Region		Southern Region	
	Inter-city services	Suburban services	Inter-city services	Suburban services
Target for completion on time	90%	95%	90%	95%
Actual % on time	82.7%	73.8%	88.3%	91.9%
% not on time, but less than 5 minutes late	7.3%	12.9%	5.6%	4.0%
% between 5 and 10 minutes late	6.0%	10.6%	2.2%	2.9%
% cancelled	3.2%	1.2%	0.1%	0.5%
	99.2%	98.5%	96.2%	99.3%
Over 10 minutes late (balance)	0.8%	1.5%	3.8%	0.7%
	100.0%	100.0%	100.0%	100.0%

Assessment of performance

Neither region has achieved its target for journeys completed on time, although Southern Region appears to be closer to achieving its targets.

Most of the late-completed journeys were completed within ten minutes of the scheduled time.

Northern Region has a fairly large proportion of cancelled trains – certainly much higher than Southern Region. However, Southern Region has a comparatively high proportion of inter-city journeys finishing over ten minutes late.

The managers of the two regions should be asked to provide a report on these aspects of performance.

30 Non-financial performance measurements

Service quality

(1) The percentage of customers who take their account away in a period (the rate of 'churn')

(2) The number of complaints in a period

(3) A measure of 'satisfaction' from responses by customers to a questionnaire about the bank's services

(4) In some aspects of service, speed of response (for example, the average time to answer telephone calls from customers: these time measures can be obtained from the bank's telephone systems).

Marketing effectiveness

(1) The number of new accounts or growth rate in new accounts in the period

(2) The growth in major business activities in the period (lending, foreign exchange dealing, and so on)

(3) Market share

Personnel

(1) The rate of absenteeism in the period

(2) The amount of staff training in the period (total training days, for example)

(3) The rate of staff turnover

(4) It might be possible to identify ways of measuring staff efficiency, but this can be difficult when much of the work is non-standard or non-routine.

31 Mission

Question 1: Meaning of corporate mission. Link to corporate strategy

A corporate mission embodies the overall purposes of an organisation. A corporate mission should answer fundamental questions such as:

- What are the values of a company?
- What is its culture?
- Why does the company exist?
- Who will be served by company and benefit from it?
- What products or services will be provided?

The majority of mission statements are presented using general concepts rather than detailed specifications.

In order to prepare an effective strategic plan, senior management should be conscious of the organisation's mission.

One view is that the mission statement is very important and a strategic plan cannot be prepared without reference to it.

An opposing view is that a mission statement is the end result of the strategic-planning process. Some critics argue that a mission statement has no practical value at all.

Question 2: The origin of a mission statement and what it covers

The mission statement should be written or approved by the company's board of directors. It does not contain quantitative targets. It might cover the following areas:

(a) The kinds of products and services the company aims to provide

(b) The customers to be served

(c) The markets in which the company expects to operate

(d) An overview of the company's philosophy or culture

(e) The company's attitude towards social obligations (corporate social responsibility)

(f) The way in which the company wants to be seen by the public (its reputation).

Question 3: Benefits of a mission statement

A company might gain several benefits from a mission statement. It should help decision-makers to focus on fundamental issues in strategic planning, and ensure that strategic plans do not conflict with the basic purpose of the organisation.

The benefits of a mission statement may be summarised as follows:

- Employees can use it to get an understanding of the company's purpose and philosophy.

- The company's aspirations are expressed in terms of a long-range vision.

- The purpose the company operates will be clearly stated. This should help management to develop co-ordinated plans that are consistent with this purpose.

- A statement about the purpose of the company should help planners to allocate resources more effectively.

32 Customer profitability

Workings

Product	Units	Contribution per unit	Total contribution	Total sales revenue
		$	$	$
A	100,000	1.20	120,000	360,000
B	150,000	0.50	75,000	375,000
C	120,000	1.20	144,000	480,000
D	180,000	0.90	162,000	432,000
E	80,000	2.00	160,000	480,000
			661,000	2,127,000

Contribution per customer category

	Total contribution	Category of customer			
		C1	C2	C3	C4
	$	$	$	$	$
Product A	120,000	12,000	24,000	24,000	60,000
Product B	75,000	30,000	0	22,500	22,500
Product C	144,000	14,400	28,800	14,400	86,400
Product D	162,000	48,600	16,200	32,400	64,800
Product E	160,000	32,000	0	32,000	96,000
Total	661,000	137,000	69,000	125,300	329,700

Rebates

	Total sales		C3		C4
	$		$		$
Product A	360,000	20%	72,000	50%	180,000
Product B	375,000	30%	112,500	30%	112,500
Product C	480,000	10%	48,000	60%	288,000
Product D	432,000	20%	86,400	40%	172,800
Product E	480,000	20%	96,000	60%	288,000
Total			414,900		1,041,300
Rebate %			5%		10%
Rebate in $			$20,745		$104,130

ABC apportionment rates

	Number of deliveries	Km per delivery	Total kilometres
C1	40	100	4,000
C2	80	200	16,000
C3	50	300	15,000
C4	100	150	15,000
			50,000

Apportionment rates

- Delivery costs: $250,000/50,000 = $5 per kilometre
- Order processing: $105,000/(30 + 70 + 50 + 60) = $500 per order
- Promotion events: $30,000/12 = $2,500 per event.

Statement of customer profitability

	C1	C2	C3	C4	Total
	$	$	$	$	$
Contribution	137,000	69,000	125,300	329,700	661,000
Rebates	0	0	(20,745)	(104,130)	(124,875)
	137,000	69,000	104,555	225,570	536,125
Activity costs					
Delivery	(20,000)	(80,000)	(75,000)	(75,000)	(250,000)
Order processing	(15,000)	(35,000)	(25,000)	(30,000)	(105,000)
Promotion events	0	0	(5,000)	(25,000)	(30,000)
Customer profitability	102,000	(46,000)	(445)	95,570	151,125
Other fixed costs					(80,000)
Company profit					71,125

33 RTC

(a)
Workings:

		Year 4			Year 5	
	Hereland	**Thereland**	**Total**	**Hereland**	**Thereland**	**Total**
Gross profit ($000)	1,450	(60)	1,390	1,520	170	1,690
Gross profit/sales	33.7%	(6.3)%	26.5%	33.8%	14.2%	29.6%
Net profit/ sales	20.5%	(18.4)%	11.2%	20.0%	(1.7)%	13.8%
Sales growth				4.7%	26.3%	8.6%
Sales/non-current assets	1.65	3.96	1.84	1.73	2.50	1.85
ROCE (%)			18.9%			19.5%
Gearing (%)			60.9%			36.1%
EBITDA ($000)			1,080			1,305

Notes:

1   ROCE = profit before interest/capital + reserves + loan stock.

2   EBITDA = earnings before interest, depreciation and amortisation.

Analysis

Total growth in sales revenue was 8.6% in Year 5. Sales growth was 4.7% in Hereland, but 26.3% - much stronger - in Thereland.

There was an increase in both the gross profit margin and the net profit margin for RTC. The gross profit margin was up from 26.5% to 29.6%, and the net profit margin was up from 11.2% to 13.8%. There was little change in Hereland, and the improvement is due to the improvement in Thereland, where a gross loss was turned into a gross profit, and the net loss was reduced.

Taking the financial performance of RTC as a whole, return on capital employed improved from 18.9% to 19.5%, and there was an increase in EBITDA from $1.08 million to $1.30 million. EBITDA is a useful approximation of cash flows from operating activities, and the growth in EBITDA would suggest that operational cash flows should be positive, in spite of the large increase in investment in non-current assets.

The ratio of sales to non-current assets remained roughly the same in Year 5 as in Year 4 for RTC as a whole. However, whereas sales per $1 invested in non-current assets went up in Hereland, it fell in Thereland.

Financial gearing fell in Year 5, partly because of the increase in equity invested, and partly due to the reduction on long-term debt. $200,000 of loan stock was redeemed during Year 5.

(b)

The following additional information would be useful:

1   Financial results for Years 1 to 3. This would make it possible to analyse the trends in performance in Homeland, and make a comparison of the early years of operations in Homeland with the initial years of operating in Thereland.

2   It would also be useful to have the financial targets or budgets for Years 4 and 5, so that actual performance can be compared with planned performance.

3   Information about cash flows would also be useful, particularly for RTC as a whole. This would provide data for the analysis of cash management.

4   It would also be helpful to have some information about the market as a whole for scientific conferences in Homeland and Thereland, and in particular the estimated size of the total market and the relative size of major competitors. This would make it possible to carry out some analysis of market share and some competitor analysis.

(c)   Tutorial note: Five suggestions are given here, but other ideas might be equally acceptable.

1   It is difficult to compare the results in Hereland and Thereland because operations in Hereland have been established for five years, and in Thereland they have been established for only three years.

2   The relative size of the total market in each country should also be considered, and the market share that RTC has in each country.

3   The number and size of competitors in each country will affect the relative performance of RTC in homeland and Thereland. Performance should be better in the country where competition is weaker, provided that the overall size of the market in each country is about the same.

4   Data about the average number of delegates at conferences in Hereland and Thereland would also be useful. Profit margins should be higher in the country where average numbers are higher.

5   The availability and cost of conference speakers in each country should be compared. This may affect the gross profit margins in each country.

34   Value for money

(a)   A value for money exercise looks at economy, efficiency and effectiveness in the use of resources.

(1)   **Economy**. A VFM study should look at major items of spending, and assess whether the school is obtaining good value for the money it is spending. For example, is it getting teachers of a suitable quality for the amount it is paying in salaries? Is the school paying sensible prices for books and other equipment, or is it possibly paying prices that are too high? All major items of spending can be investigated in this way, to

establish that resources are of a suitable quality and that the prices paid for them are not too high.

(2) **Efficiency**. A VFM study will also look at the efficiency of using resources. Key resources might be teachers' time and some teaching equipment, such as laboratory equipment and a computer centre. Efficiency can be assessed by measuring the use of these resources, such as average teaching time per teacher per week, average number of hours of computer time used per computer per day, and so on.

(3) **Effectiveness**. The VFM study must have a clear idea of the strategic aims of the school. These may be expressed in terms of the average grades expected in key examinations, or the percentage of school leavers going on to a university education. There may be other key objectives – such as providing an 'all round' education, or providing an education with an emphasis on particular skills, such as the teaching of science or art. The might also be a financial objective, such as operating the school without making a loss. The VFM study should then measure actual performance in these key areas, to establish whether the school is successful. If the school is failing to achieve its objectives, the study should try to establish the causes of the problem.

(b) The VFM study team might benefit from a benchmarking exercise – comparing the performance of the school with the performance of similar schools in the region or country.

35 Decentralisation

(a) (i) **Responsibility accounting** is the structuring of performance reports for individual managers in a way that identifies the factors that are controllable by them and for which they are responsible. Depending on the factors under the control of the manager, responsibility accounting reports may be prepared for cost centres, revenue centres, profit centres or investment centres.

(ii) An **investment centre** is an operating division within an organisation whose manager has responsibility for both the profits of the division and the investments that it makes.

(iii) **Return on investment (ROI)** = The divisional profit divided by the capital employed within that division.

(iv) **Residual income** = Divisional income – a notional interest charge for the investment in capital investment in the division

Residual income = Divisional income – Divisional investment × cost of capital

Note: Both ROI and residual income can be used as:

■ ex ante targets (planning targets) – in order to motivate divisional managers and to guide their decision-making

■ ex post appraisal measures (actual performance measures) – to evaluate the divisional manager's performance.

(b) Divisions M and W

(i) The performance of the two divisions will be evaluated using both ROI and residual income. There is no specific performance target for either division. To compare divisional performance, it is assumed that the division with the higher ROI or residual income has performed 'better'.

	Division M	Division W
ROI	20/200	410/5,000
	10%	8.2%
	$000	$000
Profit	20	410
Less: Interest on investment at 8%	(16)	(400)
Residual income	4	10

Division M has a higher ROI than Division W. However, the reason for this difference in performance may be that Division M has older non-current assets, and is reluctant to invest in new capital equipment. New investments would increase the division's profit but reduce its ROI in the short-term (because capital investment will also be higher).

Division M has a higher residual income than Division W. Therefore, in a situation where both divisional managers are motivated to accept projects that meet the firm's investment criteria (i.e. cost of capital). Division W may therefore have been more successful in finding investments that earn a return above the cost of capital. However, the difference in residual income is only $6,000, but Division W has invested $4.8 more than Division M.

Both divisions have a positive residual income, which means that they have succeeded in investing in projects with accounting returns higher than the company's cost of capital.

(ii) (i) A change in the company's cost of capital will only affect the residual income figure; it has no effect on the ROI. The revised residual income figures for cost of capital at 6% and 10% respectively are as follows:

		Division M	Division W
(1)	**Cost of capital 6%**	**$000**	**$000**
	Profit	20	410
	Less Interest on investment at 6%	(12)	(300)
	Residual income	8	110
(2)	**Cost of capital 10%**		
	Profit	20	410
	Less Interest on investment at 10%	(20)	(500)
	Residual income	0	(90)

If the cost of capital for the company is only 6%, the residual income of both Division M and Division W is higher. The larger size of the investment in Division W results in a proportionally higher RI figure.

On the other hand, if the cost of capital is raised to 10%, Division M is the better performer with a residual income of 0 compared with a negative residual income (a residual loss) of $90,000 for Division W.

36   West Division

	Sales price	Variable cost	Contribution per unit	Sales	Total contribution
	$ per unit	$ per unit	$ per unit	units	$
Product A:					
Titan brand	2.50	1.50	1.00	160,000	160,000
Unbranded	1.50	1.30	0.20	450,000	90,000
Product B:					
Titan brand	3.20	2.00	1.20	120,000	144,000
Unbranded	2.00	1.80	0.20	600,000	120,000
Product C:					
Titan brand	5.00	3.00	2.00	50,000	100,000
					614,000
				$	
Marketing costs				180,000	
Other fixed costs				375,000	
					555,000
					59,000
Notional interest: 10% × $400,000					(40,000)
Residual income					19,000

(a)   ROI = 59,000/400,000 = 14.75%.

(b)   Residual income (see above) = $19,000.

37   Annuity method

(a)   Annual depreciation = $600,000/3 years = $200,000.

	Year 1	Year 2	Year 3
	$	$	$
Average capital employed	500,000	300,000	100,000
Cash profit	300,000	300,000	300,000
Depreciation	200,000	200,000	200,000
Profit	100,000	100,000	100,000
Notional interest at 12%	60,000	36,000	12,000
Residual income	40,000	64,000	88,000

(b)   Annual depreciation = $/Year 1 – 3 annuity factor at 12%

= $600,000/2.402 = $249,792.

	Year 1	Year 2	Year 3
	$	$	$
Cash profit	300,000	300,000	300,000
Depreciation	249,792	249,792	249,792
Residual income	50,208	50,208	50,208

It could be argued that when an investment provides constant annual cash flows over its full life, it is appropriate that the change in annual performance should be a constant amount in each year.

- The annuity method of depreciation applies a constant annual charge for depreciation and notional interest, and when the annual cash flows from an investment are constant in each year, the effect on the residual income is also a constant amount in each year.

■ In contrast, the effect on residual income differs each year over the life of an investment, when notional interest is calculated on the carrying amount (net book value) of the investment.

38 Residual

(a) NPV

Year		Cash flow	Discount factor at 12%	PV
		$		$
0	Cost of investment	(42,000)	1.000	(42,000)
1 – 3	Annual cash flow	19,000	2.402	45,638
	NPV			+ 3,638

(b) ROI

Annual depreciation (straight-line) = $42,000/3 = $14,000.

Annual accounting profit = $5,000

Year	Profit	Average investment	ROI
	$	$	
1	5,000	35,000	14.3%
2	5,000	21,000	23.8%
3	5,000	7,000	71.4%
Average	5,000	21,000	23.8%

Note: Average investment, measured as the net book value of the asset, is the mid-point between $42,000 and $28,000 in Year 1, the mid-point between $28,000 and $14,000 in Year 2, and the mid-point between $14,000 and $0 in Year 3.

(c) The investment centre has been achieving a ROI in excess of 35% each year for several years. Investing in this project will therefore have the effect of bringing ROI down, although the investment is probably quite small in relation to the total size of the investment centre and its assets. The managers of the investment centre would therefore have no particular reason to undertake the investment, even though it has a positive NPV when the cash flows are discounted at 12%.

(d) Residual income

For each year, Years 1 – 3, the residual income would be as follows:

	Year 1	Year 2	Year 3
Average investment	$35,000	$21,000	$7,000
	$	$	$
Profit after depreciation	5,000	5,000	5,000
Notional interest (12% of investment)	4,200	2,520	840
Residual income	800	2,480	4,160

The residual income is positive in each of the three years, although it increases each year as the value of the investment declines.

If the performance of the investment centre is measured by residual income, its managers would be willing to undertake the investment because it will improve the divisional performance by increasing the residual income.

(e)   Residual income and annuity depreciation

If the annuity method is used to calculate annual depreciation, the annual depreciation charge will be:

Cost of investment/12% annuity factor, Years 1 – 3 = $42,000/2.402 = $17,485.

The residual income reported each year for this investment would then be:

	Each year
	$
Profit before depreciation	19,000
Annuity depreciation	17,485
Residual income	1,515

(f)   Connection with NPV

Since the annual profit before deprecation is the same in each year of the project, there is a direct mathematical connection between the residual income using annuity depreciation and the project NPV:

Residual income × Annuity factor (here, for Years 1 – 3 at 12%) = NPV

$1,515 × 2.402 = $3,639. (There is a rounding error of $1.)

39   Uncertain

(a)   Most optimistic assumptions

Year	Equipment	Benefits (+ 6%)	Costs (- 10%)	Net cash flow	Discount factor at 7%	Present value
	$m	$m	$m	$m		$m
0	(7.20)			(7.20)	1.000	(7.200)
1		6.36	2.70	3.66	0.935	3.422
2		8.44	3.60	4.88	0.873	4.260
3		5.30	2.70	2.60	0.816	2.122
						+ 2.604

Year	Net cash flow	Dep'n		Notional interest	Residual income
	$m	$m		$m	$m
1	3.66	(2.40)	7% × $7.2m	(0.50)	+ 0.760
2	4.88	(2.40)	7% × $4.8m	(0.34)	+ 2.140
3	2.60	(2.40)	7% × $2.4m	(0.17)	+ 0.030

(b) Most pessimistic assumptions

Year	Equipment	Benefits (- 6%)	Costs (+ 10%)	Net cash flow	Discount factor at 11%	Present value
	$m	$m	$m	$m		$m
0	(7.20)			(7.20)	1.000	(7.200)
1		5.64	3.30	2.34	0.901	2.108
2		7.52	4.40	3.12	0.812	2.533
3		4.70	3.30	1.40	0.731	1.023
						(1.536)

Year	Net cash flow	Dep'n		Notional interest	Residual income
	$m	$m		$m	$m
1	2.34	(2.40)	11% × $7.2m	(0.79)	(0.750)
2	3.12	(2.40)	11% × $4.8m	(0.53)	+ 0.190
3	1.40	(2.40)	11% × $2.4m	(0.26)	(1.260)

(c) The decision whether or not to go ahead with the project will depend on management's view of risk:

■ What is the probability of the most likely, most pessimistic and most optimistic outcome?

■ What is the appetite of management for risk?

40 Two divisions

(a) An optimal transfer price (or range of transfer prices) is a price for an internally-transferred item at which:

■ the selling division will want to sell units to the other profit centre, because this will add to its divisional profit

■ the buying division will want to buy units from the other profit centre, because this will add to its divisional profit

■ the internal transfer will be in the best interests of the entity as a whole, because it will help to maximise its total profit.

(b) When Division X has spare capacity, its only cost in making and selling extra units of Product B is the variable cost per unit of production, $48. Division Y can buy the product from an external supplier for $55.

It follows that a transfer that is higher than $48 but lower than $55, for additional units of production, will benefit both profit centres as well as the company as a whole. (It is in the best interests of the company to make the units in Division X at a cost of $48 than to buy them externally for $55.)

(c) When Division X is operating at full capacity and has unsatisfied external demand for Product A, it has an opportunity cost if it makes Product B for transfer to Division Y. Product A earns a contribution of $16 per unit ($62 – $46). The minimum transfer price that it would require for Product B is:

	$
Variable cost of production of Product B	48
Opportunity cost: lost contribution from sale of Product A	16
Minimum transfer price to satisfy Division X management	64

Division Y can buy the product from an external supplier for $55, and will not want to buy from Division X at a price of $64. The maximum price it will want to pay is $55.

The company as a whole will benefit if Division X makes and sells Product A.

■ It makes a contribution of $16 from each unit of Product A.

■ If Division X were to make and sell Product B, the company would benefit by only $7. This is the difference in the cost of making the product in Division X ($48) and the cost of buying it externally ($55).

The same quantity of limited resources (direct labour in Division X) is needed for each product, therefore the company benefits by $9 ($16 – $7) from making units of Product A instead of units of Product B.

On the basis of this information, the transfer price for Product X should be $64 as long as there is unsatisfied demand for Product A. At this price, there will be no transfers of Product B.

41   Training company

(a)   If the Liverpool centre has spare capacity, it will be in the best interest of the company for the London centre to use Liverpool trainers, at a variable cost of £450 per day including travel and accommodation, instead of hiring external trainers at a cost of £1,200.

Since the Liverpool centre will have to pay £450 per trainer day, any transfer price per day/daily fee in excess of £450 would add to its profit.

Since the London centre can obtain external trainers for £1,200 per day, any transfer price below this amount would add to its profit.

An appropriate transfer price would therefore be a price anywhere above £450 per day and below £1,200 per day.

(b)   If the Liverpool centre is operating at full capacity and is charging clients £750 per trainer day, there will be an opportunity cost of sending its trainers to work for the London centre. The opportunity cost is the contribution forgone by not using the trainers locally in Liverpool. Assuming that the variable cost of using trainers in Liverpool would be £200 per day, the opportunity cost is £550 (£750 – £200).

The minimum transfer price that the manager of the Liverpool centre would want is:

	£
Variable cost of trainer day	200
Travel and accommodation	250
Opportunity cost: lost contribution	550
Minimum transfer price	1,000

The maximum price that the London centre would be willing to pay is £1,200, which is the cost of using an external trainer.

The company should encourage the use of Liverpool trainers by the London centre, because this will add to the total company profit.

The optimal transfer price is above £1,000 per day, so that the Liverpool centre will benefit from sending trainers to London, but below £1,200 so that the London centre will also benefit.

A transfer price of £1,000 per day might be agreed.

(c) If the Liverpool centre is operating at full capacity and is charging clients £1,100 per trainer day, the opportunity cost of sending its trainers to work for the London centre is £900 (£1,100 − £200).

The minimum transfer price that the manager of the Liverpool centre would want is:

	£
Variable cost of trainer day	200
Travel and accommodation	250
Opportunity cost: lost contribution	900
Minimum transfer price	1,350

The maximum price that the London centre would be willing to pay is £1,200, which is the cost of using an external trainer.

It would be in the best interests of the company as a whole to use the Liverpool trainers to work for Liverpool clients, earning a contribution of £900 per day, rather than use them in London to save net costs of £750 per day (£1,200 − £200 − £250).

The transfer price should be set at £1,350 per trainer day. At this rate, the London centre will use external trainers, and all the Liverpool trainers will be used in Liverpool.

42 Shadow price

(a) The shadow price of the special chemical is the amount by which total contribution would be reduced (or increased) if one unit less (or more) of the chemical were available.

1 kilogram = 1,000 grams; therefore one kilogram of special chemical will produce 100 tablets (1,000/10 grams per tablet).

Shadow price of the chemical	$
Sales value of 100 tablets (× $10)	1,000
Further processing costs in B (× $2)	200
	800
Variable cost of making the chemical in A	500
Shadow price per kilogram of chemical	300

(b)   The special chemical does not have an intermediate market.

■   The ideal transfer price for A is therefore any price above the variable cost of making the chemical, which is $500 per kilogram.

■   The ideal transfer price for B is anything below the net increase in contribution from processing a kilogram of the chemical. This is $1,000 – $200 = $800 per kilogram.

■   There is no single ideal price. Any price in the range above $500 and below $800 should make the managers of both profit centres want to produce up to the capacity in division A.

■   A transfer price in the middle of the range, say $650, might be agreed.

(c)   The transfer price is needed to share the profit from selling the tablets between divisions A and B. It is an internally-negotiated price. Changing the price will not affect the total profit for the company as a whole, provided that division A produces the chemical up to its production capacity.

The transfer price itself should not be used as a basis for judging performance. Having agreed a transfer price, key financial measures of performance will be control over costs for division A and control over costs and the selling price for tablets for division B.

(The divisions are profit centres, and so the performance of the divisional managers should not be assessed on the basis of ROI or residual income.)

43   Bricks

(a)   Profit statements

(i)   *Operating at 80% capacity*

	Transfer price $200			Transfer price $180		
	Group X	Group Y	Total	Group X	Group Y	Total
Sales:						
External	180	240	420	180	240	420
Transfers	120	-	0	108	-	0
Total	300	240	420	288	240	420
Costs						
Transfers	-	(120)	0	-	(108)	0
Variable	(112)	(36)	(148)	(112)	(36)	(148)
Fixed	(100)	(40)	(140)	(100)	(40)	(140)
Total	(212)	(196)	(288)	(212)	(184)	(288)
Profit	88	44	132	76	56	132

(ii)   *Operating at 100% capacity*

	Transfer price $200			Transfer price $180		
	Group X	Group Y	Total	Group X	Group Y	Total
Sales:						
External	180	320	500	180	320	500
Transfers	200	-	0	180	-	0
Total	380	320	500	360	320	500
Costs						
Transfers	-	(200)	0	-	(180)	0
Variable	(140)	(60)	(200)	(140)	(60)	(200)
Fixed	(100)	(40)	(140)	(100)	(40)	(140)
Total	(240)	(300)	(340)	(240)	(280)	(340)
Profit	140	20	160	120	40	160

(b)   The effect of a change in the transfer price from $200 to $180 will result in lower profit for Group X and higher profit for Group Y, but the total profit for the company as a whole will be unaffected.

A reduction in the transfer price to $180 (or possibly lower) is recommended, because this is the price at which Group Y can buy the materials externally. At any price above $180, Group Y will want to buy externally, and this would not be in the interests of the company as a whole.

Significantly, at a transfer price of both $200 and $180, Division Y would suffer a fall in its divisional profit if it reduced the selling price of bricks to $0.32 and increased capacity by 40,000 bricks each month. A reduction in price would be in the best interests of the company as a whole, because total profit would rise from $132,000 per month to $160,000.

(c)   Ignoring the transfer price, the effect on Division Y of reducing the sale price of bricks to $0.32 would be to increase external sales by $80,000 and variable costs in Division Y by $24,000 (400 tonnes × $60). Cash flows would therefore improve by $56,000 per month. To persuade Division Y to take the extra 400 tonnes, the transfer price should not exceed $140 ($56,000/400). This is below the current external market price, although there is strong price competition in the market.

The transfer price for Division X should not be less than the variable cost of production in Division X, which is $70 per tonne.

However, if the transfer price is reduced to $140 per tonne or less, Division X might try to sell more materials in the external market, by reducing the selling price.

It would appear that although the ideal transfer price might be $140 or below, this will not be easily negotiated between the group managers. An imposed settlement may be necessary. Intervention by head office might be needed to impose a transfer price, and require Division Y to reduce its sales price to $0.32.

44   International transfers

(a)   The transfer price for Product P would be $9 less 40% = $5.40.

Division Y could buy from an external supplier at $5 per unit.

The manager of Division Y will want to maximise the profits of the division. The decision will therefore be to purchase Product P from the external supplier. This will be $0.40 per unit cheaper than buying from Division X.

This decision will be made regardless of the annual purchase quantity.

(b)   The annual profit of the company as a whole will be maximised if the marginal revenue for the company from making the transfers exceeds the opportunity cost.

(i)   Annual purchases: 50,000 units of Product P

Division X has spare production capacity for 50,000 units of Product P.

The marginal cost to Division X and to the company as a whole from making and transferring 50,000 units of Product P is therefore the marginal cost of producing them, $3.40 per unit.

A transfer price anywhere above $3.40 and below $5 would increase the annual profit of Division X and would make Division Y want to buy the units from Division X and not externally at $5.

(ii)   Annual purchases: 120,000 units of Product P

Division X has spare production capacity for 50,000 units of Product P, but producing the additional 70,000 units means that production and sales of Product Q would have to be reduced by 70,000 units.

The opportunity cost for Division X and for the company as a whole of transferring 120,000 units to Division Y is therefore:

		$
Variable cost of making 120,000 units	× $3.40	408,000
Contribution lost: 70,000 units of Product Q	× $0.50	35,000
		443,000

The minimum transfer price should be excess of $443,000/120,000 units = $3.692 per unit.

The transfer price should therefore be negotiated in the range $3.70 to $5. Any transfer price between these two amounts would result in higher profits for the company, Division X and Division Y (on the reasonable assumption that Division Y will sell Product P at a price higher than the transfer price.)

(c) If Division Y buys 120,000 units of Product P externally at $5 per unit, the after-tax position of the company as a whole would be as follows:

	$	$
Division X		
Contribution from selling 70,000 units of Product Q		35,000
Less tax at 50%		(17,500)
After-tax contribution, Division X		17,500
Division Y		
Cost of buying 120,000 units of P externally (at $5)	(600,000)	
Less tax at 30%	180,000	
Cost net of tax, Division Y		(420,000)
Cost to the company		(402,500)

(**Tutorial note:** Revenue from selling the units of Product P in Country Y can be ignored because this is the same regardless of whether the units are transferred from Country X or bought externally.)

If Division Y buys 120,000 units of Product P from Division X at $5.40 per unit, the after-tax position of the company as a whole would be as follows:

	$	$
Division X		
Transfer of 120,000 units of P at $5.40		648,000
Variable cost of 120,000 units of P at $3.40		408,000
Contribution from 120,000 units of Product P		240,000
Less tax at 50%		(120,000)
After-tax contribution, Division X		120,000
Division Y		
Cost of buying 120,000 units of P (at $5.40)	(648,000)	
Less tax at 30%	194,400	
Cost net of tax		(453,600)
Total cost to the company		(333,600)

Conclusion

It is in the best interests of the company as a whole for Division Y to purchase the units of Product P from Division X. This will result in an annual profit after tax that is higher by $68,900 ($402,500 – $333,600).

45 Long and Short

(a) **Group contribution (per unit and in total)**

	RDZ		BL	
	$	$	$	$
Selling price		45		54
Components used				
S (3 : 2)	18		12	
M (2 : 4)	8		16	
Processing costs	12		14	
Cost		38		42
		7		12
		(× 200)		(× 300)
Group contribution		1,400		3,600

Total contribution = $1,400 + $3,600 = $5,000

(b) **Divisional contribution**

(i) *Transfer price (variable cost + shadow price): supplying divisions*

	A	B
	$	$
S: (6 + 0.5)	6.50	
M: (4 + 2.75)		6.75
Less variable cost	6.00	4.00
Contribution per unit	0.50	2.75

(ii) *Buying divisions*

	RDZ		BL	
	$	$	$	$
Selling price		45.0		54.0
Less				
Transfer price				
S: (3:2)	19.5		13.0	
M: (2:4)	13.5		27.0	
Processing cost	12.0		14.0	
		45.0		54.0
Contribution per unit		0.0		0.0

(c) All contribution arises in the supplying divisions. This will be unacceptable to the buying divisions, and so will have an adverse affect on the promotion of these two products.

(d) **Transfer price**

$$\text{Transfer price} = \frac{\text{Variable cost} + \text{Opportunity cost}}{\text{(or = Market clearing price)}}$$

S = $6.00 + (5% × $6.00) = $6.30

M = $7.50 – $0.50   = $7.00

Contribution of end-products in buying divisions

	RDZ		BL	
	$	$	$	$
Selling price		45.0		54.0
Less				
Transfer price				
S: (3:2)	18.9		12.6	
M: (2:4)	14.0		28.0	
Processing cost	12.0		14.0	
		44.9		54.6
Contribution per unit		0.1		(0.6)

Therefore do not produce BL.

Strategy
Produce RDZ: Maximum possible.

Constraint?

S   2,400 units/3 units of S per unit of RDZ =   800 units

M   3,200 units/2 units of M per unit of RDZ = 1,600 units

Therefore produce 800 units of RDZ and sell the remaining 1,600 units of M externally.

Total contribution for group

	$
800 units of RDZ × $7/unit (see part (a))	5,600
1,600 units of M × $3/unit ($7 − $4)	4,800
Total group contribution	10,400

46   Balanced

(a)   The four perspectives for performance targets and measuring performance in a balanced scorecard approach are:

(1)   a customer perspective: identifying what customers value most

(2)   an internal systems perspective: identifying the processes that must be performed with excellence to satisfy customers

(3)   an innovation and learning perspective: what must the organisation do to innovate or add to its knowledge and experience

(4)   a financial perspective.

(b)   **A professional football club**

Here are some suggestions

Customer perspective

Customers value:

■   results, winning

■   an enjoyable time at football matches: being entertained (for example, with food and drink).

Targets for performance might be:

■   the size of attendances at matches

■   results (points, position in the league table, promotion)

■   revenue from catering: number of meals sold before matches.

Internal processes perspective

Processes that must be excellent to support customer expectations might include ticket selling, getting customers into the ground quickly on match days, catering efficiency, effective security and policing, and so on.

Targets for performance might be:

■   number of season ticket sales

■   targets for number of spectators per minute going through each turnstile

■   speed of producing meals in the catering area

■   number of incidents and police arrests on match days.

Innovation and learning perspective

Value can be created by developing well-trained footballers through coaching and training, and possibly selling them in the transfer market to make profits.

Targets for performance might be:

■ average fitness levels for players

■ average number of hours of training each week per player

■ revenue from transfers

Financial perspective

Presumably, the football club will be expected to make profits for its owners. Targets for performance might be profits each year, and return on investment.

Subsidiary financial targets might be average wages per player, and revenue from sponsorship deals.

47 Pyramid

(a) The performance pyramid describes a view that all measures of performance for an organisation should be linked and consistent with each other. There is a hierarchy of suitable measures of performance, with performance measures at lower levels in the hierarchy (or pyramid) supporting performance measures at a higher level.

(1) At the bottom of the pyramid, there are operational performance measures, relating to external effectiveness and internal efficiency.

(2) Operational performance measures support higher-level measures that should relate to quality, delivery, production or service cycle time and waste.

(3) These measures of performance support measures of performance at an even higher level in the pyramid, relating to customer satisfaction, flexibility and productivity.

(4) These measures of performance support measures relating to market satisfaction and financial performance.

(5) Together, measures of market satisfaction and financial performance support the achievement of the organisation's objectives.

The performance pyramid recognises that external and market measures of performance are as important as financial performance and internal efficiency in achieving the long-term objectives of the organisation.

(b) Dimensions of performance in service industries may be measured primarily by:

(1) financial performance and

(2) competitiveness.

These should be supported by performance in four other dimensions:

(1) service quality

(2) flexibility

(3) resource utilisation and

(4) innovation.

48   The Vet Centre

(a)
Profit
The profitability of the Centre should be compared with budget. (Ideally, if shared costs could be allocated fairly the profitability of each category of treatment should be measured. Profitability could also be compared with profits in previous years. However, data for making these measurements is not available.)

	Budget		Actual	
	$	$	$	$
Revenue		2,520,000		2,820,000
Salaries, full-time vets	600,000		600,000	
(10 × $60,000)				
Bonus	-		150,000	
50% × (2,820,000 − 2,520,000)				
Part-time vets	18,000		60,000	
Other costs	1,400,000		1,610,000	
Total costs		2,018,000		2,420,000
Profit		502,000		400,000

Actual profit is below budgeted profit.

Competitiveness

One measure of competitiveness might be the rate of success at turning customer enquiries by telephone into actual examinations and treatments. (Note: There could be other and better measures of competitiveness, such as growth in annual revenue and share of the local market. However, data is not available here to make these measurements.)

In the table below, 'success rate' is the percentage of customer enquiries by telephone that result in an actual examination or treatment, for which a fee is charged.

	Budget	Actual
New business		
Enquiries	5,000	9,000
Examinations/treatments	3,000	4,000
Success rate	60%	44%
Repeat business		
Enquiries	18,000	15,000
Examinations/treatments	16,000	14,000
Success rate	89%	93%

The Centre has not been as successful as expected (budgeted) at converting enquiries from new customers into 'sales', but has been more successful than expected in converting calls from 'repeat' customers into sales.

(b)

Quality

Quality of service can be measured by complaints. A useful measure might be the number of complaints as a percentage of examinations and treatments.

	Budget	Actual
Complaints	380	540
Examinations/treatments	19,000	18,000
Percentage rate of complaints	2%	3%

It would be useful to analyse complaints according to the type of animals treated in each case, but the data is not available.

The rate of complaints is higher than expected, suggesting that the quality of service is not up to the expected standard.

Resource utilisation

The key resource at the Centre is probably the time of the full-time vets. A useful measure of performance would therefore be average revenue per full-time vet. Ideally, income from the treatment of exotic animals should be excluded from revenue, but we do not know how much income was earned from treating exotic animals.

	Budget	Actual
Revenue	£2,520,000	$2,820,000
Number of full-time vets	10	10
Average revenue per vet	$252,000	$282,000

Average revenue per vet was $30,000 (nearly 12%) above budget, although some of this increase must be due to the higher-than-budgeted quantity of treatments of exotic animals.

Flexibility

A key aspect of flexibility is probably the ability of the Vet Centre to respond to requests to treat exotic animals. A suitable measure of performance might therefore be the percentage of revenue that comes from the treatment of exotic animals. The budget might state the minimum required percentage.

	Budget	Actual
Total number of treatments	19,000	18,000
Treatments of exotic animals	120	400
	0.6%	2.2%

The Centre has possibly demonstrated its flexibility in its ability to treat more exotic animals than provided for in the budget. However, this still remains a low proportion of the total annual work done by the Centre.

Innovation

There is no data for measuring innovation in a satisfactory way, although the amount spent on training (per vet) might be used as an indication of 'new learning' and so an ability to innovate and provide new methods of treatment.

	Budget	Actual
Spending on training	$75,000	$100,000
Full-time vets	10	10
Training costs per vet	$7,500	$10,000

By spending more than budgeted on training, the Centre might demonstrate its ability to innovate and offer new treatments for animals.

(c) Standards

According to Fitzgerald and Moon, the three key factors are:

(1) **Ownership.** Do the individuals responsible for achieving the performance standards 'own' them and accept them. (Were the individuals involved in setting the standards, or were they imposed by senior management?)

(2) **Achievability.** Are these standards considered achievable?

(3) **Equity.** Are the standards equitable and 'fair' for every manager responsible for achieving performance targets?

Rewards for achieving targets

According to Fitzgerald and Moon, the three key factors are:

(1) **Clarity.** Is the connection between operational performance standards and the achievement of corporate goals clear and fully understood by all employees and managers?

(2) **Motivation.** Are the rewards for achieving targets (both financial rewards and non-financial rewards) sufficient to motivate the managers responsible for achieving the targets?

(3) **Controllability.** Are there any problems with the allocation of the costs of shared services, and charging managers with costs over which they have no proper control?

49 Total quality

(a) The key aspects of Total Quality Management are:

(1) continuous improvement in operations and systems, to improve quality

(2) a policy of trying to achieve zero defects in production (getting things right the first time)

(3) the use of statistical quality control to prevent defective items reaching customers

(4) employee involvement in efforts to improve quality, for example by using quality circles

(5)   measures to improve production systems, such as minimising inventory levels, minimising the movement of materials, minimising setup times: all these take time and money but do not add any value.

(b)   Quality-related costs can be grouped into four categories:

(1)   Prevention costs: these are costs incurred in preventing quality problems. Important elements of prevention costs are costs of ensuring good product design and costs of training employees.

(2)   Appraisal costs: these are the costs of testing for quality, such as inspection costs and quality control costs.

(3)   Internal failure costs: these are the costs of faults and errors in processing, such as costs of waste, scrap and re-working rejected items.

(4)   External failure costs: these are the costs of quality problems after the product (or service) has been delivered to the customer such as the cost of handling customer complaints, and the loss of future business/sales.

In the traditional approach, the aim should be to minimise the total of quality-related costs. At this cost-minimising level of quality, some errors will occur. The TQM approach is that all errors should be avoided and sub-standard work is unacceptable. External failure costs are under-estimated, and it is worth spending money on prevention and appraisal costs to avoid internal and external failure costs, which will be higher.

(c)   Key aspects of JIT management are:

(1)   Hold no inventory. This requires just-in-time purchasing (to avoid raw materials inventory) and just-in-time production (to avoid finished goods inventory). Holding inventory is wasteful, and does not add value.

(2)   Just-in-time purchasing calls for close collaboration with key suppliers.

(3)   Just-in-time production involves trying to produce items exactly in time to meet customer needs for delivery: this calls for fast production times and avoiding breakdowns and any hold-ups or bottleneck in production.

(4)   Production systems need to be flexible, to react to changes in demand from customers.

(5)   Avoid over-production (which results in finished goods inventory).

(6)   Eliminate inefficiency and poor quality in production – eliminate waste, minimise the movement of materials (which adds no value), minimise waiting times, improve the layout of the factory floor (to minimise movement of materials), reduce setup times (which do not add value) and improve visibility in the work place (by using cards or other signalling systems).

(d)   Activity based management uses activity based costing to analyse the cost of activities within an organisation. It focuses on the cost of activities and the causes of these costs occuring (cost drivers). The aim of ABM should be to improve the value obtained from the activities, eliminate activities that do not add value or reduce the costs of activities.

50   Poole Company

(a)   Projected data

(i)   *Total production units*

	Before TQM	After TQM
Sales	5,000	5,000
Returns: (5%/2.5% of sales)	263	128
	5,263	5,128
Final inspection (12.5%/7.5% of production)	750	416
Total production units	6,000	5,541

(ii)   *Purchases of material X*

	Before TQM	After TQM
Material usage (6,000 or 5,541 × 8 m²/unit)	48,000	44,328
Processing losses: (4%/2.5% of input)	2,000	1,137
	50,000	45,465
Storage losses: (5%/3% of receipts)	2,632	1,406
	52,632	46,871

(iii)   *Gross machine hours*

	Before TQM		After TQM
Machine usage (6,000 × 0.6 hrs/unit)	3,600	(5,541 × 0.5hrs/unit)	2,771
Work on 3rd quality units (80% × 250 x 0.2)	40	(80% × 125 × 0.2)	20
	3,640		2,791
Idle time (20% of gross machine hours)	910	(12.5% of gross machine hours)	399
	4,550		3,190

(b)   Income statements

Before TQM	$	$	$
Sales:			
1st quality (5,000 × 100)			500,000
2nd quality (750 × 70)			52,500
3rd quality (200 × 50)			10,000
Scrap (50 × 5)			250
			562,750
Costs:			
Fixed			
Prevention	20,000		
Sundry	60,000		
Inspection	25,000		
		105,000	
Variable			
Inspection/storage (52,632 × 0.1)	5,263		
Material (52,632 × 4)	210,528		
Machine hours (4,550 × 40)	182,000		
Delivery costs (250 × 8)	2,000		
Product liability claims (3% × 500,000)	15,000		
		414,791	
Total costs			519,791
Profit			42,959

After TQM	$	$	$
Sales:			
1st quality (5,000 × 100)			500,000
2nd quality (416 × 70)			29,120

3rd quality (100 × 50)	5,000
Scrap (25 × 5)	125
	534,245

Costs:		
Fixed		
Prevention	60,000	
Sundry	54,000	
Inspection	15,000	
		129,000
Variable		
Inspection/storage (46,871 × 0.1)	4,687	
Material (46,871 × 4)	187,484	
Machine hours (3,190 × 40)	127,600	
Delivery costs (125 × 8)	1,000	
Product liability claims (1% × 500,000)	5,000	
		325,771
Total costs		454,771
Profit		79,474

51   Target cost

(a)

Year	0	1	2	3	4
	$000	$000	$000	$000	$000
Working capital	(400)				400
Cost/residual value	(1,400)				600
Sales revenue		1,400	2,100	1,750	700
Advertising costs	(800)	(600)	(400)	(200)	
Fixed production (cash) costs		(200)	(200)	(200)	(200)
Net cash flows, excluding variable costs	(2,600)	600	1,500	1,350	1,500
Discount factor at 12%	1.000	0.893	0.797	0.712	0.636
Present value	(2,600)	535.8	1,195.5	961.2	954.0

NPV of cash flows, excluding variable production costs = $1,046,500

(b)

Let the maximum variable cost per unit (the target variable cost) be V.

Year	Variable costs	Discount factor at 12%	PV of variable costs
	$		$
1	40,000V	0.893	35,720V
2	60,000V	0.797	47,820V
3	50,000V	0.712	35,600V
4	20,000V	0.636	12,720V
			131,860V

The variable cost per unit that will give the project a DCF return of 12% = $1,046,500/131,860 = $7.94. The DCF return will be less than 12% if the variable cost exceeds $7.94.

The current estimate of the variable cost per unit is $10. The cost gap is therefore $2.06 ($100– $7.94).

52 Cost and quality

(1) Total Quality Management

TQM seeks to reduce quality costs, where quality costs are categorised as:

- Prevention costs
- Appraisal costs (inspection costs, etcetera)
- Internal failure costs (costs of scrap, waste, re-working and so on)
- External failure costs (cost of lost customer goodwill, lost sales, returned goods from customers, warranty costs)

The aim should be to improve quality and reduce total quality costs.

TQM also seeks continuous improvement: improvement can be achieved by reducing costs or improving quality.

(2) Activity based costing

A system of ABC might identify activities related to achieving quality, such as quality planning and control, and a cost driver for those activities. ABC could then be used to identify the costs related to the quality activity.

(3) Balanced scorecard

In a balanced scorecard, cost targets could be an element for the financial perspective. Quality targets could be an element in the balanced scorecard for the internal perspective or the customer perspective.

(4) Just in Time management

JIT seeks reductions in costs through improvements in production performance. The aim is to eliminate breakdowns and bottlenecks, so that items can be manufactured as quickly as possible.

(5) Value analysis

Value analysis looks at activities and costs in the value chain, and attempts to identify ways of adding more value. Value is added by providing extra quality (where the value of the extra quality is less than any additional cost) or by providing the same quality at less cost.

Index

A

B